Learning Alternatives in U.S. Education: Where Student and Computer Meet

370.2
L47

Learning Alternatives in U.S. Education: Where Student and Computer Meet

beverly Hunter
carol s. kastner
martin l. rubin
robert j. seidel
Human Resources Research Organization

educational technology publications
englewood cliffs, new jersey **07632**

Library of Congress Cataloging in Publication Data

Main entry under title:

Learning alternatives in U.S. education: where student and computer meet.

Includes index.
1. Electronic data processing--Education. I. Hunter, Beverly.
LB2846.4.L42   370'.28'54   74-31417
ISBN 0-87778-078-1

Copyright © 1975 Educational Technology Publications, Inc., Englewood Cliffs, New Jersey 07632.

All rights reserved. No part of this book may be reproduced or transmitted, in any form or by any means, electronic or mechanical, including photocopying, recording, or by any information storage and retrieval system, without permission in writing from the Publisher.

This publication is based on a project performed by the Human Resources Research Organization (HumRRO) and supported by the National Science Foundation under Grant GJ-31153. Since National Science Foundation grantees are encouraged to express individual judgments, any opinions, findings, conclusions or recommendations expressed herein are those of the author(s) and do not necessarily reflect the view of the National Science Foundation.

Printed in the United States of America.

Library of Congress Catalog Card Number: 74-31417.

International Standard Book Number: 0-87778-078-1.

First Printing: January, 1975.

PREFACE

Robert J. Seidel and his colleagues have moved instructional technology a long step ahead in their studies of computer-based instruction. Despite the fact that they have attacked the most sophisticated and difficult, though perhaps most promising, element of that technology, the use of computers, they have come to grips with the multitude of problems which are inevitably encountered when one asks how to actually go about doing it. It is a commonplace that although a far greater investment must be made in basic educational research, possibly our greatest problem is the successful employment of the findings of research in the day-to-day processes of education. This means an effective packaging of these findings for developmental purposes that are directed squarely toward the classroom, library, and laboratory. It is here, it seems to me, that the present volume has inestimable value. It should have value not only for persons who are interested in any or all facets of the employment of computers for educational purposes, but as well for those seriously involved in other elements of instructional technology.

The authors have drawn their findings from an immense volume of research and have made their recommendations across a broad territory that embraces a numerous and various audience, ranging from educational philosophers to administrators, teachers, and publishers. It is probably a safe estimate of the worth of their work to insist that it deserves the attention of anyone seriously interested in the improvement of instruction, not only in method but also in substance. They have attacked a remarkable number of crucial questions that cut across the entire span of education and their treatment of those questions deserves the close attention of educators and all those who serve the ends of education.

Education is possibly the most conservative of all professions. This is quite understandable, for a primary function of education is induction into the culture, even though education is also properly a critic of the culture. Nevertheless, innovation is of the greatest importance in education, and ways must be found for moving education in new directions while still preserving whatever from the past deserves conservation. Educators talk and write a great deal about innovation; but we do comparatively little innovating. All of us are aware of this situation and most of us are now sensitive to the conditions and forces which produce it. We recognize that there is a wide and difficult-to-negotiate gap between the theoretical knowledge of research experts indicating what perhaps should and conceivably can be done and the capacity of administrators and teachers to actually do it. The inability to create instructional programs incorporating the new findings can contribute to a negative disposition toward doing anything at all that is a departure from the habitual ways. To make this point it is hardly necessary to employ the extreme clichés about the research reports lining the shelves while the expensive equipment gathers dust in the school closets. It should simply be obvious that one of our greatest needs is developmental work that effectively will close the gap between knowledge and practice.

Here, it seems to me, is the great merit of the present study. It is directed to the closing of that gap and may be taken as something of a model of developmental work in instruction. It is an effort to show concretely the things which can be done to employ computers effectively in education and to give assistance on how to go about it, from the dissemination of information through private and governmental agencies to the production of both equipment and instructional material to the instructor's determination of models and methods in relation to the substance of his subject. For all of this the authors have drawn on practical experience and developmental projects that involve specific fields of study as well as theory that has issued from basic educational research. Their concern is not simply with such matters as economy and efficiency. They are interested in the quality of instruction—not just the effectiveness of instructional methods, but also

Preface ix

the character of the curriculum and its relation to methods and the impact of both substance and method on the teacher and learner.

No doubt there will always be many who fear or even deplore the introduction of automated and cybernetic devices into the teaching-learning process. Their fears deserve consideration and respect because the mechanization and dehumanization of education is not beyond possibility and it is necessary to develop and maintain constant safeguards against it. It is a virtue of this study that its authors are genuinely concerned about this matter and treat it wisely. They see computers in two ways relating to education: first, that computers are now and in the future will be a basic element of the culture with which education must be concerned, and second, that computers are an extension of the intellectual equipment and capabilities of the individual and therefore the individual as a learner gains greatly through his capacity to employ them. Certainly the authors recognize the limitations of computers in learning, and they are sensitive to the possible negative impacts which computer-based learning could conceivably have on the human personality and human social relationships. But they rightly refuse to permit the prospect of negative results to destroy their enthusiasm for capitalizing on the positive possibilities when computers are employed as elements in a well-balanced instructional system that keeps humane considerations constantly in the foreground and guards against the mechanization of either the teacher or learner. It is now commonplace to admit that often the schoolroom is not as "human" as educators have usually assumed and that even computers, carefully and judiciously and expertly employed, might actually contribute to its humanization.

Instructional technology has to do primarily with the means for achieving instructional goals. But it is quite impossible to divorce means from the ends with which they are associated, to which presumably they lead. The ends must be the determinants of the means, but inevitably the means will have some determining effect upon the ends. It is not possible to wholly prevent this, and perhaps it is not even desirable. We face a very great problem, however, in the general threat of a technologizing of our culture, where the machines developed to serve us would so completely determine the ends which we seek that they would control us and our purposes. We have already moved dangerously in this direction, though certainly not fatally, and we must guard against it in our schools and colleges. For if education were to become dominated by our machines our total culture would suffer irreparable damage.

It seems to me that Dr. Seidel and his colleagues have fully recognized this serious and difficult problem in this volume on computer-based instruction. They see the close relationship of means and ends in education just as they see the relationship between instructional method and substance. This is one of the chief virtues of their work.

Finally, I would commend them for seeing their problems in a broad perspective and fashioning their recommendations in terms of the long-range possibilities of computers in education and the national scope of such problems as designing, financing, and distributing materials. The great danger is that the schools will be afraid to break new ground if they must do it in isolation and without the support of adequate research and development and without assurances of possible success. This study should be invaluable in helping to provide intelligent directives together with wise warnings and assurances.

Sterling M. McMurrin
Dean, Graduate School of Education,
University of Utah, and
Chairman, Commission
on Instructional Technology

FOREWORD

MAJOR THEMES AND FINDINGS— A GUIDE TO THE REPORT

"Computers and learning" as a subject crosses many fields of endeavor. There are many points of view regarding every aspect of the state-of-the-art, including purposes, nature, benefits, obstacles, costs, feasibility, components, and methodology. A major characteristic of this book* is that it addresses multiple audiences. The interested reader will find relevant information if he or she is: a potential developer of computer-based curricula or faculty user; a publisher or representative of some other group primarily interested in dissemination of computer-based learning materials (CBLM); an academic dean, other institutional decision-maker, or local or state administrator of public education; or a representative of a federal or private foundation funding agency.

The state-of-the-art assessment in Chapter 1 should be of interest to all such readers. Chapter 2, "Education—Trends and Visions," provides grist for planning large-scale innovative programs and is therefore relevant reading for planners and leaders in the field of CBLM system development.

---

*This volume is based on a study supported by Grant No. GJ 31153, "Strategies for Developing and Disseminating Computer-Based Curricular Materials and Instructional Concepts," sponsored by the Technological Innovations in Education Group, Education Directorate, National Science Foundation. The purpose of the project was to study development and dissemination of computer-based learning materials in the U.S. and to identify approaches for achieving beneficial, nationwide use of computers in education.

Chapters 3 and 4, dealing with the what and how of today's CBLM, should provide useful material for individual developers or adopters of innovative computer uses. (Appendix 4, the "Decision Guide," is designed to give a potential faculty user of CBLM a framework with which he can make an informed decision about the adoption of candidate materials. This guide has already proved itself useful in three different workshop settings.)

Publishers and other agencies primarily concerned with distribution of CBLM will find Chapter 5 particularly relevant to their interests.

Chapter 6 is directed toward the administrative decision-maker or potential user who is concerned with system design and its impact on economics.

State and federal administrators as well as private foundation representatives are the primary audience for the strategies proposed in Chapter 7, tailored toward potential widespread national impact of CBLM.

Chapter 8, which provides a summary of findings, conclusions, and recommendations, is directed at all readers.

In this book we have tried to represent fairly every aspect and point of view we were aware of, despite the extremely dynamic character of the field. At the same time, our own perspectives shifted continuously throughout the two-year study period. Nevertheless, certain basic themes or ideas recurred again and again, until they seemed to us to take on the character of "truths."

Each chapter of this volume contains detailed information on various subjects pertaining to computer-based learning materials. This information is organized and discussed from the perspective of one or more basic themes. These themes are summarized below, with some indication of the chapter contents that related to them.

Chapter 1, "Perspectives," provides an overview of the current state of affairs of computers in education. The basic theme is *diversity* of activities and purposes. By providing this overview of activities and obstacles to the use of computers in education, we hope to show why more coherent strategies are needed on a national scale.

Chapter 2, "Education—Trends and Visions," provides a brief glimpse of learning in some indefinite time in the future. The theme of this chapter is the *interdependence of social goals, values, educational*

Foreword

reform, and technology. Put negatively, the theme is, "If you do not know where you are going, any road will get you there." Certain ideas about, and goals for, society, man, learning, and technology which are shared by visionary educators, philosophers, and technologists are discussed in Chapter 2. The kinds of computer-based systems which would support these goals are suggested.

There are three basic themes in Chapter 3, "Today's Computer-Based Learning Methods." The first is that *computer applications to learning are important to different people for many different reasons and in many different ways*. A large number of computer-based learning experiences are described, along with reasons that have been cited for their importance (or triviality, as the case may be). The second theme is the *interdependence of the what and the how of learning*. The examples of computer-based learning are organized by discipline, so that the nature of what the student is learning can be brought out in relationship to the way he is learning. *A focus on learning activities* is the third theme. The compelling examples noted in the chapter are not categorized primarily in terms of teaching strategies or computing modes, but rather in terms of the type of learning activity the student is pursuing. This is a deliberate attempt on our part to shift the perspective of developers of CBLM from either computers or instruction to *learners*.

There are many approaches to developing innovative CBLM and all of them are risky. This is the basic theme of Chapter 4, "Developing Computer-Based Learning Materials." Whether you place your bets on creative individuals, discipline experts, systematic methodology, student or teacher involvement, powerful technology, multidisciplinary teams, magnitude of funding, or a combination of these, there are no guaranteed outcomes in quality or acceptance of the end product. But some pitfalls can be avoided, and many constraints can be dealt with successfully. Chapter 4 analyzes many of the factors involved in developing CBLM and presents a number of project stories to illustrate various approaches to development.

Chapter 5 is entitled "Ways of Achieving More Widespread Benefit from Computer-Based Learning Materials." The theme of this chapter is *coherent strategies for dissemination*. Organizations and activities involved in disseminating CBLM are described in a framework of basic functions which must be carried out if materials are to be adopted and used. The nine basic functions (such as providing technical implementation support, and financing the dissemination activity) must all be accounted for if a strategy is to be successful. Several case studies are presented, to illustrate successful coherent strategies. Recommendations for alternative national strategies are related to different purposes.

This report does not treat the subject of computer hardware and software in depth. Chapter 6, "Ways of Providing Computer Services," relates certain aspects of technology to the development and dissemination of CBLM. The theme of this chapter is *resource sharing*. The computing resources to be shared and the mechanisms for sharing are described. (Appendix 2 provides information on hundreds of organizations involved in some aspect of dissemination of CBLM; Appendix 3 identifies computing networks serving instructional users.)

Examination of the gains and problems of small-scale, relatively isolated development and dissemination efforts leads us to the conclusion that a *coordinated national program* is required to bring quality CBLM to the majority of learners. In Chapter 7, "Alternative National Models: Strategies for Change," recognition is made of the need to consider the variety of purposes for computer usage in education. The theme of *strategy coherence* is carried forward in developing alternative national models to cope with the complexities of creating and delivering CBLM nationally to the learner. The concept of "strategy" is analyzed into its components. Existing projects are described as examples of how various strategies might be implemented. Five strategies are described in detail as promising national models. Their potential impact is discussed, along with some assessment of their relative viability.

Chapter 8 provides a summary of findings, conclusions, and recommendations.

Acknowledgments

During the conduct of the study, the research team cataloged from various journals and secondary sources thousands of CBLM items. Invaluable advice and information were provided through personal interviews with national leaders in the areas of development, dissemination, and strategies for implementation of CBLM.

Foreword

We are indebted generally to over four dozen teachers, curriculum developers, and administrators for their aid in gathering the information contained in this book. Particular acknowledgment is made to Joseph Denk of the North Carolina Educational Computing Services for the wealth of information he provided on source materials and dissemination strategies. Special appreciation is also due to those individuals whom the team interviewed and who contributed ideas about potential national models for effecting widespread computer use in education: Victor Bunderson, Sylvia Charp, Thomas Kurtz, Arthur Luehrmann, Roger Levien, Harold Mitzel, Charles Morrisey, and Robert Scanlon.

Contributions to the descriptions of case studies in Chapter 3 were made by Ronald E. Anderson, social sciences; K. Jeffrey Johnson, chemistry; Donald McLaughlin, mathematics; Joseph Raken, humanities; and Charles Tidball, health sciences. Special thanks are due David Bushnell for his contribution to the discussion of potential national models in Chapter 7 and to Harvey Long of IBM for his critical review of Chapter 6.

Many of the individuals named above helped also in the review of earlier chapter drafts but the bulk of that time-consuming and demanding job was accomplished by Karl Zinn of the Center for Research on Learning and Teaching, University of Michigan; Hulda Grobman of the University of Illinois, College of Medicine, Education/Career Mobility, Chicago, Illinois; and Robert Filep, University of Southern California and formerly Associate Commissioner and Director, National Center for Educational Technology, U.S. Office of Education, Washington, D.C.

Perhaps the most difficult and yet most important acknowledgment is to the intangible guidance of spirit which kept the focus of the project on the student as the center and the purpose of any educational innovation. This view reflects implicit guidance by Thomas Dwyer, Head of Project SOLO in the Pittsburgh School System; Arthur Luehrmann, professor of physics at Dartmouth College; and Seymour Papert of the Massachusetts Institute of Technology.

Internally at HumRRO we are grateful to the secretarial staff who did a yeoman's job of keeping track of the bits of paper and retyping almost illegible scrawls. Lola Zook, HumRRO's Director of Editorial and Production, lent a helpful hand in bringing order out of a potential paper-mill chaos, ably abetted by Lala J. Curry, who served as editorial liaison. Credit for the illustrative material goes to the HumRRO Production staff.

The study was conducted at HumRRO Division No. 1 (System Operations) Alexandria, Virginia, where Dr. J. Daniel Lyons is Director. My group within Division No. 1 specializes in instructional technology.

The interdisciplinary team drawn from this group and responsible for this study was composed of Beverly Hunter, Carol S. Kastner, Martin L. Rubin, and myself. The project was conducted under my overall supervision as Principal Investigator. The major contribution to the initial writing of the book was made by Beverly Hunter. It is extremely difficult to separate out the originator of various thoughts and ideas of our effort. However, conceptualization and primary responsibility for the various chapters can best be ascribed as follows: Chapter 1, Seidel and Hunter; Chapter 2, Hunter and Seidel; Chapter 3, Kastner and Rubin; Chapter 4, Hunter and Seidel; Chapter 5, Hunter, Rubin, and Kastner; Chapter 6, Rubin and Hunter; Chapter 7, Seidel and Rubin; Chapter 8, all the authors. The resulting volume is truly a synergistic product of the four authors.

Robert J. Seidel
Principal Investigator

TABLE OF CONTENTS

	Page
Preface	vii
Foreword	xi
CHAPTER 1: PERSPECTIVES	3
Background to the Study	3
Barriers to Growth	7
Diversity of Purposes	8
The State of Affairs—Activity and Growth	15
Projections of Acceptance for CBLM	19
Summary	24
CHAPTER 2: EDUCATION—TRENDS AND VISIONS	25
Today's Trends	25
Visions and Basic Themes	31
CHAPTER 3: TODAY'S COMPUTER-BASED LEARNING METHODS	47
Overview	47
Chemistry	55
Physics	63
Mathematics	69
Business Education	78
Life Sciences	88
Health Professions	96

Humanities	103
Social Sciences	111
Education	117

CHAPTER 4: DEVELOPING COMPUTER-BASED LEARNING MATERIALS ... 123

Aims and Purposes of Development	123
Sample Development Stories	147
Organization and Funding of Development Projects and Programs	178
Development Process	188

CHAPTER 5: WAYS OF ACHIEVING MORE WIDESPREAD BENEFIT FROM COMPUTER-BASED LEARNING MATERIALS ... 207

Perspective	207
Why Is Dissemination of Computer-Oriented Curricula a National Concern?	209
Purpose and Assumptions of This Chapter	210
Organization of This Chapter	210
State-of-the-Art Overview	212
Adoption Processes	221
Dissemination Functions and Mechanisms	225
Goals and Strategies	242

CHAPTER 6: WAYS OF PROVIDING COMPUTER SERVICES ... 257

Perspective	257
Resource Sharing Via Networks	259
Data Communications Costs	273
Programming Languages	275
Terminals	279
Mini-computer Developments	284
Trade-offs Revisited	287
Summary	291

Table of Contents xix

CHAPTER 7: ALTERNATIVE NATIONAL MODELS: STRATEGIES FOR CHANGE 293
    Need for Coherent Strategies 298
    Alternative National Models 300
    Financing Comprehensive Programs 314
    Total Program Funding Levels 315
    Problems of Finance 316

CHAPTER 8: A SUMMARY OF FINDINGS, CONCLUSIONS, AND RECOMMENDATIONS 319

REFERENCES 331

APPENDIX 1: SOURCES OF INFORMATION USED TO IDENTIFY COMPUTER-ORIENTED CURRICULAR MATERIALS 355

APPENDIX 2   359
    A. Professional and Commercial Organizations Which Provide Mechanisms for Information Exchange 359
    B. Users Groups 363
    C. Major Professional Journals with Articles on Computers in Education 365

APPENDIX 3: ORGANIZATIONS AND NETWORKS PROVIDING COMPUTING SERVICES TO EDUCATION 369

APPENDIX 4: DECISION GUIDE AND CONSIDERATIONS 375

INDEX 393

FIGURES
    1. Estimated Total Expenditures for Computing in U.S. Higher Education Through FY 1980 5
    2. Summary of Projections for Adoption of Computer-Assisted Learning in Higher Education 21
    3. Summary of Projections for Adoption of Com-

	puter-Assisted Learning in Secondary Schools	22
4.	Summary of Projections of Adoption of Computer-Assisted Learning in Elementary Schools	23
5.	The Wheel of the Curriculum	43
6.	Percentage of Computer-Based Learning Materials, by Discipline	54
7.	Sample Problem: The Visual Appearance of a Rapidly Moving Spacecraft	67
8.	Outputs from LOGO Language Procedure "POLY"	73
9.	Sample Market Run	83
10.	Sample PROSIM V Capability	86
11.	Changes in FOXRAB Populations	91
12.	Results from STERL Eradication Techniques	92
13.	POLUT Graphic Output	94
14.	Computer Summary of Mental Status Interview	100
15.	Student ARTSPEAK Assignment	105
16.	Frere Jacques Procedure in LOGO	107
17.	The CARE Decision Process	119
18.	Modular Curriculum Concept	164
19.	TICCIT Courseware Design Goals	171
20.	Developer Organizations Cited for 4,900 Items of Computer-Based Learning Materials (CBLM)	179
21.	Funding Sources Cited by Developers of 2,750 Items of Computer-Based Learning Materials (CBLM)	180
22.	Funding Sources Reported by Curriculum Development Projects in the U.S.A.	183
23.	Organizational Base or Sponsorship Reported by Curriculum Development Projects in the U.S.A.	184
24.	Model for the Systems Approach to the Development of Instructional Materials	195
25.	Organization of the Chapter	211
26.	Star Network	260
27.	Satellite Network	262
28.	Distributed Computer Network	263
29.	Program Language Tree Structure	277
30.	A Potpourri of Decisions for the Potential	

Table of Contents xxi

	Educational User of Computers	289
31.	Dimensions of a Coherent Strategy	299
32.	National Program Exchange Model	304
33.	Discipline Center Model	306
34.	National Development Center Model	308
35.	Regionally Based Learning Technology Center	311
36.	Ideologically Based Center Model	313
37.	Decision Strategy for Evaluating Computer-Oriented Curricular Innovation	376

TABLES

1.	Computer-Based Learning Materials Classified by Physical Form	50
2.	Describing Dimensions of School Life	128
3.	Illustrative Statements of Purpose of Computer-Based Learning Materials	133
4.	Who Selects What for Whom	228
5.	Examples of Existing Dissemination Strategies	244
6.	Roles of National and Regional Organizations in Proposed National Strategy for Dissemination	303

Learning Alternatives in U.S. Education: Where Student and Computer Meet

Chapter 1

PERSPECTIVES

BACKGROUND TO THE STUDY

Computer-based systems are used in many ways for learning, and the benefits in some cases are very compelling. Computer-based systems can make a rich array of learning experiences available to students in a way that is not otherwise possible. The computational and information handling capabilities of computers become natural extensions of the student's intellect. Computers provide some students with new ways to represent and comprehend complex, dynamic phenomena.

One feature of computer-based instruction lies in the explicit attention to the student as an individual learner. This focus may encourage the instructor, the developer, and the administrator in the educational establishment to aid the individual learner in realizing his full potential, to take on responsibility for his educational development, and to become a more responsible individual in society. Many students now are learning to become masters of the machines which pervade nearly every aspect of our lives.

In view of this pervasive influence of computers in society, and the investment already made in developing instructional uses of computers, it is not surprising that some students thus benefit from computers. Although accurate data on total investments in computer uses in instruction are apparently not available, the following figures provide an indication of the order of investment made:

- The U.S. Office of Education alone spent an estimated $161 million between 1964 and 1969 for the use of computers in education (Grayson and Robbins, 1972), exclusive of Title I and some major administrative applications. In the same

years, an estimated $685 million was spent by USOE on educational technology and related projects.
- The National Science Foundation has specifically supported the development of computer-related innovational projects in education with nearly $40 million since 1965. In 1971 alone, the figure is estimated at $17 million. For curriculum-related projects from 1965-1974, the estimate is $17.6 million.
- In institutions of higher learning, an estimated $480 million was spent for computing activities in the year 1969-70 alone. Roughly 30 percent ($142 million) of these expenditures were for instructional uses. This was more than double the amount for 1966-67. The annual increase in computing expenditures in higher education is shown in Figure 1 (Hamblen, 1972).
- Private industry (e.g., IBM, Science Research Associates, General Learning Corporation) has invested millions of dollars in the development of computer systems and curriculum materials for educational use.

A conservative estimate of overall national investment in educational uses of computers may be approximately $2 billion.

Despite the investment nationally, in dollars, careers, energies, and intellect, it is not at all clear how many students actually use computers in their learning. A recent survey of computing activities in secondary schools indicated that under one-half of one percent of high school students used computers in any way (Darby, Korotkin, and Romashko, 1970). Data from 1969-70 indicated that about 90 percent of students engaged in higher learning were enrolled in *institutions* which had access to computing facilities (Hamblen, 1972). It cannot be determined from these data how many *students* had access to computing facilities. One estimate was that in 1967 about 6 percent of the 6 million students then in higher education used computers in some way in learning (Levien, 1972). The most recent survey by the Southern Regional Education Board provides figures on *25,000* courses of instruction using computer services in higher education. Due to incompleteness of the data, this figure might represent anywhere from 20-50 percent of actual courses in existence. Although well over half of the courses, and probably 80 percent of the expenditures, were in

Estimated Total Expenditures for Computing in U.S. Higher Education Through FY 1980

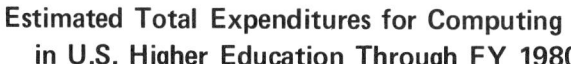

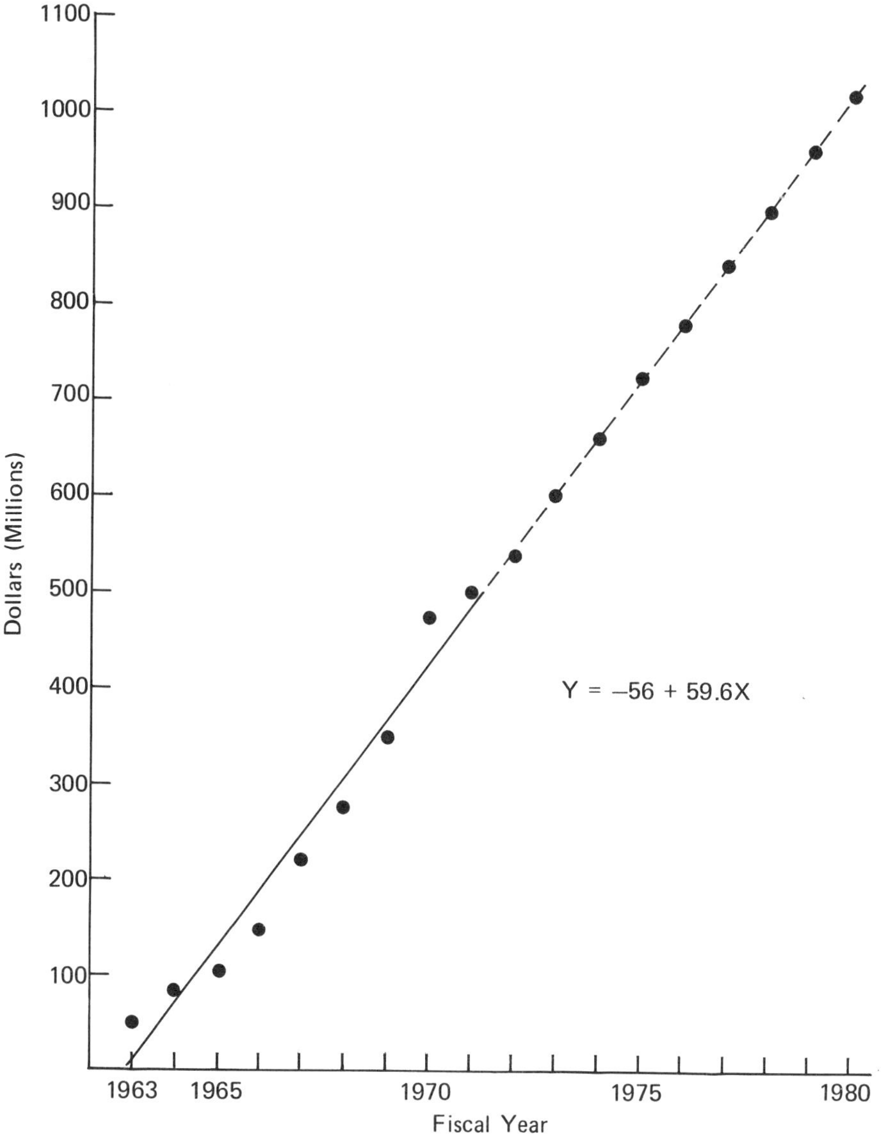

Source: Hamblen, 1972, p. III-17

Figure 1

engineering, business, and computer science areas, almost every subject area is represented to some extent (Hamblen, 1972).

Irrespective of the actual number of students involved, and whether the number is judged to be "not enough" or "too many," the phenomenon of instructional computer use has been growing and is clearly now of a magnitude that it must be taken seriously—by educators, government, and industry.

At the present stage of development, one of the most important concerns is the quality and availability of *curricular materials* required to support these uses of computers for learning.* In the present study, we accumulated data on the computer-based curricular materials for which there was publicly available information from all levels of education. These included course outlines, problem sets, instructional programs, textbooks, and similar materials, in all fields except computer science and data processing per se. These items varied from a computer subroutine for performing some calculation to complete tutorials for a two-semester course. We were able to identify about 5,650 such items, many or most of which are not actually available or operational except for use by a few people at the developing institution.** Thus, it is not surprising that a survey of experts, *Study of Factors Inhibiting the Widespread Use of Computers in Instruction,* found that the most significant obstacle to computer use by students is the lack of "... availability of adequate materials and the lack of evidence of CAI effectiveness,..." (Anastasio and Morgan, 1972, p. 47). This finding is also reflected in the recent Carnegie Commission report on instructional technology in higher education. One of their recommendations (Carnegie, 1972, p. 48) was:

> Recommendation 2: *Since a grossly inadequate supply of good quality instructional materials now exists, a major thrust of financial support and effort on behalf of instructional technology for the next decade should be toward the development and utilization of outstanding instructional*

---

*Throughout this book, such materials are referred to as "computer-based curricular materials or innovations" and as "computer-based learning materials" (CBLM).

**More data about these items are presented in Chapter 3.

programs and materials. The academic disciplines should follow the examples of physics and mathematics in playing a significant role in such efforts.

BARRIERS TO GROWTH

The barriers or obstacles to widespread use and acceptance of CBLM are complex. Anastasio and Morgan (1972, p. 47) noted the circular interrelationships among the obstacles as follows:

To provide evidence of effectiveness, one must (a) conduct a convincing high-quality demonstration. But (b) to conduct a proper demonstration, one needs good computer-based materials. But (c) to develop good materials, one needs good people who know theories and methods of instruction and are sensitive to the role of the teacher and problems of the classroom. But (d) to get good people, one needs professional recognition and economic incentives. But (e) to get professional recognition, one needs evidence of the value of the pursuit (see point a) and to get proper economic incentives one needs a formal production-distribution system (as in textbook publishing) and an active market. But (f) to establish a production-distribution system and market, one needs a demonstration of effectiveness to convince potential investors and buyers of CAI's value—and we are back at the beginning.

The obstacles can be categorized in terms of their relevance to development, adoption, or dissemination of CBLM. *Development Obstacles* run the gamut from lack of economic and professional incentives to lack of skilled personnel to produce the materials. Lack of sufficient local or outside funding presents severe problems to adequate development (as well as to adoption and dissemination). *Adoption Obstacles*, in addition to the lack of quality materials cited by Anastasio and Morgan, include important gaps in our knowledge of instructional strategies, lack of documentation, and lack of integration into curricula. Lack of skilled personnel able to train others to support and to use CBLM is also a major problem. Negative faculty attitudes stemming from fear of loss of status coupled with lack of incentives for them to spend time on integrating CBLM also are cited. *Dissemination* problems add to the above obstacles the lack of organizational structures to facilitate dissemination, poor incentives, technical problems related to incompatibility of hardware/software, and legal and financial publishing difficulties.

Critics and leaders in the field of CBLM have stressed one or more of those items noted above, i.e.:
- lack of practical understanding of the *human learning processes* (Oettinger and Marks, 1969; Bunderson, 1970; Seidel, 1971b; Stolurow, 1972; Silberman, 1970);
- high initial development *cost to industry* with small return on investment (Locke, 1971).

Congressional testimony has also touched on the same issues, as indicated in Appendix B of the House of Representatives Hearings for the Educational Technology Act of 1969 (Select Subcommittee on Education, 1971). The following is extracted from that testimony:

Obstacles to computer use in education are so interwined that it is difficult to separate them. Taxpayer resistance, fragmented sources of support, and rising demands for educational services to a broader spectrum of the population have created major problems for education in general. Only a small fraction of a school or university budget is ever applicable for *any* form of instructional materials. The implications for computer technology and other innovations are obvious. Grades, courses, credits, departments, lock-step grouping leave little room for substantive effective change in schools and colleges. One of the reflections of this problem is the lack of incentives to the innovator; promotions, salary increases, etc., are not usually based on the contribution the teacher makes to improving education.

Most of these problems are not peculiar to computers or educational technology per se, but relate to general issues of innovation in American education.

DIVERSITY OF PURPOSES

The educational panacea promised by the potential of the computer always seems to be just around the corner. The problem is that at times the corner takes on the character of the geometric anomaly called the Moebius Strip. This mathematical figure is a continuous twisted surface which loops back on itself and has no clear outside or inside dimensions. The never-ending debates over the "inside" or "outside" dimensions to the issues involved in developing and disseminating quality curricular materials using the computer seem to be characterized by the same problem.

Many different *purposes* have been advanced by educational leaders for using computers in education. Each goal implies different actions and products relevant to development and dissemination.

Computing Opportunity Purposes

Perhaps the most succinct statement of goals for computing in higher education was provided by the President's Science Advisory Committee (1970, pp. 7-8):

In all fields where computing has been used, it has added a new dimension to education, and has led the students to better comprehension of complex problems and greater insight into the meaning of quantitative expressions. In these areas undergraduates have learned, through preparation of and experimentation with computer programs, of the care required to define a problem logically and fully, and the assumptions needed to obtain answers to complex problems. We predict that in the future almost all undergraduates will use computers profitably *if adequate computing facilities are available*. There may be a few students in some fields who will not use computers at all, but they will be a small minority.

The Committee's emphasis at the time was on providing computing hardware; today we would add the provision of the need for a variety of software as well.

Discipline Advancement, Curricular Enhancement Purposes

The goal of advancing *particular* disciplines, through use of computers to enhance curricula, is implicit in the majority of the CBLM work, particularly in higher education. Examples of these purposes are described in the Conferences on Computers in the Undergraduate Curricula. One such illustration (Courtney, 1972, p. 71):

But the appearance of time-shared computer terminal facilities on many university campuses promises the possibility [through remote time-sharing] of substantive courses in business planning and control. The facilities will free students from the computational constraints presently existing and will thereby permit the realistic illustration of mathematical models as well as the behavioral dimensions of the discipline [material in brackets added].

Instructional Cost-Effectiveness Purposes

A quite different type of goal regarding uses of computers in higher education is stated clearly by Levien (1972, p. 434):

> Thus, the principal national objective concerning instruction with the computer should be: *To ensure that access to the computer and associated instructional materials is possible wherever its use would be cost-effective.* (Of course, this should be the national objective with regard to every mode of instruction.) ... Thus, a second national objective concerning instruction with the computer should be: *To improve the cost-effectiveness of instruction with the computer where such improvement will lead to a consequent improvement in the cost-effectiveness of higher education.* (There should be a similar objective for every alternative mode of instruction as well.)

In this case, the computer is a means of instruction, to be compared against alternative means in terms of costs and effectiveness.

Computing Literacy Purposes

Computing literacy needs and goals have been articulated by a number of observers, including the recent report by the Conference Board of the Mathematical Sciences Committee on Computer Education (1972, pp. 1-2), *Recommendations Regarding Computers in High School Education*. They recommend:

> A_1. ... the preparation of a junior high school course in "computer literacy" designed to provide students with enough information about the nature of a computer so that they can understand the roles which computers play in our society.

Perspectives

- A₂. ... the process of preparing the text materials for the above course be such as to provide wide and rapid dissemination of information about the availability and feasibility of the course.
- B. ... text materials for a number of other courses be prepared, ... introduction to computing, as a follow-up to the computer literacy course, ... integrate computing into high school mathematics courses, ... in simulating the behavior of physical or social phenomena and ... in the study of courses outside mathematics.
- C. ... the development of special programs for high school students showing unusual aptitude and promise in computer science.
- D. ... a major effort aimed at making vocational computer training more generally available and at the same time improving the quality of such training.
- E. ... the National Science Foundation provide financial support for the development of a variety of programs for the training of teachers and of teachers of teachers of high school courses involving computers.
- F. ... the establishment of a clearinghouse for information about high school computer education.

Educational Reform Purposes

The computer and other aspects of educational technology are often viewed in terms of overall educational reform (Commission on Instructional Technology, 1970, pp. 6-7):

> ... Formal education is not responsive enough: the organization of schools and colleges takes too little account of even what is now known about the process of human learning, particularly of the range of individual differences among students.... Technology, we believe, can carry out its full potential for education only insofar as educators embrace instructional technology as a system and integrate a range of human and nonhuman resources into the total educational process.... The changes required will probably be as thoroughgoing as those which industry underwent when it

shifted from hand labor to mechanization. But a society hurtling into the age of the computer and the satellite can no longer be held back by an educational system which is limping along at the blackboard-and-textbook stage of communication.

A number of experiments are being conducted, and a variety of writers are advocating institutions and systems for learning that are alternatives to the traditional educational institutions. Some of these require computer support in one way or another (e.g., Leonard, 1968; Silber, 1972).

Silber (1972), in describing an "open learning system," draws heavily upon computer technology to facilitate the learner's contact with resources. His proposed "open-ended" bank of learning objectives would require an immense computing facility for storage and retrieval. The ideal learning facility would include a computer terminal at home, featuring color television, cathode ray tube (CRT), with a light pen and interactive capability, and a video-telephone.

Toffler (1970) to a less dramatic degree advocates varied organizational structures devoid of grades and based on an interactive, individualized, and independent work setting. Community and schools are to be closely intertwined through use of experts as mentors and local businesses as learning settings. The role of the computer and other technological advances are to support the differences in organizational structures. This trend will be sharply encouraged by improvements in computer-assisted education, video recording, holography, and other technical fields.

In a more conservative vein, Saxe (1972) focuses on the need for alternatives to augment, supplement, and complement but not necessarily replace or eliminate the institutions of the public schools. He is a proponent of independent study, solicitation of student ideas, and inclusion of "cafeteria-type," student-selected experiences. Computers and other technologies fit his search for alternatives that would open up the schools.

The traditional educational institutions are as aware of the need for reform. This is exemplified in the recently adopted goals of the State of Virginia (*Standards of Quality and Objectives for Public Schools in Virginia, 1972-74*):

- to acquire competence in using the fundamental learning skills and to acquire basic knowledge needed for participation in today's society;
- to acquire skills and knowledge needed for education beyond high school or for employment;
- to acquire a sense of personal worth and dignity;
- to develop attitudes and values that lead to responsible participation as a citizen of our republic;
- to develop understanding of one's relationship to his ecological, physical, economic, and social environment;
- to understand and appreciate people of different nationalities and ethnic groups and their contributions to the development of our nation and culture;
- to develop personal habits for continuing physical and mental health; and
- to appreciate beauty and to understand its contribution to daily life.

The problem for real reform may well lie in the *implementation* of such goals. The foregoing are desirable-sounding, lofty aims but require careful translation into meaningful, measurable objectives at the level of classroom use. And it is likely that a traditional system may have more difficulty than an alternative system because of accumulated resistance to change.

The Carnegie Commission on Higher Education (1972), recognizing emerging alternatives, stated in *The Fourth Revolution: Instructional Technology in Higher Education* (p. 52):

> But a realistic appraisal of current progress suggests that the most significant advances, in the coming decade [in educational technology], will be generated by emerging institutions and extramural educational systems that are being created alongside traditional ones.

The Commission went on to state (p. 53):

> We recommend that major funding sources, including states, the federal government, and foundations, recognize not only the potential of new and developing extramural education systems for expanding learning opportunities, but also the

crucial role such systems should play in the ultimate development of instructional technologies. Requests of these systems for funds with which to introduce and use new instructional programs, materials, and media should be given favorable consideration.

These differing points of view undoubtedly have contributed also to an unnecessary and potentially harmful conceptual confusion regarding roles of the computer in instruction.

A *de facto* distinction often appears in literature and projects, between "computing literacy" applications of computers in learning and "surrogate instructor" roles of computers. This distinction is reflected in:

- leadership of computer instruction projects (e.g., discipline experts versus educational technologists);
- computer software systems which have been developed for instructional applications (e.g., IMPRESS vs. Coursewriter);
- sources and amounts of funding for projects (OE 1966-71: $5,985,027 for "Problem-Solving"; $52,725,366 for "Computer Presented Instruction") (Grayson and Robbins, 1972);
- national statements of goals for computer use in education (e.g., Report of President's Science Advisory Committee, 1967 vs. Carnegie Commission, 1972);
- various studies regarding computers in education (e.g., Levien's 1972 "instruction about" vs. "instruction through" the computer);
- the ways in which instructional computing applications are evaluated (e.g., new benefits vs. cost-effectiveness);
- common classifications for types of applications (e.g., "problem-solving" versus "tutorial"); and
- the instructional materials themselves.

We view this distinction as not only unnecessary, but as an obstacle in the long run to the development and adoption of potentially useful and beneficial computer-based educational innovations. Students in a "computer as surrogate instructor" environment are often deprived of the opportunity to develop computing skills relevant to the very subjects the surrogate instructor is teaching. Students who benefit from "computing literacy" or "problem-solving" materials and programs often must do so in a lock-step classroom environment without the benefits of adaptive individualized instruction the computer could provide.

This summary of types of purposes is not exhaustive. It is intended to point out the difficulty in working *in general* on strategies for computer-oriented educational materials, without reference to specific goals. A strategy to provide computing opportunity on a widespread basis may not, and should not, be expected to further other goals, such as educational cost-effectiveness or broad educational reform. A strategy for enhancing curricula in a particular discipline is not the same as a strategy for achieving universal computing literacy or developing alternative educational systems.

In this book, different strategies for developing and implementing CBLM are related to the various purposes of learning systems in general and computer-based learning systems in particular.

THE STATE OF AFFAIRS— ACTIVITY AND GROWTH

Despite many obstacles to computer use in education, activity and development in the field continue to increase rapidly. There are indicators of this activity in commission reports, studies, conferences, organizations formed, research and development projects, and many other areas discussed in various chapters of this book. Following is a sampling of what has been occurring.

Studies

• Comprehensive statistical surveys for higher education have been made by the Southern Regional Education Board (Hamblen, 1972) under NSF grants. The inventory provides a comprehensive statistical base of usage, types of use, and expenditures on computers in higher education.

• A major review of the uses of the computer in higher education was conducted in 1970 by the Rand Corporation (Levien, 1972). The study was sponsored by the Carnegie Commission on Higher Education, NSF, and the Rand Corporation, and drew on other statistical surveys, such as Hamblen's, in its coverage of all uses of the computer: research, administrative, library, and instructional. The report contains informative descriptions of the various applications in each area of use, as well as considerable analytical information on current trends in computer use. The last section of the report is oriented to the prospects of computers in instruction in higher education over the next two decades.

• Studies of the role of computers in elementary and secondary education have been less extensive than for higher education, and even less has been done on community and junior colleges. The American Institutes for Research, under an NSF grant, conducted an empirical *Survey of Computing Activities in Secondary Schools* (Darby, Korotkin, and Romashko, 1970). The emphasis was on instructional uses of computers, although some data on other uses were gathered from the 12,396 public secondary schools responding to the survey.

• A more detailed study of the uses of computers in instruction in all institutions was conducted at the University of Michigan under the sponsorship of USOE (Zinn, 1970). The report from this study provides case study information on research, development, ongoing activities, dissemination, and facilities for the use of computers in instruction. Unlike the Hamblen, Levien, and Darby reports, it does not provide statistical information on the extent and utilization of computers in educational institutions.

• An overview of "Computer Innovations in Education" was provided by Andrew Molnar of the National Science Foundation (Molnar, 1972). It highlights recent developments nationally and internationally.

Commission Reports

• The President's Science Advisory Committee (1967), under the chairmanship of John Pierce, established goals for computing in higher education. They recommended that computing opportunity be provided to all students.

• The Commission on Instructional Technology (1970) prepared an evaluation which resulted in recommendations for a comprehensive national program of Research, Development, and Applications in the form of a National Institute of Education (NIE) and a National Institute of Instructional Technology (NIIT).

• The Carnegie Commission on Higher Education prepared a report and recommendations on Instructional Technology in Higher

Education. In this report, the Carnegie Commission urges (Carnegie, 1972, p. 45) that "colleges and universities, industry, governments, and foundations concerned with educational endeavors make an effort to advance the time when currently available technologies will be fully utilized for the instruction of our youth and the continuing education of our citizens."

CBLM Development

- A wide range of instructional programs and materials for the computer have been developed. Denk (1971a) found over 3,000 such programs. Thousands of articles, books, and periodicals exist on subjects related to the use of computers in instruction. The fourth edition of a CBLM index (Hoye and Wang, 1973) documents 1,766 instructional programs. Our own study uncovered 5,560 items, including programs and related text materials about which there exists some published information. Most of these materials have been developed in the past eight years.

Users Groups

- Special users groups have been formed to exchange information, ideas, and materials for use of computers in instruction—groups such as the Association for the Development of Computer-Based Instructional Systems (ADCIS); National Association of Users of Computer Applications to Learning (NAUCAL); Association for Computing Machinery, Special Interest Group on Computer Uses in Education (ACM SIGCUE); an American Educational Research Association special interest group (AERA SIGCAI); and Interuniversity Communications Council (EDUCOM-EIN).

Conferences

- National and international conferences have been held, such as: International Federation for Information Processing (IFIP) World Conference on Computer Education (Sheepmaker and Zinn, 1970); Iowa, Dartmouth, Atlanta, and Claremont Conferences on Computers in the Undergraduate Curricula (Luehrmann, 1971, and *Proceedings*, 1970-1973); and the Commission on College Physics Conference on Computers in Undergraduate Science Education (COMUSE) (Blum, 1971).

Projects

• Research, development, and demonstration projects are underway in every type of educational institution. The two demonstration projects most widely publicized recently are TICCIT (the Mitre Corporation) and PLATO (University of Illinois). They are collectively receiving $9 million support from NSF to show that ". . . a CAI system can function economically and effectively in practice, . . ." (Hammond, 1972, p. 110).

The basis for the TICCIT approach is the targeted development, packaging, and delivery of CBLM by means of teams of specialists. The hardware system is built around small, stand-alone computers with color TV student terminals and is designed to serve 128 students simultaneously.

PLATO is based on teacher-oriented preparation of CBLM. The student terminal is unique—the Plasma Panel, which displays graphic information permanently without auxiliary storage. The computer system is based in a large general purpose machine (four central processors) with the intention of serving thousands of students simultaneously over telephone lines.

• Currently some 225 schools are participating in 16 regional and state computing networks. The networks comprise four-year colleges, universities, two-year colleges, and secondary schools. The NSF Office of Computing Activities in its Regional Cooperative Computing Activities Program originally supported the networks.

• The Advanced Research Projects Agency (ARPA) has established a nationwide computer communications network among 20 universities, with the goal of making every local resource available to any computer in the net in such a way that any program available to local users can be used remotely (Roberts, 1972).

• NSF has sponsored CONDUIT, a project joining five major regional networks in higher education. The purpose is to determine critical factors in the transportability of computer-oriented curricular materials across networks and to examine potentially feasible strategies for accomplishing transport. The participants are North Carolina Educational Computing Service, Dartmouth, Oregon State, Iowa, and the University of Texas.

• NSF through EDUCOM sponsored a series of seminars held

during the winter of 1972-73, directed toward establishing parameters for a National Science Information Network. Millions of dollars will be spent within the next few years to bring NSIN into existence.

Commercial Organizations
• Several new organizations have been established to provide computing services and curricula materials to schools. Time Share Corporation in Hanover, New Hampshire, provides computing services and guidance and instructional materials to high schools. They have joined forces with Houghton Mifflin, the publisher, in developing and marketing CBLM. Computer Curriculum Corporation in Palo Alto, California, markets computer-based drills in mathematics and reading to elementary schools. They also provide complete hardware and software systems. There are a number of others, including Digital Equipment Corporation and Hewlett-Packard Corporation.

Federal Programs
• Between 1965 and 1971, the U.S. Office of Education funded more than 500 projects that use computers in education. The USOE is composed of numerous bureaus and national centers, each of which focuses its activities on a particular level or area of education. Virtually every bureau and national center has supported computer activities related to its area of concern. The USOE support has been provided under 14 different legislative titles and acts administered by almost every bureau and center (Grayson and Robbins, 1972).

• The National Science Foundation Office of Computing Activities since 1965 has supported hundreds of projects in computer innovations in education as well as basic research in computer science and computer applications in research (Molnar, 1972).

PROJECTIONS OF ACCEPTANCE FOR CBLM

Given today's dynamic, diverse state of affairs, and the obstacles in the path of development, adoption, and dissemination, a remaining question is: When can we expect that computers will become an accepted part of American education?

Descriptive projections regarding the adoption of computer technology for instructional purposes are available in three studies, all of which used some version of a Delphi technique. Doyle and Goodwill (1971) of Bell Canada have prepared "An Exploration of the Future in Educational Technology" which covers a variety of topics related to technology and education, including values, school design, role of teachers, computer-based systems, terminals, and chemical learning. The panel was composed of educational technologists, educators, administrators, and government officials.

Bernard Luskin's *An Identification and Examination of Obstacles to the Development of Computer Assisted Instruction* (Luskin, 1970) included projections of "breakeven points" in adoption of CAI, by three separate panels of educators, administrators, and industry representatives. Jarrod Wilcox, of the Sloan School of Management at MIT, prepared a report of a Delphi, *A Survey Forecast of New Technology in Universities and Colleges* (Wilcox, 1972). The Wilcox report includes two surveys: one of technologists and the other of college and university faculty.

The projections of the three studies with regard to higher education are shown in Figure 2 (black arrowheads represent median response; direction and spread of interquartile range are shown by tails of arrows). All the panels place the routine use of computer-assisted instruction systems in the majority of institutions at 1985 or before. The faculty panel in the Wilcox study places some interesting qualifications on this, however. The faculty response to a projection that CAI has "largely supplanted the traditional live teacher classroom instruction in some courses taught in my department" was the year 2020, or *never* with regard to all types of technology systems.

As shown in Figure 3, adoption of computer-assisted instruction in the majority of secondary schools was placed at some time in the 1980's by all but Luskin's administrator panel. However, Luskin reports a high tendency toward pessimism* by all panels, with interquartile range spreading to *never*.

For elementary schools, the general expectation is that adoption will come later than secondary or higher education. As shown in Figure

---

*It should be carefully noted that Luskin's use of the term "pessimism" assumes that widespread use of CBLM is desirable. Some readers may disagree with that assumption.

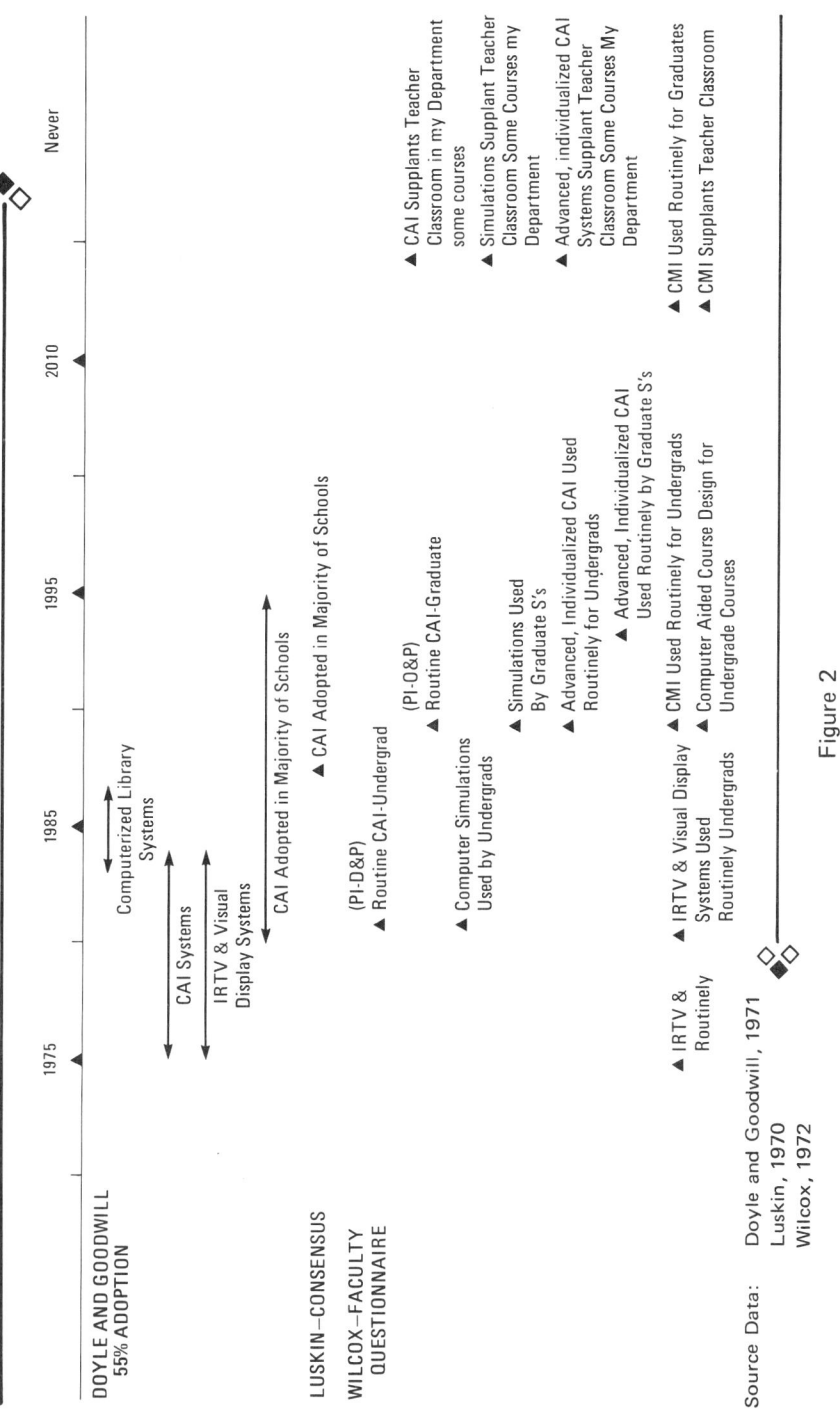

Summary of Projections for Adoption of Computer-Assisted Learning in Higher Education

	1975	1985	1995	2010	Never

DOYLE AND GOODWILL
55% ADOPTION
- ▲ (1975)
- Computerized Library Systems
- CAI Systems
- IRTV & Visual Display Systems

LUSKIN—CONSENSUS
- CAI Adopted in Majority of Schools
- ▲ CAI Adopted in Majority of Schools
- ▲ (2010)

WILCOX—FACULTY QUESTIONNAIRE

(PI-D&P)
- ▲ Routine CAI-Undergrad
- ▲ Computer Simulations Used by Undergrads

(PI-O&P)
- ▲ Routine CAI-Graduate
- ▲ Simulations Used By Graduate S's
- ▲ Advanced, Individualized CAI Used Routinely for Undergrads
- ▲ Advanced, Individualized CAI Used Routinely by Graduate S's

- ▲ IRTV & Routinely
- ▲ IRTV & Visual Display Systems Used Routinely Undergrads
- ▲ CMI Used Routinely for Undergrads
- ▲ Computer Aided Course Design for Undergrade Courses
- ▲ CAI Supplants Teacher Classroom in my Department some courses
- ▲ Simulations Supplant Teacher Classroom Some Courses my Department
- ▲ Advanced, individualized CAI Systems Supplant Teacher Classroom Some Courses My Department
- ▲ CMI Used Routinely for Graduates
- ▲ CMI Supplants Teacher Classroom

Source Data: Doyle and Goodwill, 1971
Luskin, 1970
Wilcox, 1972

Figure 2

Summary of Projections for Adoption of Computer-Assisted Learning in Secondary Schools

	1975	1985	1995	2010	Never

DOYLE AND GOODWILL
55% ADOPTION

- Computerized Library Systems
- CAI Systems
- IRTV & Visual Display Systems
- CAI Adopted in Majority of Schools

LUSKIN

EDUCATORS ▲ CAI Adopted in Majority of Schools

ADMINISTRATORS ▲ CAI Adopted in Majority of Schools

INDUSTRY ▲ CAI Adopted in Majority of Schools

CONSENSUS ▲ CAI Adopted in Majority of Schools

Source Data: Doyle and Goodwill, 1971
              Luskin, 1970

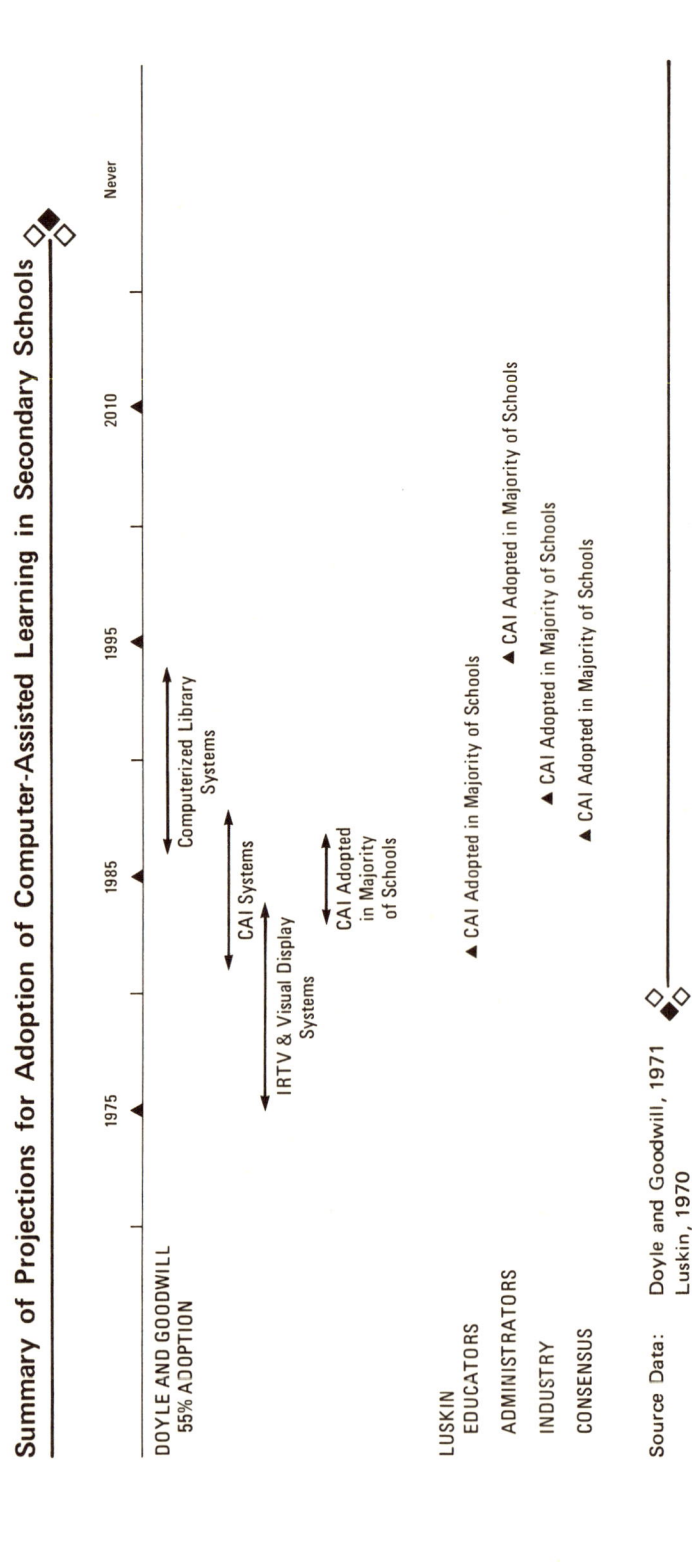

Figure 3

Summary of Projections of Adoption of Computer-Assisted Learning in Elementary Schools

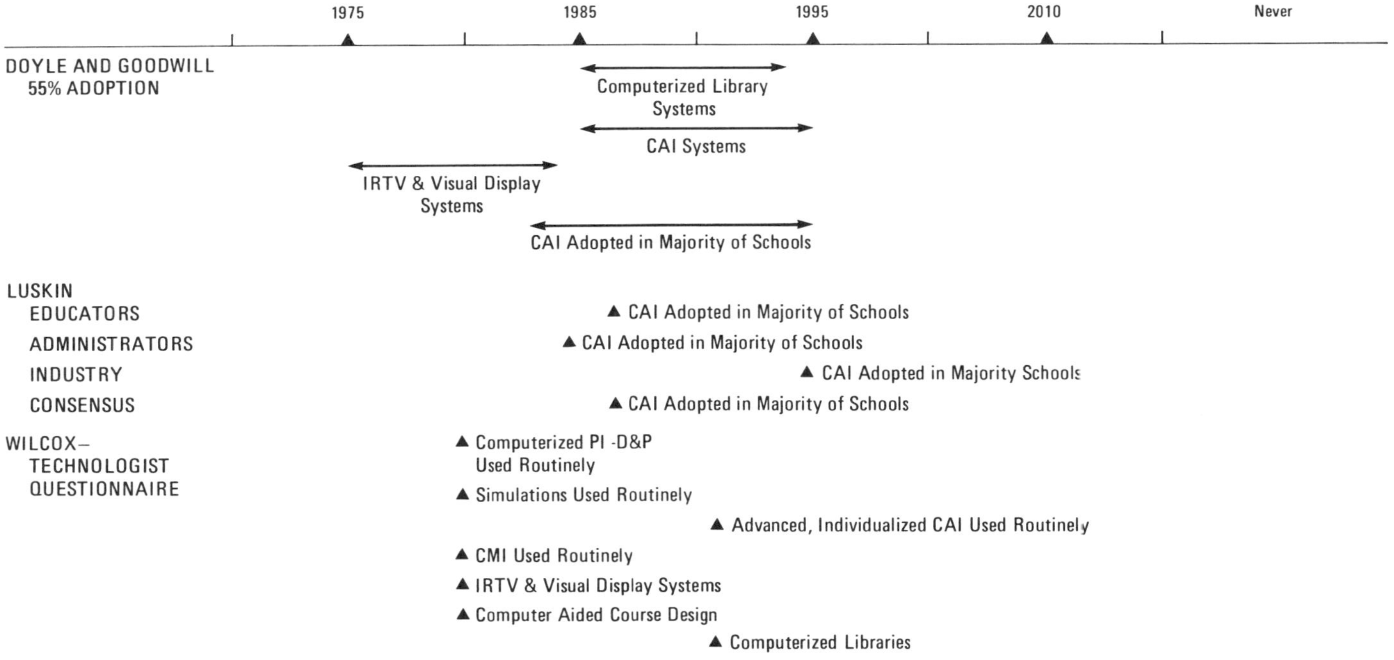

	1975	1985	1995	2010	Never

DOYLE AND GOODWILL
55% ADOPTION

IRTV & Visual Display Systems (1975–1985)
Computerized Library Systems (1985–1995)
CAI Systems (1985–1995)
CAI Adopted in Majority of Schools (1985)

LUSKIN
EDUCATORS — ▲ CAI Adopted in Majority of Schools (1995)
ADMINISTRATORS — ▲ CAI Adopted in Majority of Schools (1995)
INDUSTRY — ▲ CAI Adopted in Majority of Schools (2010)
CONSENSUS — ▲ CAI Adopted in Majority of Schools (1995)

WILCOX—TECHNOLOGIST QUESTIONNAIRE
▲ Computerized PI-D&P Used Routinely (1985)
▲ Simulations Used Routinely (1985)
▲ CMI Used Routinely (1985)
▲ IRTV & Visual Display Systems (1985)
▲ Computer Aided Course Design (1985)
▲ Advanced, Individualized CAI Used Routinely (1995)
▲ Computerized Libraries (1995)

Source Data: Doyle and Goodwill, 1971
Luskin, 1970
Wilcox, 1972

Figure 4

4, sometime around 1990 the majority of elementary schools are expected to use CAI routinely, though once more Luskin's panels are pessimistic, i.e., there is a spread toward "never" among the third and fourth quartiles of the responses.

Expectations are for widespread computer use to take place first in higher education. This projection centers around 1985, with the provision that some teacher replacement by computer teaching may not occur until 2020 or later. Common acceptance at the secondary education level is seen as occurring shortly after higher education. Elementary education is expected to be the last to use computers routinely; this occurrence is projected somewhere in the early 1990's.

SUMMARY

Although computing has not directly affected the schooling of a large percentage of students in this country to date, considerable resources are being expended to provide computing facilities and curricular materials for education. There are several quite different reasons why various individuals and organizations support computer use in education. There are a variety of obstacles to developing and adopting computer-based innovations. Strategies to provide computer-based learning materials nationwide to students and their schools must take into account these various purposes and obstacles.

Chapter 2

EDUCATION — TRENDS AND VISIONS

Motto for the Twenty-first Century:
"Anything Is Possible."
Thomas Hanna (1970)

The interpretations and conclusions that one draws about computer-based curricula in education—the importance of such curricula, the nature and form they should take, the significant variables involved, whether and how to go about developing materials and systems to support such curricula, how large an investment to make—such conclusions rest largely on basic assumptions about society and education, both today and in the next decades.

Some points of view on educational reform were discussed in Chapter 1. What educational purposes would proposed reforms serve? What trends toward reform can be seen in the near term? What vision of the future might these trends presage? Do any implications follow for the role(s) of the computer in education, and types and quantity of computer-based materials needed? Information resources? Total computer-based learning centers? Entire communities' needs served by large computing resources? What dangers exist in adopting computer-based learning materials—dehumanization? Amplifying the bad qualities of education by creating technological mousetraps?

TODAY'S TRENDS

A succinct statement characterizing emerging educational purpose is exemplified by leading educators (e.g., Burns and Brooks, 1970, p. 6) as follows: "What will future generations call this age? Whatever the designation it will imply 'change.'" To educate for change will necessitate (1) efficient learning of skills with wide transfer value (emphasis on process orientation), and (2) ability to learn independently of the formal setting (flexibility, problem-solving, etc.). Burns and

Brooks cite the area of science instruction as leading the change in orientation toward an information processing approach to learning. But no reforms "... have gone far enough to produce the curricula needed for today's education" (p. 4). They go on to describe a host of growing societal pressures which are continuing to force the required changes in American education. It is useful to list and briefly discuss these pressures because they imply technological and, in particular, computer needs in emerging education (pp. 5-6).

1. We are living in a global society.
2. We are living in a rapidly changing world.
3. Our culture is experiencing an information explosion.
4. Present curricula are information-oriented rather than process-oriented.
5. There is a lack of relevancy between in-school education and out-of-school life.
6. There is a prohibitive time lag in education between the discovery of new techniques and the incorporation of these techniques into educational practice.
7. General education and core curricula are presently too survey-oriented.
8. There are new technical innovations for which new curricular patterns can be designed.
9. Urban living, a decreasing emphasis on family structure, and the increasing mobility of the population demand greater individual responsibility.
10. There is an increased recognition of the needs of minority groups and minority group problems.
11. Our knowledge of what is true is constantly changing.
12. There is an increased understanding of how people learn.
13. The behavioral definition of learning products has revealed deficiencies in our present curricula.
14. Productivity has released men from the necessity of long labor.

The information-explosion phenomenon (item 3) is especially pertinent to computer-based curricula. Some recent estimates are that at the current rate, knowledge doubles every seven or eight years (Chapanis, 1971; Licklider, 1966). Data on the numbers of new book

Education–Trends and Visions

titles published each year illustrate the explosion in information available. In the field of sociology and economics, the number of titles for new books and new editions published annually increased from under 800 in 1960 to over 6,400 in 1972 (*The Bowker Annual of Library and Book Trade Information*, 1971, 1973).

Further, the effects of knowledge are felt more rapidly. In technology, for example, photography took roughly 112 years to move from discovery to application; the x-ray tube approximately 18 years; the atomic bomb, 6 years; and recently solar batteries, 2 years (*Futurist*, 1970). These apparent trends toward more and more rapid explosion of knowledge and its effects imply to some observers the need for massive changes in education to enable people to cope with this rapid pace of change (e.g., Boulding, 1967; Kemeny, 1972). And, in fact, the results of our inability to cope are being felt, for example, in our dilemmas about the environment, food supply, pollution, energy sources, and global economy.

Computer-based systems are intimately bound up with the knowledge explosion and the rate of technological change. An illustration of the increasing importance of computing in the U.S. is seen in the rapid growth rate, 213 percent, for general purpose and 1233 percent for dedicated application of computer use over the past seven years (*EDP Industry Report*, March 30, 1973).

Belief in the importance of computer-based curricula stems largely from the assumption that these rates of change in knowledge and technology will continue to accelerate. If man is to be able to cope with the rapid change, it seems obvious that he must acquire skills which will enable him to learn how to learn: to learn more things faster, continually learn, and learn independently of a formal educational setting. Since computer systems are basic to our capabilities for handling large, complex sets of information, the need seems obvious for increasing computing literacy on the part of the populace.

Another consideration accompanying the above is the rise in numbers and importance of computer-related jobs and the pace of change in jobs in general. It has been estimated (Molnar, 1970) that 70 percent of the jobs which will face our children who are in elementary schools today do not currently exist. Following the foregoing logic, awareness of, and skill in, computing would seem to be an essential part of our emerging education.

However, it cannot automatically be assumed that past rates and types of change can be projected into the indefinite future. There are limits to growth. There are checks and balances in the systems producing these phenomena. As one simple illustration, consider the rapid, increasing trend in book title output in the decade from 1960-1970 (Hokkanen, 1970). The smallest growth rate was a doubling of output, in Science, with other fields showing varied exponential increases (the largest being Sociology and Economics, with 785 percent growth). Federal aid to education made more textbooks available to more students than ever before. Federal aid also supported libraries, which in turn support the book industry. The unprecedented national wealth and personal prosperity, combined with leisure time and increased level of education, created the economic conditions for a very successful publishing market. However, many of these variables are subject to change, and in fact by 1972 there were a number of signs of pessimism in the book industry, as reported in the *Library Journal* (Nyren, 1973). Diminishing federal funds for research, diminishing federal support of libraries, problems in finding a new financial base for support of schools, and drops in school enrollments are examples of these signs. This is not to suggest that the increase in new book titles is going to level off or decrease in rate. It is simply to point out that the particular growth curves of the past few decades are not necessarily indications of the future state of things.

Growth might be dramatically altered, for example, by a long-term energy crisis and its side-effects. The educational implications of critical fuel shortages are just beginning to surface. Over time, lower temperatures, shorter hours, and longer vacations must inevitably affect educational programs. And these early attempts to conserve energy resources might be followed by drastic measures. The consequences would probably deal fatal blows to many curricular innovations. The hardware orientation of much educational technology could mean an early grave for programs that depend on elaborate facilities with gluttonous appetites for the consumption of electricity. On the other hand, technology could help solve the problem of taking school to the student who works at home, in the dorm, or in other places selected for maximum utility of energy resources.

Various aspects of the societal characteristics cited by Burns and

Brooks clearly place great (and often conflicting) pressures on the educational systems. Although the basic responses on the part of educators to solving the resulting problems will be in the nature of social and organizational arrangements, technology is expected by many to have a significant role in solving many of the problems. For example, students can learn to use computer-based libraries and information retrieval systems.

Libraries of information are easily stored, and rapidly accessed and updated with computers. Students could begin using such computerized libraries as everyday tools, thus helping them find and use information more efficiently than today. Individually administered, adaptive instruction could also be computer-based and complemented by other media. Computer-based capabilities for individual inquiry, text handling, computation, simulation, and management information systems all may lend themselves to satisfying educational needs. The computer and CBLM curricula could be natural parts of such an emerging educational scene.

On the other hand, a leading critic of the American educational establishment, Charles Silberman (1970) states as the purpose of education "... to develop sensitive, autonomous, thinking, humane individuals," and asserts that today's system is failing to accomplish this. Silberman fears that the instructional use of computers and other technologies will simply amplify current failures in American education.

Although he shares Silberman's general assessment of problems with the status of the educational system, another educator (Kapfer, 1970, p. 37) is optimistic about today's trends in American education. In particular, Kapfer sees "a new breed of teacher" emerging, working with students to develop a more humanized atmosphere, and holding to the view that "... learning is a natural human enterprise, that students want to learn, ..." and can do so effectively and efficiently when given responsibility in the determination of their own learning activities. Kapfer sees this trend toward individual responsibility emerging as compatible with the use of instructional technology. In particular, he focuses on the value of behavioral objectives given that adequate instructional implementation of new curricula takes place. To date, he feels, limits in the use of behavioral objectives have been a function of the limitations of the school environment, not the concept of objectives.

Wedemeyer's recent assessment (1972) of the status of technology in education yields a perspective against which the romantic fears of Silberman, the projected societal needs of Burns and Brooks, and Kapfer's assessments can be resolved. Wedemeyer asserts that the philosophical trend in education today is coming to grips with three differing points of view of the human being. The "radical romantic" desires the individual to be free, to unfold naturally. The behaviorists with the techniques to disambiguate much of the previously obscure objectives of education have contributed important advances on a limited scale. The major criticism has been a mechanistic, shortsighted view of man.

The third philosophical position, which Wedemeyer attributes to the majority of Americans, especially the teachers, is consonant with the "cognitive-developmental theory of learning." The value system or philosophy of most Americans today is to place man and society in the context of "individualism, freedom from cruel and unusual restraint, democratic participation, value-oriented and idiosyncratic life styles, and authority-seeking rather than authority-following behaviors..." (p. 9).

Wedemeyer concludes that if this characterization of trends is correct, American education is at a readiness stage to benefit from technology—but this "new educational harvest" will require more philosophical maturation first. A significant aspect to this required maturity is discussed by Mitzel (1972, p. 1) as a need to "eliminate the current adversary atmosphere in American education." Part of the philosophical resolution necessitates the growth of "... human warmth between adults and children" in the typical elementary and secondary school classroom. It is essential to note that such growth is within the province of human interaction and beyond the limits of computer aids. If, as Mitzel proposes, the teachers of the future are to concentrate on "higher order skills . . . diagnosis . . ., mediating a dispute, assessing the impact of a pupil's home environment upon his in-school behavior and expressing comfort for a wounded spirit or an injured body" (p. 2), then a change in the existing adversary system must occur as a concomitant part of the general maturity of purpose. The computer (or any other technology, for that matter) can be a powerful resource to aid human goals but cannot supplant interpersonal needs and social transactions.

Against this backdrop of projected maturation of education, the many different types of computer applications may be seen to be useful. Apparent conflicts between proponents of the computer as surrogate instructor versus as a tool of the student may well vanish.

The visions discussed in the remainder of this chapter can be viewed as different future projections of present-day uses of computer-based learning materials. Geometrically, these visions can be viewed as compatible mappings onto a hyperplane of social space.

Leonard (1968) describes a personalized, adaptive "learning dome" which might be viewed as a futuristic extension of the *tutorial concept* into a multi-modal, all-encompassing, learning environment. Silber's open learning system (1972) maps the *computer as a tool* onto the surface of an entire community as the independent learner's resource. Fuller's geoscope (1971) paints with a broader brush the creative possibilities that technological tools place at the disposal of the independent learner—"communication of phenomena ... not at present communicable ... many motion patterns such as ... hands of a clock ... the solar system planets ... molecules of gas in a pneumatic ball ...," etc. From still another perspective, Rossman's vision (1972) is best described as presenting in hyperbole the requirement for curricular flexibility and relevance. While not explicitly outlining the role of the computer, Rossman's view projects continuous and cyclical change as an integral part of society's future. It implies a demand for complex, adaptive, individualized curricula to encompass the requirements of recurring basic skills. The computer enters here as a natural aid in design, updating, and administration of such curricula.

These and other visions are discussed in greater depth in the following section of this chapter.

VISIONS AND BASIC THEMES

There are differences among visionaries regarding purposes and functions of education, assumptions about human nature, relationship of the individual and the state, the nature of learning, the relationship of schooling to education, and the roles of technology in education.

There are, however, certain themes which all visionaries seem to share. These are present whether the visionary is a professional educator, a humanist, a technologist, or a social critic. This section highlights those common threads which seem to have implications for the design of computer-based systems. Hopefully, this will provide one vantage point from which the reader may devise strategies for developing and disseminating computer-based materials and systems for learning.

The basic themes discussed here include:
- the synergism of humanism and technology;
- respect for the uniqueness of individual humans;
- free learning resources for all, rather than compulsory schooling for some;
- a variety of learning resources—more options;
- a variety of places for learning;
- the importance of human relationships; and
- relationships between technology and learning outcomes.

The Synergism of Humanism and Technology

Synergism is the cooperative action of discrete agencies such that the total effect is greater than the sum of the effects taken independently. The general message of all the visionaries seems to be that education will be transformed through the synergistic effects of humanism and technology. From humanism we get new visions of the potential of individual humans for self-actualization, new respect for the variety and uniqueness of each whole person, and the energy to pursue new goals and establish new premises. From technology we get a new sense of possibilities, of the options that can be provided, of the tools which can be used to support self-actualization of individuals—and which can be used to support cooperation among them.

Humanism and technology, far from being antithetical to one another, are already intertwined. Harold Mitzel, a pioneer in the development of computer-assisted instruction for many years at Pennsylvania State University, has testified to the U.S. House of Representatives' Committee on Education and Labor that "one of the first things we must do to reform schools is to markedly increase the manifest expression of human warmth between adults and children" (Mitzel, 1972).

Isaiah E. Robinson, former President of the Board of Education of the City of New York, has described his vision of a "computerized and automated school system" in which the primary objective is "to imbue each student with the habit of success." Robinson (1972) believes the habit of success is developed through:
- evaluating each student by his own progress and not against the progress of others;
- cooperative experiences instead of competitive ones; and
- reinforcing curiosity, imagination, aptitude to inquiry, viability of notions, purpose, and intellectual excitement.

The essence of Robinson's vision is close to that of the humanist and visionary George B. Leonard who, in *Education and Ecstasy*, describes a "Learning Dome" of the year 2001. The relationship of technology and humanism in Leonard's vision is exemplified in the EID (electronic identification device) which every child wears at all times whenever he is on the school grounds. The central computer continually tabulates how much time he spends in each educational environment, and records the details of his interaction with computer-assisted dialogues. Leonard (1968, p. 154) says of the EID:

> This allows educators not only to keep track of each child's educational development with a minimum of effort, but also to evaluate the drawing power and effectiveness of each environment. The first principle of free learning is that if an environment fails to draw or to educate, it is the environment's, not the learner's, fault. Visiting educators from educationally underdeveloped nations sometimes find it hard to understand that EID tracking serves not to enforce conformity, but just the opposite. In fact, "asymmetry" is highly valued.

Respect for the Uniqueness of Individual Humans

This *respect for, and encouragement of, the uniqueness of individual learners is* a common theme among visionaries. Realization of the potential of individual humans is regarded not only as possible, but as necessary to survival of post-industrial, knowledge-based society. Thus, Leonard makes clear that the basic premise of *Education and*

Ecstasy is (p. 115):
> that the highly interactive, regenerative technological society now emerging will ... *require* something akin to mass genius, mass creativity, and lifelong learning.

This "mass genius" of which Leonard speaks is not the purely academic genius of the intellectual half-man. It is the genius of self-actualizing, whole human beings, with self-awareness, sensitivity to others, and the ability and confidence to manage their own lifelong learning. Thus, Papert and Solomon (1972, pp. 15-16) speak of the children who, through learning to program the computer, are learning to take conscious control over the programming of themselves.

> Quite clearly, using the child to program the computer is a good thing. He is deeply active and using his knowledge to get results. But that is not really what it is about. What you really want to teach the child to program is not the computer but *himself*. Really, the task of education has got to be to bring the child to the point where he does not need to be taught, where he does not need to be dished out the stuff according to good learning schedules or bad learning schedules; in other words, to the point where most of us grownup people would like to think we are at. If I want to learn something new, I do not go and take a course in it. I might consult experts, I might read books, I try to solve problems, I think about it, I put it together with pieces of knowledge I have in mind, and so on. I *know* how to go about looking for a new kind of knowledge in a new area, and we must bring the child to that point.

Buckminster Fuller (1971, pp. 50-51) has phrased it this way:
> Real education ... will be something to which individuals will discipline themselves spontaneously under the stimulus of their own ticker-tapes—their individually unique chromosomes. Everyone has his own chromosomal pattern. No two persons have the same appetite at the same time. There is no reason why they should.... We must make *all* the information immediately available over the two-way TV's ready for the different individual human chromosomal ticker-tapes to call for it.

This theme of individual growth recurs whether the visionary is in the role of school administrator, a technologist, a social critic, or a humanist. The National Conference of Professors of Educational Administration, in the book *Educational Futurism 1985* (Hack, *et al.*, 1971, p. 78) point out the importance of this theme to the organization of schools of the future:

> We anticipate that the basic principle of organization in 1985 will be preoccupation with individual freedom and fulfillment that are unknown today except in the dreams of visionaries such as George Leonard, P.W. Jackson, and A.S. Neill. This concern for human dignity and integrity in formal education systems will be attained not at the expense of organization, but as a result of alternative understanding about the possibilities of organization.

Free Learning Resources for All

A major implication for organization of education is the *shift from compulsory schooling for some to free learning resources for all*. According to Conrad Briner and Gerald Sroufe in "Organization for Education in 1985" (Hack, *et al.*, 1971, p. 83):

> Probably future organization will be based on a "free" system. . . . The obvious implication of this principle is, of course, the elimination of compulsory education. The school as an organization would then become a place where individuals meet by choice and with a common purpose, and would not be, as it is now, a regulatory, and in many cases, penal, institution. . . . The usual bureaucratic hierarchy will be eliminated or sharply reduced in favor of an organizational rationality based on individual freedom.

Computer-based systems are essential components in vision of "organizational rationality based on individual freedom." Ivan Illich, whose version of "organizational rationality" involves the disestablishment of schools altogether, envisions "Learning Webs" in which computer-based information systems are used to bring individual learners in contact with learning resources appropriate to their needs. One such service, for example, would be "peer-matching" (1970, pp. 91-93).

At their worst, schools gather classmates into the same room and subject them to the same sequence of treatment in math, citizenship, and spelling. At their best, they permit each student to choose one of a limited number of courses. In any case, groups of peers form around the goals of teachers. A desirable educational system would let each person specify the activity for which he sought a peer. . . . The operation of a peer-matching network would be simple. The user would identify himself by name and address and describe the activity for which he sought a peer. A computer would send him back the names and addresses of all those who had inserted the same description. It is amazing that such a simple utility has never been used on a broad scale for publicly valued activity.

In Silber's Learning System, all citizens of the city would participate, voluntarily, in learning and teaching (Silber, 1972). The Carnegie Commission on Higher Education envisions educational opportunities more appropriate to lifetime interests and more available to more people, including women, employed persons, older people, and persons from the lower income levels. They advocate increased accessibility of education for "those to whom it is now unavailable because of work schedules, geographic location, or responsibilities in the home." Perhaps more importantly, according to Illich (1970), the social decision to allocate educational resources preferably to those citizens who have outgrown the extraordinary learning capacity of their first four years and have not arrived at the height of their self-motivated learning will, in retrospect, probably appear as bizarre. Buckminster Fuller put it more strongly: we are going to have to pay our whole population to go to school and pay it to stay at school (Fuller, 1971).*

A Variety of Learning Resources—
More Options

If the schools (or non-schools) of the future are to satisfy the needs of individual learners, one requirement is that a much wider range of learning resources be available than is presently the case. Two of the

*The possibility and necessity for this is inherent in Fuller's approach to economic accounting. See, e.g., Fuller, 1973.

ways in which computer-based systems make this feasible (there may be more) are by (1) assisting the learner in finding materials appropriate to his learning objectives and present skills (interactive guidance systems which assist the learner in defining his goals, assessing his skills, and identifying learning materials or people or environments which can help him learn); and (2) by actually delivering instructional materials such as drills, interactive tutorials, films, and videotapes.

Silber has described his vision in the form of a scenario for "The Learning System" (Silber, 1972) which is defined as follows:

- A Learning System has as its purpose to bring people into contact with resources for learning.
- A Learning System is a system which provides:
a compilation of data about resources for learning;
a means for creating and storing learning resources; and
a means for access to learning resources.

Learning resources include people (always learners—not full-time educators); tools and equipment; materials; facilities; activities; and evaluative instruments. The functions of such resources include consulting; providing skill models; peer learning; group facilitating; and tutoring. In Silber's vision, each citizen is both a learner and a learning resource. Therefore, the computer system must function to help citizens create and store learning resources as well as help them gain access to resources.

A Variety of Places for Learning

In Silber's vision, as well as most visions of future education, learning takes place in a variety of places, not only in a specific building called "school." Although the role of specifically designated school buildings varies from vision to vision, all include a much wider variety of places for learning than the present formal educational system does. The importance of "place" in alternative education for the future is reflected in such titles as "The City as Classroom," "The Whole Town Is Their High School," "New Learning Places for High School Students in the St. Louis Public Schools," for the papers in the book *Opening the Schools* (Saxe, 1972). Irrespective of the percentage of learning that takes place in the home, specialized learning centers, offices, community centers, museums, or other places, it seems clear that formal educational systems of the future will include more diverse places and facilities.

Computer-based communications networks provide essential links among these people, places, and materials. Robinson (1972) envisions small decentralized learning centers throughout the city, linked to a central Information System which would serve the needs of the city's school Chancellor, Diagnosticians, Facilitators, Curriculum Developers, and Students. Silber (1972) envisions computer terminals in homes, in order to:

- send messages to all Learning System components;
- receive data from the Learning System;
- receive learning resources from the Learning System:
    see a film . . .
    read parts of books . . .
    draw and alter drawings . . .
    do programmed materials;
- send messages to other learners; and
- receive messages from other learners.

In his early appraisal of educational technology, Oettinger (1969) had a vision of a "common information pool" serving as the basic tool for virtually all formal education. From terminals at "innumerable local points of access," a student has access to (p. 5):

(1) the catalogs of great libraries, hence access to their collections;

(2) the catalogs of new videotape or film libraries, hence access to the collections which include recorded lessons on specialized topics (possibly in the manner of an illustrated encyclopedia) and also source materials such as records of significant contemporary events, of outstanding dramatic productions, of clinical recordings (perhaps of a difficult operation particularly well performed in a leading hospital), and so on;

(3) teaching programs of the kind already in widespread experimental use; and

(4) tools to aid symbol manipulation and concept formation such as numerical and algebraic manipulators, dictionaries, thesauri, editing programs, etc.

Michael Rossman (1972, p. 30) derives his vision of the future of

Education—Trends and Visions

higher education from his perception of the "alternative system" of education which exists today in the form of networks. In "How We Learn Today in America" he says:

> The network includes the many sorts of groups that have organized to connect people directly with the learning and learning action they now feel they need: free clinics, free schools, underground papers and radio stations, crisis centers, free universities and student-run experimental colleges, media collectives (from video to posters), minority liberation groups, anti-war and military resistance groups, tutorials, yoga/meditation/aikido/"growth" centers, ecology and consumer-action groups, and so on. Each of these categories currently includes between 200 and 800 nodes. Each node consists of a group of ten to a hundred people, their energies focused on work that involves the lives of many others. (Thus even this "countercultural" fraction of the alternate system may be seen to involve numbers of "teachers" and "students" on the same order as the official system.)

The Importance of Human Relationships

A rich array of learning resources, conveniently accessible to free learners, is only a part of the vision. Supporting mechanisms are required in order to help the learner define his goals, assess his skills, and choose his learning activities. These functions assume far greater importance in the learner-centered system envisioned for the future than they do in present schools. Most importantly, this involves a warm, accepting relationship between human beings. The counselor is variously labeled a "learning facilitator" (Robinson, 1972); "consultant" (Silber, 1972); "sympathetic resource" (Doyle and Goodwill, 1971); or "warm human beings sensitive to the personal needs of children" (Mitzel, 1972). Computer-based systems are expected to support this type of relationship between learners and counselors in two ways: first, by providing information to enable counselors to be informed about the progress and capabilities of the learners; and, second, by performing lower-order functions such as exposition and record-keeping, thereby freeing humans to perform higher-order functions such as encouraging, inspiring, and sharing in intellectual and emotional growth.

Relationships Between Technology and Learning Outcomes

The visions of future education in terms of delivery of educational services—the who, when, where, and how of learning—show fairly concretely the relationship of technology to new purposes and values in education. What has not emerged clearly is the relationship between technology and *what* people will be learning. The Carnegie Commission on Higher Education, for example, in its *The Fourth Revolution: Instructional Technology in Higher Education* (Carnegie, 1972), states a variety of goals and benefits for use of technology in higher education, but gives not even a hint that the "media" they review (including computers) may have profound implications for the *nature* of the skills, intellectual tools, knowledge, and approaches to inquiry that are developed by learners and scholars.

Similarly, the Commission on Instructional Technology, in its summary of benefits of instructional technology (Tickton, 1970, pp. 32-35) makes almost no mention of the substantive contribution of technology to the outcomes of learning. Their six points were:

1. Technology can make *education* more productive.
2. Technology can make *education* more individual.
3. Technology can give *instruction* a more scientific base.
4. Technology can make *instruction* more powerful.
5. Technology can make *learning* more *immediate*.
6. Technology can make *access* to *education* more equal.

An assessment of the possible effects of all these "benefits" in terms of what people learn, what kind of individuals and societies will or can result, what old or new values are thereby promulgated, is lacking. Yet, as Marshall McLuhan and Quentin Fiore (1967, p. 8) have pointed out: "It is impossible to understand social and cultural changes without a knowledge of the workings of media." Technology and media do influence cultural change. Words and their meanings ". . . fostered and encouraged a fragmenting process, . . ." in thought and culture. Electronic technology, on the other hand, facilitates unification of self and society. To understand potential cultural and individual effects we must have a thorough knowledge of media, they note.

Few attempts have been made at understanding the relationship of computer technology and the nature of learning outcomes. The

Education—Trends and Visions

following illustrate some of the connections which have been drawn.

Oettinger, in Prologue II to *Run, Computer, Run*, attempts to suggest something of the ways in which computer uses affect the nature of scientific inquiry. In speaking of the computer's promise for learning, Oettinger opines that fiscal concern over the use of computers in education is well-justified if their promise is limited to page-turning or "witless calculation." However, imaginative, more subtle use—to meld theory and calculation, building structural models and paradigms make computers

> ... capable of profoundly affecting science by stretching human reason and intuition, much as telescopes or microscopes extend human vision. I suspect that the ultimate effects of this stretching will be as far-reaching as the effects of the invention of writing. Whether the product is truth or nonsense, however, will depend more on the user than on the tool (Oettinger, 1969, p. 36).

Similarly, Arthur Luehrmann's thesis is

> ... that *a computer is not a mere delivery system for instruction* in remedial English or math, for example. On the contrary, *computing itself is a new and fundamental intellectual resource. It is a fundamental intellectual resource in the same sense that counting or reading and writing are basic intellectual resources.* Like them it shapes, or more properly, it represents our thoughts and perceptions of the world. The terms algorithm, iterative loop, feedback, and bug—terms that Seymour Papert speaks so excitedly of—are not just pieces of technical jargon. They are new intellectual structures (Morton, 1972a, p. 10).

There are some examples provided in Chapter 3 of this volume of the ways in which the use of computer systems can affect the nature of what is being learned.

Leonard's vision (1968) of a Basics Dome of the year 2001 provides some hints as to the types of skills and concepts a young child might learn in a future computer-based dialogue system. The Basics Dome incorporates an advanced form of what is now generally called "computer-assisted instruction."

The raw material of the "content" is traditional knowledge, which it has in common with today's "computer-assisted instruction." Thus, the traditional "subject-matter" forms an important component of the learning environment; what the child is learning, however, is not (except incidentally) the traditional "subject-matter," but rather he is learning to invent creative ways of his own of understanding and using the store of accumulated knowledge. The student's freedom and control over the system are a matter of deliberate engineering by the educators. Leonard's vision is unique in that it represents a positive, constructive, deliberately designed approach to developing unique capabilities of the individual. Where most critics of education want merely to do away with authoritarian control and enforced conformity, Leonard presents one constructive alternative, in which technology plays a key role in determining the nature of what is being learned.

In Leonard's vision, five variables are always responsive to each student's needs and contribute to the ecstasy of the learning experience: (1) a complete data bank of common cultural information in dialogue form; (2) basic material arranged to provide novelty and to aid insightful leaps of discovery; (3) personally analyzed brain wave patterns, depicting short-term memory and consciousness states; (4) analysis of the student's overt responses, spoken or typed; and (5) a communal interconnecting capability to link the material on various nearby displays where learning would be enhanced.

Michael Rossman's perspective on the interdependence of technology and the content of learning is that of the curriculum *process* (1972, pp. 32-33).

> ... Picture the human being, surrounded by the comprehensive wheel of our needs in a society [see Figure 5]. The curriculum of alternatives moves within this wheel, focusing on subject after subject as the years go by. Its perambulations follow developmental logics, as in the sequence "psychedelics/body/paranormal," for example, and are modulated by all the forces at play in the society. Slowly and surely the curriculum moves through the whole wheel, passing on, looping back. *Have no fear. What you did not learn this time will come around again, in some appropriate way. And we shall have to deal with it all before we are through.*

The overriding point is that it is the *process* as much as the

The Wheel of the Curriculum

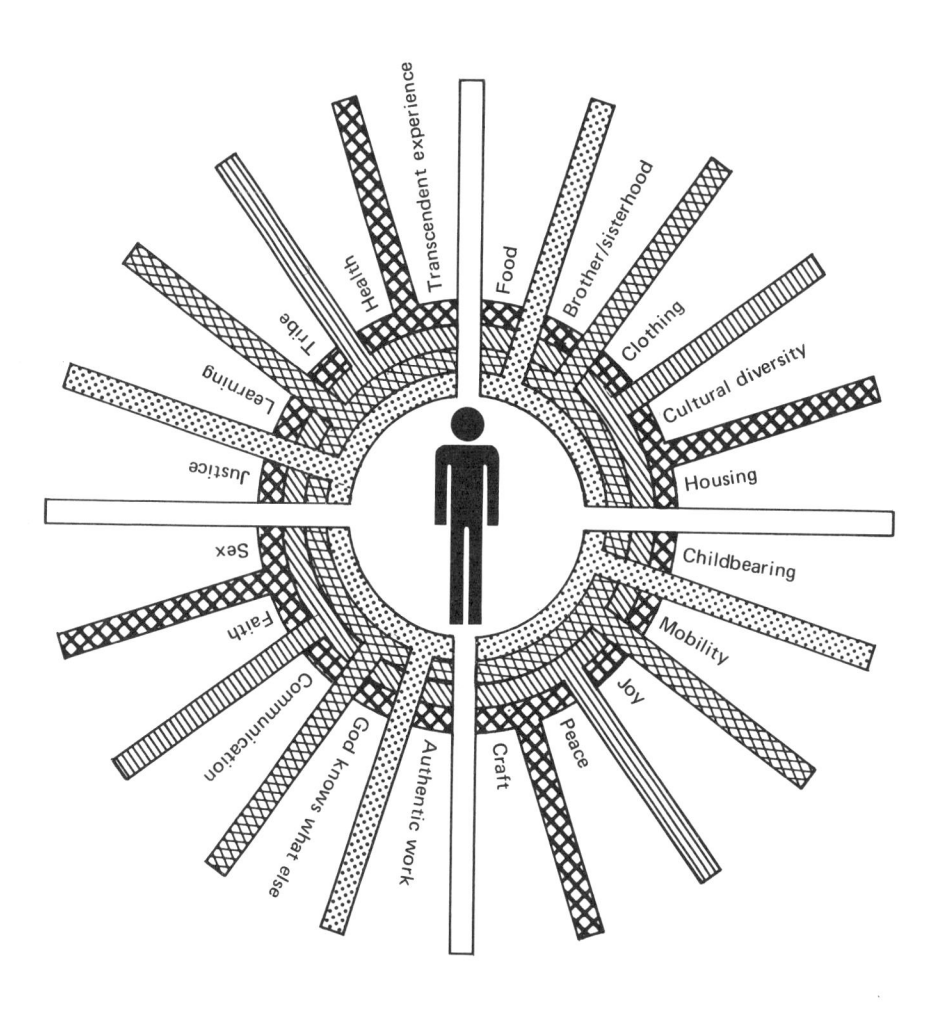

Source: Rossman, 1972, p. 32

Figure 5

content that is being taught and learned—"The process of becoming new people, larger than the limits that we were taught bound us; and thus of creating an unknown and just society, and ultimately refiguring our way in the cosmos."

For computer technology the implications are flexible, rapid design and updating of curricula to match the relevance of the moment. This is coupled with individualized, adaptive administration of the curricula to satisfy personal needs.

Implications for Development of Computer-Based Learning Resources

The primary purpose of this chapter has been to present visions of leaders and innovators of computer-based systems. Hopefully, this chapter has demonstrated the interdependence of visions, values, social relations, and technology. Deeper investigation of the visionary ideas introduced here should make it clear that we have alternative futures, and that the technologies we design and disseminate today have strong implications for the type of vision that will become reality tomorrow. Conversely, the clearer our vision is today of where we want to be in the year 2001, the more likely we are to develop technologies supportive of our vision and values. As one educator said with regard to the design of computer-based counselor training systems: Carl Rogers and B.F. Skinner would probably design very dissimilar counselor training systems (Meany, 1972). Meany's article is unusual in the field of computer-related instruction in that it examines some of the alternatives available in system design, including the programming of the computer itself, as these alternatives relate to different value orientations.

Visions and goals of education, personal and social values, and design of technological systems are highly interdependent. Surely the pioneers in the automotive industry did not regard themselves as the inventors of a new lifestyle for the members of our society. They were simply making more efficient the process of transportation. Yet the automobile and highway systems are woven into the warp and woof of our entire society, values, lifestyles, economy, and natural environment. What we are suggesting here is that it may be time to take a less simplistic view of technology than our predecessors have had.

Emmanuel Mesthene, in his paper "Instructional Technology and the Purposes of Education" (Mesthene, 1971) has emphasized the importance of including external—social, cultural—values and criteria in the development and evaluation of educational technology systems (p. 239):

> The implicit claim of many researchers in the field of educational technology is a modest one: we are only trying to do better and faster what is now being done less well and slowly. But much of what we are doing now in education may be wrong, and if technology helps us to do it very efficiently, it may lead us beyond the point where we can detect and correct our errors. This leads me to a final danger, which is the unconscious reinforcement of the values of efficiency and achievement that can result from technical improvement of present educational processes. There is more to education than the promotion of efficiency or the imparting of occupational skills. Education also has the functions of socializing individuals, of shaping their values, of preparing for citizenship, of conserving traditions, and of imparting some sense of awe before the wonders of the universe. To apply technology to the improvement only of the instrumental function of education may thus become an obstacle to a society that is trying to redress the balance of the heyday of achievement and economic productivity in favor of a greater pluralism in our values and our culture. And if that happens, educational technologists could find that they have contributed to technical richness at the cost of moral poverty.

Chapter 3

TODAY'S COMPUTER-BASED LEARNING METHODS

OVERVIEW
Definition of CBLM

We use the phrase "computer-based learning materials" (CBLM) to denote a very wide range of educational materials and computer applications. The phrase encompasses materials variously described in the literature as "computer-assisted instruction," "computer-managed instruction," "simulations," "problem-solving," "computer-based instruction," "computer-assisted learning," and others. The materials themselves take many forms: books, problem sets, computer programs and programming systems, films, course syllabi, and data bases. The common denominator of this wide range of items is the support they give to the educational use of computers by learners and teachers. Although books and courses in the field of computer science and data processing would also logically be included in this collection, we have not specifically addressed ourselves to these. We have focused primarily on computer applications to learning and instruction in other disciplines.

Within the range of "computer-based learning materials," the computer has a variety of roles. A firm distinction often is made in the literature between the computer as an *object* of study and the computer as an *agent* of instruction (e.g., Levien, 1972). However, we have not pursued this distinction because it does not seem to be an operational reality. In reality, a student is likely to be simultaneously learning how to use computers in his discipline, using the computer as a tool to help him learn concepts and skills of the discipline, and at the same time viewing the computer as an agent of instruction. A student who is using a computer-based drill in arithmetic is receiving instruction from the computer and at the same time is certainly learning something about computers (whether or not what he is learning about computers was intended by the developers of the drills). In effect, we have found it difficult to separate medium from message.

Purpose

This chapter makes some observations about the quantity and nature of existing computer-based learning materials (CBLM) in the United States. The information in this chapter is intended to:

(1) provide a more comprehensive picture of the wide spectrum of computer applications to learning than is available in other publications;

(2) indicate the quantity and quality of CBLM available for various purposes;

(3) describe existing materials in particular disciplines; and

(4) provide sources of information for those who are interested in learning about computer-based materials.

Sources of Information

There is no single course of information on CBLM. In our study, we did not conduct any new surveys of materials, but rather depended on the many, varied, formal or informal published sources.* (We call this the "diffuse data base" because in many cases the sources did not contain any indication of the availability, quality, or creation date of the materials.) The most comprehensive sources were Hoye and Wang (1973), the ENTELEK CAI-CMI literature and Program Abstracts (ENTELEK, 1965-1973), PALS (Program and Literature Service of the North Carolina Educational Computing Service) (Hege and Denk, 1972), and the proceedings of various conferences. Other sources were program library catalogs and newsletters of college and university

---

*A list of sources actually used in building our diffuse data base is provided in Appendix 1. Other sources of information on CBLM are provided later in this chapter, organized by discipline. Additional sources are given in Appendix 2. Still another group of sources is comprised of the networks listed in Appendix 3, each of which has some catalog and/or newsletter describing programs.

computer centers, computer-assisted instruction centers, and professional journals and interest group newsletters.

CBLM Items

The definition of "items" of materials is arbitrary, and non-comparable across applications. A textbook on computer-oriented calculus is an "item" in our diffuse data base. A two-semester, computer-assisted instruction tutorial program—a sizable package—is one "item." A canned program to calculate given values is an "item." There are computer programs, subroutines, and data bases which have potential utility as learning materials, but are not presently known to be used as such. Which are actually used in undergraduate curricula, and which have potential utility in curricula is impossible to ascertain on the basis of catalog information. We included in the data base information on those that mentioned or implied instructional use.

Physical Form of Materials

One of the ways we categorized materials was in terms of their physical form—books, computer programs, data bases, etc. Table 1 shows the number of CBLM items we found in each of these categories. The books, canned programs, and animated films are the most readily available and usable of the categories. The availability, transportability, and usability of the other categories of items vary widely, depending on how well they are documented, the type of computer required for operation, and their developmental status.

In computer-oriented *books*, the traditional subject-matter treatment is different in that computer methods or problems are included in the texts. The majority of computer-oriented books (75 percent) were in the area of mathematics or business, with only a few computer-oriented texts and problem books in natural science and social science subjects.

Data from the Southern Regional Education Board indicate that three to five thousand college courses of instruction in the physical sciences used the computer in 1969-70 (Hamblen, 1972). This suggests a large potential user market for computer-oriented text materials in those courses. Printed materials, including textbooks, are the traditional form of curriculum materials. Hence, one would expect that if an

Computer-Based Learning Materials Classified by Physical Form

Item Type	Description	Example	Number of Items
BK	textbooks, workbooks, problem books	CRICISAM Calculus— A Computer-oriented textbook	260
CAI	tutorials and drills presented and controlled by computer	Stanford Arithmetic Drills	1600
SYS	programming systems and packages	SPSS—Statistical Program for Social Sciences	130
CAN	canned programs and subroutines	Canned routine to calculate eigenvalues	2500
SIM	simulations and games with some computer support	TEXG—the Executive Game	600
DB	computerized data bases used in learning	Voter opinion from 1968 presidential election	300
AF	computer-animated films	film on magnetic force fields	20
PSC	problem-solving courses or labs described in the literature	a course in computer art described in conference proceedings	180
CMI	computer-managed instruction program systems and packages	Project PLAN	60
			5650

Source: Project data base.

Table 1

adequate supply of CBLM were available in any form it would be in printed materials. However, we have found that compared to the publication of over 300,000 new and revised book titles in the fields of business, education, medicine, psychology, science, sociology, economics, and technology between 1960-1971, the number of computer-oriented texts is insignificant (Bowker, 1971, 1973).

It was not possible to show a detailed trend for each of the types of materials, since not all items included a development date. However, based on the dates of the references, it can be surmised that developments in the early 1960's were mainly *CAI* programs. A pronounced shift toward problem-solving applications, simulations, and data bases occurred in the late 1960's and continues today. At this writing, CAI is being revised with a number of new materials presently under development.

The absolute count of *systems* does not provide an indication of their importance relative to other types of materials. Integrated statistical systems, which make up the majority of the count, are the workhorses of educational computer use. These systems are used across all fields, in both physical and social sciences. An individual system may have as many as 50 to 100 programs, each performing a separate statistical operation. The survey did not include automated retrieval systems used for performing library searches because they have not yet been offered for student use.

Canned programs are a dominant factor (47 percent) in the count of items. These programs are not so significant educationally as the count suggests because most are not accompanied by written materials. Most canned programs are developed for local use and do not appear in published literature; thus, the count in this study is understated.

The upsurge in the published use of computer-based *simulations* in education has occurred primarily since 1970. These simulations vary from simple to complex models that include a large number of variables. Many of these simulations were originally intended to be a device to stimulate student interest, but in certain cases they have now been expanded to become the focal point of entire courses.

Nearly all computerized *data bases* identified in the literature search fall into the broad area of social science. The majority of these data bases were originally created as part of research studies concerning such topics as attitudes toward minorities, factors affecting voting behavior, etc. No attempt was made during the survey to identify the numerous data bases which exist in industry, government, and research that have potential for adaptation for educational purposes. Nor does the figure reflect data bases developed by students as part of individual research projects. The educational value of the wealth of information contained in data bases has only recently been recognized, as evidenced by the fact that projects to adapt these data bases for educational usage have been instituted only recently.

Animated *films* play a relatively small role in the overall picture of educational computer use. One of their significant characteristics is that they can visually depict physical phenomena. Most films made to date have been very short, lasting only a few minutes, and have been used primarily to demonstrate techniques of computer animation.

Courses oriented around the computer are an important indication of the growing impact of computers. The literature points out that earlier computer use was grafted onto existing curricula. Now, however, individual courses are based on the application of computer capabilities by combining such areas as quantitative methods, computer techniques, and subject-matter problems amenable to computer solution. The count of these courses is also understated, since many courses developed by individual professors would not appear in the literature.

Computer-managed instruction applications appear early in the literature and have maintained a status quo with very few new developments. It is suspected that their lack of growth relates to required changes in administrative procedures that their use requires. As individualization of curricula increases, it is reasonable that computer-managed instruction will become a more efficient, feasible approach to management of the instructional process.

Development of Materials by Educational Level

Our data highlight the concentration of computer-based materials, 68 percent, at the college level. This presents a contrast to the approximately 16 percent of CBLM at the secondary school level, and the relatively insignificant amounts for graduate and professional, continuing, and elementary education. The latter percentages are 10, 4, and 2, respectively. This relative concentration is consistent with the history of the computer in that the applications were initially developed for research purposes. College faculty members were thus able to acquire the skills and knowledge needed to use computers educationally. If programs are instituted in order that secondary school faculty can obtain the necessary computing literacy, there will be a corresponding need for computer-based learning materials. This need can be filled in part by some materials in use at the college level which can be used for or adapted to secondary level education. The remaining amount of curriculum materials developed at the elementary school level has been in CAI programs (118 out of 152 falling into this area).

Development of Materials by Discipline

The physical sciences, engineering, mathematics, and business curricula have made the greatest use of computer-based learning materials, as can be seen in Figure 6. Quantitative methods in these disciplines are well established, and thus they lend themselves more easily to computer use. More recently, growth has occurred in the area of social sciences, especially in the use of data bases and simulations.

The area of business is dominated largely by simulation in the form of games and by canned programs used for financial analysis.

It is surprising that the life sciences account for less than .5 percent of the total count. This is one area where a large investment in a comprehensive curriculum is needed. There is an enormous store of environmental information already in computerized form which, when properly condensed, could be used for educational purposes.

Humanities is an area of special interest, since it would appear at first glance to be incompatible with the use of computers. Quite to the contrary, however, new fields of study are appearing, such as computer-generated music, and computer graphics as a medium of art.

Nature of the Materials

In addition to the diffuse data base, which provides very sketchy information on CBLM, we collected more detailed information on the nature of several dozen computer applications to learning. These applications were selected by asking experts in the field of educational computing to tell us about applications they considered compelling or important, by their own criteria. The criteria included:

Percentage of Computer-Based Learning Materials, by Discipline

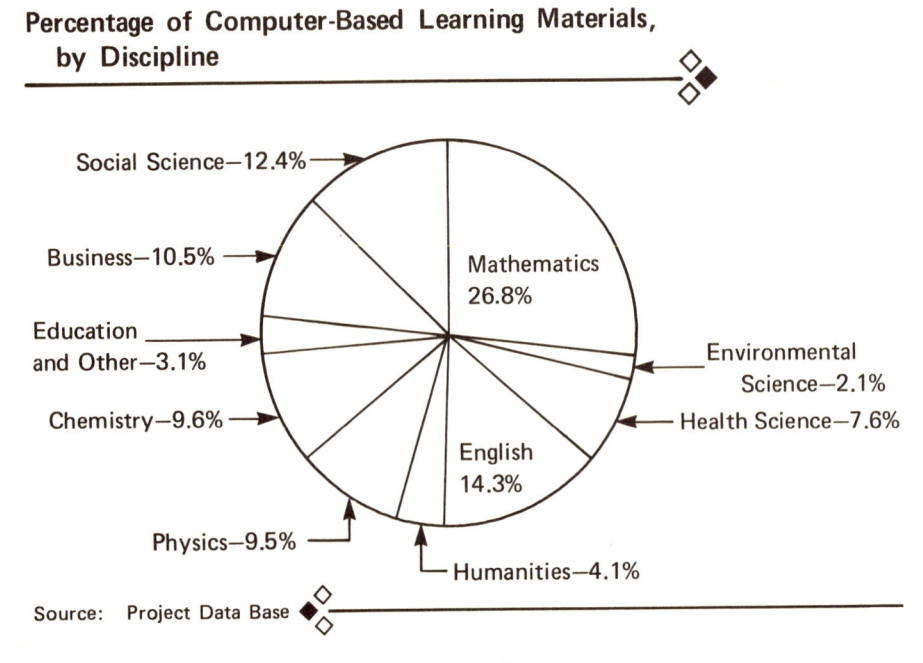

- Social Science—12.4%
- Business—10.5%
- Education and Other—3.1%
- Chemistry—9.6%
- Physics—9.5%
- Humanities—4.1%
- English 14.3%
- Health Science—7.6%
- Environmental Science—2.1%
- Mathematics 26.8%

Source: Project Data Base

Figure 6

- Commercial marketability or widespread acceptance
- Potential for curricular reform in a particular discipline
- Utility to students
- Completeness or quality of packaging, documentation
- Useful in helping students deal with complex phenomena
- Innovative content, learning outcomes
- Fills a widely recognized need for materials in a particular subject
- Cost-effectiveness advantage over alternative materials or methods
- Feasible, workable, within traditional educational environment
- Makes possible independent study projects.

The nature and value of CBLM is best understood in the context of the discipline or subject-matter of study. Therefore, information on the "compelling examples" is organized in this chapter *by discipline*. We prepared short descriptions of the compelling examples, trying to represent all the important types of applications in the discipline. In many cases, there is disagreement among experts in the discipline as to the value or importance or quality of the materials. These points of view are presented insofar as we were aware of them.

Organization of the Chapter

The remaining sections of this chapter are organized by discipline groups. The sections, in order, are:

Chemistry
Physics
Mathematics
Business
Life Sciences
Health Professions
Humanities
Social Sciences
Education

Each section includes:
- "Compelling examples" of computer applications in the subject area, at all levels of education where appropriate;
- major issues and problems related to computer applications in the discipline; and
- major resources and sources of information.

CHEMISTRY

Computer applications in chemical education will surprise no one who is familiar with the overall use of computers in the field. K. Jeffrey Johnson of the Department of Chemistry of the University of Pittsburgh has provided us with the background story.*

Chemists have been heavy computer users from the beginning of the computer revolution. The crystallographers and quantum chemists were among the first to take advantage of the computer as a "number

---

*This section is an edited version of material specially written for this book by Dr. Johnson.

cruncher." The power of the computer for simulation and data reduction soon became obvious to chemists generally, and computer programs became valuable tools for research. More recently, chemical educators have recognized that computers can be used in a number of ways to assist in teaching.

It is convenient at the outset to differentiate between computer-assisted instruction (CAI) and computer-augmented learning (CAL). In CAI a computer program attempts to simulate a human tutor. The students interact with the computer in conversational mode, usually at a remote terminal. The program presents information, asks questions, provides hints, and responds appropriately to a variety of student answers. The student has relatively little control over the program. An example of this tutorial-drill interaction will be presented.

With CAL the student uses the computer with varying degrees of independence. For example, he may use a Fortran program at a computer terminal to stimulate a family of weak acid-strong base titration curves. The objective may be simply to check the student's hand calculations and relieve him of the tedious numerical work required to calculate a titration curve. Alternatively, such a program may be part of an optional assignment in which the student can discover how sensitive the titration curve is to changes in the concentration and the dissociation constant of the weak acid. Here the student controls the execution of the program by entering values for certain parameters. At a higher level a student may be required to write a program or modify an available program to solve a particular problem.

The following CAL applications will be discussed: computer-generated repeatable exams, simulation and data reduction programs, chemistry courses involving computing, on-line data acquisition and experimental control, and graphics.

In the following examples the computer is being utilized as a learning aid which either relieves the student and/or the instructor of tedious numerical work or makes available to the student a tool for solving a problem that would not be attempted without the computer.

Applications

Computer-Assisted Instruction

A number of chemistry CAI systems have been described in the literature. The objective is to establish a dialogue between a student and a tutor, the latter being represented by the CAI program. This dialogue is frequently pitched at a remedial tutorial-drill level. The degree of sophistication is, however, an arbitrary decision of the lesson designer.

CAI is particularly useful in large freshman chemistry classes. A significant number of students in these classes require outside assistance to master such fundamental concepts as stoichiometry and the gas laws. Frequently, it is a matter of sharpening dull algebraic skills as well as clarifying chemical and physical concepts.

Some of the topics in which CAI materials have been developed include the following topics in freshman chemistry: stoichiometry, gas laws, atomic structure, oxidation and reduction reaction, and simulation of experiments; organic chemistry, e.g., qualitative analysis and synthesis; electrochemistry; instrumental analysis; and radiochemistry.

The University of Pittsburgh CAI library currently contains some 30 lessons relevant to the general chemistry curriculum. This represents approximately 10 hours of tutorial-drill interaction for the students. These lessons are written in the CATALYST and PIL languages.

With this approach, the computer is programmed to execute one of several branches based on the student's response. If the student does not know how to solve the problem, he may type "help" and a hint will be provided. If he types "calc," PIL is loaded into the core memory and the student may use the computer as an extremely powerful desk calculator. The keyword "return" reloads CATALYST and the CAI lesson continues. The keywords "skip" and "back" allow the student to branch to a harder or easier question. The computer is programmed to anticipate two or three incorrect responses and respond accordingly. The branching feature is particularly useful, since the student is informed immediately not only that his answer is incorrect but why it is incorrect.

The library of CAI materials is made available to freshman chemistry students at Pitt on an optional basis. The student feedback has been highly favorable and development of CAI materials for the freshman chemistry curriculum will continue.

Computer-Generated Repeatable Examinations

A number of papers have appeared on computer-generated

repeatable examination systems (CGRE). Most of these generate exams from a large data base of complete test items. The approach at Pitt is to write a series of FORTRAN subroutines, each one of which defines an item format. For example,

How many grams of . . . . , ... , can be made from
. . . . grams of . . . . and . . . . grams of . . . . ?

The blanks are filled in by a subroutine that identifies this item, and contains lists of compounds and elements, ranges for random numbers, etc.

The CGRE system was first used during the fall term, 1972. The distribution of items in the CGRE system at that time was: Stoichiometry, 67; Gas Laws, 28; Nomenclature, 2; Solids, 8. The instructor specifies the number of items per exam, the coverage, and the difficulty of the items.

There were approximately 800 students in five sections of the first term general chemistry course during the fall term, 1972.

The Computer Center generated 400 tests. Each contained six easy, nine moderate, and five difficult items. The students took four exams on the average. The average of the highest scores was 80 percent. The average would have been 60 percent or lower if an exam of this coverage and difficulty were given conventionally.

Simulation and Data Reduction Programs

The CAI and CGRE systems discussed above require a major investment in hardware and software. Simulation and data reduction programs are usually considerably easier to implement. Most of these programs are written in FORTRAN. They do not require extensive hardware facilities. Many programs have been implemented on desk-top programmable calculators. The *Journal of Chemical Education* and the proceedings from several conferences on the uses of computers in education give examples of computer programs used for simulation and data reduction purposes.

A simulation program allows a student to manipulate a mathematical model that approximates a chemical system. The model is usually represented by a function

$$y = f(x; \alpha_1, \alpha_2, \ldots \alpha_p)$$

where y and x are the observed dependent and independent variables, and α_1, and $\alpha_2, \ldots \alpha_p$ are the adjustable parameters. For example the M^{2+} - EDTA titration system is a three-parameter problem,

$$pM = f(V; K_f, pH, C_m)$$

where pM is the negative logarithm of the free $[M^{2+}]$ in solution, V is the volume of titrant EDTA, K_f is the formation constant of the M^{2+} - EDTA complex, pH is the acidity at which the titration system is buffered, and C_m is the initial concentration of the metal ion. It is a relatively simple task to write a Fortran program to simulate this titration. The input to the program should include K_f, pH, C_m, the initial volume of the M^{2+} solution and the concentration of the titrant EDTA. The output should include the data for verification purposes, and a table containing pM and V.

One use of such a simulation program would be to let students verify hand-calculated values as part of a homework assignment. A more exciting application is that well-motivated students can use such a program to take on problems that go beyond the problems at the end of the chapter. Programs of this sort allow inquisitive students to get an answer easily to the question, "what if ...." Some examples of simulation programs are described briefly below:

Name	Description
BOX	Calculates eigenvalues of a particle in a finite and infinite well potential. Parameters: mass of the particle, width of the well, magnitude of the well potential.
CONTOUR	Calculates and displays using "teletype graphics" electron density contour plots of certain atomic, hybrid, and molecular orbitals. Parameters: the orbital, the effective nuclear charge, and for molecular orbitals, the internuclear distance.
EDTA	Simulate the M^{2+} - EDTA titration system. Parameters: K_f, pH, C_m.
ENTROPY	Calculates the molar entropy of a gas from spectroscopic data. Parameters: number of atoms in the molecule, linearity, mass, and coordinates of each atom relative to an arbitrary origin, temperature, pressure, symmetry factor, multiplicity, and the fundamental vibration frequencies.

A data reduction program not only relieves the student of tedious numerical work, but often allows a more penetrating analysis of student data. For example, a linear regression analysis program can provide the intercept and slope of the linear function that gives the "best fit" to the observed data in the least squares sense, but these parameters can be obtained with a desk calculator. However, it is trivial to extend the computer program to provide the standard deviations of the intercept and slope, the correlation coefficient and a table containing the observed data, the calculated ordinates and the differences between the observed and calculated ordinates. A rate constant can therefore be reported as $1.0 \pm 0.2 \times 10^{-2}$ sec^{-1} instead of 1.027×10^{-2} sec^{-1}.

A library of numerical analysis programs can allow students to solve complex numerical analysis problems, e.g., nonlinear regression analysis. Examples of some data reduction and numerical analysis programs are described below:

Name	Description
JACOBI	Matrix diagonalization routine (Jacobi method).
MATINV	Matrix inversion routine.
NEWTON	Solves systems of nonlinear simultaneous equations using the Newton-Rapheson method.
NONLIN	Nonlinear regression analysis (curve fitting).

Courses Involving Computing

The ability of students to use the computer as a tool to solve problems adds an exciting new dimension to education. Perhaps the best example of how computers have impacted undergraduate education is the Dartmouth College time-sharing system. The students at Dartmouth learn to write computer programs in the BASIC language. With this facility they can then handle assignments which would not be attempted in the traditional undergraduate courses.

This facility can be provided if a reliable time-sharing system and a sufficient number of computer terminals are available to students. Most time-sharing systems provide an interpretive language like BASIC. This greatly facilitates the mastery of the fundamental programming skills, e.g., input and output, looping, testing, etc. Pitt has offered an optional, no credit, no grade course in PIL programming. All well-motivated chemistry students (freshman through faculty) are invited. It is usually offered during the evening, once a week for four weeks. This short course provides an adequate introduction to PIL programming for most students. They can now use the computer and take on special projects in their chemistry courses.

An upper-division elective, "Numerical Methods in Chemistry," also has been developed. This course attempts to review Fortran programming and several topics in numerical analysis from a chemical applications point of view. The students are required to write two fully documented programs in this course. There are two exams emphasizing programming techniques and a take-home exam on numerical methods. No "cake" elective, this course attracts only well-motivated juniors and seniors. They realize that this course provides a unique opportunity to learn how computer programming and numerical analysis can be applied to chemical problems they will encounter in industry or in graduate school.

Other Applications

Small computers interfaced to instruments are having an enormous impact on chemical research. These computers not only facilitate the acquisition and reduction of data, but also they can be programmed to control the experiment. For example, in a thermochemistry experiment the computer can control the amount of heat supplied to the sample until the desired temperature is reached, and then begin to collect data. A number of schools are now beginning to incorporate courses on interfacing data acquisitions and experimental control in the undergraduate curriculum.

An interactive graphics system significantly enhances the power of the computer as a tool for simulation and data reduction purposes. For example, the Culler-Fried system allows the user to enter data and parameters from a keyboard and inspect the results in graphical form. The main output device is a storage oscilloscope and the graph is an arbitrarily large set of points connected by straight line segments. Some of the programs implemented at Pitt on the Culler-Fried system include simulation of kinetic schemes, NMR spectra, titration systems, potential-pH diagrams, electron density contour plots, and others.

Effectiveness Considerations

It is difficult to evaluate the effectiveness of CAI. The oral and written feedback from the students in freshman chemistry courses has been reinforcing. The lessons have been made available on an optional basis for the past five years. They are an adjunct learning aid, like the optional programmed instruction book and the optional problems book also provided for these courses. Approximately half the students use CAI. They say they find the lessons useful and urge the continuation of the development of the CAI library. This is being done. The development of a CAI system is an expensive project, however. There are many requirements: a reliable and responsive time-sharing system, an adequate number of terminals, sufficient memory for execution and storage of lessons, an appropriate programming language, a lesson designer, programmers, etc. It is a time-consuming undertaking to design, code, debug, and edit a CAI lesson. Using graduate student programmers, the development of one course hour requires approximately 300 hours. The Pitt CAI library currently contains about 10 hours of tutorial-drill CAI. These require approximately 50,000 36-bit words of disk storage. To execute CATALYST, PIL, and one of the CAI lessons, the student requires approximately 21,000 36-bit words of core. In execution time alone, the cost is approximately $1.00 per CAI hour. The CGRE system requires approximately 14,000 36-bit words of memory to generate a single 20-item exam and costs about $0.10 per exam in execution time alone.

The simulation and data reduction programs are relatively easy to implement on a time-sharing or batch system. By teaching a programming language and/or making available a set of programs with which students can solve some interesting and pedagogically useful problems, we can significantly impact chemical education.

With care, we can provide tools with which our students can both more easily grasp the traditional chemical concepts and also explore phenomena that are beyond their grasp using conventional techniques.

Sources of Information

Chemistry applications are some of the most widely transported of computer-based materials. There are at least two exchanges for chemistry programs; the Quantum Chemistry Program Exchange (QCPE) at Indiana University and the Center for Exchange of Chemistry Computer Programs (CECCP) at Eastern Michigan University. Several universities have large libraries of chemistry programs, including the Illinois Institute of Technology; St. Olaf's College, Northfield, Minnesota; Xavier University, New Orleans; University of Pittsburgh; Project C-BE at the University of Texas; and Project PLATO at the University of Illinois. Another excellent and widely disseminated resource is the *Journal of Chemical Education*, published by the American Chemical Society.

In the field of chemical engineering the CACHE (*C*omputer *A*ids for *Ch*emical *E*ngineering) Committee was organized by the Committee on Education of the National Academy of Education* to promote digital computing in chemical engineering education, through interaction and program exchange among universities. CACHE publishes a newsletter several times a year, and also has published several volumes of computer-oriented homework problems which correspond to the course structures in chemical engineering.

PHYSICS

Physics was one of the first subjects in which computers were used in instruction. Physics is second only to mathematics in number of computer-based learning materials developed for secondary school level, according to the data collected during this study.

In physics we find good examples of how the computer can be used in a variety of ways in one integrated lesson—as a tutor, a calculator, and a simulator. In such cases, the distinction between "computer-assisted instruction" and "problem-solving" applications dissolves rapidly.

The computer-based dialogues developed at the Physics Computer Development Project (PCDP) at the University of California at Irvine exemplify this integrated approach.

*Information on CACHE is available from the Committee on Education, National Academy of Engineering, 2101 Constitution Avenue, NW, Washington, D.C. 20418.

Computer-Based Dialogues

PCDP began under the direction of Alfred Bork in 1969, with the support of the National Science Foundation. With an initial goal of searching for areas where the computer might yield significant advances in teaching physics, the project has concentrated on developing a variety of dialogues (Bork, 1971).

Interactive proof dialogues, used as replacements for or supplements to lectures, aid the student in proving the concepts on which the course is based. An example of a dialogue, CONSERVE, starts from the Laws of Motion to aid the student in doing a one-dimensional proof deriving energy conservation.

Some dialogues assist a student with a problem he has previously attempted unsuccessfully. This type of dialogue has proved particularly useful for large classes where the instructor has only minimal time for individual attention. Some dialogues may be used within a physics course for remedial assistance in mathematics.

Another type of dialogue was intended for an introductory course taken by non-physics majors. Its underlying concept was that of a series of "threshold" quizzes, which were the minimal performance standards for passing the course (Bork and Ballard, 1972).

One dialogue, MOTION, is described by Bork and Ballard (1972, p. 6) as their "most ambitious attempt in combining graphic, dialogue, and computational facilities interactively." The dialogue studies graphically the motion of a single mass under a wide range of forces, aiding the student in achieving "an intuitive understanding of the effects of the force law and the initial conditions."

Graphics

Several innovative graphic systems are used by physicists. Examples include the Culler-Fried system, the BRAIN system from Harvard, and a system at Dartmouth (in conjunction with Project COEXIST).

At Oregon State University, GROPE (a system funded by NSF) has been developed so that interactive graphics can be used in the physics classroom (Kelley, *et al.*, 1972). The philosophy motivating the development of this application system was the importance of a student being able to appreciate and visualize the parameters used to formulate a problem. The system develops and displays families of curves for undergraduate physics students.

During the class session, the instructor can issue commands using a keyboard and receive his graphic output on TV monitors or a projection screen. The displays created can be continually changed, modified, or augmented according to the instructor's need to effectively integrate them into his presentation.

Some of the benefits of the graphics system are that the student can now visualize evaluations of approximations, and successively refine models. Mathematical analysis is made real by using it in a classroom investigation.

It is not necessary for the physics professor using it to have had prior experience in programming languages and computers. Compared to other graphic applications, the system is relatively simple and inexpensive.

Animated Films

Computer-animated films are used in physics more than in other disciplines. One set of films on thermal equilibrium has been developed by Jon M. Ogborn, F. Robert Hopgood, and Paul J. Black (1971) from the University of London. The purpose of the films is to promote students' understanding of the Second Law of Thermodynamics and to help them become familiar with the concept of entropy. The approach is statistical, using random games to show what probably will happen. Students play the game of exchanging quantum of energy between two forms until the game has reached a steady state. The computer starts slowly, playing the game as it simulates the random process of diffusion of heat and energy, and predictions of the transition of a crystal. Later the speed of playing is accelerated, and the distributions may be analyzed, each film taking on new dimensions of complexity.

Simulation

At Bowling Green State University in Ohio, Ronald Stoner has developed several simulated experiments which can be utilized with limited resources (e.g., programmable calculator) to understand the visual appearance of a rapidly moving object.

The students are introduced to the experiment by being asked to recall their experience hearing a fast-moving, noisy aircraft. The airplane is much farther along its trajectory than the sound indicates, because the sound does not reach the observer's ear until sometime after leaving the source. Similarly, if a source of light is moving at speeds near the speed of light, it will be further along its trajectory than an observer would infer. The students learn through their experiment to determine the apparent position of each point. The calculator simulates the object as it travels close to the speed of light. Figure 7 depicts a sample problem dreamed up by a student and reproduced from his laboratory report.

These experiments can be done only via simulation. Traditionally, undergraduates have rarely been able to visualize relativistic effects. Students are intrigued by designing their own experiments. In addition, the cost of these simulations is modest.

Several schools have developed simulations of a rocket ship landing on the moon for use in a physics curriculum (e.g., University of California, Park College). Both have been successful in terms of stimulating student interest immediately.

Another use of the computer in physics is to simulate expensive laboratory equipment, such as a mass spectrometer. An undergraduate physics student rarely gets to use a mass spectrometer, and many small schools cannot afford it. All they can hope for is an experiment from the textbook, never really having the opportunity to work directly with the kinds of material a spectrometer yields. With a simulator, the student can get experience with both manipulating the data and analyzing the output.

Similarly, the simulation of an accelerator laboratory is described by R.C. Mikkelson (1969) as it has been used at Macalester College in St. Paul, Minnesota. The computer is not used as a calculator but rather as a black box representing a physical process. Students are asked to predict the results of high energy particle actions in a nuclear bubble chamber. The student then tests his predictions by his "experiments," which consist of running his cards through the computer-simulated accelerator laboratory. When Mikkelson used this simulation, he added an extra dimension corresponding to the actions of a scientist. Students were able to "publish" their positive findings on a class bulletin board.

Courses

Extensive work on integrating the use of the computer into the

Sample Problem: The Visual Appearance of a Rapidly Moving Spacecraft

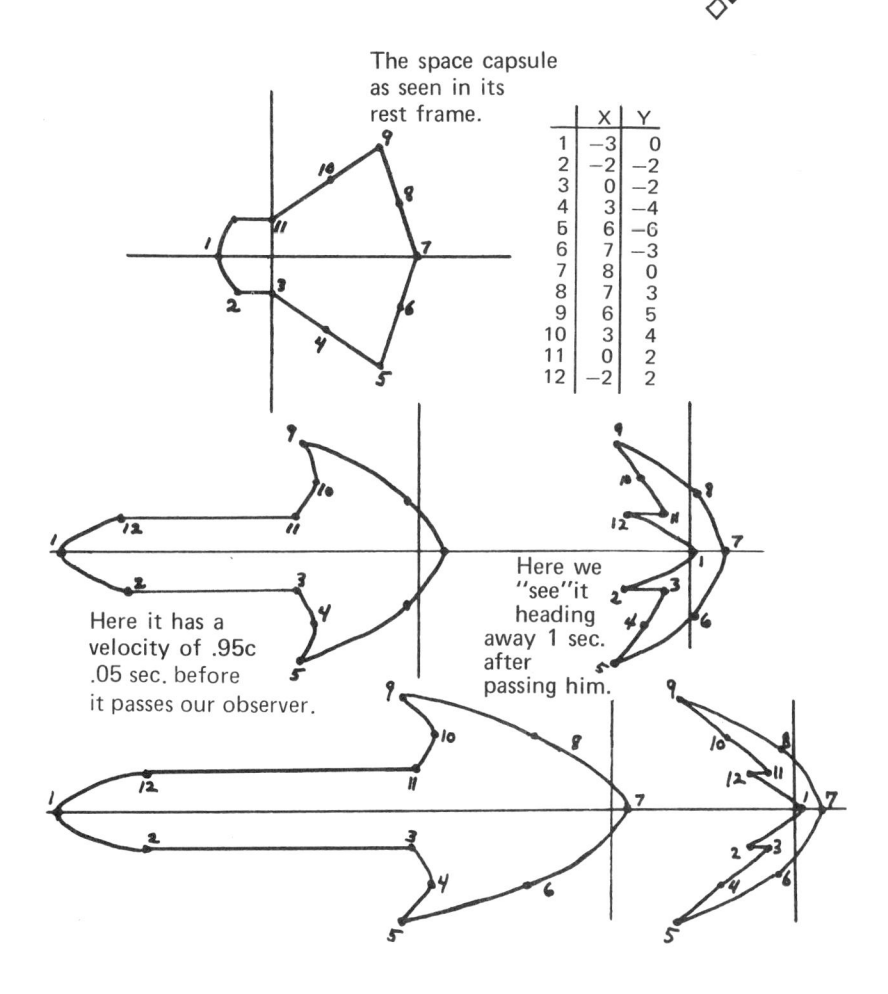

The space capsule as seen in its rest frame.

	X	Y
1	-3	0
2	-2	-2
3	0	-2
4	3	-4
5	6	-6
6	7	-3
7	8	0
8	7	3
9	6	5
10	3	4
11	0	2
12	-2	2

Here it has a velocity of .95c .05 sec. before it passes our observer.

Here we "see" it heading away 1 sec. after passing him.

Here the only change is the relative vel. This capsule is traveling with velocity .98c.

Source: Stoner, 1971, p. 254

Figure 7

Physics Curriculum has been done by Project COEXIST at Dartmouth. The computer work is supplementary and used in conjunction with standard texts. There is considerable consensus as to what is included in introductory college physics. Therefore, COEXIST restructures the kinds of problems students do, rather than the overall course. The purpose is to give the learners the idea that a solution is a procedure rather than an idealized quotation, making the problems more real. COEXIST attempts also to help solve one of the largest problems in physics instruction, the students' lack of a mathematical background.

The COEXIST materials are directed so that the student will do the programming of problem solutions and have real experience with the procedures. In certain instances canned programs are used, and an x-y plotter produces graphic representations of physical phenomena.

Views

With the exciting possibilities of graphics, many developers see it as the way of the future. Still, the large costs for both hardware and software for many graphics applications make its availability impossible for some users. Alfred Bork has described the difficulty of designing high quality simulations, mainly due to student differences (Bork and Ballard, 1972). This is also a problem in other disciplines (e.g., Business).

The mathematical background of physics students is an important variable to be considered in the design of physics curricula. Should or could the computer be used so that students do not need mathematical expertise? Should drills and/or tutorials for remedial math be available by computer?

When to use the computer? When is the application trivial? Instructors and developers have very different points of view on this issue. Some people believe that a particular concept is worthwhile to study analytically; others feel that using a computer experiment to study the concept is valuable. If you can derive it by simple analysis, why use the computer?

Sources of Information

The Commission on College Physics was a leader in promoting the use of the computer in undergraduate physics courses. In 1970, the

Commission held a conference at the Illinois Institute of Technology called Computers in Undergraduate Science Education (Blum, 1971). The proceedings were published and are a primary source of information about a wide range of instructional uses of the computer in Physics.

The Commission on College Physics has also published *Computer-Based Physics: An Anthology* (Blum, 1969).

The *American Journal of Physics* has taken a large role in providing information through both its articles and a column on instructional uses of the computer in physics. *Physics Today* also has articles on computing.

Additional sources of information include the specific projects themselves—in particular the Physics Computer Development Project at the University of California at Irvine, and COEXIST at Dartmouth; Florida State University also has developed a physics course on which information is available from their CAI Center.

Institutions identified in the data base as major developers of physics programs include the United States Naval Academy, the University of California, Brooklyn Polytechnic Institute, and the University of Pittsburgh.

MATHEMATICS*

Examples in this section illustrate the variety of ways computers are used in both traditional and innovative approaches to mathematics education.

Computer Systems for Mathematics

Computer systems have been designed especially for use by mathematicians and college-level mathematics students.

MATHLAB was developed by the Mitre Corporation and MIT (Schey, 1971). The developers designed MATHLAB as a computational aid to relieve the mathematician of drudgery.

MATHLAB is an on-line experimental system providing machine assistance for the mechanical symbolic processes encountered in

---

*This section was reviewed by Dr. Donald McLaughlin, Department of Mathematics, Augustana College, Rock Island, Illinois.

analysis of mathematical expression. It is capable of automatically performing such common procedures as differentiation, polynomial factorization, direct and inverse Laplace transforms, indefinite integration, and solving linear differential equations.

The role of the user in MATHLAB depends on his expertise in the particular class of mathematical problems being addressed. In one case the user may guide the computer on a line-by-line basis, and in another case, the computer dominates the problem-solving process. MATHLAB was designed so that the user could try out an idea, see the results, and quickly experiment with another idea, without investing a large amount of computational time and energy.

The *Culler-Fried system* developed at the University of California at Santa Barbara, is a unique computational tool which a mathematically oriented person can use to perform complex mathematical operations through a specially designed man-machine interactive system (White and Fried, 1971). The system allows development of solutions through a trial-and-error approach. The Culler-Fried system virtually eliminates the trivial procedural steps necessary to use the computer. As with MATHLAB, the Culler-Fried user may carry out complicated mathematical operations without having to write a computer program. The user performs mathematical computations through the operation of a special console suited to a mathematics-oriented person. The upper keyboard contains the mathematical operators and the lower keyboard is used to enter the operands. The Culler-Fried user communicates with the computer in the natural language of his discipline, i.e., in functional terms. There is a one-to-one correspondence between the mathematical functions and the console keyboard buttons, e.g.,

SIN — sine function
SQRT — square foot
MAX — find maximum value
MOD — modulus: take the absolute value

The user does not have to know anything about the on-line system itself, but he must pay careful attention to the logic of the mathematical operations performed.

A System for Children

Under the leadership of Seymour Papert, the MIT Artificial

Intelligence Laboratory has developed a unique learning environment for children. Like MATHLAB and Culler-Fried, a digital computer and specially designed terminals form the bases of the system. However, the systems are very different in terms of purposes, users, and the nature of the mathematics involved. The MATHLAB and Culler-Fried systems are especially designed so that computer-based procedures are *invisible* to the mathematician. Papert's system is designed to teach children to create computer-based procedures.

Irving, the robot "turtle," is part of this environment (Papert and Solomon, 1972). The robot "turtle," is a remote-controlled, wireless vehicle, about one foot in diameter, capable of moving freely under computer commands via a radio transceiver attached to a teletypewriter terminal.

Children can make the computer move Irving forward and backward an increment of distance, turn specific angles, sound a horn, or encounter an obstacle. The idea behind the "turtle" is for the children to *discover* the power of mathematics through doing exciting things with a computer. The child uses a specially designed computer language called LOGO to write procedures that direct the turtle's movements and actions.

Imagine a child's excitement when he first moves Irving from the center of the room through the doorway (this will typically require a sequence of 10 or 15 basic commands). Then the child makes Irving turn the corner and disappear from sight; now he makes Irving reappear, bringing it back in the room. (A *seven*-year-old has no difficulty mastering this procedure.)

> The notion that there is an algorithm for doing this is not at all obvious to them. And the particular scheme of reversing Irving's path by doing the operations opposite to the ones that moved him away (i.e., RIGHT is the opposite of LEFT and FRONT of BACK) sequenced in the reverse order, is a mathematical idea of considerable power and simplicity, normally introduced much later, often in a purely algebraic way. But use of the turtle makes it accessible to beginning students. Furthermore, this straightforward reversal idea can easily be formalized and greatly extended in terms of LOGO procedures (Feurzeig and Lukas, 1972, pp. 5-6).

A more difficult area of study is associated with written procedure to form geometric shapes.

> For example, we can start with the problem of recognizing a simple polygonal shape using the turtle as probe. A very difficult problem—recognizing connectivity of given configurations soon follows. Here we are well within the realm of finite topology problems encountered in artificial intelligence. Thus, use of sensors, spans an enormous range of teaching possibilities (Feurzeig and Lukas, 1972, p. 11).

In its simplest form the procedure in LOGO may be written as (Papert and Solomon, 1972, p. 12):

```
TO POLY :STEP :ANGLE
1 FORWARD :STEP
2 LEFT :ANGLE
3 POLY :STEP :ANGLE
END
```

The following pictures show the effect of involving this procedure with different inputs for angle and step size. (See Figure 8.)

There are many questions and hypotheses about the nature of the skills being learned by the student using the system, the relationship of these skills to existing and future mathematics curricula, the long-term effects on problem-solving skills and mathematical creativity, and many related issues. Some of these questions are being addressed in various research efforts, for example, at the MIT Artificial Intelligence Laboratory; at the Xerox Research Laboratory in Palo Alto, California; and at Syracuse University.

Researchers at Syracuse University are conducting a study of children's creativity in using the Papert system. The researchers discovered that individual personality differences were major variables in the children's learning experience. The researchers expected to see some differences in motivation and learning style, but were startled by the subtle differences among children, as there were changes in the degree of need for teacher approval, levels of emotionality, amount and need for direction, etc.

Courses

Computer use has been incorporated in many thousands of

Outputs from LOGO Language Procedure "POLY"

POLY 150 120

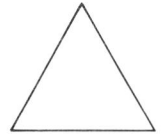

POLY 75 60

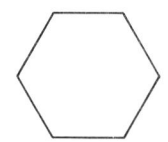

POLY 4 3

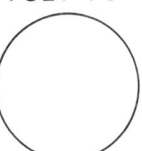

POLY 75 40

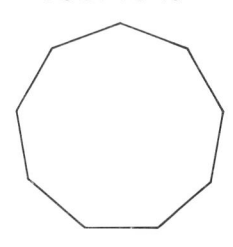

POLY 150 144

POLY 300 156

Source: Papert and Solomon, 1972, p. 12

Figure 8

mathematics courses at all levels of education, in many different ways, and for a variety of purposes. Although the vast majority of these courses are undocumented, a few textbooks, problem sets, and computer program packages have been published.

Calculus: A Computer-Oriented Course (Stenberg and Walker, 1968) was developed by the Center for Research in College Instruction in Science and Mathematics (CRICISAM). The course is designed to introduce students to calculus and to provide a rewarding experience in solving calculus problems using a computer.

A two-volume text presents an introductory one-year computer-oriented course in single variable calculus. Numerical calculation and problem-solving are emphasized to strengthen the student's understanding of the concepts and processes of calculus. To this end, extensive use is made of the concept of an algorithm, its construction, improvement, and refinement. Stressing the algorithmic approach causes a departure to be made from the traditional sequence of presentation of some concepts. Such changes in the ordering of concepts are not unique to this book. Other, much older, texts on calculus have been written in violation of the traditional sequencing of concepts. A more radical change, caused by the algorithmic approach, appears in the statements and proofs of some of the theorems.

The book gives a more rigorous treatment of the single variable calculus than the majority of introductory calculus texts. Such treatment has always been a goal of mathematicians. A more rigorous approach was chosen by the authors to avoid the criticism that a computer-oriented text would place more emphasis on heuristics. Unlike most of the texts that satisfy modern criteria for rigor, CRICISAM is not difficult for students and it contains a good set of problems. Traditionally, problems are few and difficult and are usually oriented toward the theoretical aspects of calculus. The difficult conceptual part of calculus, for a student, is the understanding of limit processes. Practice in a variety of problems is essential to achieve this understanding of limit processes, enabling him to test his knowledge against problems too time-consuming and complex to solve without a computer.

Problems in CRICISAM are given whose numerical solution requires the use of a computer. Solutions to all of these problems

require the development of approximating sequences and estimation of the associated error bounds. The problems thus are selected to deepen the student's understanding of the limit process. Example problems include:
- Find the zeros of given equations using Descartes' theorem and Newton's method.
- For given infinite series, compute the number to which it converges.
- Determine if given sequences converge and, if they do, find the limits.
- Compute the area under a curve by constructing upper and lower approximating sums.
- Find limits experimentally by computing function values at various points approaching a particular point. Not all limits need to exist.

Some mathematicians have strong reservations regarding CRICISAM calculus. One leading expert centered his reservation of CRICISAM around his feeling that there is no room for the instructor to modify the materials; they are a set piece, difficult to teach, and difficult to diverge from.

Another leader in the application of computer-based learning materials felt that CRICISAM was "too much calculus and too much computer," and, therefore, too difficult for most instructors to use.

Computer Resource Book—Algebra. Dwyer and Critchfield (1973) provide computer-oriented materials on 12 first-year algebra topics. The book is designed to help high school algebra teachers integrate computer use into a traditional course. The materials were an outgrowth of Project SOLO in Pittsburgh, in which high school students and their teachers worked together to devise computer programs and problems to help them learn mathematics and related subjects.*

Computer-Assisted Instruction

Several programs have been developed to provide individualized drill and practice for achieving authentic skills. The Arithmetic

*Project SOLO is described in Chapter 4.

Proficiency Training Program (Kratochvil, 1972) is a CAI program to be used as a supplement in an elementary classroom—traditional or innovative. It was developed by Science Research Associates, a subsidiary of IBM. Although designed for children in grades one through eight, APTP can be used for remedial work at an older age. The target population of APTP consists of all students in need of additional proficiency in computational skills.

The long-range goal of APTP is to individualize the learning of computational skills by students. By helping students master such skills through drill and practice and at their own level and rate, APTP is designed to free the teacher from the supervision of practice so that he can develop concepts, present ideas, and facilitate the student's understanding of arithmetic. A fundamental assumption of APTP is that the student "must be able to *do* things, not just understand them." In APTP, the student works at a computer terminal that is similar to an electric typewriter. The student spends about 20 minutes a day, or whatever length of time is considered appropriate, at the terminal.

The student's work on each arithmetic "molecule" is divided into two phases—placement and development. The placement phase is designed to determine the student's current level of ability in a "molecule," while the development phase is designed to take him from his current level to mastery of the most difficult skill at the top of the "molecule."

There are four options for use of the program: basic; flexibility for the teacher to adjust parameters (e.g., speed criteria); teacher specifies a particular "molecule" and mode (i.e., test or practice); and spiral, where the learners follow the spiral curriculum chosen by the teacher.

Views

The growing influence of computers on mathematics education is beginning to receive serious attention. "Until quite recently the mathematical community has given relatively little consideration to the possible impact of the computer on its undergraduate educational programs" (Committee on the Undergraduate Program in Mathematics, 1972, p. 1). The Committee formed a panel to study the potential impact of the computer on undergraduate level courses. The panel felt that there was an urgent need for experimentation, since there was no consensus about the role of the computers in basic mathematics curriculum.

Many issues have been raised about the relationship of math to computer science, the role of the mathematician, and the approach to problem-solving. Mathematicians have strong opinions about the relative roles of math and computer science. In one of his essays, Schwartz (1969) compared mathematics to diamond mining and computer science to coal mining. The former reduces masses of raw material to small exquisite gems. The latter produces masses of useful bulk material.

Other mathematicians disagree, as they see the computer as having profound effects on the mathematician—to the point of changing his role. Engleman (1971, p. 104) conceives of the computer as having far more power than a computational aid:

> The computer would act as a mechanical amplifier which would allow the mathematician to almost flit from idea to idea, painlessly testing the consequences of each and with no undue investment in any of them. It is a power which, quite frankly, might be resented by those accustomed to less frequent demands being placed upon their thinking. But its consequences for young mathematicians are beyond our imagination.

Another view is that "mathematics and computer science are distant and very different disciplines. Neither is in a position of being taken over or dominated by the other; however, neither dares continue to exist in total ignorance of the other" (Leinbach, 1971, p. 13).

Traditionally, math students have spent most of their time developing proofs of the existence of solutions to mathematical problems rather than developing actual solutions. The computer's development as a problem-solving tool has spawned the algorithmic approach to teaching mathematics. The student spends his time stating the problem, and analyzing the solution produced by the computer. The Committee on the Undergraduate Program in Mathematics strongly recommended this approach for applied mathematics students but cautioned against the misuse of the computer.

Sources of Information

Organizations of mathematicians and mathematics teachers realize the necessity for the effective utilization of computer-oriented curricula in their curricula, and several have formed committees to study the problem and a future course of action. The Mathematical Association of America has a Committee on the Undergraduate Program in Mathematics which has prepared two important documents. One concerns the impact of the computer on the content and organization of introductory courses in mathematics involving computers ("Recommendations on Undergraduate Mathematics Courses Involving Computing," October, 1972). Another is called "Recommendations for an Undergraduate Program in Computational Mathematics" (May, 1971). The Conference Board of Mathematical Sciences has a Committee on Computer Education. With the support of the National Science Foundation, they have prepared a document titled "Recommendations Regarding Computers in High School Education."

The Minnesota Council of Teachers of Mathematics has published a position paper on computers in the classroom (Hewlett-Packard, 1972). The National Council of Teachers of Mathematics began in 1968 to distribute a selected annotated bibliography on "Computers in the Mathematics Classroom," which has been continuously updated. It describes both mathematics and computer science materials.

Several large projects are also good sources of information on computing in the mathematics curriculum. These include Project SOLO at the University of Pittsburgh, for high school students; Papert's project at MIT; and Stanford's math project, for elementary children.* Some of the published materials from the Dartmouth Secondary School Project are also interesting sources. At the college level, the University of Iowa has available math materials, the results of an NSF development grant.

BUSINESS EDUCATION

The fields of business and accounting rank high among disciplines

---

*Project SOLO, Department of Computer Science, University of Pittsburgh, Pittsburgh, Pennsylvania 15213. Dr. Seymour Papert, MIT, Artificial Intelligence Laboratory, Cambridge, Massachusetts 02139. Institute for Mathematical Studies in the Social Sciences, Stanford University, Stanford, California 94303. Regional Computer Center, University of Iowa, Iowa City, Iowa 52240.

in numbers of computer-based learning materials available. There are more published books with computer-oriented treatment in business and accounting subjects than in any other field (we identified about 70). This does not include the many hundreds of books in the data processing area.*

Accounting

Accounting education has provided a real "success" story on integrating computers into the educational process. The *Computer Augmented Accounting* series, authored by Dr. Wilbur Pillsbury of Knox College, is published by South-Western Publishing Company as an integrated system of over 80 programs with accompanying workbooks (*CompuGuides*).

Emphasizing planning and analysis in accounting, the materials are used in hundreds of colleges and universities throughout the nation in introductory accounting courses.

Four goals for using the computer in an accounting curriculum include (1) allowing the students to become intelligent users of available computer facilities; (2) using the computer as a tool for better understanding the accounting material being studied; (3) saving faculty and student time; and (4) extending quantitative analysis in an accounting course (Pillsbury, 1971).

Students work problems similar to those in traditional accounting courses but, in addition, they are also able to create their own data for testing. The computer performs many of the clerical chores, such as organizing and calculating, leaving the student free for the more creative tasks, such as developing analysis techniques. This approach enables students to learn and apply theory and concepts of accounting much earlier in their curriculum than with traditional approaches.

Finance

At the Amos Tuck School of Business Administration, computer usage has most heavily influenced the areas of finance and investment.

---

*Although data processing curricula are often offered as part of a business or accounting program, we did not specifically address data processing training in our study.

Examples of how the computer has altered the curriculum include:

1. *Case Studies.* The pertinent analytical information for a company or an entire industry is stored on a computerized data base. The CRIII (Computer Research Involving Investment Information) contains 72 financial facts on each of 94 corporations over a 20-year period. The students using the computer can sift through large amounts of actual data about a company (the data normally found in an annual report). For example, a company may be having financing problems, and the students may be asked to propose a solution. The students can compare their approach to the actual one taken by the company being studied.

2. *The Stock Market Investment Curricula.* The students are now examining in a weekly assignment questions that would have been considered proper to raise only in a doctoral thesis a few years back. The students consider complex questions on measuring mutual fund performance, and the validity and practicality of various investment theories. For example, the students may learn that the theory is perfectly sound but the data to implement it are inaccessible.

3. *Utilization of Real Data.* Data files used by the investment community have been adapted to instructional use.

4. *Quantitative Expertise.* Certain mathematical techniques have become standard tools. Exemplary of this phenomenon is multiple regression, now frequently used via computer. Previously a student would be required to do one, by hand, consuming hours, never to be done again.

Games

Business games are commonly classified as either functional or general purpose. Before 1966 few games for functional areas were used, but since that time the number has expanded greatly. Still, only nine percent (average) of the computing budget in a business school is spent on computerized games.

FINANSIM (Greenlaw and Frey, 1967) is a commercially published text. The simulation included in the book concentrates on financial management problems. Also included in the text are materials that concern how the basic principles and concepts taught in a traditional financial management course can be applied by the students in their efforts to manage a FINANSIM firm.

Two characteristics of FINANSIM make it attractive to a wide audience. First, its level of sophistication can be varied according to the students and the objectives of the instructor. Thus, it can be used both in undergraduate and graduate business education. Second, the computer program is so easy to use that the faculty user does not need to have computer experience.

The purpose of the game is to aid learners in making decisions that relate to acquiring and using capital (e.g., what alternative sources of funds are available). These are the kinds of decisions faced by a financial manager.

Students are first exposed to the concepts basic to finance and making these decisions and then are given the opportunity to apply them in the simulated environment. Decisions are made in the other functional areas.

Either an individual or a group may comprise a firm that not only makes decisions on production schedule, marketable securities, debentures, loans, common stock, plant capacity, capital improvements, and dividends, but learns to live with them from quarter to quarter. Certain decisions, such as demand, price, and unit cost, are beyond the control of the participants, providing built-in contingencies.

A cousin to FINANSIM is MARKSIM (Greenlaw and Kniffin, 1964). The two are similarly organized, but MARKSIM concentrates on concepts relating to marketing management. It was designed to be applicable in introductory marketing management courses.

The central activities of the marketing manager (setting prices and determining advertising outlays) are experienced by the student in his application of fundamental concepts such as price elasticity or breakdown analysis.

The firm produces a product in competition with two other firms. They make decisions on such items as retail list price, production volume, quality, advertising, units sent to distributors, research information, and debts. The seasonal and cyclical fluctuations of the economy are built into the game but beyond the control of the competing firms.

A firm must decide the amount of product going to distributors versus the amount to wholesalers. They must vary the quality of products to satisfy three segments of the market, a demand for low, medium, and high quality products. Each firm is not making decisions with all the data given. This helps them develop another critical skill—being able to predict the behavior of both customers and competitors.

Although most of the computer-based materials in business were created for college students, the Huntington Two Project has developed a simulation game in elementary marketing, called MARKET, for high school students. This game generates competition between two companies selling the same type of product. (See Figure 9.)

The game allows the learners to manipulate variables in order to make their own decision about their companies. In addition to being motivating, the students are able to experience the results of both good and bad decisions. This experience furthers the learner's understanding of the relationships between the marketing variables.

As the game begins, the players are informed of production costs to market their goods. Each company is given an initial inventory, cash on hand, and total assets. Marketing decisions are made by the student about quarterly production levels, advertising budget, and unit price of the product. When the quarterly decisions are made, reports are issued from the computer showing the results of the decisions with respect to performance on the market. A company report lists the following items: profit, percentage share of the market, cash on hand, number of units sold, inventory, and total assets. Players use the reports to make decisions for the next quarter. The computer can also randomly produce contingencies which may require changes in strategy throughout the game. A winner is named when a company attains $12 million dollars in total assets, or the other company is bankrupt (*MARKET Teacher Handbook*, 1972).

The Executive Game (Henshaw and Jackson, 1966, 1972) is a general-purpose business game developed at the University of Michigan. The game is designed for beginning students in business. This management simulation involves industry in an oligopoly requiring quarterly decisions in such areas as product price, marketing and research budgets, volumes, dividends, etc. Nine teams can play—and it is easy to evaluate which team won.

The Executive Game simulates a business environment in which

Sample Market Run

MARKET SIMULATES THE COMPETITION BETWEEN TWO COMPANIES
SELLING A PRODUCT DIFFERENTIATED BY BRAND ADVERTISING.
THE QUANTITY EACH COMPANY SELLS IS DEPENDENT UPON PRICE
AND ADVERTISING BUDGET. THE GAME ENDS WHEN ONE
COMPANY GOES BANKRUPT OR REACHES 12 MILLION IN
TOTAL ASSETS.

ARE YOU BEGINNING THE GAME OR CONTINUING
(TYPE 1 FOR BEGINNING, 2 FOR CONTINUING)? 1

> This option allows you to enter the MARKET game at any point you desire. In this case, the program will start at the beginning, i.e., Quarter 0.

FIXED PRODUCTION COST=$ 250000 / QUARTER
VARIABLE PRODUCTION COST=$ 20 /UNIT
WITH NO ADVERTISING AND A SELLING PRICE OF $50/UNIT
A COMPANY WILL SELL 25000 UNITS (PRINTED AS   25)
WAREHOUSE CHARGE FOR INVENTORY= 5 PER CENT
INTEREST CHARGE ON BORROWED MONEY= 5 PER CENT

> At this point the computer prints out the values for all of the variables at the start of this run.

UNITS AND DOLLARS BELOW ARE IN THOUSANDS

QUARTER 0

PROFIT	MARKET SHARE	CASH ON HAND	NUMBER SOLD	INVENTORY	ASSETS
0	0	5000	0	100	7000
0	0	5000	0	100	7000

Source: Huntington Two Computer Project, 1 May 1972, p. 34

Figure 9

students play the role of top-level managers. The outcome of the game is determined by interactions of the participating teams in the economic structure and probabilistic elements such as chance errors and luck. The game is a general-purpose game in that it forces the participants to deal simultaneously with all of the functional areas—production, marketing, finance, competition, etc. Simulated practice in dealing with these problems obviously does not guarantee that the participant will become an expert manager (Henshaw and Jackson, 1966).

INTOP (Thorelli and Graves, 1964), developed at the University of Chicago, is a general-purpose business simulation oriented toward problems of overseas operations and international markets. It is a sophisticated game, somewhat difficult to manage in undergraduate education. It is often used not only for graduate students but also as a training tool for business executives and as a business planning and research instrument.

INTOP has a dual purpose—to be a tool in general management training while concentrating on increasing the learner's understanding of international operations and the problems of a multi-national corporation. The functional areas of a company (including finance, marketing, production, and research and development) are all represented, in addition to the possibilities of encountering problem situations with personnel.

This dual purpose aims to force participants to be entrepreneurs, to be challenged to change the business, to expand rather than just operate efficiently.

Student teams of four to eight people comprise an individual company. The decisions made by teams and their subsequent consequences enable the learners to experience the principles of marketing, production, and finance not only in isolation but as they relate to one another. This knowledge is, hopefully, integrated and assimilated into a working management philosophy (Thorelli and Graves, 1964).

Computers in Operations Management

Two computer-oriented books on operations management published in 1972 are important not only because of their educational value, but also because of their availability as commercially published books. Each book is an "integrated package," i.e., self-instructional training for a potential faculty user.

Computer Models in Operations Management by Harris and Maggard (1972) includes 12 computer models to be used by undergraduates in learning how a manager would use the computer for management analysis and decision-making. The student is given a problem or situation and uses the computer as a tool to analyze and solve portions of the "case."

Operation and Logistics Management by Berry and Whybard (1972) contains a series of 10 cases. By using the computer as a tool in studying the cases, the student is able to increase the depth of his analysis—well beyond that possible for the undergraduate business student in a traditional curriculum. Since the cases are already created, the student can concentrate on the analysis rather than writing programs. The varied foci and complexity of the cases have also provided a new stimulus for student discussions.

Production System Simulator

PROSIM V was developed to help students gain experience controlling a total production system, applying concepts and ideas, and getting feedback on the results of their decisions. The simulation is flexible enough to simulate almost any operating environment that outputs a product or a service: There is also flexibility in the type of production control system that can be designed. Figure 10 depicts a typical inventory-production-sales system that PROSIM V is capable of simulating.

The PROSIM V program is available at cost from Professor Joe Mize, Department of Industrial Engineering, Oklahoma State University, Stillwater, Oklahoma 74074.

Views on Computing in Business Education

As the complexity of the business world increases and its participants rely more and more heavily on the computer, schools of business are also finding innovative means of increasing learning and/or motivating students by integrating instructional uses of the computer into the curriculum. Business educators are using simulations, games, and models as tools in aiding students to learn problem-solving,

Sample PROSIM V Capability

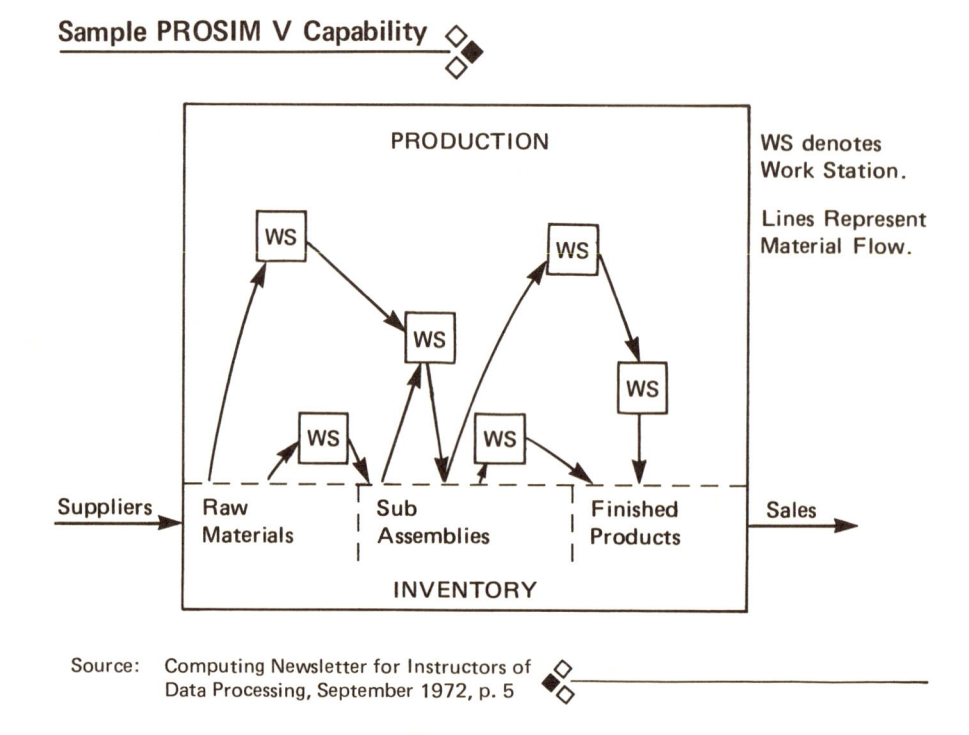

[Diagram: A box labeled PRODUCTION at top and INVENTORY at bottom. Inside are multiple WS (Work Station) boxes connected by arrows showing material flow. Below the dashed line: Raw Materials, Sub Assemblies, Finished Products. Arrows come in from "Suppliers" on the left and exit to "Sales" on the right.]

WS denotes Work Station.

Lines Represent Material Flow.

Source: Computing Newsletter for Instructors of Data Processing, September 1972, p. 5

Figure 10

analysis, and decision-making processes in a multi-variable environment. They are relying particularly on simulation games to give students an opportunity to experience situations similar to those in the real world, make decisions, and live with the results of their decisions. They expect students, after exposure to the theory and concepts, to be able to apply these in their decisions.

Issues center around the educational value of simulation games. Some of the reasons games have been criticized are: They are either so simple that they are trivial and give a false impression of the real world, or so complex that they are unmanageable.

Other professors overlook any deficiencies in the games, believing that the greatest value of the simulation is in forcing a student to consider all aspects of a problem situation rather than the traditional approach of dealing with one variable in isolation. One author introduces his game by saying:

> While the details of these problems will differ from any specific situation facing the students in real life, the principal elements, their *general* linkage and their *dynamics* will be sufficiently similar to offer the students a taste closer to "the real thing" than that of almost any other potion educators are in a position to offer (Thorelli and Graves, 1964, pp. 3-4).

Another concern is how to use a game. For example, an advanced class might do research of greater depth into a topic after playing a game, or they might evaluate the game and attempt to make it more sophisticated or more similar to the real world. The effectiveness of the game depends on how it is used with the particular students.

The "number crunching" capabilities of the computer also have been cited as valuable to business education. The computer can relieve the beginning accounting student of the tedium of calculating a long column of numbers and allow him to concentrate on analytic problem-solving. Faculty also view the time-saving capabilities of the computer as calculator and as a means of providing more time for the development of simulations and models.

Another value of integrating computers in business education is that it gives students the ability to do original research. J. Peter Williamson (1971) of the Amos Tuck School of Business Administration describes such a learning environment to include a substantial set of computer programs and data banks. Using these, MBA students can do original research for term projects and even on daily assignments. They can, with these tools, develop and test hypotheses of ideas and questions. They can come to the realization that the original research is not beyond their means.

Sources of Information

Clifford Gray and Robert Graham (1969) have written a book which includes not only abstracts of approximately 150 games, but readings on business games in general, information on choosing a game to meet the needs of a particular target audience, and when and how to use them, and a bibliography.

The *Computing Newsletter*, edited by J. Daniel Couger and published by the Center for Cybernetics Systems Synergism in Colorado Springs, is an excellent source of the most current computer innovations in business education. The January, 1973 edition contains a bibliography of books that are useful in teaching business applications of the computer, listed according to target audience and/or purpose.

The American Institute for Decision Sciences and its publication, *Decision Sciences*, is another source of information for business education. Many of the business games are commercially published texts and available in most libraries. South-Western Publishing Company publishes a good selection of computer-oriented materials in business. Most of these texts also include general information on the games and their use.

At Dartmouth, the Amos Tuck School of Business Administration has assembled a large data base of programs that aid in problem-solving. Good documentation is available on these applications and how they are integrated into specific courses.

A few of the other major developers of CBLM in business and accounting include: Babson Institute of Business Administration, Dartmouth College, Ohio State University, and the University of Minnesota.

Studies by the American Institute of Certified Public Accountants and the American Accounting Association are explicit in stating the need for including instruction on computers and programming in accounting education.

LIFE SCIENCES

Curricula in life sciences have been undergoing rapid change due to a variety of factors, including the greater use of quantitative methods and greater focus on complex ecological systems. The potential of computer-based methods and systems for educational purposes is just beginning to be explored in such subject areas as botany, zoology, microbiology, ecology, population, genetics, and oceanography. The majority of computer applications to date have been simulations of organisms, populations, and ecological systems.

Ecological Models

It is often difficult to teach students the concepts of genetic-environment interaction which are basic to the study of ecology (Salter, Pitts, and Bateman, 1972).

A simulation model has been developed at the University of Southwestern Louisiana and Cottey Junior College which allows a student to observe the interaction on a closed population of a single species or to predict the results of such an interaction for various contemplated environmental changes. The student can change the input factors on species development (individual gene content, and dominant and recessive gene characteristics) or on the environment factors (population size, number of predators, food supply, water supply, and accident ratio). The student is able to obtain feedback on the genetic and environmental effects after a given number of years (Salter, Pitts, and Bateman, 1972).

Robert Gill states that the students who use computer-based approaches "should be excellently prepared to meet the challenges of work with current ecological problems, either as technicians in research institutes or as graduate students in programs in ecology and environmental management in our various colleges and universities. In addition, other students who have been exposed to one or more of these uses of computers may be able to understand and appreciate some of the intricacy and complexity of ecological processes, be better prepared to evaluate the progress of ecology, and be critical of simplistic solutions to ecological problems" (Gill, Bryant, and Mellon, 1971, p. 174).

Models of population growth, competition, and predation are difficult for beginning students to comprehend, since these models use sophisticated matrix operations. At California State College, the biology curriculum requires the students to take a course in basic programming skills. These skills are later used by the student to build models and for analyzing and summarizing data. By using the computer, the students overcome resistance to employing mathematics, and they understand better the workings of mathematical relationships. The students learn to extend the formula in the textbook to changes in the situation (e.g., partial selection in changing gene frequencies) (Owen, 1971).

Fox-Rabbit (Moxley and Denk, undated) developed at the Illinois Institute of Technology, is one of the best-known computerized population models. The model establishes the environment as an island on which only foxes and rabbits live, where the foxes (predators) feed on the rabbits (prey) and the rabbits feed on some substance (such as grass) that is in limitless supply. The mathematics involved in the model represent projections of future population trends for both species. The model quantifies rates for the birth, hunting success, and natural mortality in the fox population, and rates for birth, escaping success, and mortality (natural and violent) in the rabbit population.

Since FOXRAB exists in a time-sharing environment, the user inputs his requests and receives the resulting projections all while sitting at a keyboard terminal. The student enters his estimates for the birth and survival factors he projects for the island, and he requests population projection information. Output of population projections are tabular and graphical, clearly portraying the spectrum of possibilities. After his requested projections are returned, he may modify his study or explore the effect of different factors on the model while remaining in contact with FOXRAB. A tutorial is included in the program. The tutorial helps the student formulate his requests. A sample output from a FOXRAB run is shown in Figure 11.

The Huntington Two project also has developed a series of computer simulation models on ecological systems. These simulations are designed to be used in the 10th to 12th grades.

STERL simulates the problem of pest control of the screwworm fly. One pest-control technique, proven to be very successful, is the "sterile male" technique in which male flies are raised in a laboratory, sterilized, and then released in infested areas. The technique depends on the fact that females mate only once.

The simulation program permits the student to explore the relative merits of pesticides, sterilized males, and any combination of the two techniques. The student is able to develop and try out policies of pest control which the student could not try directly nor study analytically because of the complexity of the equations (Huntington Two Computer Project, 1 September, 1971).

The results obtained under two pest eradication program techniques are shown in Figure 12. Surprisingly good results are obtained from releasing 100,000 sterilized males and using pesticides only once at the outset.

Young learners study problems of water pollution using POLUT

Changes in FOXRAB Populations

```
TIME  RABBITS  FOXES  FOXES/RABBITS
 .10   5.67    2.54    .45              F                            R
 .20   5.77    3.33    .58                    F                      R
 .30   5.08    4.21    .83                           F    R
 .40   3.87    4.82   1.25                        R       F
 .50   2.74    4.90   1.79                 R                F
 .60   1.99    4.55   2.29           R                  F
 .70   1.56    3.99   2.56        R                 F
 .80   1.35    3.40   2.51      R              F
 .90   1.30    2.86   2.20      R           F
1.00   1.36    2.41   1.78      R         F
1.10   1.52    2.06   1.35       R  F
1.20   1.80    1.80   1.00        RF
1.30   2.20    1.64    .74        F R
1.40   2.75    1.56    .57      F      R
1.50   3.46    1.58    .46      F           R
1.60   4.30    1.74    .40       F              R
1.70   5.15    2.08    .40        F                 R
1.80   5.74    2.67    .46           F                       R
1.90   5.70    3.50    .61             F                     R
2.00   4.87    4.36    .89                    F  R
2.10   3.64    4.88   1.34                 R       F
2.20   2.57    4.86   1.89            R             F
2.30   1.88    4.45   2.37       R              F
2.40   1.50    3.88   2.58    R             F
2.50   1.33    3.29   2.47    R          F
END OF RUN NUMBER  1
DO YOU WISH TO CHANGE YOUR INPUT VARIABLES AND TRY AGAIN?
N
```

Source: Moxley and Denk, undated, p. 11

Figure 11

Results From STERL Eradication Techniques

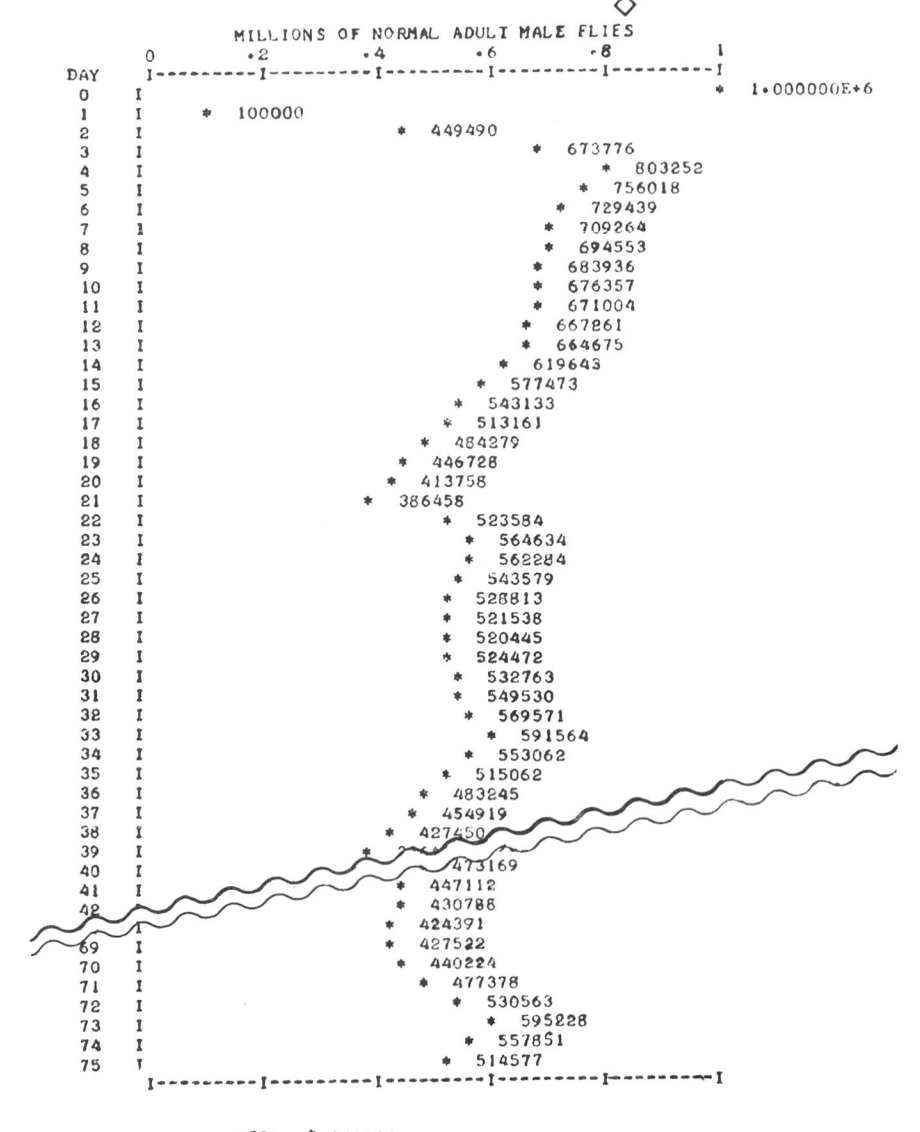

```
              MILLIONS OF NORMAL ADULT MALE FLIES
            0        .2        .4        .6        .8        1
  DAY       I---------I---------I---------I---------I---------I
   0        I                                                *    1.000000E+6
   1        I    * 100000
   2        I                     * 449490
   3        I                                 * 673776
   4        I                                       * 803252
   5        I                                    * 756018
   6        I                                  * 729439
   7        I                                 * 709264
   8        I                                * 694553
   9        I                               * 683936
  10        I                               * 676357
  11        I                               * 671004
  12        I                              * 667261
  13        I                              * 664675
  14        I                            * 619643
  15        I                           * 577473
  16        I                          * 543133
  17        I                         * 513161
  18        I                        * 484279
  19        I                       * 446728
  20        I                      * 413758
  21        I                     * 386458
  22        I                          * 523584
  23        I                           * 564634
  24        I                           * 562284
  25        I                          * 543579
  26        I                          * 528813
  27        I                         * 521538
  28        I                         * 520445
  29        I                         * 524472
  30        I                          * 532763
  31        I                          * 549530
  32        I                           * 569571
  33        I                            * 591564
  34        I                           * 553062
  35        I                         * 515062
  36        I                        * 483845
  37        I                       * 454919
  38        I                      * 427450
  39        I                        *
  40        I                       * 473169
  41        I                      * 447112
  42        I                     * 430788
             *                    * 424391
  69        I                     * 427522
  70        I                      * 440224
  71        I                       * 477378
  72        I                         * 530563
  73        I                           * 595228
  74        I                          * 557851
  75        I                        * 514577
            I---------I---------I---------I---------I---------I
```

COST OF FLY CONTROL: $ 174000

Source: Huntington Two Computer Project, 1 September 1971, p. 3

Figure 12

(Huntington Two Computer Project, 15 September, 1971) as a simulated laboratory. The students are faced with complex economic issues and scientific decisions associated with the water pollution problem. The POLUT unit addresses a manageable portion of water pollution problems and provides a context that enables the students to acquire an understanding of basic scientific factors. It allows the students to investigate effects of variables, make comparisons of pollution control strategies, examine hypothetical situations, and make and test hypotheses. Such student involvement is in contrast to that which is traditionally available.

The students study water pollution by changing such variables as type of body of water, water temperature, type of waste dumped, the rate of dumping, etc. The results of three student investigation runs are plotted in Figure 13.

Oceanography

With the increasing number of students studying oceanography, oceanography schools have found it increasingly difficult to provide adequate shipboard experience to complement the classroom instruction.

The space that is available on ships is at a premium, and is expensive in terms of both money and lost experimental opportunity if that space is not occupied by an experienced scientist. When students first go to sea, they seldom are able to understand what is going on scientifically, usually due at least in part to physical discomfort. The obvious solution (at least to the scientific problem) is to provide the student with as much familiarization with the scientific process before he goes to sea.

At the University of Washington, a new curriculum uses computer-based models of oceanographic phenomena. The models include new forms of student-computer interaction using graphic input and output. The graphic devices are used to display student charts and graphs of data collected during the scientific cruise. The cruise simulator provides the weather which often determines the fate of real cruise operation.

Genetics Laboratory

Many genetic phenomena cannot be shown in a three-hour lab or

POLUT Graphic Output

```
BODY OF WATER? 3
WATER TEMPERATURE? 60
KIND OF WASTE? 1                                    RUN 5
DUMPING RATE? 14
TYPE OF TREATMENT? 1

DO YOU WANT: A GRAPH(1), A TABLE(2), OR BOTH(3)? 1

AFTER DAY 6  THE FISH BEGIN TO DIE, BECAUSE
THE OXYGEN CONTENT OF THE WATER DROPPED BELOW 5 PPM.

          0...OXYGEN-SCALE....5...OXYGEN-SCALE...10...OXYGEN-SCALE...15
          0..WASTE.10..SCALE.20..WASTE.30..SCALE.40..WASTE.50..SCALE.60
   DAY    I---------I---------I---------I---------I---------I---------I
    0     I               W                                            O
    1     I                     W                      O
    2     I                        W                O
    3     I                           W           O
    4     I                             W      O
    5     I                             O W
    6     I                           O     W
    7     I                          O        W
    8     I                          O         W
    9     I                          O         W
   10     I                          O         W
   11     I                          O         W
   12     I                          O         W
   13     I                         O              W
   14     I                         O               W
   15     I                         O               W
   16     I                         O               W
   17     I                         O               W

THE WASTE CONTENT AND OXYGEN CONTENT WILL REMAIN AT
THESE LEVELS UNTIL ONE OF THE VARIABLES CHANGES.

***********
BODY OF WATER? 3
WATER TEMPERATURE? 35
KIND OF WASTE? 1                                    RUN 6
DUMPING RATE? 10
TYPE OF TREATMENT? 0

DO YOU WANT: A GRAPH(1), A TABLE(2), OR BOTH(3)? 1

          0...OXYGEN-SCALE....5...OXYGEN-SCALE...10...OXYGEN-SCALE...15
          0..WASTE.10..SCALE.20..WASTE.30..SCALE.40..WASTE.50..SCALE.60
   DAY    I---------I---------I---------I---------I---------I---------I
    0     I    W                                                       O
    1     I               W                                 O
    2     I                     W                        O
    3     I                          W                O
    4     I                              W         O
    5     I                                 W   O
    6     I                                  O W
    7     I                                 O     W
    8     I                                O        W
    9     I                               O           W
   10     I                              O             W
   11     I                             O               W
   12     I                            O                  W
   13     I                            O                  W
   14     I                           O                    W
   15     I                           O                    W
   16     I                           O                    W
   17     I                           O                    W
   18     I                           O                    W

THE WASTE CONTENT AND OXYGEN CONTENT WILL REMAIN AT
THESE LEVELS UNTIL ONE OF THE VARIABLES CHANGES.
```

Source: Huntington Two Computer Project, 15 September 1971, p. 22

Figure 13

even an entire semester using living organisms for experimentation. Therefore, genetic experiments must be simulated in a course of instruction. Such simulations require lengthy and tedious calculations which generally "turn off" the students. The learning process is effectively blocked, so that students neither fully understand the genetic processes or the application of mathematical modeling in genetics.

A desk-top computer is ideal for performing the laborious calculations required for mathematical modeling of genetic phenomena (Spain, 1970; Tan, 1971). For example, the students might develop a population genetics model for living organisms (plants) in different geographic regions. The students observe change in population for successive generations.

One example of a genetics simulation is GENE1, developed by the Huntington Two Project. GENE1 (Huntington Two Computer Project, 1 June, 1971) is a program used to study the transfer of genetic traits from part to offspring. GENE1 is built upon the Mendelian assumptions that: (1) genetic traits are non-sex-linked and independent; (2) each allele of a trait has an equal probability of being transmitted from the parent to the offspring (allele is a form of a gene, usually arising through mutation that is responsible for hereditary variation); and (3) one allele is clearly dominant, while the other is clearly recessive.

Genetics students have difficulty appreciating the *probabilistic* nature of the transfer of genetic traits. The main purpose of GENE1 is the development of an understanding of the fact that Mendelian ratios apply only when large numbers of offspring are involved.

The student inputs into a computer run the two alleles of the genetic trait selected and specifies which of the two is dominant and which recessive, assigns a dominant or recessive classification to each of the two genes, and the number of offspring for a particular run. The computer program determines the two genes received by a particular offspring as well as his phenotype, i.e., the appearance of an organism resulting from the interaction of the genotype and the environment.

Sources of Information

Information sources in life sciences are scattered, centering around projects rather than published books, journals, or catalogues.

The University of Iowa is a distribution center for modules in undergraduate biology education.

Extensive research in computer simulations models in oceanographic education is being conducted at the University of Washington. Funded by NSF, the project reports are good sources of information.

The data base indicates the University of the South and the University of Iowa to be the major institutions that have developed biology applications.

HEALTH PROFESSIONS

Of all professional and graduate fields of study, the health professions have been most active in developing pedagogical applications of computers.

Computer-Based Tutorials

At Ohio State University Medical School the first two years of undergraduate medical education have been radically revised in the past few years. A major program modification allows incoming students to choose between an independent study program (ISP) or the traditional curriculum. A computer-based system is an important component of the ISP. The computer system, called TES (Tutorial Evaluation System) "helps a student achieve short-term goals by giving him some idea of where he is going" (Ingellsore, 1970). TES helps the student check out how well he is learning, and provides remedial materials to students who are not doing well.

TES assesses the students' understanding of the course material. It is a self-evaluation tool used by the student to check his own subject-matter mastery. TES corrects any misconceptions he may have and provides additional information. Some of the evaluation material has a flavor of drill and practice when the student is learning a skill such as body organ identification.

Ohio State is also using the computer to assist doctors with their "bedside teaching." Under the program, patients seat themselves at typewriter-like computer terminals in hospitals and receive instructions that otherwise would be provided by physicians, nurses, or allied health professionals. The system can be used to learn about post-operative activities and restrictions, diet, or practical day-to-day care information.

Health professionals are now using the system to update their skills in their own individualized refresher course (*Automated Education Letter*, October, 1972).

Simulated Clinical Experiences

The University of Illinois is well known for its system titled CASE, which simulates clinical encounters with patients. In CASE, the role of patient is played by the computer with the student performing diagnosis and prescribing therapy. CASE is most applicable to the last two years of undergraduate education and for continuing education (Harless, 1971).

The three broad educational purposes of the CASE system are:

(1) to simulate the clinical encounter;

(2) to provide feedback at the end of the success of the students' treatment, including an optimal path to the diagnosis and treatment of the CASE; and

(3) to establish a library of CASE's which allows the student to interact with a representative and potentially unlimited variety of disease situations.

Although patient encounter and experience with a variety of patient ailments are central elements of medical education, the average medical student sees only a small number of patients in his first four years of training, and may assume full responsibility for perhaps as few as 30 cases. Few medical students have the opportunity to observe patient care from beginning to end and experience the consequence of their own independent decision-making.

The simulated clinical encounters allow conditions that normally are not allowed with the real patients.

> In almost every field of study except medicine, a student is permitted to make mistakes. In fact, this is often considered a very valuable way for him to learn. But in medicine, the loss of a patient is not regarded as a valuable part of a student's training (Hammadi and Fonkalsrud, 1970, p. 123).

During the CASE clinical encounters, the student talks directly with the patient (the computer). He asks the patient about his symptoms, performs tests, administers treatment, and modifies treatment according to patient reaction. The patient may have medical complications where the affects of one disease mask the effects of another. The patient may get progressively sicker until treatment is changed—or even die. During the course of conversation with the patient, the student formulates his directives in his own words and in most situations the computer will recognize them. If the "doctor" requests a physical examination of the heart, he will be presented the sound of the heart beats on an on-line tape recorder, which he listens to through a stethoscope. If the "doctor" requests an X-ray, it will be shown on the slide projector adjacent to the terminal console.

Massachusetts General Hospital has a wide variety of simulations of disease syndromes, biochemical models, and clinical encounters. They are applicable both for undergraduates and practicing physicians (Hellerstein, 1970).

One such program helps students identify body organs by presenting blow-ups which magnify the normal view from 1 to 200 times to show details like cell structures and follicles.

The computer asks the student a question about the physical appearance of organs or is asked whether a particular organ is correct. If the student correctly identifies an organ, he moves on to the next organ. If he is incorrect, he is forced to consider other organs before being led to the correct identification.

Another type of simulation was developed by students at the University of Southern California. They created an ingenious computer-controlled life-like mannequin lying on an operating table.

The SIM ONE mannequin was developed to train anesthesiology residents to administer anesthesia during an operation. The mannequin allows the difficulty of problems presented to the resident to be *gradually increased* and particular phases *repeated* as necessary for additional practice (Abrahamson, Denson, and Wolf, 1969). The left arm of the mannequin is extended ready for intravenous injection, the right arm fitted with a blood pressure cuff.

The mannequin *breathes*, has a heart beat, blood pressure, opens and closes its mouth, blinks its eyes, and has both a temporal and carotid pulse.

The physiological responses to what is done to the mannequin are in real time and provide the student immediate feedback on his performance.

A formal evaluation of using a patient-simulator in training has yielded the following results: (1) residents achieve desired proficiency level in a smaller number of elapsed days of training; and (2) residents achieve desired proficiency level in a smaller number of trials in the operating room.

Information Retrieval

The Vision Information Center was established at Harvard University by the National Institute of Neurological Disease and Stroke to disseminate information on areas related to the eye and vision. The Vision Information Center serves both the needs of physicians doing postgraduate work in ophthalmology and scientists carrying out vision research. Vision is a large interdisciplinary subject. It includes ophthalmology, biological and psychological research on the eye and visual processes, physiological optics, and environmental factors relevant to the eye or eye diseases.

The Vision Information Center assists users (students and researchers) to sort through masses of books, reports, and other documents for specific bits of information (Eichhorn and Reinecke, 1970).

The student begins by taking a course of instruction from the computer through short sequences on specific topics. A bibliography is available on-line. The combination of computer tutorial with information retrieval provides a unique service to a person new to a subject area.

A computer-based medical history system has been developed at the University of Wisconsin in order to provide a technique that will prove useful to physicians both in clinical and long-range research efforts. The computer program collects medical histories from patients through a typewriter conversation. Simultaneously the computer is monitoring the heart rate and the response latency of the patient for each question frame. The program can branch to an alternative line of questioning based on the patient's heart rate and time of response. For example, the interview may be altered from questions on physical problems to questions on the patient's psychiatric history.

The computer prints out a patient's response in a form useful to the clinician and stores the information for research and patient follow-up observation. Figure 14 shows a summary printout of patients' responses in that format.

Computer Summary of Mental Status Interview

```
PROGRAMMED MEDICINE UNIV. OF WIS.
COMPUTER-BASED MENTAL STATUS EXAM

1.  GENERAL MASTERY OF COMPUTER INTERVIEW
    --HEART RATE AT START OF INTERVIEW  112 BPM--
    SATISFACTORY MASTERY OF COMPUTER OPERATION
    --HEART RATE AT FINISH OF ORIENTATION  112 BPM--
2.  ORIENTATION
    A.  NAME
        AGE 31 YEARS, BORN 1938 FEMALE, OCCUPATION PROGRAMMER
        EDUCATION HIGH SCHOOL, COLLEGE COMPLETED
    B.  PLACE
        RESPONSES TO QUESTIONS ABOUT PLACE OF INTERVIEW
            CITY-MADISON, STATE-WISCONSIN, BLDG.-HOSPITAL
    C.  TIME
        YEAR-1970, MONTH-FEBRUARY
3.  MEMORY
    A.  REMOTE
        REMEMBERS TEACHERS NAME--GRADE 8
        PRESIDENTS OF U.S. PRECEDING RICHARD NIXON LISTED AS FOLLOWS
            JOHNSON, KENNEDY,
        PRESIDENT PRECEDING EISENHOWER--TRUMAN
        YEAR OF RESPONDENTS BIRTH--1938
    B.  RECENT
        TACHYCARDIA HERE--PATIENT ADVISED TO RELAX
            HEART RATE 121 BPM AT THIS POINT, HEART RATE 116 BPM WITH NEXT FRAME
        JULY 4TH 69
        UNABLE TO REMEMBER ROOM NUMBER, UNABLE TO REMEMBER FLOOR NUMBER
    C.  RETENTION
        CORRECT RECALL OF 6 DIGITS, CORRECT RECALL OF 2ND SET OF 6 DIGITS
        CORRECT RECALL OF 3 DIGITS BACKWARDS,
        CORRECT RECALL OF 4 DIGITS BACKWARDS
        RECALL OF INFORMATION GIVEN IN STORY--ERROR, CORRECT, CORRECT
4.  GENERAL INFORMATION
        ALASKA GIVEN AS LARGEST STATE, PARIS GIVEN AS CAPITAL OF FRANCE
        LONDON GIVEN AS CAPITAL OF ENGLAND.
5.  SUSTAINED MENTAL ACTIVITY
    A.  SERIAL 7S                    B.  ARITHMETIC EQUATIONS
        93, 86, 79, 72, 65, 58, 51       3 x 12 = 36, 4X = 24, X = 6
6.  VOCABULARY
        CANDID-TRUTHFUL, COMBINE-JOIN, DISPUTE-ARGUMENT, REPUTE-REPUTATION
7.  LOGIC
        1ST SYLLOGISM CORRECT, 2ND SYLLOGISM CORRECT
        1ST GENERALIZATION CORRECT, 2ND GENERALIZATION CORRECT
        3RD GENERALIZATION CORRECT, 4TH GENERALIZATION CORRECT
8.  BRIEF PSYCHIATRIC HISTORY
        STUTTERING PROBLEM, NO PHOBIAS, ANXIETY SYMPTOMS,
        NOT COMPULSIVE,
        NO PSYCHIATRIC TREATMENT, NO ADMISSION TO MENTAL HOSPITAL,
        NO CRYING PROBLEM, NO DEPRESSION, NO SUICIDAL THOUGHTS,
        COULD NOT MAKE SUICIDAL GESTURE, NO INSOMNIA.
9.  SUBJECTIVE REACTION
        DIFFICULTY 2, DISLIKE 2, FUN 1, INTERESTING 1, BORING 2, TIRED 2,
        PREFER MD 2, PREFER COMPUTER 1, WIRES BOTHERED 2,
        KEYBOARD EASY TO USE, PERMISSION GRANTED.
10. CONCLUSION
        INTERVIEW TIME 13 MINUTES
        HEART RATE 109 BEATS PER MINUTE
```

NOTE: Computer summary of mental status interview. Respondent (name withheld) gave permission for the use of her responses for research purposes. The responses in category 9 ("Subjective Reaction") are numbered "1" for yes and "2" for no. (BPM, beats per minute.)

Source: Slack, 1971, p. 85

Figure 14

Views

The computer role in the health professions is now coming to fruition:

> The computer can act as a true extension of the mind if you worry more about getting jobs done and getting more people cared for than you do about who does it. There is no evidence that the stethoscope and typewriter kept us from being less true physicians than our fathers were, and we should not assume that the new tools will make the next generation any less humanitarian (Schwartz, 1970).

Someday a significant portion of a doctor's work will be taken over by a computer.

> It has been estimated that if you could increase the productivity of all doctors practicing by 4 percent you would have the equivalent of another graduating class from all medical schools. It is hard for me to believe that there is not at least 4 percent of a doctor's work that could be done by a computer, and I think that when we talk about the physician shortage this is one place we should look (Jason, 1970).

CAI, simulations, information retrieval, process control, and graphics all have potential to aid education:

> The ESSENTIAL FEATURES OF A GOOD MEDICAL EDUCATION are the acquisition of a vast quantity of factual knowledge and a broad exposure to patients, and perhaps even more important, the opportunity to develop judgment and the decision-making capacity necessary for good medical practice (Feurzeig, 1970).

The information-processing capacities of the computer may revolutionize health sciences.

The highly diverse student demands have brought the issue of curricula reform to the forefront. Inflexible curricula are no longer *relevant* to the needs and interests of incoming students.

Dr. Lloyd R. Evans has raised the issue that the computer may be threatening to medical practitioners who traditionally cherished their capacity for storing knowledge, formulating a differential diagnosis, and carrying on decision-making activities.

Introduction of the computer into these processes could well be viewed by the doctor as devaluating his hard-won medical education and as undermining his intellectual contribution to medical care.... Such a loss of status could have serious social, economic, and political consequences for a profession that has historically enjoyed eminence in the public mind (quoted by Schwartz, 1970).

Sources of Information

Three medical centers have been identified by the National Library of Medicine as notable in the application of computers to undergraduate and continuing medical education: Ohio State University Medical Center; the University of Illinois Medical Center, Chicago; and the Laboratory of Computer Sciences of Massachusetts General Hospital and Harvard Medical School in Boston. Each of these centers has its own computer and its own set of teaching routines, and each is willing to share its resources with others in the form of articles, information, and/or access to programs.

The Lister Hill Center's Biomedical Data Network has provided the capabilities of sharing curricular materials in order to improve medical education.* This network has been described in the *Journal of Medical Education*, and in pamphlets available from the National Library of Medicine. The National Library of Medicine has also produced a booklet describing all the programs of the network (Lister Hill, 1972).

Several conferences have been held of which published proceedings are available. These include *Computer Applications in Dental Education* (1971), the report of a working conference held in San Francisco during late October, 1969. ENTELEK published *Computer-Assisted Instruction in the Health Professions*, the proceedings of a conference at the Harvard Medical School in 1970 (Stolurow, Peterson, and Cunningham, 1970).

The *Journal of Medical Education* is an important resource for knowledge about computers in the health sciences.

A conference held in 1973 by the Federation of American

---

*Lister Hill Network is described in Chapter 4.

Societies of Experimental Biology (FASEB) devoted one day to a teaching session on computer-assisted medical education.

HUMANITIES

Although the amount of computer use in humanities education is less than in other areas, a great variety of computer applications to learning have been developed. The majority have been drill-and-practice programs in spelling, reading, and foreign languages. A variety of other computer applications have been developed in which the computer is used as a creative artists' tool or medium.

Computer-animated films are one type of application in creative arts. "A computer environment for film animation is a unique application of the computer for artistic purposes" (Csuri, 1970). The "real time" environment allows the artist to see results of his artistic decisions almost as rapidly as he can make them. He can try out different ideas (shapes, size, arrangement, etc.) before he commits his decisions to film. The words and symbols can be made to move about in time and space, and provide the effects of an animated motion picture. Through the use of a special device, the animator can control the rotation, speed, and the viewing angle of his image. The animator can use a light pen to draw the path in which his images (e.g., a car pulling into a parking lot) are sectioned into the individual frames (24 are required per record) to make it appear as a motion picture.

Computer art films involve skills that require knowledge of art, mathematics, and computer programming. The animator must make aesthetic judgments about the color, positions, and the effect of movement. He has to understand the mathematics required to create figures which are pleasing to the eye.

Computer Graphics

Computer-aided graphics have already achieved some status as a new art form. Art galleries have held special shows to display the works of computer graphic artists.

At Chico State College, there is now a course for artists to explore this art form (Hertlein, 1972). The course objectives are: (1) to develop an acceptance of computer graphics as an art form by exposure to computer-aided creation; (2) to afford in-depth experimentation of machine capabilities relating to known art techniques and unknown computer techniques; and (3) in-depth study and use of art materials and design techniques.

The art students learn to write computer programs and to perceive mathematical relationships symbolically. At first the students, who are not accustomed to the logical thinking required to develop computer programs, have considerable psychic difficulties accepting the computer. Because of having to analyze and define their artistic problems, the students discover that "the world of science is more demanding than the world of art" (Hertlein, 1972, p. 320). It would be far easier for the students to work with watercolors or sculpt a head than to use a computer, but the artists emerge with a new intellectual independence as they learn a new discipline.

The computer language, ARTSPEAK, developed at the New York University Linguistic String Project, is designed for art students. With an hour's instruction, the student is able to write his first computer program.

The student employs the special language for drawing pictures, designs, and graphs connected by straight lines or curves. An ARTSPEAK program and computer output is shown in Figure 15.

Computer Music

The computer has caught the fancy of a small but dedicated group of researchers and educators for whom electronically generated music holds a special fascination. The composer may also use the computer to write music which will ultimately be played on conventional orchestral instruments.

Other researchers have worked on sound synthesis that involves challenging problems of pitch, tone, and rhythm.

BEDLAM, developed at Dartmouth College, is an example of a computer-based system for music students. BEDLAM is a computer which plays musical compositions which are programmed on punched paper tapes in computer-readable format. The student can have his composition played as often as necessary. He can test variations and modifications of his music and get feedback as often as he likes by playing it on BEDLAM.

A teacher can program BEDLAM to produce combinations of

Student ARTSPEAK Assignment

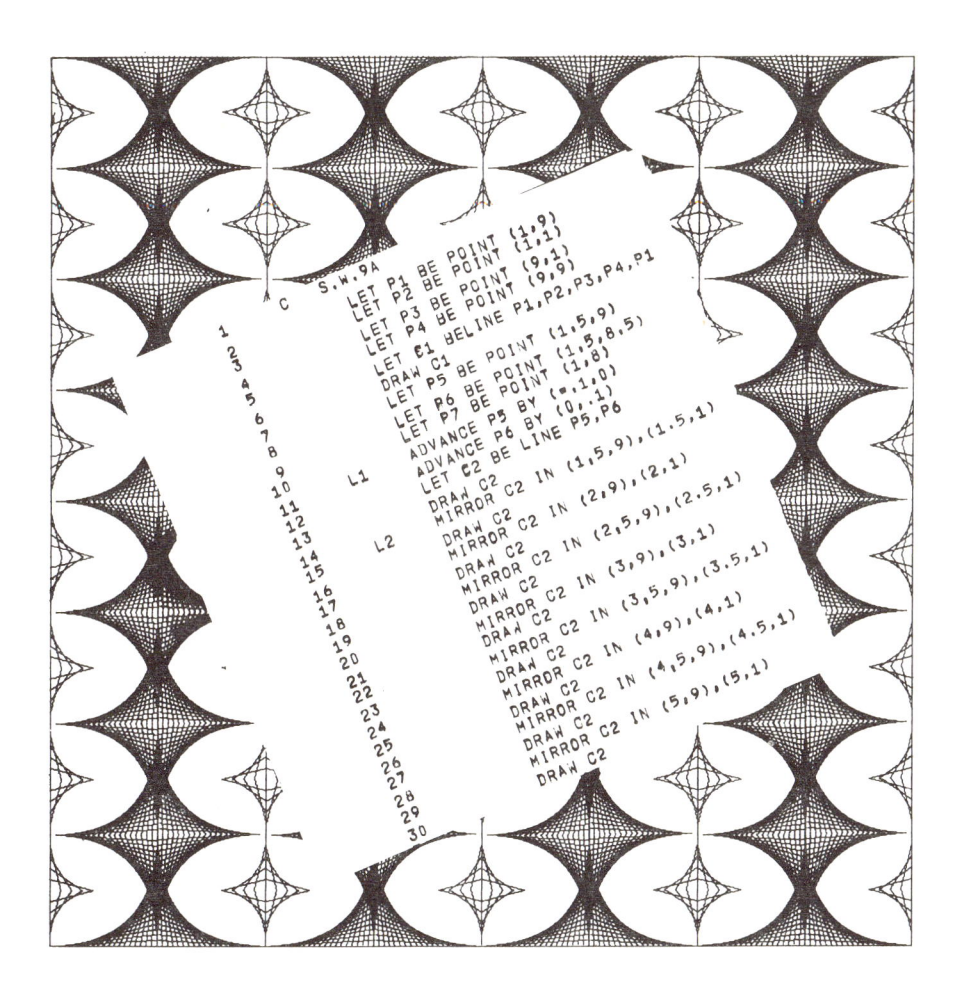

```
S.W.9A
   C
        LET P1 BE POINT (1,9)
        LET P2 BE POINT (1,1)
        LET P3 BE POINT (9,1)
        LET P4 BE POINT (9,9)
        LET C1 BELINE P1,P2,P3,P4,P1
        DRAW C1
        LET P5 BE POINT (1,5,9)
        LET P6 BE POINT (1,5,8,5)
   L1   LET P7 BE POINT (1,8)
        ADVANCE P5 BY (0,1,0)
        ADVANCE P6 BY (0,-1)
        LET C2 BE LINE P5,P6
   L2   DRAW C2
        MIRROR C2 IN (1,5,9),(1.5,1)
        DRAW C2
        MIRROR C2 IN (2,9),(2,1)
        DRAW C2
        MIRROR C2 IN (2,5,9),(2.5,1)
        DRAW C2
        MIRROR C2 IN (3,9),(3,1)
        DRAW C2
        MIRROR C2 IN (3,5,9),(3.5,1)
        DRAW C2
        MIRROR C2 IN (4,9),(4,1)
        DRAW C2
        MIRROR C2 IN (4,5,9),(4.5,1)
        DRAW C2
        MIRROR C2 IN (5,9),(5,1)
        DRAW C2
        MIRROR C2
        DRAW C2
```

Source: Mullish and Lewis, 1972

Figure 15

sounds for students who are learning to recognize various musical pitches, intervals, rhythms, etc. In this mode, BEDLAM becomes a drill-and-practice aid for mastering basic musical ideas.

Young children are delighted with composing their own tune and hearing the musical effects of their creativity. General Turtle, Inc., manufactures a music box that can play a five-octave range of notes, with as many as four at a time. The children "play" the music box by writing a program in LOGO, a computer language.

Terry Winograd and Jeanne Bamberger have experimented with various notions with which to describe the music. One example is described below:

> One octave is chosen as the base, and its twelve chromatic tones are numbered 1 through 12. Notes in the next octave up can be indicated either by continuing beyond 12 or by using the sign "!". Thus 13 and 1! represent the same note. The LOGO command SING takes a sequence of notes as input and plays them in order. Thus SING "1! 3! 5! 6! 8! 10! 12! 1!" will cause a major scale to be played. To add rhythm to the tune we use a LOGO operation MUSIC which takes two inputs: one a sequence of notes, the other a sequence of durations and combines them in the obvious way (Papert and Solomon, 1972, p. 14).

A Frere Jacques procedure written in LOGO is shown in Figure 16.

A music box can produce any of 60 pitches (i.e., five 12-tone chromatic octaves on four channels or "voices"). The instructions to the channels are buffered internally so that they produce simultaneous voices, making attractive chords. The music box also generates two distinct percussion sounds.

MUSIC 360 is a computer language, developed by Barry Vercoe at MIT, which is used to create musical compositions. A student uses MUSIC 360 to describe his own "instruments," which in combination form an "orchestra." His program then describes the notes to be played by each instrument. A program written in MUSIC 360 is run on a digital computer (IBM 360) and produces a tape. The tape is converted to analog on an analog-to-digital converter. After conversion, the tape can be played; what exists is an original composition of computer

Frere Jacques Procedure in LOGO

```
TO FRERE1
1  SING MUSIC OF "1! 3! 5! 1!"  "2 2 2 2"
END


TO FRERE2
1  SING MUSIC "5! 6! 8!"  "2 2 4"
END


TO FRERE3
1  SING MUSIC "8! 10! 8! 6! 5! 1!"  "1 1 1 1 2 2"
END


TO FRERE4
1  SING MUSIC "1! -8! 1!"  AND  "2 2 4"
END


TO FREREJACQUES
1  FRERE1
2  FRERE1
3  FRERE2
4  FRERE2
5  FRERE3
6  FRERE3
7  FRERE4
8  FRERE4
9  FREREJACQUES
END
```

Source: Papert and Solomon, 1972, p. 15

Figure 16

music. The only documentation which exists on MUSIC 360 is an unpublished programming manual.

Computer-Assisted Music Lessons

System Development Corporation, Santa Monica, California devised a system to give music lessons to children. Thirty electronic pianos were connected to a computer. The project, funded by USOE, was conducted in cooperation with the Wichita, Kansas, Public School System and the Wurlitzer Company. The overall aim of the study was "to evaluate the use of a computer-assisted program for teaching melody, rhythm, harmony, and creative music concepts." Visual devices are also included in the system (e.g., a rear screen projector above each piano so the student could visualize in written form each note being played). The child wears earphones to hear instructions and musical notes he or the computer plays. For example, a child might play melody with the computer providing the accompaniment.

The music education department at Penn State has used CAI to individualize learning of skills critical for musicians. For example, a student could view a display of a musical excerpt with question marks inserted in the place of missing notes. The taped excerpt may then be played in full, the student deciding on the missing notes and rhythmical varieties. Skills in melody and harmonic dictation, aural-visual discrepancies, and style can be learned through minor variations of this technique.

Computer-Assisted Language Drills

Linguistic experts, educators, and psychologists have been interested in the potential of computers for providing individualized learning in acquiring language skills.

ELSEVOC, developed by John Allen of Dartmouth College, is a computer program which provides individualized language drills. Students of several foreign languages (including Spanish, French, Latin, and Danish) are able to participate in individualized drills, which are

> continually adapting to concentrate on what the student shows he does not know and ignoring what he shows he has mastered. Similar to the language laboratories, these programs take much of the drudgery away from instructors in

drilling students, but unlike many language laboratories, they do not bore students by making them repeat over and over again the same unchanging mechanical drill (Allen, 1971).

The student goes to a teletype terminal, signs on, and ELSEVOC is called into memory. The computer then asks a series of questions determining what the student wants to study. The computer selects a random phrase which the student is asked to translate. ELSEVOC avoids the mistake of deciding whether the student's answer is exactly similar to the "correct" answer! Instead, ELSEVOC determines whether the expression is spelled correctly without worrying about accent marks or punctuation.

Computer-based programs have also been used in teaching early reading. A CAI reading curriculum for grades K-3 was developed at the Institute for Mathematical Studies in the Social Sciences at Stanford University. In the original design of the curriculum the computer would tutor the child in reading and provide nearly all of his reading instruction (Atkinson, *et al.*, 1970).

However, school tryouts of this approach led to the conclusion that economically and pedagogically, many aspects of reading instruction should be left to the classroom teacher. The aim was switched to the development of a low-cost, supplemental curriculum.

Students spend a 12-minute session on the terminal each day at a cost of 40 cents per session. The CAI program uses a simple teletype terminal equipped with an audio headset. The student receives his instructions on the drills through the audio headset and responds via the teletype terminal.

The program is designed in seven "strands." Each strand is composed of a series of drill exercises of increasing difficulty. In any given session on the terminal, the child may perform exercises in one or more strands, depending on his skills at that point in time. The selection of strands and exercises is made by the computer program, which analyzes the student's ability based on his performance in the program.

Stylistic Analysis

Researchers have found the computer to be an invaluable tool for stylistic analysis. The computer is able to take a multi-dimensional view of the text, and recognize the patterns in the writing.

The University of Michigan has developed an educational application of computer style analysis. Beginning journalism students receive guidance on their writing techniques via a computer (Bishop, 1970). The teachers are more concerned with substantive content of the student's writing and the social issues that are raised. They have less time or interest in developing writing skills.

The student may write a report of his own choice and then feed it into the computer for analysis. The program computes the average sentence length and the number of polysyllabic words in order to judge reading difficulty. The computer provides an overall rating and pinpoints paragraphs giving the most trouble. The computer can recognize articles, adjectives, and passive verbs that are associated with dull writing. The computer can also be used with pre-selected stories. In this mode, the computer can check the accuracy of the story, looking for key names, dates, or other facts. Completeness can be checked, at least superficially, by searching for key terms or phrases.

Sources of Information

An excellent source of information on the utilization of computing in humanities education is the journal *Computers and the Humanities*. Its information is varied, with articles about the increasing number of computer courses for the humanist, lists of related conferences, and descriptions of a sophisticated linguistically oriented text processing system.

Discipline journals such as the *Journal of Research in Music Education* also promote awareness of these applications. Articles are now also beginning to appear with increasing frequency in both computer and educational magazines of a general nature.

Several commercially published books are valuable resources in the humanities. *The Computer and Music* (Lincoln, 1970) is the most comprehensive book available in this area. *Computers in Humanistic Research* (Bowles, 1967) is valuable because it samples several areas across the humanities. *Techniques of Film Animation* (Halas and Manwell, 1968) is an important specialty book.

Conferences concentrating on similar topics are becoming more ordinary. An International Conference on Computers in the Humanities was held at the University of Minnesota in July, 1973.

Centers of excellence, which concentrate on humanistic research using computers, also are being developed. Examples include linguistics studies at the University of Kansas and chronological data bases at the University of Wisconsin.

Creative Notebook is a newsletter published at the University of Florida about "A Humanistic Computer-Assisted Creativity Center for the Common Man." This concept promises exciting possibilities for the future.

SOCIAL SCIENCES*

Compelling computer usage in the social sciences, although of heterogeneous types, relate in most cases to social data analysis. Although social and behavioral scientists were utilizing computers much earlier, not until the early 1960's were instructional materials published. Cooley and Lohnes (1962) produced a book to aid the simultaneous teaching of social statistics and computer programming. Other instructionally oriented books soon appeared (Green, 1963; Janda, 1969) but most instructional computer applications remained unpublicized until the 1970's. The annual Conferences on Computers in the Undergraduate Curricula provided the vehicle for many curricular uses to surface; these conferences still remain the richest source of data on social science computing for the classroom.

Pioneering Effort

Project IMPRESS, under the direction of E. Meyers, was the pioneering effort (Meyers, 1970). The goals of the IMPRESS project were set high and consequently their realization resulted in considerable impact on the field. The key features of IMPRESS are (1) accessibility of a variety of large social data bases, (2) availability of a wide selection of statistical and data transformational techniques, and (3) relatively uncomplicated procedures for system use. Combining all these features yields a package with many possible teaching applications, but two major limitations inhibit its utilization: (1) IMPRESS is not readily

---

*This section is composed primarily of an edited version of a specially prepared paper by Dr. Ronald E. Anderson.

transportable to other computer installations, and (2) few student exercises or learning units are available. One major exception to the second limitation is a course manual developed by Davis (1971).

IMPRESS includes a large data bank of social surveys, census data, anthropological materials, economic time series figures, etc., permanently stored in the memory of the computer. A user goes to any convenient teletype terminal, calls the program IMPRESS***, and begins a conversation in English with the machine. The system asks him to choose a specific study, next to select from two to eight variables in that study, and then to map his data as he chooses (as raw numbers, dichotomies, grouped categories, normalized values, or whatever). This done, the system allows him to order a variety of statistical routines ranging from simple percentage tables to fancy multiple regression analyses.

The system is designed to be inviting: there are no cards to punch, no problem of turnaround time, no programming skills required as it is a library (canned) program, and the entire process is conducted in reasonably straightforward English questions and answers. One may think of IMPRESS as a computational analogue of a library—ample, comfortable, and open stack.

University of Iowa Data Analysis Kits

The University of Iowa series of data analysis packages is one of the few sets which can be used with the IMPRESS system as well as SPSS (Statistical Package for Social Sciences). These kits consist primarily of student exercise manuals, which include instructions for accessing a data base with the aid of a statistical package. The University of Iowa data analysis kits are not the only such packages, but they have been selected for special note here because (1) a rich variety of data bases are included, (2) the packages have been widely disseminated and utilized, and (3) they can serve as useful models for creation of new packages.

IMPRESS and the University of Iowa Data Analysis packages have had wide appeal because they afford the method of research which most social scientists find comfortable: the social survey. IMPRESS compellingly organizes or extends the statistical techniques many instructors are already using in their research. The University of Iowa packages tailor data analysis exercises to interesting substantive issues students can explore.

Data Simulation and Gaming

The data simulation and gaming approach of DATACALL (Johnson, 1971) demonstrates the interesting potential of less popular techniques such as computer simulation. DATACALL, developed by Richard Johnson, generates artificial data for analysis by students. The artificial data are created according to the theoretical model specified by the instructor or simulation designer. The student structures his own data set by specifying certain parameter values. The data then are generated within these parameter limits and the variables interrelated according to a substantive model, which the instructor previously translated into a computer program. This procedure duplicates the essential steps in experimental research, with the exception that data collection is greatly reduced from long tedious laboratory sessions to a simple program run. The pedagogical significance of this exercise is that the student has to concentrate upon the difficult but challenging decisions of experimental design and data analysis. DATACALL can be used as a game by placing a cost on each computer run with a payoff for useful results. Johnson reports successful results utilizing this game format. The primary advantages of the DATACALL approach are: (1) Many more "experiments" can be run and more complex designs used than is possible in an ordinary laboratory-oriented psychology course; and (2) students become motivated to pursue and learn about such related topics as statistics and experimental design.

Taking DATACALL as a model, Dana Main and her associates at the University of Michigan developed and released several simulation packages under the name EXPERSIM. Models for (1) Imprinting, (2) Schizophrenia, and (3) Motivation are described in *EXPERSIM: Computer Simulations for Teaching Elementary Research Design in Psychology* from the Center for Research on Learning and Teaching. The EXPERSIM programs are now being used at several schools around the country.

Level of Education

All the examples discussed above were constructed with undergraduate education in mind and all can be used by large lower division classes. These packages, however, can be used at other learning levels as well. IMPRESS is used enthusiastically at both the high school and graduate levels. DATACALL was designed for an introductory laboratory course but is appropriate for many other applications in courses and fields other than psychology. The University of Iowa Data Analysis packages were designed for introductory "principles" courses, yet they are frequently used in more advanced courses and in methods/statistics courses.

Economics Models

Undergraduate economics students at the University of Michigan are using computer-based macro-economic models in their courses. Developed by R.S. Holbrook, these models are at various levels of complexity.

One of the more complex models is a representation of a world composed of 10 essentially equal countries interrelated by capital flows and international trade. These, in turn, can affect domestic policy.

A student group has responsibility for the policy of one country. With a goal of achieving full employment, price stability, growth, and balance of payments, decisions are made on taxes, government spending, and the money supply. Each team must be familiar not only with its own economy and try to predict its behavior patterns, but also those of other countries.

Students are expected to apply economic theory to analyze the historical behavior of the country and approximate the multipliers for forecasting the future. Decisions are inputted via computer terminals—students are even given a chance to change their minds—and data are stored and printed upon request. Decisions for a quarter are made between class periods—therefore, three-quarters of a year can be covered in a week.

In micro-economics, DYNSIM was developed at Oberlin College in order to integrate the advantages of the computer as a tool for economic analysis into the undergraduate curriculum. It offers undergraduates direct experience with research methods.

Students using DYNSIM have two options for their analysis. They can either create their own models or investigate a previously invented and stored model. In the creation mode, the student has complete control over the structure, variables, and running of the model. During execution, the learner can also modify his model.

The student must go through three procedures in order to invent his simulation, specify the model, initialize the variables, and create the controls. DYNSIM is running at several schools in addition to Oberlin.

Economics Courses

Small colleges have used computer models in both macro- and micro-economics courses. Professors feel the models bring a more dynamic atmosphere to the course, using different variables as the basis for policy-making.

The most widely used text adapted for this type of use is a book written under the direction of George Treys of MIT, *Computer Problem Kit for Economics*, published by Macmillan.

Views

The social and behavioral sciences have utilized the computer in ways that are relatively congruent with previous instructional practice. This is equally true of the specific packages described above. These instructional materials are all data-oriented with the objective of exposing students to experiences typical of research activity. A primary advantage of this approach is the first-hand knowledge students gain in empirical techniques and in formulating decisions that must accompany use of such techniques. At a broader level the approach is designed to teach students a mode of thinking with an emphasis upon inquiry to obtain an answer for a question. Inquiry is important as a way of dealing with most problems that arise in the social world.

Few self-contained, distributable, computer-related curriculum packages can be found in the social and behavioral sciences. It is not that instructors are not using computers in classroom applications, but rather that their usage is generally idiosyncratic and undocumented. Typically, the data and method of utilizing the data are unique to these instructors and hence not amenable to export. Even some of the published materials, e.g., Vargus and White (1971), suffer from such difficulties. Since the compelling models of computer utilization are of fairly recent vintage, it is not surprising that there are so many examples of mediocre or unsatisfying computer use in social science education. Classroom computer use must involve a change in the structure of instruction, especially in the role of the teacher. As we increasingly recognize this fact, it will be possible to plan much improved pedagogical activities involving computer technology.

Sources of Information

The most complete compilation of literature on social science computing was produced by Ronald E. Anderson at the Social Sciences Research Facilities Center at the University of Minnesota (Anderson, 1972).

Social science research centers are often good sources of information, particularly for their own activities. One of the best examples is the Laboratory for Political Research at the University of Iowa, which houses the Regional Social Science Data Archives. The Archives hold over 400 data sets dealing with research activities. About 130 of them are accessible through SPSS with documentation available. It publishes a newsletter, *SS Data Quarterly*, which reports on activities of the archives, newly published books in the field and other news. Another example is the National Opinion Research Center (NORC), affiliated with the University of Chicago.

Dartmouth has a large, well-documented library of applications of the computer in the social sciences. James Davis (1971) has written a book, *Elementary Survey Analysis*, with which one may easily integrate the utilization of computerized data bases.

The University of Wisconsin has a Central Program Inventory Service for the Social Sciences. They provide an index to a collection of abstracts for social science-oriented computer programs, and an associated information circular.

For sources of applications programs in the social sciences, the HumRRO data base shows that the following institutions have developed the greatest numbers of programs: University of Pittsburgh (sociology), Coast Community College (political science), Notre Dame (economics), and the University of Michigan (psychology).

The Commission on College Geography of the American Association of Geographers has published two papers about computing in geography, "Computerized Instruction in Undergraduate Geography"

(Fielding and Rumage, 1972), and "Computer-Assisted Instruction in Geography" (Fielding and Rumage, 1969).

A Geography Program Exchange (GPE) is located at the Computer Institute for Social Science Research, Michigan State University, East Lansing. The Exchange maintains a library of computer programs useful in geography and a list of programs available for distribution.

EDUCATION

The category "educator training" includes materials designed for use in education curricula—both materials to teach teachers and administrators about educational uses of computers and materials which use the computer to teach other "education" subjects, such as educational measurement.

The relatively limited use of computers in the formal training of educators is reflected in the small number of curricular materials which have been developed. Of the few materials we identified, the majority are short demonstration programs to introduce educators to computer-assisted instruction techniques or systems.

Computing Literacy for Educators

The "computing literacy" type of education course ranges from a survey course on ways computers are used in educational institutions (American University; Florida State University) to seminars on learning to develop your own CAI materials (Montgomery County, Maryland).

At the University of Louisville there is a course open to senior and graduate education students to prepare prospective secondary-level mathematics teachers to use computers (Greeslin, 1972). The purpose of the course is threefold: to teach mathematics teachers a programming skill, to give them experience in problem-solving, and to help teachers consider alternative means of introducing the use of the computer into a course. The importance of learning a programming skill is emphasized during the course because so little time is available when teaching, and students tend to dominate the terminals.

A package of curricular materials designed to educate educators about computers has been developed by the Northwest Regional Educational Laboratory. The package, called REACT, emphasizes "hands-on" experience with computers. Three courses were developed, each providing 30 hours of instruction. Materials for the courses consist of 24 instructional booklets. The courses can be used for independent study, in college courses, or in structured seminars or workshops.

Computer-Assisted Instruction

Although quite a few computer-assisted instruction programs have been developed for use by students in education curricula, nearly all of these have been short demonstration type programs used to illustrate technical or pedagogical features of various CAI systems.

CARE (Computer-Assisted Remedial Education) is an exception to this. CARE is a complete series of courses of instruction developed at Pennsylvania State University.

CARE is a special education course designed for undergraduate education students. It is also used by inservice teachers and paraprofessionals.

Use of the program by teachers in rural areas is facilitated by a mobile van which houses the computer system and moves from location to location.

CARE teaches teachers to identify characteristics of handicapped children and to be aware of symptoms of learning disabilities. The teachers are taught to screen the children, use diagnostic procedures, profile the children, and make appropriate decisions about referral.

The teacher (student) spends 25-30 hours interacting with the computer system, primarily in a tutorial mode. Some simulation and inquiry also are used. The student can inquire of the system, and the system can use its data to make some decisions on preferable alternatives for the learner. In addition to different approaches, a variety of media are utilized during the instruction. For example, samples of handwriting are displayed by slides on the terminal. While studying speech defects, the audio portion of the system is used. The steps in the CARE program are presented in Figure 17. CARE I is described here, but CARE II, CARE III, and CARE IV are also in development by Penn State, addressing other areas of special education (Cartwright and Cartwright, 1972).

The study of supplementary materials, such as a CARE Handbook, is an important activity of the learner when not working directly with the computer system.

The CARE Decision Process

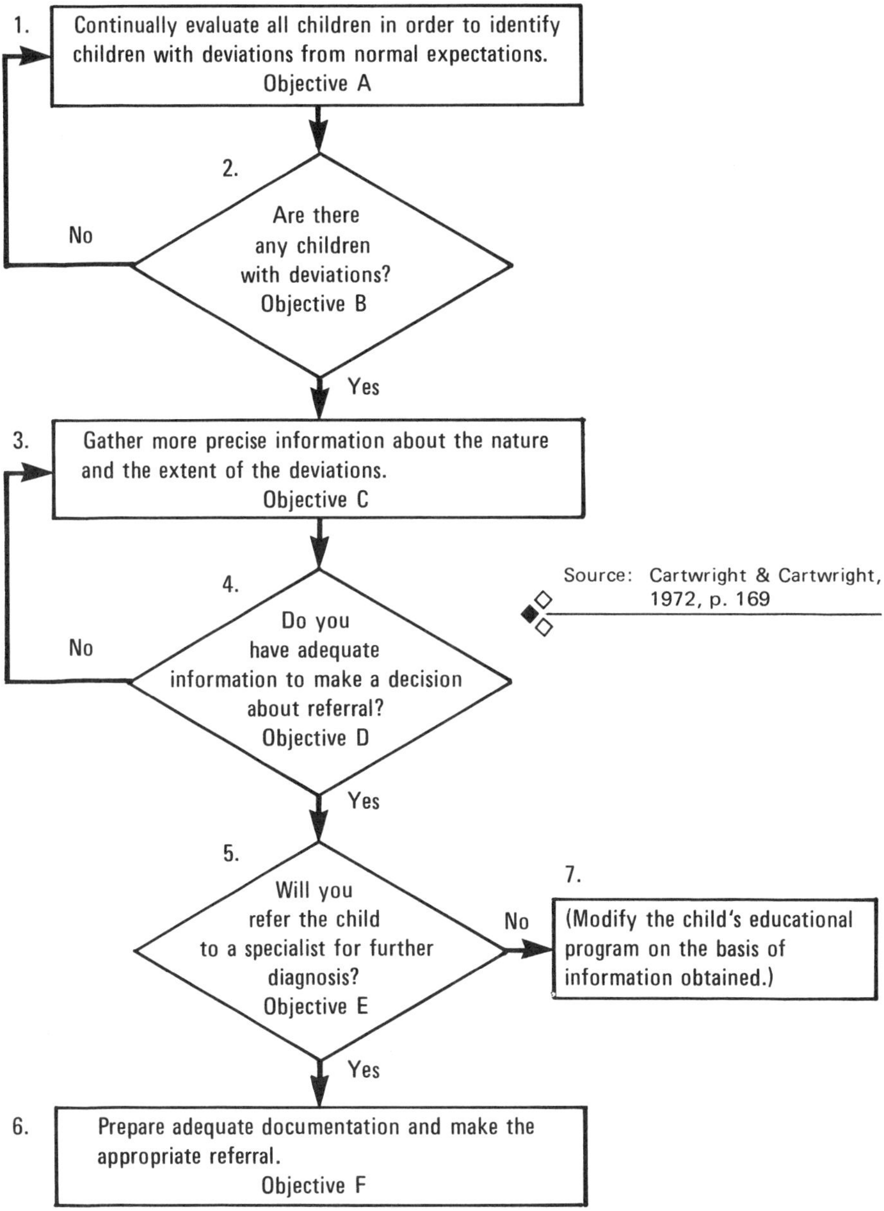

1. Continually evaluate all children in order to identify children with deviations from normal expectations.
   Objective A

2. Are there any children with deviations? Objective B
   - No → return to 1
   - Yes ↓

3. Gather more precise information about the nature and the extent of the deviations.
   Objective C

4. Do you have adequate information to make a decision about referral? Objective D
   - No → return to 3
   - Yes ↓

5. Will you refer the child to a specialist for further diagnosis? Objective E
   - No → 7
   - Yes ↓

6. Prepare adequate documentation and make the appropriate referral.
   Objective F

7. (Modify the child's educational program on the basis of information obtained.)

Source: Cartwright & Cartwright, 1972, p. 169

Figure 17

Views

Many people feel an urgency for preparing teachers, administrators, and students to use the computer effectively. A few courses have been developed, but they have not had widespread impact. A recent study stresses the need for faculty training, probably taking the form of continuing education.

One issue for discussion is the effectiveness of teaching programming versus receiving the instruction via computer. In a course developed at Western Washington University, the computer both presents information and manages student progress. The theory is that a teacher is more likely to use the computer if he/she has been taught in this manner.

There is also a lack of personnel within traditional schools of education to develop and organize such a course. This problem might be alleviated by getting help from the university computer center and outside experts.

Sources of Information

There is no single source of information on computing literacy training for educators. A variety of organizations, including computer manufacturers, time-sharing companies, universities, and professional societies offer seminars and workshops for teachers or administrators. The educator desiring to improve his skills and knowledge on computer-related subjects faces the problem of sifting useful information out of an overwhelming array of publications and seminars.

There are a number of books addressed to educators on the subject of computers, such as:

The CAI Author/Instructor, J.C. Meredith, 1971

Layman's Guide to the Use of Computers, AEDS, 1971

Using the Computer in Education, Paul G. Watson, 1972

Educational Uses of the Computer: An Introduction, M. Clemens Johnson, 1971.

The Teacher and the Computer, B.L. Hicks and S. Hunka, 1972.

Preparing for Computer Assisted Instruction, Charles A. Dyer, 1972.

The Association for Educational Data Systems (AEDS) is a useful resource for communication among educators on computer-related subjects.

For teachers, discipline-related sources of information are probably most relevant and useful. At the present time, undergraduate education majors must look to other departments, such as computer science, for training in computer-related subjects.

Chapter 4

DEVELOPING COMPUTER-BASED LEARNING MATERIALS

This chapter is designed to help make decisions about the purpose, organization, funding, and methods of developing computer-based learning materials. There are so many different purposes and contexts for producing computer-based learning materials that it seems neither useful nor possible to seek general principles or optimum strategies for development. The first discussion below will help those planning and organizing projects to clarify the purposes of a particular development project or program. Next, a series of case studies illustrates the variety of approaches to and contexts for development of computer-based learning materials. Then, issues and alternatives for organizing and funding projects are discussed. Finally, this chapter addresses processes of development and evaluation of computer-based curriculum.

AIMS AND PURPOSES OF DEVELOPMENT

Computer technology is used in support of many different educational aims and purposes. This section is designed to help those who are initiating, directing, or funding development projects to clarify purposes along several dimensions.

Target Situation—Schools and Teachers

The resources, constraints, and characteristics of the target school environment—including the administrators who make decisions on adoption and implementation—are an essential part of the definition of aims. Some of these considerations are important in the case of any educational materials—such as compatibility with existing curricular objectives, credit requirements, scheduling, staffing patterns, and budgets. Computer-oriented curricula add more considerations to the definition of target situations. These cut across all aspects of schooling, from budgets to facilities to staffing to curriculum objectives to instructional management. The answers to questions about the intended school environment place definite constraints on the design and implementation of the materials/systems.

Developers of computer-based curricula nearly always have aims which entail some modification of and compromise with a traditional school environment. Teacher role and functions, instructional management, facilities, student scheduling, costs, present curriculum, and decision-making are the areas which need to be examined closely. These considerations and others are listed in more detail in Appendix 4.

The Commonwealth Computer-Assisted Instruction Consortium, formed by the School Districts of Pittsburgh and Philadelphia, the Department of Education of the Commonwealth, and the Pennsylvania State University, conducted a pilot program to develop, implement, and evaluate computer-assisted instruction for urban high schools. Two mathematics courses, consisting of 150 on-line hours of computer-assisted instruction, were used in public high schools in Philadelphia and Pittsburgh. One of the major conclusions of the experiment is stated by the project leaders as follows:

> To try to insert an individualized program of the type developed by the Consortium into schools with widely divergent philosophies of mass education is not recommended. Other subjects are being taught following a traditional pattern, with traditional expectations. Students had some difficulty adjusting to the relative freedom of the CAI classroom ... [teachers] were concerned, for instance, because not all students covered the material in the given amount of time. ... The school is a social system, and produces better results when the way in which all courses are taught is in agreement with its general overall philosophy. A fundamental reorganization of schools is needed in order to adapt them to new individualized methodologies. ... The course materials must be revised for a program of continuous progress instead of the current restrictions of the semester or bi-semester plan of scheduling (Mitzel, *et al.*, 1971, pp. 76-77).

One leading computer-assisted instruction center at a major university developed a CAI program to provide remedial instruction in basic language arts for incoming students deficient in these skills. The program was demonstrated to be highly effective, and clearly met a need of many students in the university. After it was developed, the CAI project staff was dismayed to discover that the academic departments would not endorse the program, that academic credit would not be given to students taking the course, that there were no financial mechanisms available in the university for making the course available to students—that the program did not fit into the overall curriculum.

A project, if it is to be successful in providing learning materials useful to students, must realistically address how it intends to deal with the existing structure. If it accepts aspects of existing structure as given, then the materials and systems will be designed to fit into, and interact with, that structure. Supplementary materials would fit into existing courses and tie into widely used textbooks. Existing teacher roles and classroom management would be part of the overall design. Traditions about what topics are covered at what grade levels would be respected. School finances would be taken into account. Teachers' conceptions about the subject-matter would not be seriously violated.

The Stanford CAI lab spent many years and millions of dollars in public funds in designing and redesigning computer-based learning materials that would not only be effective in themselves but more importantly would *work* in a traditional school structure. The Division of Instructional Systems in Philadelphia has been working directly in the public school system for over eight years, developing and revising systems and materials that will both work and provide benefits within a school structure. It is not a trivial task to devise innovations and alternatives that will *work* within the structure, much less show some unique benefit.

If a project aims to change major elements of existing school structure, and if it hopes for computer-based systems to play a key role in this reform, then it would not develop the computer-based system in isolation of major school reform efforts. For example, the computer-based project might be part of a larger effort by a community or institution which shares this aim, and the computer-based system would be designed to support the larger effort (not vice versa). One example of such "larger efforts" is the University Without Walls, a program of the Union for Experimenting Colleges and Universities, that provides learning resources and experiences tailored to the objectives of the individual adult learner, of whatever age or background.

If a computer-based education project has as a major aim the reform of educational structures, it is not likely to achieve its aims by building a computer-based system or course of instruction and plugging it into a traditional institutional environment. The Rand Study of Computers in Higher Education concluded:

> The high resistance to change of most existing institutions of higher education suggests that the most rapid and extensive adaptation to the capabilities of computer-based instruction is likely to occur in institutions intended to serve populations not enrolled full time in conventional institutions (Levien, 1972, p. 533).

Similarly, the Carnegie Commission on Higher Education believes that

> a realistic appraisal of current progress suggests that the most significant advances [in educational technology], in the coming decade, will be generated by emerging institutions and extramural educational systems that are being created alongside traditional ones.... Although traditional institutions may employ the new technologies for 10 to 20 percent of their instruction by the year 2000, extramural education may use them for up to 80 percent of their instruction (Carnegie, 1972, p. 52).

Similarly, the Commission on Instructional Technology found that:

> Our study has shown that one-shot injections of a single technological medium are ineffective. At best they offer only optional "enrichment." Technology, we believe, can carry out its full potential for education only insofar as educators embrace instructional technology as a system and integrate a range of human and nonhuman resources into the total educational process (Tickton, 1970).

Oettinger and Marks (1969) pointed out the difficulty in trying to realize the potential of educational technology. Part of the reason is that the "structure" of education involves far more than the administrative hierarchy of schools themselves. Oettinger's description of the actors involved in keeping the educational structures include, for example, parents, mass media, churches, and foundations—from both "inside" and "outside" the system of schools.

There have been a number of attempts in the past decade at a major revision of educational structure in a particular community. The Ford Foundation, for example, has supported a number of experiments in community-based schools. The U.S. Office of Education is supporting an "experimental schools" program involving large public school systems (HEW,USOE, 1972). However, we found no cases where pioneers in computer-based learning were involved in these major attempts at educational reform. Most computer-based learning projects have proceeded in isolation from substantive attempts at school reform.

The curriculum development project which targets its products to a non-traditional school environment is undertaking an enormously complex and costly task which is far larger than development of materials and programs. Novel staffing patterns alone can take *years* to implement in a school district (see *Strategies for Differentiated Staffing*, English and Sharpes, 1972).

A salient problem in accomplishing educational reform is the difficulty of describing and quantifying the important dimensions of educational structure. A possible tool to aid in this effort is described by Traub, *et al.* (1972). They have developed and tested an instrument for quantifying the dimensions of school life (see Table 2). This instrument might be used to measure the degree of *openness* in any specific institution and thereby to predict the chances of success for programmatic, broad educational innovation. Briefly, the more *open* the school is on their scale (e.g., greater scheduling flexibility and student participation in decision-making) the greater the likelihood that a given innovation will succeed.

Such an analysis of the school environment may help the CBLM innovator to (1) make realistic assessments of likely candidate schools for his project, and (2) more precisely identify the preconditions requiring change at all schools prior to attempting application of his particular curricular reform.

In summary, if the aim of the project is to provide materials and systems that will be widely used in traditional educational environ-

Describing Dimensions of School Life

Dimension	Items*
Setting Instructional Objectives	23. Defining Objectives 24. Use of Objectives
Materials and Activities	6. Availability of Curriculum Programs 7. Materials Usage 11. Media Usage
Physical Environment	9. Learning Environment
Structure for Decision-Making	1. Assignment of Teachers 18. Subgrouping Criterion
Time Scheduling	2. Time Structure 3. Unstructured Time 16. Attendance 17. Independent Study Time
Individualization of Learning	14. Student Methods 15. Pace of Materials 19. Number of Student Groups
Composition of Classes	20. Range of Age 21. Vertical Organization
Role of Teacher	8. Selection of Materials 10. Decision-Making 12. Teacher Focus 13. Teacher Role
Student Evaluation	22. Promotion Timing 25. Evaluation Audience 26. Timing of Evaluation 27. Student Role in Evaluation 28. Evaluation Procedures
Student Control	4. Rule-Making 5. Rule-Enforcing

*Item numbers refer to those in the instrument.

Source: Traub, Ross E., et al. "Closure on Openness: Describing and Quantifying Open Education." *Interchange*, Vol. 3, Nos. 2, 3, 1972, p. 79.

Table 2

ments, then the materials and systems should be designed to *work* within these environments or reasonable modifications of these environments. If the aim is to *reform* the structure of educational institutions, then the computer project probably should be undertaken in a reform context, part of a larger effort along many dimensions. Isolated development of computer-based systems by technologists who hope that one day educators will see the light or who imagine that the machine will revolutionize the structure has been demonstrated to be an ineffective strategy. Therefore, a statement of aims in keeping with the targeted school structure (of whatever type) is a key ingredient to success of the project.

Intended Learner Population

Parameters commonly used to describe intended learner population are: immediate history, long-term history, and goals. For example:
- Age
- Academic background
- Career interests
- Ability groupings

Some projects are concerned potentially with all students at a given "grade level" in a particular subject area; some are targeted toward students with a more specific learning need, e.g., remedial English for community college students; some projects are concerned with learners in a broad range of ages and grade levels in a particular subject area; some are restricted to certain socioeconomic or geographic groups, e.g., an ecology course designed for students with access to a particular forest or lake as a laboratory.

One approach to curriculum development is to begin with a specific population, analyze their needs, and develop materials to satisfy those needs. (For a discussion of a "systems approach" as applied to curriculum development, see Geis, 1970.) In this case, one begins with a careful description of the learner population as a matter of course.

It is more common, however, for a project to begin with an interest in a particular subject-matter, e.g., introductory calculus; develop instructional materials in that subject area; and then find out who learns effectively using the materials.

Or a project may be particularly interested in a method of instruction (e.g., a computer-based tutorial strategy); develop some instructional materials incorporating that methodology; and then try it out to find out who can benefit from the materials.

The Sullivan Reading Program is a notable example of a curriculum which began with a methodology. The decision to work with programmed lessons was the

> most momentous decision involved in the development of the Sullivan reading materials.... The development of the reading materials was not a case of wanting to improve reading instruction and then seeking the means to do so. It was instead a case of discovering a valuable teaching tool and seeking a deserving subject to teach with it. Had Sullivan (and others) not taken up the programming aegis in 1956, the teaching of reading might be plodding along in the tradition of centuries (Thompson, 1971, p. 45).

This focus on method rather than target population at the outset did result in some "false starts." Sullivan initially prepared foreign language programs for high school students, but found the students unable to master the materials. "He was sure that his programs were not at fault; the high school students simply could not read well enough to follow the programs (Thompson, 1971, p. 12). It was this experience that led Sullivan to focus on teaching reading, to remedy this situation. (The foreign language materials are being used currently to teach *adult learners*.)

Purposes may also be clarified in terms of the potential *extent* of use. The potential number of students who may use the materials in a given period of time and potential number of institutions adopting the materials/systems has implications for the amount of resources that can reasonably be invested in development of the materials, in addition to having strong implications for the type of dissemination strategy planned. In order to demonstrate on a large scale the benefits of computer-based curricula, some experts advocate beginning with an identification of the largest potential audience and working back to a definition of the qualitative characteristics of the audience. This was the approach, for example, of Mitre Corporation in devising a strategy for large-scale demonstration of the market potential of the TICCIT system for computer-assisted instruction. They determined that introductory and remedial courses for junior college students would have a numerically large potential audience. The design of the TICCIT system and the curricular materials to be delivered on this system were based on a careful definition of the target audience. For example, it was determined that in junior colleges, decisions on adoption of curricula would be more likely to be based on a cost/effective tradeoff than in other institutions, and that these decisions would be made by administrators rather than faculty. The TICCIT curricula are being designed to minimize the per-pupil time spent by the human instructor, which reduces the student/hour cost of delivering instruction.

Careful analysis and definition of the target audience should reveal some information as to the extent and nature of *user tailoring* to be provided. For example, the Huntington Two simulation materials for high school students are designed and packaged in such a way as to allow for user tailoring in several ways. They are packaged in modules which can be used in the context of different courses in different ways, depending on the skills and purposes of the teacher, the computing resources of the school, and the interests and skills of the students. A module could become the basis for a six-week course; it could be used as an enriching demonstration for a day or two; it could be an independent study project for a small group of students; or it could be a departure point for development of a new curriculum within a school or school district. This characteristic of the Huntington materials is consonant with the aim of providing adjunct materials which can be readily adapted into the existing curricula of traditional public high school environments.

Purpose for Using Computers in the Curriculum

In Chapter 1 of this book, several types of *purposes* for using computers in learning were identified. To review briefly, these were:
- Computing opportunity purposes
- Discipline-related curriculum improvement purposes
- Computing literacy purposes
- Instructional cost-effectiveness purposes
- Educational reform purposes

These purposes are by no means mutually exclusive, but usually projects focus on one of these more than others. Underlying rationale depends on perceptions of what improvements and reforms are needed in education, and in perceptions of how computer applications can contribute to learning. An "illustrative statements of purpose" for improving the educational process, developed in the present study, is shown in Table 3.

There are several reasons why we stress the importance of clarifying the purposes for using computers in the curriculum project or product:

- Careful analyses of purpose may suggest that a less expensive alternative to computers may be used to accomplish the same end.
- Careful analysis of purposes may suggest related changes or reforms in the educational environment or curriculum required to achieve the purpose. This is surely the case where the purposes relate to "individualization" and "learner independence," which are intimately bound up with the overall organization, structure, and culture of schools.
- Potential users of the curriculum products need to be able to relate the products and methods to their own needs and purposes, in order to make decisions on adoption and implementation.
- Funding agencies need to be able to relate the project purposes to their mission, goals, and program purposes.

Intended Learning Outcomes—
Schemes for Classifying

Educational aims in terms of learning outcomes are often described in terms of three major domains—affective, cognitive, and psychomotor. The cognitive domain includes recall of knowledge of various types and intellectual skills and abilities, such as analysis, synthesis, and evaluation (Bloom, 1956). The affective domain includes such abilities as receiving (attending), responding, and valuing. The psychomotor domain includes such activities as attending to and selecting from sensory stimuli, imitating acts, and performing motor tasks.

Illustrative Statements of Purpose of Computer-Based Learning Materials

- Enable students to develop new skills and tools for handling information.
- Provide opportunity for students to practice writing and testing algorithms.
- Provide students with access to wide range of data for checking out hypotheses.
- Enable students to develop richer intuitive grasp of complex phenomena through graphic visual representation.
- Enable students to develop a variety of tools for describing phenomena, e.g., graphic, mathematical, algorithmic, statistical, logical.
- Enable students to learn how to deal with factors which limit and define experimental accuracy; e.g., learn to distinguish systematic from random errors in data and processing.
- Enable students to learn more of the complexities of phenomena, e.g., through modeling and simulation.
- Enable students to apply concepts and abstract laws to a variety of concrete problem situations.
- Enable students to visualize implications of theory.
- Enable students to take a more active role in learning.
- Encourage learner independence.
- Increase students' motivation to learn the subject.
- Encourage students to value computer as a tool.
- Encourage students to tailor their learning experiences to meet their own objectives.
- Emphasize intrinsic joy of learning and deemphasize competition with peers as motivating force.

Table 3

Other taxonomies also have been proposed (e.g., by Gagné, 1965; Merrill, M.D., 1971; and Merrill, P.F., 1971). Bloom's principal goal was to aid in classifying and communicating instructional objectives. The cognitive domain taxonomy has been widely used but the affective categories in the main have lacked operational meaning. Gagné developed a hierarchical model to relate eight hypothesized types of learning with conditions required for their occurrence. Thus, he hoped to provide a basis for instructional sequencing. Many have felt that Gagné's approach was too limited to aid practical development of curriculum on a broad scale. M.D. Merrill (1971) broadened Gagné's categories to 10 and added an instructional paradigm to deal with learned emotional behavior. To date, they have all been successfully applied to some form of cognitive curriculum development.

Most curriculum development projects, computer-related or not, have cognitive aims as the primary explicit focus. As many critics of education have pointed out, however, the affective domain is in fact involved in learning irrespective of stated cognitive goals. Grobman (1970, p. 96) states, for example:

> Thus, it seems quite likely that the achievement of cognitive and psychomotor aims involves prior or concomitant achievement of some affective outcomes, whether or not these are identified by the project. Regardless of the long-term, primary goals of the curriculum project, perhaps such affective outcomes should be the most important areas for project concern, since without achieving some positive affective outcomes ... achievement of any other goals in the cognitive and psychomotor domains may be precluded.

Even where cognitive aims are primary, the computer is usually expected by developers to have a salutary effect on certain affective characteristics of the learner, such as attending to the learning task at hand. According to Licklider (1962, p. 238), for example:

> It seems possible, by exploiting the computer's constant capability for quick response and reinforcement, to develop techniques of instruction and intellectual exploration that will "trap" the attention of students and divert their energies from amusements and other less constructive pastimes to education.

Computer-based curriculum projects do not usually have aims in the psychomotor domain other than achievement of typing or keypunching skills. Driver and flight training simulators are the primary exception to this statement.

In the cognitive domain, computer-based projects often emphasize "process" learning as contrasted with "knowledge." Such abilities as applying concepts to concrete examples, producing procedures, analyzing errors, and organizing data are emphasized in computer-based learning.

Two frequently cited aims of computer-based learning are increased learner independence and increased interest and motivation in a particular subject area. Another related aim is to have the students learn to be masters of the computing machines and thereby learn to be masters rather than slaves of technology in general. Such learning is advocated most strongly by, for example, Thomas Dwyer of Project SOLO, Seymour Papert of MIT, and Arthur Luehrmann of Dartmouth.

Learning Outcomes—
Specificity of Aims

The development of computer-based curricula has heightened the already existing controversies regarding specificity of aims. Advocates of detailed behavioral objectives for describing short-term learning outcomes see in computer-based systems an opportunity or requirement to become extremely precise. Critics of detailed behavioral objectives see the computer as a tool for open-ended learning in which the learning goals are stated in fairly global terms.

As Grobman (1970, p. 100) points out, "The way in which objectives are stated—whether the statement is general or highly specific, and whether objectives are stated in terms of immediately observable behavior—influences a number of aspects of the project." It influences the ways in which materials are prepared, the manner in which achievement of goals can be evaluated, and the type of learning materials and systems produced.

One example of the interdependence of these factors is the case of the Intermediate Science Curriculum Study, one of the past decade's "high impact" curriculum projects. The planners of the project intended first to produce objectives for the materials, then develop the materials, and evaluation instruments, and finally try out the materials. The plan also called for preparation of the materials in four-week summer writing conferences of junior high school science teachers and content specialists. However, the approach did not work with the writing teams.

> For the first several days of the conference, the morale of the writers was quite obviously low, and at the end of the first week of the four-week conference, no progress had been made. When quizzed as to their lack of progress, the writers reported that they found it extremely difficult to prestate objectives and that they felt uncomfortable trying to do this ... "I am a creative person, let me produce something first, and then you write what it will do" (Kratochvil and Crawford, 1971, p. 22).

The writers felt it was impossible to know in advance what they seek to accomplish with science instructional materials; that good science instruction is aimed at accomplishing things that cannot be stated in specific terms; and that prestating specific objectives was unduly constraining and reduced their perspective.

At this point the project leaders had the choice either of training the writers to write objectives or of modifying their approach. The developers felt the content experts were indispensable but that it would be too difficult to get them to work productively under the original approach. So they modified the approach. Under the new approach, a general plan was first specified, then materials were developed, then the materials were tried out, then objectives and formal evaluation instruments were developed, and finally, the materials were formally tried out. The objectives are not part of the product available to users.

The statement of goals in behavioral terms facilitates the task of preparing materials for writers trained in this approach; and it makes evaluation much easier. Computer-based systems may be useful in the role of managing the instructional process for an individual learner, but only if objectives are clearly specified. An instructional manager program built into the computer system can continually monitor an individual learner's progress toward meeting the objectives, and prescribe learning activities which will help him meet specific objectives of the course or program.

Developing Computer-Based Learning Materials

Critics of the behavioral objectives approach raise the following kinds of objections, particularly with regard to computer-based materials:

- Computers are a new tool for learning; we do not yet know what all kinds of learning outcomes are possible. Therefore, a more experimental approach should be taken in which materials and learning outcomes emerge from day-to-day experience in the classroom. This, for example, was the philosophy of Project SOLO in Pittsburgh. Learning modules and programs emerged from the work of students and their teachers on a day-to-day experimental basis (Dwyer, 1971a).
- Computer-based systems provide the opportunity for more open-ended learning than is possible through other means. Each student should have the opportunity to explore the subject area in his own creative, unique way, and computer systems make this more possible.*
- Behavioral objectives are specified in immediately observable terms, and there is a difficulty in insuring that what is immediately observable is related to the long-run desired outcome. Also, since affective outcomes are difficult to state in specific terms or measure, they are likely to be ignored.†
- Specific statements of behavioral objectives tend to place a ceiling on learning for an entire group. This stifles the individual creativity of a learner.†

In brief, on the one hand, computer-based tutorials, drills, and computer-managed instruction, if they are to be effective, require detailed statements of both terminal and enabling objectives. The value of a computer-managed system is lost if there are no clearly specified criteria for management of the learning process (Seidel, 1971b). On the other hand, computer-based inquiry systems, problem-solving facilities, design aids, games and simulations, and other open-ended systems do not lend themselves well to a detailed behavioral objectives approach. Overall, however, if there are no guidelines at all as to the expected

---

*Personal communication with Ronald Blum.

†Personal communication with Joseph Denk.

learning outcomes, a number of problems arise. It is difficult for the developer to evaluate the programs and systems or to know in what ways to improve them; it is difficult for school administrators and faculty to make decisions on adoption of materials; it is difficult to integrate materials or courses into an overall program of studies when it is unclear what the prerequisite skills and learning outcomes are; it is difficult for the student to evaluate his own experience if there are no guidelines as to the abilities he can develop using these tools; in a free learning situation, it is difficult for a student to decide whether to engage in a program of activities if he does not know what kinds of learning he can expect to gain. Many computer-based games and simulation programs in particular suffer from these problems.

The difficulty in developing, selecting, using, and evaluating simulations which do not have learning objectives specified is illustrated by the remarks of a physics educator who is an expert on the uses of computers in undergraduate instruction. His remarks were in response to a conference presentation concerning a lunar landing simulation:

> It is essentially a game in which the student tries to set his rocket ship down on the moon. Now I am not sure how much a student actually learns by going through a simulation like this. He may learn how to drive a LEM, but I do not know if he is going to get a very strong feeling for physics as a result. I would have to try out the program personally to get any idea what physics might be learned from it.*

Recognizing this problem, the Project COMPUTe staff wrote in its guidance to faculty developers:

> Simulations are frequently more fun to write and play with than they are useful as instructional tools.... We feel it is of paramount importance to the success of these instructional materials for authors to assess carefully the nature of the student's interaction with a simulation. For instance, what tasks or problems is it appropriate to assign a student with respect to the simulation? What ultimate objective should the student achieve as a result of working with the simulation? What, in other words, should he be equipped to do after his

---

*Interview with Ronald Blum, 1972.

Developing Computer-Based Learning Materials

exposure to a given simulation that he could not do before? From the point of view of Project COMPUTe, a working simulation is *not* the objective of a writing effort, although it may well serve as a beginning. Careful consideration of the instructional value of such a tool may make the difference between its being merely a game or a valuable resource.*

Definition of Curriculum:
What Is to Be Developed

There is no commonly agreed-upon definition of "curriculum." As Goodlad points out in the epilogue to *Curriculum Design in a Changing Society*, "There is not agreement even on what *a* curriculum or *the* curriculum is" (Goodlad, 1970, p. 350).

A project's definition of "curriculum" and what the project aims to do with it, often emerges over time with experience.

A project may simply plan to do something to improve a situation in a given discipline, study the situation, and perhaps decide to prepare some kind of student materials. After preparing these materials, it may find that something more is needed, since teachers are not ready to use the materials. The project may then decide to conduct teacher-training sessions. Or it may prepare teacher materials. Or it may supplement or modify student materials with other kinds of materials to facilitate teaching and learning. Or the project may want teachers to develop their own materials and so it may start with teacher training in the subject area. It may then realize that, even after special training, the individual teacher, who is teaching full time in the classroom, has neither the background nor the time to develop classroom materials. This realization may lead the project into materials development, when it had not initially intended to do this (Grobman, 1970, p. 114).

To some this process may sound unnecessarily inefficient; a more careful analysis of the needs of the target population at the outset, and a broader definition of "curriculum," would ensure against such costly

*From "Description of Project COMPUTe Materials."

shifts in direction and aims. Grobman, on the other hand, believes that "This ability to change when such change is indicated is one of the greatest strengths of the developmental movement" (p. 115).

Although considerable flexibility is needed in the definition of what is to be developed, it would seem that some mistakes of past projects could be avoided. The history of computer-assisted instruction is replete with examples of projects that developed materials under a fairly narrow definition of curriculum as being instructional programs or devices—which then did not turn out to be usable in an operational school environment because other components of the curriculum were not taken into account in the design. Edwin Taylor (1970) in "History of a Failure in Computer Interactive Instruction" describes an elegant and technically successful computer interactive display, developed to teach special relativity, which is not used by students. Although the display system had obvious (to the developers) pedagogical value, its developers ignored its relationship to other facets of the curriculum and school environment such as class size (600 students), budgets (duplication of the system would cost $150,000 per display), faculty interests and skills, textbooks, student interests and skills, and so on.

Purpose of the Development Activities

The purpose of a project to develop computer-oriented curricula may be described in terms of the development process itself. That is, the *process* of developing the materials is viewed as an important learning experience for those involved. In this case the development process itself is a sufficient *raison d'être* for the project.

One of the more articulate supporters of the process orientation to development is Dr. Thomas Dwyer of the University of Pittsburgh (see the Project SOLO development story later in this chapter). In "Some Principles for the Human Use of Computers in Education," Dwyer (1971b) delineates some basic requirements for development projects with this orientation. The principles are "based on a belief in the value of learner control of certain key aspects of his education" (p. 221). According to Dwyer, "one of the most interesting uses of computers we have employed in our high school work involves the creation of tutorial, review, gaming, and simulation programs by students (not teachers) for the improvement and individualization of various courses.

The students are acting at the organization-of-knowledge level, while simultaneously participating in improving the curriculum to which they have been assigned" (p. 223).

One characteristic of a process-oriented approach is that it is open-ended. As Dwyer says, "The development of curricula that involve computing systems has to proceed on a basis that is open to new insights. It is important, in particular, to be wary of the 'logical' sequence of fixing objectives first, and then developing the curriculum to match. The present vision of changes that can take place in learning when educational technology is properly mastered is too dim to make more than initial estimates of what our goals can or should be. We must, of course, make such estimates, but we must view them as subject to considerable refinement" (p. 224).

Some projects emphasize learning on the part of the teachers involved in development. The Cooperative Venture in College Curriculum Development led by IIT (see later in this chapter) had as one of its major goals faculty training and involvement in curriculum development with the computer as an instructional tool in specific discipline course work (Illinois Institute of Technology, 1971). Some participants in the IIT Venture concluded that CBLM development by untrained faculty was not a successful strategy either for getting materials developed or for increasing use of computers in the classroom. They found that most of the participating faculty lacked essential skills in computing and curriculum development. At Coast Community College District in California, the Office of Educational Development has supported a variety of projects, including faculty training programs in educational technology, in which the faculty develop curriculum modules as part of their own learning process (Luskin, 1970).

The process of developing and refining a computer model can be a useful learning experience for a teacher-student group. For example, Brian Vargus and Douglas White of the University of Pittsburgh designed and taught a course in urban sociology for undergraduates in which an experimental computer simulation played a key pedagogical role (Vargus and White, 1971). In this course, the students went into a neighborhood in Pittsburgh and collected observation data on 10 variables, such as traffic on streets, condition of houses, and family cycles. This information was fed by the students into a provisional computer model designed by Vargus and White. An option in the program required the student, at the end of the run, to evaluate the accuracy of the output statements and the degree to which his input data were accurate. These evaluations were stored by the computer for later use by the designers of the model in their revisions. In other words, the students became participants in refining the model and the kinds of equations used in generating it. Vargus and White (1971, p. 367) describe the students' learning experience in this way:

> Most students found something wrong with at least 20 percent of the output statements in their simulation. They were stimulated to suggest changes in the model so that the authors could improve the predictions for the particular neighborhood the students had observed. This resulted in a large number of papers from the students showing a new appreciation for informal social interaction in an urban context and the influence of all sorts of variables on neighborhoods. Beyond this, the papers showed a surprising awareness of the potential usefulness of a simulation model in understanding neighborhood dynamics.

The development of computer programming aids and tools for use by students in a particular subject area can itself be a learning experience for a teacher/student group. Grace Hertlein conducted an interesting experiment at Chico State College, California, in a course on computer-aided graphics as an art form for the artist (Hertlein, 1972). She arranged a course in which half of the students were computer science majors and half were artists. Through the interaction of the teacher and the two groups of students, a number of artistic techniques, pedagogical techniques, and programming subroutines were developed. The computer science students developed multi-purpose, complex subroutines for artist use, and the artists learned to understand more complex programming from their more "sophisticated" classmates.

The view that the process of developing computer-oriented curricular materials is an important learning experience in its own right has been a significant factor in the state-of-the-art of instructional computing. A growing cadre of enthusiastic devotees of instructional computing has been established through personal involvement on the part of teaching faculty in developing their own materials and programs.

The process orientation has also contributed to the state of affairs which presently exists, in which the "lack of high quality, readily available" curricular materials is the most serious obstacle to widespread use of computers in instruction (Anastasio and Morgan, 1972). This state of affairs, sometimes referred to as the "cottage industry" for curriculum development, is largely a result of the fact that there are more rewards (i.e., creativity, learning, fun) in the process of developing new applications and programs than there are in polishing and packaging a transportable product.

Purposes and Evaluation
One of the most important and yet ambiguous issues regarding CBLM development is evaluation of the quality of materials. The importance of assessing the value of the CBLM is generally recognized but confusion about the specific criteria for, and even methods of, evaluation abounds in this innovative field. The thesis offered here is that a significant part of the confusion rests in the fact that (1) different purposes are the *raison d'être* for the various development efforts and (2) in turn each purpose implies different evaluation requirements. Only when the purpose is made explicit can evaluation criteria be applied and only then can appropriate judgments of CBLM learning outcomes be made.

In general, the problem is one of deciding the relative validity of instructional curricula in accomplishing stated project goals. The types of goal can and do vary, such as: development of computing literacy, providing novel learning experiences with the use of the computer, enhancing motivation to learn, helping a student to learn (how to learn) more appropriate or efficient strategies for processing information, enabling a student to solve problems independently, or increasing the effectiveness and/or efficiency with which students can reach specified performance-based, behavioral objectives.

Cost-Effectiveness Purpose
Considering the cost-effectiveness goal first, the easiest criterion upon which to evaluate new materials occurs when the new and old curricula are designed to teach the same thing. But even this can be a deceptively simple judgment. It requires that the objectives of both sets

of instructional materials be explicitly stated in achievement terms and that mastery criteria be stated. Do both kinds of instruction have the same short-term purpose? Long-term (weeks, months, years)? Retention? (See Brennan, 1973 for detailed discussion of necessary data points to consider.) If the answers are "yes," then comparisons of differences in effectiveness, efficiency, and relative *cost-effectiveness* can be measured. In order to make the analysis complete, it is also essential that the criterion tests for both curricula be equivalent and that the pedagogical techniques for student-materials-instructor interactions be made *explicit*. Thus, given that these control procedures are followed, costs and effectiveness of new and old instruction can be measured and compared. Then and only then can the interested potential user decide whether the added gain is worth the added cost (or, conversely, is less cost worth a loss in effectiveness?).

Examples serving this type of purpose can be found in most of the surrogate-instructor or CAI studies. Unfortunately, the necessary controls cited above have not been generally applied. Consequently, definitive studies are difficult to find. Vinsonhaler (1970), for example, reviewed CAI studies in which CBLM was added to the other instruction. The only safe conclusion is that more instruction resulted in better learning. The clearest illustration of projects tailored to this cost-effectiveness purpose is the on-going one called TICCIT, for which a formal evaluation is planned (see the TICCIT case study later in this chapter).

Discipline Enhancement Through Curricular Improvements

In many instances the purpose for computer usage may be to advance the discipline. In these cases, the objectives may still be performance-based as in the above cost-effectiveness purpose; however, reforming the discipline generally means establishing new curricular objectives. Therefore, it is improper to attempt comparisons between old and new instruction. Evaluation of the new instruction must take a *value added* approach. This involves (1) appraisal of the value of new objectives by discipline experts; (2) if these are found acceptable, measuring with appropriate students the degree to which the new materials meet the new objectives; and (3) if the instruction is deficient, iterative revision of the materials and retesting with more targeted students until the desired criterion is achieved.

Examples of this type of CBLM are COEXIST in physics and CRICISAM in mathematics. Even though both sets of materials deal with "basic" physics or "basic" calculus, they require evaluation specific to new objectives. (More detailed descriptions of these curriculum projects are given later in this chapter.)

Both of the above types of computer usage have in common the goal of increasing achievement or mastery of specified objectives. Perhaps this is one reason evaluation tends to get confused in projects serving one of these two distinct purposes. Evaluation probably becomes most difficult when only parts of a course are modified. It occurs when modules of new CBLM are developed. The evaluation task must separate old objectives from new and, secondly, relate particular instruction to particular old or new objectives. Most of the over 5000 items in the HumRRO data base fit this "gray" area of CBLM, yet to our knowledge no such detailed evaluation has been conducted on these materials.

Computing Literacy and Providing Computing Opportunities

Other purposes for which computers have been introduced into instruction can be generally classed as experiential or process-oriented as opposed to objectives-oriented. Teaching students to become literate in using the computer as a tool and providing them with computing opportunities have been behind much of the effort at Dartmouth (see Luehrmann, 1972, for example). The goal of such efforts is to enrich the educational experiences of the student through his mastery and use of computers as a tool for learning. Evaluating the quality of materials designed to serve such purposes takes on a different character. Broader areas of focus are involved. Performance-based objectives may or may not be included. Longer range "value added" is generally part of this purpose. Therefore, criteria for evaluation of quality must perforce be less precise and more process-oriented. Long-range (beyond the formal schooling years) judgments become the criteria for evaluation. The behaviorally oriented criteria of mastering immediate objectives are per se inappropriate. Categories of measurement include assessment of acceptance by teachers and students alike of the novel experiences made possible by the new tools. Project SOLO is an example of such an approach (described later in this chapter).

Educational Reforms and Alternatives

As may be apparent from the discussion so far, evaluation becomes more judgmental and takes on a broader context as the goals of a project change from specific, immediate performance-mastery to providing novel experiences and enhancing a student's general and long-range capabilities to solve problems. The extreme of this direction is the goal of relating the computer usage as a contribution to overall educational reform. Questions addressed might be: How can the computer enhance an alternative open educational system by providing tools for independent learning, enhancing self-reliance, creativity, self-actualization, and discovery of personal meaning?

No existing CBLM projects are this broad or far-reaching in their goals. Examples can be found which deal with subsets of educational reform. Papert's approach of having students learn problem-solving skills by programming complex movements of a "turtle" deals with part of the issue. Relating computers to art is an attempt to enhance humanities with technology. Project IMPACT (see Seidel, et al.,1969) has been a research attempt to study effects of changing the instructional model via technology and evolving a totally automated tutorial environment for the individual student. The Oakland Community College Project (Hill, 1971) is an attempt to open education by providing an adaptive, computer-based system relevant to cognitive styles of individual students.

Generally speaking, however, the closest illustration of such a broad purpose is seen only in the visions described in Chapter 2. These visions await concrete attempts at implementation. The reasons are not difficult to find. Evaluation of broad proposals is rooted in the belief and value structure of society. Criteria are first and foremost judgmental and must initially involve a consensus that such an all-encompassing project is valuable to fund. No consensus on educational reform exists, much less an agreement that various all-encompassing projects are useful or viable.

In sum, we see a paradox of major importance to be emphasized.

The most adequate and highly developed evaluation instruments and methodology exist for measuring specific, course-related, short-term, behavioral effects. But the broader, long-range, pervasive educational outcomes suffer from a lack of available evaluative tools.

SAMPLE DEVELOPMENT STORIES

The variety of factors in development of computer-oriented curricula—approaches, purposes, staffing and funding patterns, development processes, and products—is reflected in the sample development stories in the present section of this chapter.

The projects described in this section were selected because they represent a variety of approaches and illustrate different factors in development. Material for case studies is not readily available, and there is a scarcity of case studies of development in the literature. In our study of the development process, we felt greatly hampered by the lack of any systematic documented information or assessment of actual projects. We relied heavily on personal contacts and unpublished documentation.

The development stories in this section are more illustrative than systematic. We attempted to provide information on each of the following facets of the projects:*

- Aims, Purposes, History
- Organization and Finance
- Development Process, People
- Evaluation
- Dissemination
- Delivery Systems

In most cases, information on all these facets of a project was not readily available and the scope of the study did not allow for the in-depth data collection needed to complete the picture.† However,

---

*The curricular materials developed by the projects described here are often themselves described in Chapter 3. Hence, the project stories do not include a detailed description of the products.

†One very good model of case studies is the AIR evaluation of high impact educational projects (Crawford, *et al.*, 1972). We would recommend that such systematic case studies of computer-based curriculum development be undertaken.

most of the key people associated with the development stories supplied additional material when reviewing the manuscript.

The projects and the development themes they represent are:

Pillsbury	Innovative Professor Model
Commission on College Geography	Professional Society Leadership for Innovative Professor
Social Sciences Instructional Programming Project (SSIPP)	Innovation in a Small College Environment
Project COMPUTe	Support for the Innovative Professor
IIT Cooperative Venture	Regional Network Cooperative
CRICISAM	Multi-University Team Development
Huntington Projects	University Leadership for High School Authors
Project SOLO	High School Students as Developers
Stanford Reading	Educational Research-Based Development
REACT	Regional Education Laboratory
TICCIT	Market-Oriented Development by Non-Profits
APTP	Manufacturer-Inspired Publisher Development

Developing Computer-Based Learning Materials 149

Bio Medical Network

Computer-Assisted
Remedial Education

Discipline-Based Computer Network

Computer-Assisted Instruction
Laboratory

We believe that very few if any general conclusions about development can be drawn on the basis of these project stories. They represent a wide range of purposes, organization, products, delivery systems, and costs. All of them would be regarded as "successful" by some criteria, "unsuccessful" by others. The only common element among these stories is the use of digital computers in some way in the learning activities of the student. The total development cost of all of these projects, taken together, is somewhere in the neighborhood of $10 to $20 million, most of which came from the federal government. If these $10 to $20 million had been spent in a more systematic, coherent way, would the benefit be greater? We do not know of any way of measuring collective benefit in a way that would permit an answer to that question. It seems clear that more curricular materials would have been developed, and that they would be more widely used, if *quantity* of materials and users had been the central focus of all this activity. If, on the other hand, systematic *assessment* of the value of certain types of computer-based materials had been a central focus, there would be today a larger body of knowledge in the form of research reports and papers. There are dozens or hundreds of similar "if—then" type statements which could be made about these development efforts. But, unless there is an agreed-upon objective or goal, trade-offs cannot be made.

SAMPLE PROJECT STORIES:
Innovative Professor Model

The Pillsbury Story

Computer Augmented Accounting, by Wilbur F. Pillsbury, is a highly successful computer-based curriculum package used in over 240 colleges and universities. It illustrates the reasons why the individual author-publisher model for development rarely works in computer-based materials. It took enormous dedication and energy on Pillsbury's part to overcome the technical, administrative, economic, and educational obstacles to development of *Computer Augmented Accounting*, even given a considerable amount of assistance from many individuals.

In September, 1968, Dr. Pillsbury returned to Knox College in Galesburg, Illinois, to begin his 21st year of teaching economics and accounting. In his class was a student who had attended a summer institute in computing. Shortly after the first homework assignment was made, the student approached Pillsbury. Could he use the newly installed IBM 1130 computer to do his accounting problems?

Pillsbury was pleased at his student's initiative, but the best he was able to do was give him an encouraging pat on the back and introduce him to the computer center director.

As the semester went on, Pillsbury became more and more fascinated with the work his student was doing on a financial analysis program. Pillsbury applied for and received an NSF "starter grant" of $500 to pay for some supplies and computer time for his student. After considerable time filling out forms and writing reports, Pillsbury decided to avoid any further grants. Instead, he applied for and received a sabbatical, his first in 21 years.

Dr. Pillsbury spent a month in "Executive Introduction to Data Processing," "Introduction to the 1130," "IBM'S Introduction to 360," and the like. At the same time, he was formulating a plan for a collection of accounting programs to be used in his course.

He next took FORTRAN courses at Stanford and worked on his accounting programs with much help from staff and students. He then returned to Knox with a partial set of accounting programs for his students to use in their introductory course.

By September, the Knox College 1130 had a disk loaded with 70 accounting programs. Pillsbury and his students began the first tryout: queues at the keypunch machine. The keypunch errors: account numbers not right-justified; transposed digits in the five-digit account numbers; asset amounts in the wrong card column. The voluminous output: reams and reams of balance sheets, income statements, ledgers cranking all too slowly out of the 1132 printer.

Developing Computer-Based Learning Materials 151

By January, Dr. Pillsbury's experiment was drawing the attention of the IBM Education marketing division. He was asked to make a presentation in Poughkeepsie to 200 education marketing representatives from all over the country. In his presentation, of course, he told of the endless keypunch errors. A university liaison manager in the audience asked a simple question: "Why don't you write a free-form input subroutine for your programs?" "What's that?" asked Pillsbury, the non-computernik.

From this encounter in Poughkeepsie resulted two important developments in the Pillsbury story. First, Pillsbury received a grant from IBM of $9,000 to revise and test his programs. Second, the need for the programs was demonstrated. No sooner had Pillsbury returned home than the phone calls and letters started coming. The 200 IBM marketing representatives wanted to know, "Can I get a set of your programs?" "Can you send me a copy of your student workbooks?"

"No, not yet," was Pillsbury's reply every time he thought of the keypunch errors, the output reams, and the class management problems.

Further encouraged by a Sloan Foundation grant of $9,000 and an Esso grant of $5,000, Dr. Pillsbury hired an IBM programmer to build a free-form input subroutine for the 1130 so that students would not be making errors in card column spacing. He redesigned his programs to take out some of the "overkill" printouts like the income statement which students should learn to prepare manually themselves. He replaced 5-digit account numbers with 2-digits, which avoided most input errors.

He arranged for tests of the materials at three other institutions: a community college with an open-door policy; a large urban university in an underprivileged area; and a large university with a graduate program. An experimental design was planned, so that the educational value of the computer materials could be established.

In September, 1970, the experiment began. Dr. Pillsbury announced to his incoming class at Knox that they would be divided into three groups. Group 1 would do 90 percent of their accounting problems by hand, and 10 percent with the computer. Group 2 would do 50 percent by hand and 50 percent with the computer. Group 3 would have the computer for 90 percent of their work, and do 10 percent by hand. In response to some groans of dismay, he reminded them that this was all in the interests of science and the improvement of education.

After two weeks, Dr. Pillsbury's first venture into scientific experimentation had proved a disaster. The 90-10 and 50-50 students cried discrimination and demanded access to the computer for their work. He relented, and had his most successful accounting class in 23 years of teaching.

His "experiment" at Knox in a shambles, Dr. Pillsbury turned to his other three tryout schools for data. At one school the department chairman in his enthusiasm for the Pillsbury materials had required all 20 accounting instructors to use the computer version for over 800 students. The logistic and management problems were horrendous. The computer center had three- and four-days turnaround time on student problems. Keypunch queues were longer than the local movie house queues. Simply sorting out the printouts for students took an army of clerks. Instructors unprepared for the new approach tried desperately to retain their traditional posture as the "expert."

Once a month, Pillsbury made the rounds of his tryout schools, making notes on revisions needed, mimeographing supplements to workbooks, revising programs and printouts, checking on control groups, counseling instructors on their new role as managers of their classes rather than dispensers of wisdom, checking on the progress of conversion from OS to DOS.

By the end of the 1970-1971 school year, a field rep from South-Western Publishing had found out about the materials being used so successfully at one of the schools. South-Western had been looking for computer augmented accounting materials for some time. Would Dr. Pillsbury be interested in publishing his package? Staring at the stack of requests on his desk for programs and workbooks, Dr. Pillsbury happily responded, "yes." But what about the computer programs? Twenty-three thousand dollars of grant monies had gone into the development of them. They should be in the public domain and distributed free, or at the cost of reproduction of the decks.

And so a packaging and publication arrangement evolved. South-Western would publish and market the *CompuGuide* booklets and teacher manuals, on which Pillsbury would receive royalties. The programs and their documentation would be distributed at cost to the schools who bought the booklets.

But Pillsbury had further provisos. He insisted that the field reps for the *CompuGuide* materials control the way in which the materials were implemented in a school. *Start small*. Try only one class the first semester. Get only the most enthusiastic professor to adopt at first. Prove the value of the materials at the school before adopting wide scale.

Despite the limited adoption policy, 28,000 copies of *CompuGuide* were sold to 200 schools by the end of the first year. In September, 1972, over 40,000 copies were in use.

In the meantime, what has happened to the students, Pillsbury's guinea pigs? They have learned 25 percent more about accounting in 25 percent less time than before. Only three of Pillsbury's 250 students have failed accounting in three years. Only five have not gone on to second semester accounting (three of these switched to a computer science major). Managerial and mathematical aspects have been added to the course, and have taken the place of rote computations. Students are free to bring in their own cases, their own data. They are no longer constrained by prespecified "class" cases. A student who works at a gas station does the accounting for his boss as part of his course work. Another does the accounts for his uncle, a dentist.

SAMPLE PROJECT STORIES:
Innovation in a Small College Environment

Social Sciences Instructional Programming Project (SSIPP)

The Social Sciences Instructional Programming Project (SSIPP) was sponsored by the National Science Foundation and Beloit College. Funding for the development of the curricular materials themselves was less than $20,000. Beloit received additional monies for computer hardware and development of a time-sharing system.

Work on the project began in August, 1968 under the leadership of Michael Hall. The unique approach followed throughout the development was based on Hall's style, personality, development philosophy, and awareness of the needs of the small college. A dedicated SSIPP staff could be found at the computer center at almost any time (day or night) debugging their computer programs. The computer center was available 24 hours a day—staff members were given a key to the center.

Beloit College offered a non-credit course in FORTRAN IV. The SSIPP instructional programmers were selected from students who completed the course. Over 50 students, altogether, participated in the project. About $13,000 of project monies were used for student wages (representing 90 percent of the funds available for personnel). Hall was adamant in his belief that students could play a key role in instructional program development. "I have found that undergraduate students are the only reliable, low cost, high-output resource in educational computing" (Hall, 1971).

The Joint Statistics Committee of Beloit College (consisting of professors from psychology, chemistry, biology, anthropology, education, geology, government, and speech departments) provided a continuing link between the students, the computer center, and SSIPP. The committee members guided the students in their instructional development efforts.

The project team created programs that would make the best possible use of a small computer memory and slow, inelegant, inexpensive input-output devices. Because the SSIPP programs were interactive and required a time-sharing system to be resident in core, the task was especially difficult.

The SSIPP programs used a *simple* version of FORTRAN IV to maximize their transferability to other small college computing environments.

The prolific SSIPP staff developed over 60 programs in probability and statistics. A smaller number of programs (35) were developed in other fields—economics, accounting, operations research, psychology, sociology, and geography. Separate documentation was produced for each program.

While SSIPP had no formal plan for dissemination, the SSIPP

products were publicized through a number of channels (Hall, 1970). Demonstrations and presentations were given at symposia and conferences, such as the June, 1970 Conference on Computers in the Undergraduate Curricula, at the University of Iowa, and the American Statistical Association annual meeting. SSIPP programs and descriptions of Beloit courses involving them were featured in material published as a paperback book by IBM. Quarterly project reports contained brief descriptions of programs completed, and interested parties were encouraged to place their names on the mailing list. The computer center mailed out single copies of the program documentation free of charge, and the programs could be ordered for a nominal charge. Over 200 requests were received for the SSIPP programs from such diverse places as Troy State University; Perkin-Elmer Corporation; Sloan School of Management, MIT; Michigan State University; and Wabash College.

SAMPLE PROJECT STORIES:
Professional Society Leadership for Innovative Professor

Commission on College Geography

The Commission on College Geography (CCG) was established in 1963. It operates under the auspices of the Association of American Geographers, and its activities were supported by grants from the National Science Foundation.

Several "computer-assisted learning units" have been developed by members of the Commission. Topics are in such areas as Energy-Water Balance and the Hydrological Cycle, Land Use Decisions, Central Place Theory, and Relative Location Advantages. The primary role of the Commission is to initiate this development in order to provide usable computer-based educational programs for colleges and provide a pool of persons trained in educational uses of computers in geography education. The Commission's goal is to establish a critical mass of materials and trained persons so that CAI work in the future can be done by local institutions and individuals. The Commission and its sponsor, the AAG, provide demonstrations and seminars on the CAI materials at national conferences and conventions of geographers.

SAMPLE PROJECT STORIES:
Support for the Innovative Professor

Project COMPUTe

Although hundreds of teaching professors, like Dr. Pillsbury, have developed computer applications to improve their courses, few have found incentives or mechanisms to package and disseminate the materials so that others can benefit. Project COMPUTe is designed to bridge this gap.

Arthur Luehrmann, Kent Morton, and the Kiewit Computation Center, at Dartmouth College, are providing support and guidance to authors of computer-oriented materials in a variety of disciplines. An NSF grant of $450,000 pays summer salaries, housing, and partial travel expenses for the authors to come to Dartmouth to revise, refine, and package their materials.

Project COMPUTe plans to provide camera-ready copy to a publisher and to negotiate as agents for the authors to "enter into individual agreements with each author under which the author may receive a portion of the royalties received by the grantee up to a ceiling amount to be agreed to by the author and grantee." Printing, physical packaging, and distribution will be up to the commercial sector for all marketable manuscripts. Separate packaging and distribution may be required for extensive computer software packages. COMPUTe itself expects to duplicate and distribute copies of these to persons who purchase the textual materials. This is a somewhat awkward arrangement, and it is difficult to anticipate what percentage of the total production will require this separate packaging. COMPUTe personnel feel that the pedagogy contained in the textual materials is the most important aspect of COMPUTe products, and therefore is discouraging production of large-scale computer software as part of the products.

A Board of Overseers composed of eminent educators experienced in instructional uses of computers has been established for COMPUTe. Selected primarily from the environmental sciences because of the project's initial emphasis on that field, the Board's purpose is to advise on priorities and educational needs in environmental areas and to provide general guidance for the project in terms of policy and procedures. They evaluate, with the assistance of others in various fields, the educational value and quality of the materials produced by the project and seeing that it gets used by appropriate persons.

SAMPLE PROJECT STORIES:
Regional Network Cooperative Curriculum Development

IIT Cooperative Venture in College Curriculum Development

A logical approach to curricular materials development is a cooperative venture among the colleges in a regional network. A common delivery system, ability to share courseware without technical difficulties, and geographic proximity of the developers are some advantages inherent in this approach.

In 1968, the National Science Foundation made a grant to the Illinois Institute of Technology and nine participating colleges and universities in northern Illinois and southern Wisconsin for a joint program involving the introduction of the computer as an instructional tool in undergraduate courses. The purposes of the Venture were to develop a regional computer network, train faculty, and develop computer-oriented curricular materials.

The project was successful in developing the regional computing facilities. Although some useful instructional materials also resulted, a number of difficulties were encountered in materials development and faculty training. As the project final report points out, a key aspect of the organization and funding of the Venture was that the grant support for curriculum development was made directly to the participating institutions rather than to individual faculty. This turned out to be a mistake, as the administrators *assigned* faculty members to participate who in many instances had no interest in computers. The grants were made with the requirement that the computer be administered as a utility for use by all faculty. Hence, there was no direct responsibility on the part of specific faculty to develop curricular materials.

Except for IIT, none of the participating institutions had computer facilities prior to the network project. IIT, as the leader institution in setting up the cooperative program, had a computer facility and extensive experience for many years in programming language instruction. None of the institutions had any experience in developing curriculum materials which made use of the computer.

Seven discipline-oriented groups of teaching faculty (mathematics, physics, chemistry, biology, psychology-education, sociology, and business-economics) from the network schools prepared computer programs and related documentation. The groups varied in their methods of development, depending on the level of involvement of the individual members of the group. Major problems encountered were the lack of computer skills on the part of the faculty developers and lack of commitment to computer-oriented instruction.

The programs and related documentation were made accessible to IIT network schools through a program exchange library. An unknown number of the programs were distributed to other schools and networks.

Probably more far-reaching in effect than the curricular materials themselves were a number of concepts and influences which resulted directly or indirectly from the project. A number of participating network schools greatly increased their level of educational computing activity including homegrown faculty training and development projects. Several national and international conferences were held as an outgrowth of the IIT project, including a Conference on Computer Impact on College Curricula in 1969, a forerunner of the annual Conferences on Computers in Undergraduate Curricula which have been so successful and influential. (See discussion of these conferences in Chapter 5.)

An indirect outcome of the project was the establishment of the Computer Impact on Society programs at the National Science Foundation, through the efforts of Peter Lykos, Director of the IIT project.

SAMPLE PROJECT STORIES:
Multi-University Team Development

The CRICISAM Story

Calculus, A Computer-Oriented Presentation (Stenberg and Walker, *et al.*, 1968) is a two-volume text which represents the first comprehensive computer-oriented introductory course in calculus (see Chapter 3, Mathematics section). It was developed by CRICISAM, the Center for Research in College Instruction of Science and Mathematics.

CRICISAM was an organization for the investigation, development, and dissemination of new materials and techniques for collegiate instruction in the various fields of science and mathematics, with emphasis on interdisciplinary cooperation.

The planning for CRICISAM lasted over a three-year period in which a number of conferences and committee meetings were held to iron out the functions and objectives of the proposed organization.

As many as 20 institutions were invited to become members. It was considered an honor to be asked, since the requirements were stiff—Ph.D. programs in four out of five science disciplines.

It was anticipated that the organization would become self-sustaining but the schools showed disinterest in an annual membership arrangement. They did accept a one-time assessment of $2,000 each.

A total of $500,000 in government and private foundation support was obtained, but funds dried up after five years.

One of the main tenets of the organization was that it be directed by scientists so that quality of the materials would be the foremost consideration.

The development cost for the CRICISAM calculus materials is estimated to be a little under $200,000.

A team of mathematics professors from a variety of institutions planned the structure of the text and, in summer writing conferences, produced sample chapters. The final writing was done by Warren Stenberg (University of Minnesota) and Robert Walker (Cornell University). The authors received a stipend for their time, but no incentive royalty arrangement. According to Dr. Walker, a major obstacle in development was the difficulty in finding competent writers who could spend the amount of time required for the project.

The CRICISAM materials can be used with almost any computer and in fact have been used with such diverse computer systems as GE time-sharing, IBM 360/65, IBM 1130, Honeywell 200, PDP8, a commercial time-sharing company, IBM 1401, and a CDC 6400. The CRICISAM newsletter provided data on the operating cost-per-student under these various delivery systems.

The CRICISAM material received extensive publicity primarily through discipline-based channels such as the Mathematical Association of America. The text was displayed at mathematics conferences and provision was made for obtaining free desk copies. Over 2,000 sets were mailed out directly to mathematics departments. Articles appeared in a math educational journal and talks were given on the materials.

Each year a letter was mailed to departmental chairmen (about 2,500) asking their intentions on using the text. About 10,000 CRICISAM texts have been distributed. There are currently 50 to 60 schools using the text. According to Dr. Walker, this is "a lot more than I expected."

An arrangement was negotiated with NSF under which the material entered the public domain as of June, 1972. It was expected that the materials would be revised and polished, appearing as a commercially published text after this date.

While there was no formal evaluation, the textbooks were revised based on the suggestions of experimental users. The CRICISAM newsletter served as an open forum for teachers to comment on the classroom use of the materials, and to share information on costs and management of the course.

SAMPLE PROJECT STORIES:
University Leadership for High School Authors

The Huntington Projects

The Huntington Computer Project was initiated in 1968 as an

outgrowth of the Engineering Concepts Curriculum Project (ECCP) which had developed a high school course called *The Man Made World*. In *The Man Made World* students are introduced to complex problems of modern society and technology—for example, problems of pollution and complex decision-making. The role of digital computer simulations to help students understand these complex phenomena became obvious. Ludwig Braun worked for two years with some 80 high school teachers training them in the use of the computer for instruction. The major product of this effort was a teacher's manual containing 80 programs in various disciplines. Non-exclusive copyright *licenses* were awarded to Digital Equipment Corporation, Hewlett-Packard, and Independent Data Processing Corporation for publishing and selling the manuals.

Experience gained in this two-year project led Braun and his staff to the decision that simulations were the most promising uses of small computers for high school curricula. A two-year grant of $300,000 from NSF enabled the project, renamed Huntington Two, to begin development of more comprehensive educational packages based on computer simulations. The redirected effort had as its purpose the development of high quality, well-documented, and well-supported simulations for high school biology, physics, and social studies.

The individual packages were developed by high school teachers in their own school environment, with university subject-matter experts as consultants. A few high school students were involved in development, but were replaced when they became so familiar with simulations that they were no longer representative of the typical student. Computer help was provided by Brooklyn Polytechnic Institute undergraduates.

In the 1971-1972 school year, 30 packages were distributed to 100 high schools and 25 colleges in the United States for a large-scale tryout by 250 teachers and 8000 students. The materials were requested by at least four times that many schools, most of whom already had access to computing facilities but few instructional materials to use with them.

For evaluation purposes the schools were grouped with an area coordinator responsible for communication between schools and the evaluation chairman. The principal evaluation instrument was a Student Opinion Inventory of the simulation programs in terms of their value, ease of use, and interest to themselves and their teachers. The evaluators ran into problems with teachers cooperating on the data gathering, even though the schools had agreed to cooperate in return for having *free* use of the materials.

After a 1971-1972 evaluation project was completed and the complete set of 30 packages was ready for widespread dissemination, the materials were published and marketed by DEC under an exclusive license. The Huntington Computer Project arranged with the National Science Foundation to have all royalties received from DEC to remain with the project for future development work.

SAMPLE PROJECT STORIES:
High School Students as Developers

Project SOLO

Project SOLO was *not* a typical curriculum development project. SOLO cannot be evaluated in the customary terms of educational validity, cost-effectiveness, or marketability of the materials. Project SOLO can only be understood in terms of its unique process, philosophies, and view of student learning behavior. SOLO attempted to actualize the potential of students and teachers through their co-exploration of the complexities of technological innovation.

The Project SOLO people wholeheartedly believed in the natural *genius* of students and teachers which has to mature through a *sophisticated* environment and sympathetic encouragement.

A two-year grant was provided by NSF to Project SOLO through the University of Pittsburgh Computer Science Department. Thomas Dwyer of the University was the creative force behind this project.

Three Pittsburgh high schools participated in the project. The Project SOLO staff consisted of the Project Director, two curriculum specialists, and a research assistant. The Project SOLO staff drew upon the talents of the teachers and students in the three participating schools to develop many of the curricular modules.

Dr. Dwyer conducted a summer institute to provide the teachers with the basic programming skills necessary to develop their own programs. He also made frequent visits to participating schools for personal consultation.

A central motivation of SOLO was to stimulate students to synthesize and organize knowledge on their own with interactive computing as the catalyst. The Project SOLO newsletter carried announcements of student accomplishments, e.g., a CAI program for vocabulary drill in German written by a high school freshman.

The concept of peer teaching with computers was one of the many novel approaches tried in Project SOLO. Students wrote programs that would help their fellow students. For instance, an 11th grader developed a tutorial game to help younger students learn measurement conversion factors.

The SOLO curricular modules were designed to stimulate the students by providing interesting topics for exploration with a computer. The Project SOLO philosophy is alien to notions of comprehensive curricula developed from a precise set of learning objectives. SOLO modules can be organized by the individual learner into a sequence consonant with his individual interests. The modular curriculum scheme is illustrated in Figure 18. The figure shows the multiplicity of entry points and paths.

The SOLO computer resources were provided by a commercial time-sharing organization called COMSHARE with teletypewriters linked to the XDS 940.

Three schools were involved with the project: one in the suburbs and two in the inner city.

Each student was provided one 45-minute shot on the computer each week. Students complained that this was not an adequate amount of time!

Project SOLO staff learned that it did not take long for the students to become sophisticated.

Project SOLO, therefore, developed in conjunction with COMSHARE a new software system called NEWBASIC to explore the value of an advanced language tailored to the needs of education (Dwyer, 1971a).

The computer education was force-fitted into the normal school administrative routine. A student in the *middle* of a problem-solving

Modular Curriculum Concept

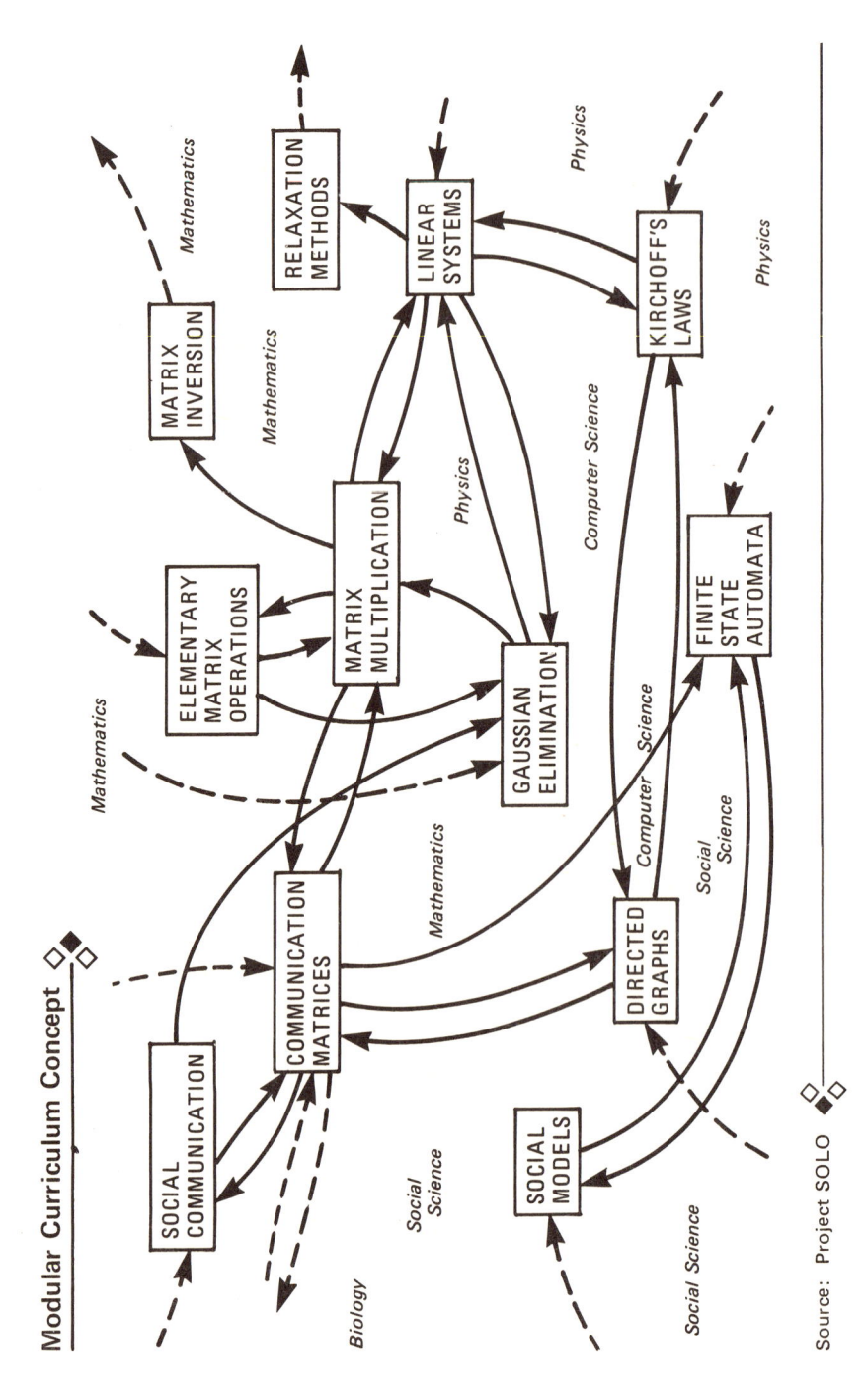

Figure 18

Source: Project SOLO

session had to quit when the bell rang announcing the end of a period. Also, it is interesting to note that if the study halls did not exist, Project SOLO would not be able to get students for their work!

The students' learning experiences in Project SOLO were new in both the cognitive and affective domains. It follows that an evaluation relying on performance measurement through a standardized achievement test would be inappropriate. Project SOLO felt that observation of the learner was more to the point and five students were chosen as case studies. Their learning experiences were recorded on a sound film which is available on request.*

Secondly, Project SOLO collected the opinions of the users (students, teachers, administrators, visitors, researchers) and the results are evidence of the enthusiasm that Project SOLO engendered.

The original budget called for a good deal of dissemination, but this item was not funded. Despite this, as of this date, SOLO has sent newsletters and curriculum modules to over 600 schools. Dwyer has also worked hard at dissemination through publication (eight articles), numerous addresses, two films (*Project SOLO* and *My Computer Understands Me*),† and most recently a multi-media show called *Midnight to Midnight*.

SAMPLE PROJECT STORIES:
Educational R & D Based
Curriculum Development

Instruction in Initial Reading Under Computer Control: The Stanford Project

The "right to read" is the most fundamental educational value in our society. An innovation in materials, methods, or curriculum which

---

*Available from Association-Sterling Films, P.O. Box 272, Pittsburgh, Pennsylvania 15139.

†Available from Film Library, DEC, Maynard, Maryland 01754.

enables more children to learn to read or does so at a lower cost has a high payoff in terms of numbers of people affected.

The Stanford Initial Reading Project began in 1964 with a detailed analysis of the obstacles encountered by culturally disadvantaged children in acquiring reading skills. The purpose of the project was to provide a comprehensive, individualized curriculum which would reduce the inequities among children in the basic reading skills they acquire.

The project, headed by Richard Atkinson, was funded by the USOE for $920,000 from 1964-1967. Related work in computer-assisted instruction at Stanford was supported by USOE from 1966-1968 for $944,000.

The 1964-1967 project was designed to provide a comprehensive computer-assisted instruction program for a four-year (K-3) reading curriculum. All of the child's instruction was presented and managed by the computer, and depended very minimally on a classroom teacher.

The reading program was implemented on an IBM 1500 instructional computer system and tested at Brentwood, California. Major conclusions resulting from this experience were:

- The additions of the CAI program to the regular program did enable more students to learn reading than did the traditional classroom instruction.
- Of the two basic types of skills in reading, namely decoding and communication, the computer is best suited to teaching the decoding skills. Communication skills are best learned with a classroom teacher.
- The costs of a comprehensive computer-assisted instruction system were unacceptable to schools. The computer program should be redesigned from a *service* use to a supplemental use type of program.
- The costs of the IBM 1500 instructional system were too high. The materials should be implemented on lower cost terminals and a large time-shared computer which could serve more students simultaneously.

A reoriented project was conducted from 1967 to 1970 with a grant from NSF. Its aim was to design and implement a low-cost CAI curriculum that would act as a supplement to normal classroom instruction.

More recently the emphasis has been on optimization of presentation strategies to make the instructional sequence more sensitive to student ability and item difficulty.

Distinct from the above Reading project is the Computer Curriculum Corporation (CCC) founded in 1967 by Dr. Patrick Suppes as a marketing outgrowth of research and development in CAI at Stanford University. CCC retains close contact with educational research and bases its curriculum design on explicit learning theories.

CCC has a pragmatic marketing approach of:
(1) going out with a *proven* project;
(2) showing that the product benefits *teacher* and *pupil* (performance summaries *help* the teacher to gauge the class's progress); and
(3) offering the products for a *reasonable* price.

SAMPLE PROJECT STORIES:
Regional Educational Laboratory Development

Project REACT–Relevant Educational Applications of Computer Technology

The purpose of Project REACT is to improve the computer literacy of educators. School administrators and teachers are the target population for the REACT materials. The goals are short term and designed to meet the immediate need for improved skills on the part of educators. The product is a training program for school administrators and teachers. This program of training is currently organized into three courses, each providing 30 hours of instruction. The course materials comprise a total of 24 instructional books. Computer programs written in BASIC are provided with the booklets.

REACT represents a unique organizational arrangement between the U.S. Office of Education, the Northwest Regional Educational Laboratory, and the Technica Education Corporation. The program was funded by the U.S. Office of Education ($320,000 for the first two years and $146,000 for the third year) and developed by the Regional

Educational Laboratory, tested in public schools and universities, and published and disseminated by the Technica Education Corporation.

The training program was developed by the Regional Educational Laboratory over a period of two years. During development and evaluation, the REACT courses and materials were tested in a variety of settings. The program was presented as a graduate course for preparing school administrators at two universities and as an inservice program at a small rural school. The course materials can be tailored to suit the specific target group both in terms of the content and the way in which the materials are studied.

Technica Education Corporation held an exclusive contract with the Laboratory to publish and disseminate REACT material and was responsible for conducting the REACT training programs for school administrators and teachers. Royalties were shared between the Laboratory and the Office of Education. A portion of Technica's profits were placed, by the terms of the contract, into an escrow account to maintain the system.

The computer programs will run on any computer with a BASIC compiler, including mini-computers. The interaction on a teletype terminal is a key element of the courses.

The federal government's investment in Project REACT was a half-million dollars. The computing literacy training program has not yet had widespread use; however, not all the course material had been printed until recently. Many potential users have been reluctant to purchase any courses until all three courses are available.

NWREL has continued to develop student materials as well as additional teacher and administrator training materials. A new series is ECC, *Elements of Computer Careers*, a high school curriculum package for computer career skill training.*

---

*Information on ECC may be obtained from NWREL, 400 Lindsay Building, 710 Southwest 2nd Avenue, Portland, Oregon 07204.

SAMPLE PROJECT STORIES:
Market-Oriented Development
by Non-Profits

The TICCIT Community College System

The National Science Foundation funded MITRE, a large, not-for-profit corporation, to "catalyze the mass dissemination of CAI" through a five-year program aimed at achieving a major market success for computer-assisted instruction. The entire system is targeted to meet instructional needs in junior colleges.

> What became apparent was that neither a lower cost, higher performance CAI computer system nor an improved theory of instructional psychology would get CAI in the schools. The real problem is the making of a market (i.e., creating a supply/demand situation) for Computer-Assisted Instruction (Stetten, June, 1972).

Community colleges were selected as the target institution because of:
- their rapid growth;
- their receptivity to innovation;
- their emphasis on educational effectiveness; and
- the wide spread among student abilities.

The spread in student abilities creates a dramatic need for individualized instruction, which the TICCIT Community College System is attempting to fill.

Earlier, NSF had funded MITRE's TICCIT computer system concept as a potentially economically viable CAI system. The TICCIT innovations included the incorporation of mini-computers, the use of television technology, and cable distribution.

In a separate but related contract, NSF had sponsored CAI course development work in freshman English and mathematics at the University of Texas under the directorship of Dr. C. Victor Bunderson.

A market study conducted on the instructional needs of junior college students found that the *major* need lay in so-called remedial mathematics and English.

These subject areas were selected for TICCIT because of the

potential high density (a third or more entering students require this help); and the fact that they are not threatening to faculty, since they are not considered desirable subjects to teach and historically have been neglected.

The TICCIT system, including the hardware, software, and "courseware," is being developed jointly by the MITRE Corporation and Brigham Young University, under Dr. Bunderson. MITRE is developing the hardware-software and is responsible for the overall project. Brigham Young is developing software and hardware design requirements and the courseware, under subcontract to MITRE.

The TICCIT courseware is being developed by teams of instructional psychologists, subject-matter specialists (experienced in teaching the subjects), media specialists, and programmers at BYU. The teams are using carefully engineered assembly line production techniques. One goal of the project is to demonstrate the feasibility of systematic courseware production procedures using differentiated staffing (Bunderson, 1972). Each team member is assigned a separate task in the highly proceduralized course development process. Standardized forms are filled out, based on a predefined instructional strategy. For example, the "subject-matter expert" may be asked to write on a form several English sentences which are examples of a particular grammatical concept.

Independent evaluators have made a preliminary review of the development process. They have raised the issue that standardization of procedures and pedagogy without classroom tryout may be premature. Because the course development proceeds in parallel with the development of the hardware and software, there is little time allowed in the course development process for tryout and revision.

The subcontract for courseware development is for $1.5 million, and it is estimated that the cost of courseware per student contract hour will be 15 cents based on the expectation of 20 schools eventually adopting the system (Stetten, 1972). Courseware design objectives are outlined in more detail in Figure 19.

The NSF grant also covers the cost of installing and operating TICCIT (for two years) at two community colleges: Phoenix Junior College and Northern Virginia Community College. MITRE is counting on the demonstrations and their evaluation to create a market success for CAI.

TICCIT Courseware Design Goals

COST GOAL

    < $1.00 per contact hour
    25% less time
    Increase enrollment significantly

CONTENT GOAL

    Small step forward in content
    Clarify objectives
    Design for flexibility

GOALS FOR STUDENTS

    85% of students will achieve mastery
    Efficiency — $\geq$ 50% improvement
    Improved strategies — Efficiency up, advice down, balanced profile
    Voluntary approach — Attitude scores, # options involved
    Responsibility — % of scheduled time met

GOALS FOR EDUCATORS

    Define new professional roles in development
    Define new roles in counseling-management
    Stimulate teachers to demonstrate humane values in follow-on
        or coordinate instruction

Source: Personal communication from C. V. Bunderson, September 6, 1973

Figure 19

> The real selling of CAI will be done by the students and teachers who use the system and the administrators who overlook its operation.... To add credibility and statistical strength to the demonstration, a separate firm ... will evaluate the success of the demonstration (Stetten, 1972).

There is no apparent plan for widespread dissemination (e.g., marketing staff, junior college administrator workshops) beyond the demonstration phase. The success of this demonstration strategy, then, depends on the eventual takeover of the project by a commercial firm such as a computer manufacturer.

Attainment of the four major goals of the project shown earlier will be evaluated by Educational Testing Service under a contract with NSF. As part of the plan to evaluate the greater efficiency (25 percent less time) and general cost/effectiveness, ETS will be comparing student mastery in the CAI format to a comparable non-CAI version. Since broader goals of student, faculty, and community acceptance also are part of the project, many indirect measures of success will be used. These will include survey questionnaires which measure the affective results in students choosing to use additional library materials in the topical area being studied, changes in faculty/student relations, and long-term results such as student choice of follow-on courses and choice of major field. Many survey instruments are also planned to obtain data on community acceptance as well. The results of the study are programmed to be available in 1976.

SAMPLE PROJECT STORIES:
Computer Manufacturer and Publisher Join Forces

APTP CAI*

The Computer-Related Instructional Systems Center of Science

---

*This story is based on a more detailed case study by American Institutes for Research (Kratochvil, 1972).

Developing Computer-Based Learning Materials

Research Associates, Inc., was the developer of the Arithmetic Proficiency Training Program (APTP). For three years, the Center operated largely as a laboratory where a great deal of intermingling of persons and ideas took place. Interdisciplinary work was encouraged; there was much opportunity to experiment with various ways in which the computer could be used in instruction. At its zenith, the Center had an organizational structure consisting of a director and managers of curriculum design, evaluation, programming, and computer operations with a total of 35 people on the staff.

Initial work on a formal development plan for APTP occurred in late 1967. A decision was made to develop instructional products for off-the-shelf hardware (specifically, the IBM system 360 and standard typewriter terminals). APL was the choice for the CAI language because of its power relevant to trying out ideas and revising programs quickly. Later APTP was shifted to Coursewriter III.

Educationally the computational skills of elementary arithmetic were selected as being a manageable piece of material—large enough to be of significant use to schools and yet small enough that development time would not be excessive.

The APTP materials were developed by an interdisciplinary team of subject-matter, curriculum design, computer programming, evaluation, and management specialists. Science Research Associates invested about 20 man-years in product development and the price tag was established by AIR to be one million dollars.

Beginning in October, 1968, the Computer-Related Instructional Systems Center and the Chicago Public Schools entered upon a field trial of the Arithmetic Proficiency Training Program in grades 6, 7, and 8. Almost 300 students in the program who were attending one of the eight schools were initially included in the sample. In the course of the seven-month study, daily performance of the students was recorded; subjective opinions of students, teachers, administrators, and parents were assembled; and final achievement results were obtained for the involved students and a comparison group. A number of modifications were made as a result of the trial.

A second trial was held in Memphis in conjunction with the Memphis Community Learning Laboratory. The experimental group performed significantly better than the control group as indicated by their computation, problem-solving, and concepts scores.

APTP was marketed by the Computer-Related Instructional Systems Center of SRA. They found that their traditional marketing approach, using "staff associates" (marketing representatives) and publicity brochures, did not work. It became apparent that the sale and installation of the program are costly and complex. Installation includes training teachers, training proctors, educational counseling, helping the school design its evaluation studies, and acquiring computing facilities. Therefore, the job of marketing the product became the responsibility of the Center rather than the general staff associates. APTP was licensed by SRA to customers at an annual use charge of $9,000.

At the present time, APTP is being used by under 10 schools. Essentially, APTP suffers as a product without a delivery network. Very few elementary schools have access to a time-sharing computer and terminals for instructional purposes (an IBM 360 Model 30 is the smallest system for which the program is available). The product has been marketed by the Data Processing Division of IBM, parent of SRA, since 1971.

SAMPLE PROJECT STORIES:
Discipline-Based Computer Network

Computer-Based Information Network for the Medical Professions
The Lister Hill Center

The educational component (known here as the Network Program) of Lister Hill's Biomedical Data Communication Service is experimental. The network provides mechanisms by means of which inter-institutional cooperation and sharing of resources can be used to meet some of the needs of medical education and medical practice. The objective is to encourage and facilitate serious investigation into the usefulness of CAI in the using institutions (usually, but not always undergraduate medical).

The Network Program is unique in several respects:

- The development of materials is tied into a physical computing network.
- The physical network provides built-in mechanisms for dissemination of the materials.
- The physical network provides the facilities (hardware and software) for development and tryout of materials.

Therefore, the physical network eliminated many of the dissemination and delivery barriers encountered by other projects.

The Lister Hill Center chose three "centers of excellence" as contractors: the Ohio State University Medical Center; the University of Illinois Medical Center in Chicago; and the Laboratory of Computer Sciences of Massachusetts General Hospital. The computers at these three centers are accessed by users at remote institutions via a data communications network.

The contractors' services and the communications network were supported by the National Library of Medicine for approximately $450,000 per year in 1973 and 1974.

The contractors provide packages of biomedical instructional materials, development know-how, software, and guidance to new people getting started in the field. An unusual feature of the project is the obligation incurred by Network Program users. Users who wish to obtain an operational status agree to add to the repertoire of materials and to evaluate contractor-developed materials.

After an initial rough beginning, contractor-user cooperation has grown, although there are still problems arising from differences in philosophies and curricula of contractor-developer and user-developer institutions.

The Network Program has many issues to resolve regarding the development of new curricular materials by users, e.g., quality control mechanisms, training of developers and users, standards, and selection of subject areas for development.

This approach to cooperative development is highly innovative and it will take some time before the results can be assessed.

SAMPLE PROJECT STORIES:
Development by
Computer-Assisted Instruction Laboratory
Pennsylvania State University

CARE

CARE (Computer-Assisted Remedial Education) fulfills a special need to improve the quality of inservice teacher preparation in the area of special education. The course enables preschool and primary teachers of seemingly typical children to identify children who might be educationally retarded or handicapped in some way. The CARE course incorporates a novel mobile delivery system that is able to reach teachers in remote rural areas who otherwise would not have access to the instruction.

The project was organized under Harold E. Mitzel, Associate Dean for Research, College of Education, Pennsylvania State University. The project was divided into two main areas: the development of the mobile van and the development of the CARE course. Professor Phillip Cartwright supervised the team of authors in programming the course of instruction. Professor Keith A. Hall supervised the technical development and field operation staff. The Gerstenslager Company constructed the specially designed mobile van to house the computer facilities.

Funds for constructing the specially designed mobile van were provided in part by the Penn State Foundation. The CARE course was developed under grant support from the Bureau of Education for the Handicapped, and operation of the program in the field is being supported by the Bureau of Personnel Development, USOE.

The development process followed in the CARE 1 course illustrates the effort required to produce an operational CAI course. The development was divided into five phases, with the first two devoted to defining the overall strategies for presenting the materials and specifying the behavioral objectives for individual course segments. The development expertise came from the Computer-Assisted Instruction Laboratory, which came into existence in 1964 with four part-time faculty and has grown to a present total of 53 university employees (faculty, graduate assistants, technicians, and clerical staff) equivalent to 38 full-time persons. It is important to note that these systems have been operating in the field with a rich terminal configuration of audio, image projections, and video terminals since 1970.

CARE is unique since it is both a new delivery system for educational services and an individualized instructional system. The mobile van contains 16 student stations. The delivery system is brought into the teachers' neighborhood and set up adjacent to centrally located school buildings.

The individualized instruction system is a completely self-contained three-credit, college-level, computer-assisted instruction course.

Generally there is little basis for comparative evaluation to test the educational validity of instructional materials, since more often than not the old conventional course and the new computer-based course are non-comparable. The CARE course is an exception to the general case in that there was a conventional course at Penn State designed to teach the same objectives as the CAI course. A summative evaluation was conducted and the results were favorable to CAI in that the students instructed by CAI obtained a mean score 24 percent higher on the final examination and finished the course in 33 percent less time than students in the conventional lecture course.

CARE 1 is a thoroughly "documented" CAI course, because the authors recognized that documentation was necessary to make CAI a viable instructional mode. An automated documentation program provides the technical documentation, and the complete package of documentation includes a guide to the instruction and a comprehensive syllabus to be handed out to students.

Three additional courses in the CARE series are now available: CARE 2, Diagnostic and Prescriptive Teaching of Preschool Handicapped Children; CARE 3, Diagnostic and Prescriptive Teaching of Primary Handicapped Children; and CARE 4, Teaching the Visually Impaired.

The mobile van is normally parked at one location for seven weeks, during which time 150 educators will be able to complete the course. In 33 months of operation, a single van could reach approximately 3 percent of the elementary and secondary teachers and supervisors in Pennsylvania.

ORGANIZATION AND FUNDING OF
DEVELOPMENT PROJECTS AND PROGRAMS

The development stories in the preceding section illustrate a variety of funding and organizational arrangements for developing CBLM.

Although there are a wide variety of organizational and funding arrangements possible, the vast majority of CBLM development has taken place in universities and colleges, as indicated in Figure 20. The majority of the materials have received funding support by the National Science Foundation and the educational institutions; however, many other agencies and organizations have supported CBLM development (see Figure 21).

Figure 21 does not indicate funding amounts, but only number of materials or projects. Although it is impossible to get comparable figures from USOE and NSF on funding of computer-based curricular materials, USOE has spent, by conservative estimate, over twice as much on computer-based curriculum development as has NSF since 1965.

The two legislative authorities which have provided the principal OE support of computer activities are Title III of the Elementary and Secondary Education Act and the Cooperative Research Act. These two authorities together supported about 80 percent of the computer-related projects supported by USOE (Grayson, 1972). ESEA Title III authorized grants directly to local school districts to stimulate them to seek creative solutions to local educational problems. After 1969, the states assumed administration of Title III funds. By far the largest amounts of Title III funds for computer activities, however, were in the years 1965-1968. Projects under Title III to develop computer-based curricular materials, therefore, were not *intended, organized, authorized,* or *funded* to prepare packages for widespread dissemination. The Cooperative Research Act as amended by the Elementary and Secondary Education Act of 1965 did allow support for dissemination.

Our point here is that curricular materials do not get developed, disseminated, and used by accident. Although some computer-based educational projects did receive considerable OE funding in the past, it should not be surprising that few generally useful curriculum packages have resulted, since this was not the intent of the legislative authority or programs.

Developer Organizations Cited for 4,900 Items of Computer-Based Learning Materials (CBLM)

Categories
- Universities
- Colleges
- Public Schools
- Private Sector
- Non-Profit
- Community Colleges
- Military

Number of CBLM Items

Developer Organizations: Univ., Colleges, Public Schools, Private, Non-Profit, Comm. Colleges, Mil.

Source: Project Data Base

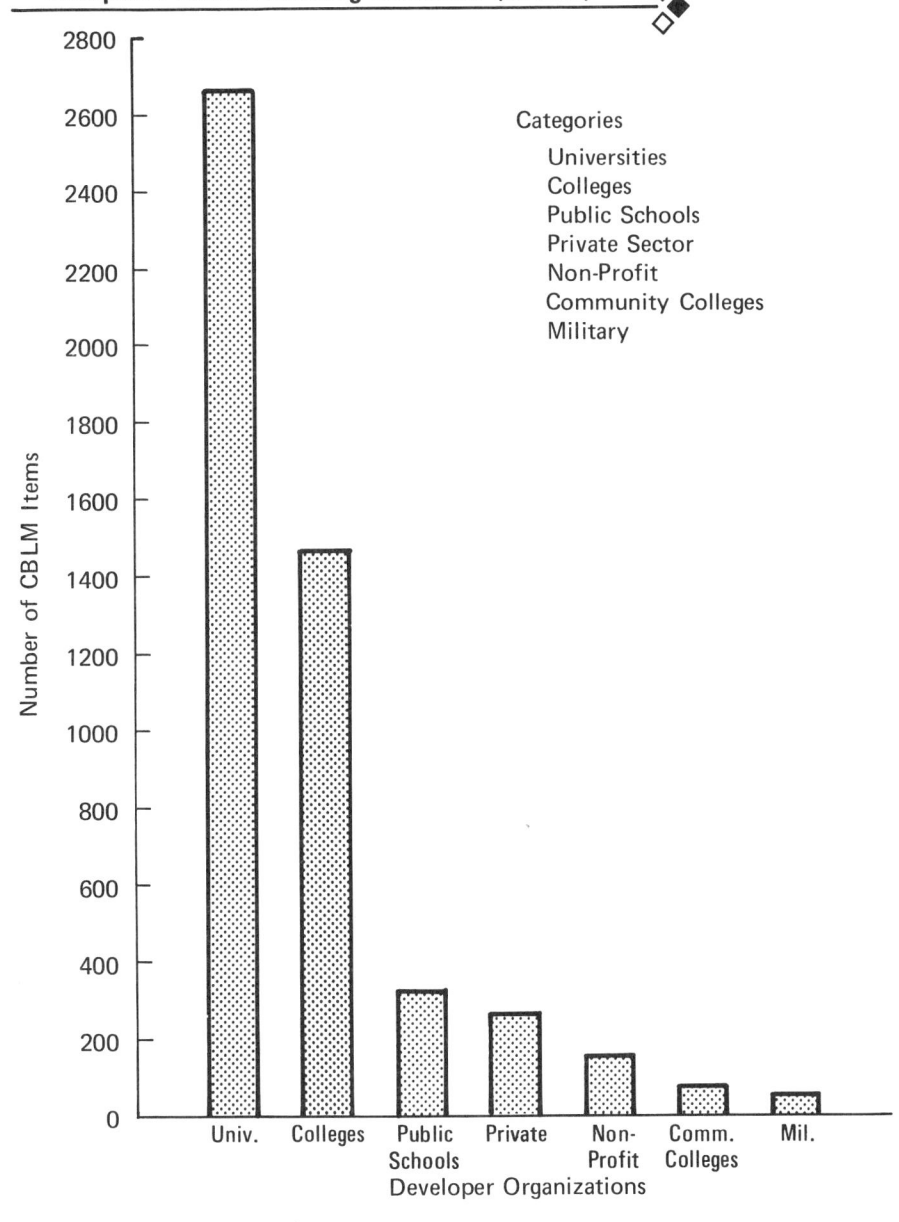

Figure 20

Funding Sources Cited by Developers of 2,750 Items of Computer-Based Learning Materials (CBLM)

Categories

National Science Foundation
Colleges and Universities
Military
U.S. Office of Education
Private Sector
Public Schools
National Institutes of Health
Other Federal Agencies
Other — Foundations,
  State Agencies,
  Community Colleges,
  Professional Societies

Number of CBLM Items (vertical axis, 0 to 800)

Funding Sources: NSF, Col./Univ., Military, OE, Private, Public Schools, NIH, Other Federal, Other

Source: Project Data Base

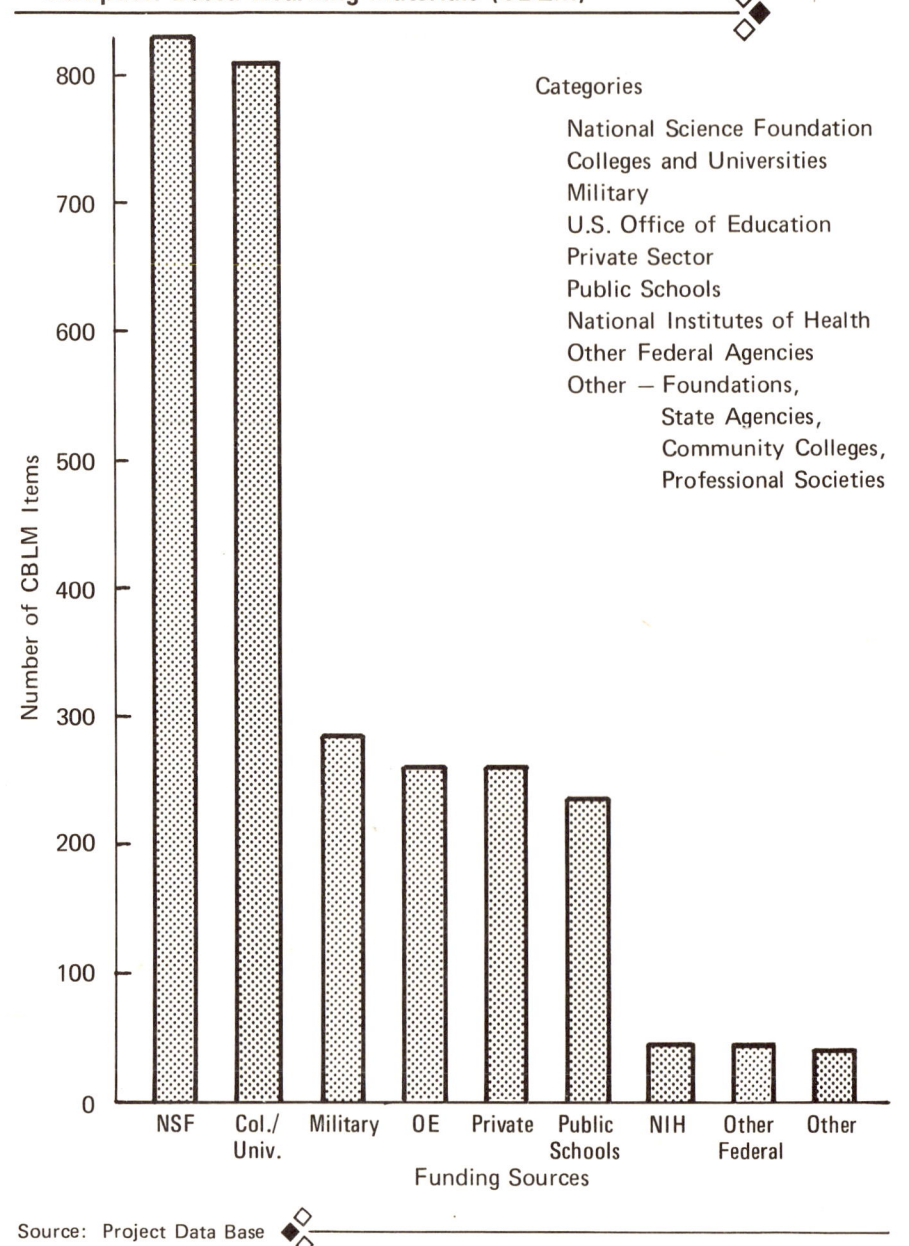

Figure 21

The influence of federal funding on CBLM development is further illustrated in the types of computer applications OE has supported in the past. Half of the OE support for computer-based instruction development was for "computer-presented instruction"—over $50 million. This was 10 times the amount spent on problem-solving applications. One "computer-presented instruction" product might be a full semester course presented on-line in tutorial fashion on the computer.

Further evidence of the key federal role in CBLM development is found in the 1972 *International Clearinghouse on Science and Mathematics Curricular Developments* (Lockard, 1972). It reports 20 projects which use the computer in some way in instruction. The NSF supports a dozen of these, USOE, eight. Public school districts, either individually or in cooperatives, provide funding for six of the projects. Other sources of funding for these projects include private foundations, state boards of education, private business and industry, non-profit organizations, and one community college. Many projects have multiple funding sources.

Who might be expected to provide organizational and financial support in the future for projects to develop computer-based curricular materials? It may be instructive to review briefly the history of curriculum development in general.

Every educational institution, at any level of education, supports curriculum development in some way. Every textbook publisher as well is contributing to curriculum development. However, the two single agencies which have contributed the most financially to large-scale curriculum improvement efforts have been the U.S. Office of Education and the National Science Foundation. Between 1957 and 1969, the U.S. Office of Education spent over $2 billion in support of education product development. The National Science Foundation spent an estimated $68.6 million from 1954 through 1965 in support of course improvement projects. From 1965 to 1972, NSF spent over $500 million on improvement of pre-college and undergraduate science curricula, including development of curricular materials and teacher training (estimated from NSF Annual Reports). (The NSF spent about $13 million on computer-based curriculum development during the same period.)

The USOE and NSF are the most frequently cited sources of funding support by curriculum development projects reported in the *International Clearinghouse on Science and Mathematics Curricular Developments* (Lockard, 1970, 1972). There is, however, considerable variety in the funding support, as indicated in Figure 22.

About half of the projects indicated funding support from NSF and about a third indicated OE support. About 1/5 indicated support from foundations, about 1/5 support from states, and about 1/5 support from public schools. Financial support from colleges or universities was cited in about 1/10 of the projects. A handful of projects cited support from private corporations, professional societies, and other organizations.

The AIR study (Crawford, *et al.*, 1972) of high-impact curriculum products found that 48 percent of the projects were supported totally by federal agencies, 28 percent with both federal and private funds, and 24 percent with private funds. The amount of funding support for the 20 high-impact products ranged from $50,000 to $14 million. About half of the products had cost $2 million or more before they reached the user. About one-fourth of the products cost less than half a million by the time they reached the user.

The above data indicate to us that, if history is to be a guide, the major financial factor in any large-scale attempts at computer-based curricular improvement would be expected to come from the federal government.

As far as organizational support for curriculum development is concerned, the majority of projects in the past have been university based.

The organizational basis or sponsorship for curriculum development projects is most frequently a college or university. Over half of the U.S. projects described in the *Clearinghouse* are based in a college or university. Figure 23 shows the relative frequencies of various organizations involved in the projects listed in the 1970 and 1972 Clearinghouse Reports. About one-third of the projects in the 1972 Clearinghouse Report have some commercial affiliation, usually the publisher of the products.

In the AIR study of 21 exemplary high-impact products, an attempt was made to represent the range of organizational arrange-

Funding Sources Reported by Curriculum Development Projects in the U.S.A.

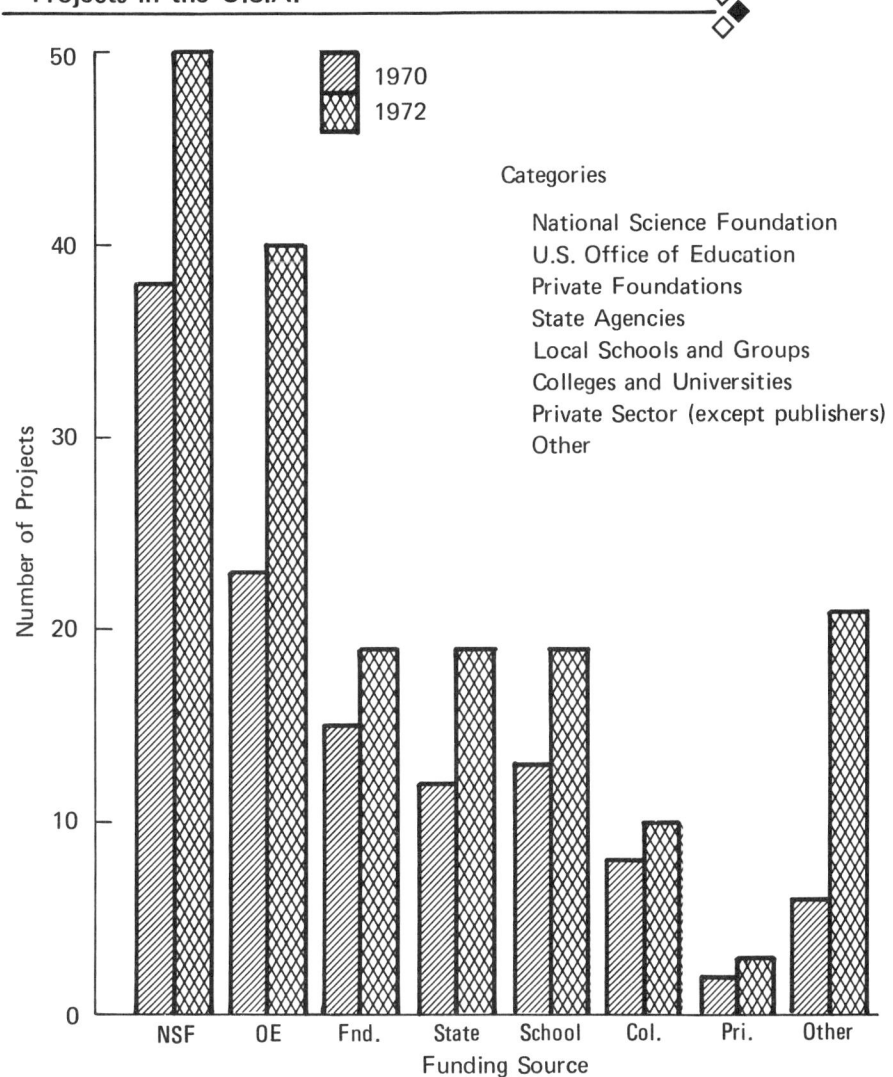

```
                    ▨ 1970
                    ▩ 1972
```

Categories

National Science Foundation
U.S. Office of Education
Private Foundations
State Agencies
Local Schools and Groups
Colleges and Universities
Private Sector (except publishers)
Other

Number of Projects vs Funding Source (NSF, OE, Fnd., State, School, Col., Pri., Other)

Note: Total projects — 1970, 103; 1972, 140. Some projects did not report funding sources and some reported more than one source.

Source Data: Lockard, 1970 and 1972

Figure 22

Organizational Base or Sponsorship Reported by Curriculum Development Projects in the U.S.A.

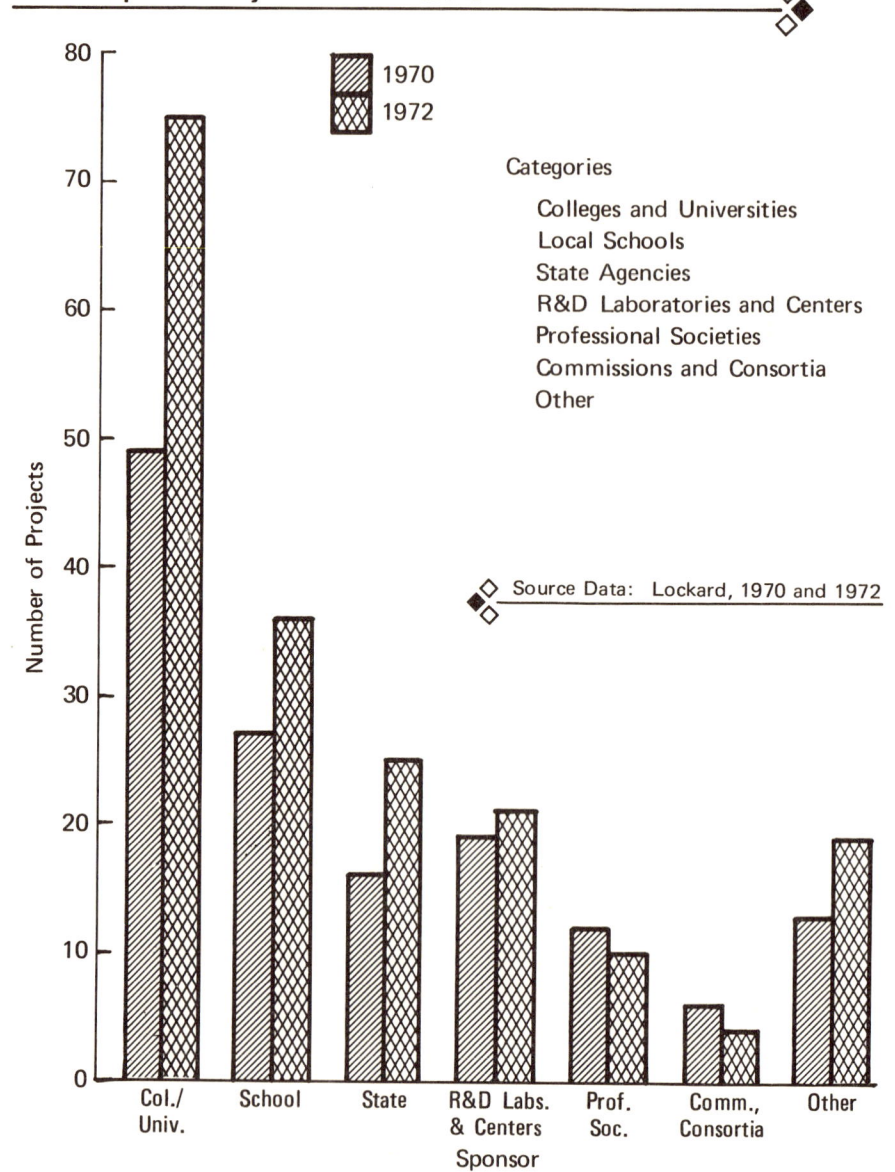

Categories
- Colleges and Universities
- Local Schools
- State Agencies
- R&D Laboratories and Centers
- Professional Societies
- Commissions and Consortia
- Other

Source Data: Lockard, 1970 and 1972

Note: Total projects — 1970, 103; 1972, 140. Some projects did not report sponsorship and some reported more than one sponsor.

Figure 23

ments. The projects represent development by Regional Laboratories, Educational R & D Centers, universities, governments, private non-profits, profit-makers, and professional societies—in various combinations as well as individually.

How do organizational and funding arrangements affect the outcomes of the project and how can the constraints be minimized?

Although it is difficult to show clear-cut cause and effect relationships, the end products of a curriculum development project do appear to be strongly influenced by the *source* of organizational and funding support. Grobman (1970) describes the myriad constraints on curriculum development arising from organizational and funding arrangements. The major areas she discusses are situational constraints, funding constraints, age and life-span of the organization, sponsorship, degree of centralization, degree of external control, internal management, and decision-making. Although these considerations apply to any curriculum development project, some areas are of particular concern to computer-based developments.

Funding Constraints. Grobman (1970, p. 37) says: "Funding sources work in different ways, and the eccentricities of their requirements and ways of handling grants circumscribe the freedom of the developmental project in ways beyond the control of the project." As she points out, the problems in funding relate not just to *amounts* of funding needed and available for a project, but equally importantly, "the *time* when funds become *available*, the *strings* attached to the funds, and the funding *uncertainties*." Funding is further complicated by the number of separate proposals and grants needed to put together a *coherent* program. For example, "according to Harvard Project Physics, its carefully coordinated, long-range, teacher-preparation program, covering seven facets of teacher training over a five-year period, required thirty-five different proposals, one for each facet of the program, for each of the five years" (Grobman, 1970, p. 39).

The facility and staff requirements of a curriculum project using computers makes the problems of uncertainty and fragmentation of funding more pronounced. It is very difficult for a project organization to keep the required staff and facilities together through the vicissitudes of funding.

It is difficult for a complex curriculum development project to maintain a coherent development effort in the face of changing priorities and policies on the part of funding agencies. One year's work may have to be oriented (at least by rhetoric), for example, around improved education for the disadvantaged. The next year the priority of the project may be focused on its accountability and systematic evaluation plans. From time to time the work may be sold on the basis of the computer technology involved; occasionally the focus and selling point must be the novel instructional strategies. The ability of a project to plan early for dissemination (the importance of which is discussed in the next section of this chapter) does not depend only on the foresight of the project planners—more importantly it depends on the policies of the funding agent in supporting dissemination efforts. Often the dissemination function is presented as a follow-up phase, which is likely never to be funded.

Grobman may be only partially right when she says that these constraints are outside the control of the project.

It is probably wise at the outset to have a *comprehensive* development and dissemination plan, with many contingencies accounted for and fall-back positions ready. There are a number of different dimensions along which a complex project can be described and sold as a worthwhile effort for government or foundation support—the importance of the *target population* (e.g., disadvantaged); the importance of the *subject-matter* (e.g., ecology); the potential of the *technology* (e.g., graphics terminals); and the *cost-effectiveness* of the product or process. If the project leaders can plan a coherent, long-term development program which includes these and other dimensions, then the shifting of gears on the part of project staff can be minimized from one grant period to another.

The problems resulting from funding uncertainties and fragmentation can also be minimized if funders and project planners take these into account in their planning. Some projects, for example, purchase computing equipment early in the development rather than lease, so that they will still have their equipment during periods when funding is held up. Funding agencies can help by allowing this purchase. Another tactic is to keep the permanent staff to a minimum, so as to retain continuity during lean times. Manpower for the high production periods is then acquired through summer writing conferences, consultants, and the like. Another approach is to plan the work in such a way that fairly discrete products are produced over short periods of time, rather than producing one very large indivisible product over the entire project time, which may be as long as 10 years. Similarly, evaluation products and dissemination activities can be built into very early stages of the development for these partial products, so as to achieve at least a part of the project objectives in full before funds are cut off. Furthermore, if the early products achieve acceptance or show educational benefit, the probability of continued funding, or funding from other sources, is increased.

Some developers, especially academic faculty, regard the proposal writing and funding process as a troublesome detail unbefitting their scientific stature. There are, however, some people who enjoy the very creative and inventive process of putting together a meaningful program through careful planning and marketing of the various aspects of the project. Perhaps the skills of "grantsmanship" should be included in any list of requirements for personnel skills on a development project.

Other sources of funds besides federal should be considered. Although private industry is still reacting to the fiascos of the late 1960's in CAI development, publishers and computer manufacturers and new types of educational companies are likely to reenter the market eventually. As David Engler (1971, p. 98), formerly of McGraw-Hill, has said: "Eventually, I believe publishers, in the broad sense, will provide most of the capital for the development of computer-based instructional materials; publishers will contract with development groups and various individuals to develop such materials; they may also develop some of these in-house; publishers will market their own programs, as well as programs developed by others."

The AIR study of high-impact educational projects found that "the striking success of private enterprise typically occurred when it built on prior development funds supported by federal sources" (Crawford, *et al.*, 1972). Even if the commercial firm is not willing to provide funds at the outset of a project, it may be profitable for both the project and the company, in the long run, for the project personnel to utilize the services and expertise of a commercial firm, in some way, from the beginning.

The EDUCOM study of *Factors Inhibiting the Use of Computers in Instruction* suggested that publishers "might be induced to make a considerable investment, on a shared-risk basis, if comparable government or foundation support could be provided" (Anastasio and Morgan, 1972, p. 22). The publishers' contributions would be used for activities related to packaging, production techniques, dissemination, and teacher training, rather than the basic work on instructional technology.

Another approach to coping with the funding problems of curriculum development is to invest considerable time and effort at the outset in a carefully conducted and documented *feasibility study*. The needs, aims, resources, and problems can be analyzed, and a well-informed judgment as to potential impact of the project can be formed. The existence of such a feasibility study considerably reduces the uncertainty and risk of the project, from the point of view of potential funding agents. The conduct of a feasibility study was the first *key* step in the success of *Sesame Street*, according to the study by AIR of high-impact educational products.

> Mrs. Cooney's feasibility study, summarized in "The Potential Uses of Television in Preschool Education," was the first critical breakthrough in the struggle to change the message of television. This report spelled out the untapped potential of television in meeting the present crises in education concerning the disadvantaged child. It was the first step toward obtaining substantial funds to tap the potential of television (Kratochvil, 1971a, pp. 39-40).

We are now at the point, especially in certain disciplines, where a considerable base of experience has been built up in developing computer-based learning materials. This experience can be drawn upon, directly or indirectly, in assessing the feasibility of proposed development projects, and setting the policies under which the projects are funded.

DEVELOPMENT PROCESS

This section provides information and ideas on the process of developing CBLM. This information should be useful in making decisions on development approaches to be taken by a project.

Personnel

Of all the factors involved in development, personnel is one of the most, if not the most, critical to success of the project.

The history of *Sesame Street* is an illustration of the perceived importance of personnel. According to the AIR case study of high-impact products:

> It was quite apparent to the developers of the proposal and to the funding agencies that the director, the producer, and the link to the educational world would have a lasting influence on the quality, the scope, and the overall impact of the effort. *Thus, the emphasis was initially placed on people rather than on programs or organizations* (Kratochvil, 1971a, p. 40) [Italics added].

Two main aspects of personnel are significant: (1) the existence of one or few key people who are the driving force behind the project, who will initiate, sustain the project through lean times, and fight for support; and (2) a mix of specialists and skills on the part of the people who do the actual preparation of materials.

There are many examples of the critical importance of the key leader who sustains a project. Individuals with an idea or a vision may pursue it through many years of research and development, despite vicissitudes of funding programs, staff changes, tryout failures, or public disinterest. This type of inner drive or motivation is especially important in the case of highly innovative curricula, such as computer-based materials, because of the uncertainty of external rewards. The problem of incentives for developing computer-based materials has been widely discussed. (This problem is not peculiar to computer-based materials but it is particularly acute in this case because of high risk and long-term development requirements.) There was a high degree of consensus among panel members in the EDUCOM study of *Factors Inhibiting the Use of Computers in Instruction* (Anastasio and Morgan, 1972) that incentives are a significant problem.

> At the university level the lack of professional incentives stems from the general disinterest in improving teaching methods. Current academic incentives practically ignore the development or improvement of instructional techniques. Thus the participants generally agreed that more resources

should be directed toward recognition of technological applications in education and toward revising the academic reward system (Anastasio and Morgan, 1972, p. 20).

The Luskin study (1970) also found incentives for development to be a critical obstacle.

Types of incentives which have been suggested, and found occasionally, include royalties; a legitimized publication vehicle; research and publication credit by universities and academic departments for selection, promotion, and tenuring of faculty; provision of resources (equipment and staff support) for innovative faculty; and faculty release time for developing curricular innovations.

Although our study team heard many anecdotes and opinions regarding the subject of incentives, we were unable to discover any systematic research having been performed on this subject.

One suggested approach to dealing with the incentives problem is to take advantage of the climate which exists in many smaller colleges and junior colleges, where excellence in teaching is given high priority. That is, an alternative to trying to change the reward structure in universities is to provide resources for faculty in small colleges to develop computer-based curricular innovations. NSF, for example, has done this to some extent in the past, by providing grants to faculty at small colleges for computer-based curricular innovations.

From the information gathered in the present study, it appears that an equally important characteristic of a development project is a mix of staff experience and specialties. This conclusion is also highlighted in the AIR study of high-impact curriculum products (Crawford, *et al.*, 1972).

The lack of an adequate mix of skills and orientation in development teams is reflected in many existing computer-based curricular packages and materials. Some are technically very sophisticated and clearly take advantage of computer system capabilities, but are highly impractical for use in educational environments. Some are practical and usable and technically interesting, but the student or faculty user has no clue as to the instructional objectives or educational validity of the materials. Some have carefully specified instructional objectives and considerable evaluation data to show that students achieve the objectives, but discipline experts regard the objectives and content as inappropriate, inaccurate, or trivial.

There are advocates of many different approaches to staffing for curriculum development. Some stress discipline expertise as primary; some relegate the "subject-matter" people to a trivial role; some stress pedagogical expertise; some depend entirely on classroom experience; some ignore the classroom teacher altogether; some emphasize student involvement; others seem to forget students are relevant. If there is any such thing as an "optimum" staff mix, it is yet to be discovered. However, it does seem clear the major and fairly obvious flaws in design and implementation of curricular products could be avoided if staff mix includes in some form:

- discipline expertise,
- recent teaching and learning experience in the subject area involved,
- computing applications in the discipline,
- instructional computing experience,
- curriculum development and evaluation skills,
- "grantsmanship,"
- curriculum product implementation experience, and
- dissemination skills.

The priority or weight given to these various areas of expertise depends largely on the aims and purposes of the project, and on the biases of the project initiator. A project director who is not at all knowledgeable in a particular area could compensate for this in his staff. Unfortunately, the reverse is often the case. A project director with little or no experience in computing, for example, may underestimate the importance of staff expertise in this area. Then the project staff may get so hung up on technical computer problems that the instructional materials suffer immeasurably. Our impression is that people who have computing experience in research in the discipline have been underutilized in many projects to develop computer-based instructional materials.

The mix of specialties may be acquired in a number of ways. If the project is not based at a university, for example, the discipline expert with research-computing experience may contribute only on a consulting basis.

Summer writing conferences are sometimes the mechanism for

classroom teacher involvement in materials preparation. On the other hand, teams of students and their teachers working on a day-to-day basis together in the classroom may develop, try out, and revise materials. Students may be involved only as part of a tryout and evaluation step; on the other hand, they may be involved in the design of the materials or may contribute computer programming support. In the COEXIST project at Dartmouth, students contributed significantly to the design and programming of exercises and problems, but their professors felt students were not able to write the conceptual text materials in a way that communicated well to faculty. In the development of IMPRESS at Dartmouth, the programming contribution of students has been an acknowledged part of its success. In the Social Sciences Instructional Programming Project (SSIPP) at Beloit College, students did an important percentage of the programming. In Project SOLO, students and their teachers together designed and programmed the instructional modules. Advocates of a high degree of student involvement in development stress that the purpose is not simply to get low cost programming help, but rather to benefit from the insights of a student who himself is just learning the subject, as to the problems and exercises which are useful and relevant for other students. Many of the advantages of peer instruction may hold in the case of writing computer-based instruction as well as in personal peer interaction.

Development Procedures

In a review of the technology of development, Baker (1973, p. 249) makes the following observation:

> Much of the process of curriculum development cannot be properly considered in a chapter on the technology of development, since the defining element of technology is the production of replicable materials through relatively codified means. The bulk of school-initiated curriculum development until recently would fail both criteria: it rarely described replicable procedures and the manner of its production can hardly be recounted. Instead, most curriculum activity persists as anthropological "rites of convocation" where the activity is sufficient in itself and useful materials are both rarely expected and infrequently realized.

Developing Computer-Based Learning Materials

No procedures are complete and final solutions to the problem of curricular development. Moreover, the use of systematic development procedures can give a false sense of security to a developer. The necessary and sufficient conditions for useful development must include *implementation considerations*, which are usually not accounted for in formalized development procedures. The state and local political environment, administrative attitudes of an institution, and other orthodox educational practices can, singly or collectively, easily negate an expected instructional gain based on systematic procedures of formative and summative evaluation. Such procedures are, therefore, only guides to facilitate the translation of a creative idea into useful instruction. The initial critical ingredient to instructional innovation is the inventive individual. But if his inventions are to benefit other teachers and students, his intuitions must be given explicit, operationally defined meaning.

A number of theoretical approaches to systematic instructional design and development exist—any of which can be viewed as *aids* to the developer.* None can claim exclusive value but the essential features they all possess are the principles relating to: explicit specification of end-of-course student performance requirements, clear-cut identification of particular skills and knowledge tasks in order to reach end-of-course proficiency, requirements for explicitly stating prerequisite relationships, if any, among the parts of the course (especially as they refer to student performance), and the requirement for iterative testing, feedback, and modification until a mastery criterion is met. The following descriptions are presented as illustrative

---

*Merrill (1973), for example, has developed an approach for analyzing content and instruction of cognitive curricular tasks (classifying instances of rules, using rules, or finding rules). This is being used by the TICCIT project team as part of their systems approach to course development. Dick and Gallagher (1972) emphasize analysis of the instructional tasks in terms of identifying correct and incorrect conceptual units (cognitive tasks), constructing a product according to some pre-set requirement (productive tasks), and combinations of these. Thomas (1973) has highlighted the value of the computer as an aid to instructional design per se: *information retrieval* for task analysis and behavioral objectives, *composition* and *editing* for developing test items and instructional materials, and *computation* and *analysis* for evaluation of the course.

of useful alternative approaches which have resulted in the development of effective courses.

Attempts have been made at providing useful taxonomies of learning objectives. The principal goal of such taxonomies has been to aid in establishing a consistent basis for classifying instructional objectives. It has worked to some degree in the cognitive area but with difficulty in maintaining clear-cut distinctions among levels of hypothesized hierarchies (knowledge, comprehension, application, analysis, synthesis, and evaluation). Gagné's hierarchical model (1962, 1965, 1970) provides a basis for establishing instructional sequencing. Other instructional theorists (e.g., M.D. Merrill, 1971; P.F. Merrill, 1971; Olivier, 1971; Seidel, 1971a; Stolurow, 1972) have felt for various reasons that the language and/or structure of Gagné's hierarchy are too limited to aid practical development of curricula on a broad scale. Others (e.g., P.F. Merrill, 1971; Seidel, 1971b) have attempted to remain relatively free of perceived restrictions in the classic learning theory approach to instructional development, advocating an *information processing* approach to facilitate the organization of instructional materials. P.F. Merrill (1971) in particular describes this approach as particularly useful where partial achievement or *output* from learning one subskill is required as *input* for learning a succeeding subskill. If no prerequisite is established for a given subskill, then it may be learned independently of others. Stolurow (1972) has attempted an eclectic approach toward an instructional grammar to aid the developer. He feels that "current basic (psychological) research is providing fundamental findings useful to the more general conception of educational technology, and particularly for the development of the contingency grammar needed by this conception of instruction" (p. 13). Drawing upon examples from the literature, he feels one can make a number of prescriptive instructional judgments. For example, *if* the student has aptitude + (or personality a, or ethnic characteristic b), then give him materials A, and so forth.

One item about which all of the above-cited theorists agree is that research is required to verify many of their concepts (see Okey, 1973). Application of their approaches also implies the need for instructional technology specialists to aid the curriculum developer or the need for the curriculum developer to obtain training in the techniques of

Developing Computer-Based Learning Materials 195

instructional analysis. M.D. Merrill (1971) has outlined a teacher training program designed to accomplish the latter.

A phrase commonly used to denote a set of formalized development procedures is "systems approach."* A general schematic representation of a systematic development process is shown in Figure 24.

Model for the Systems Approach to the Development of Instructional Materials

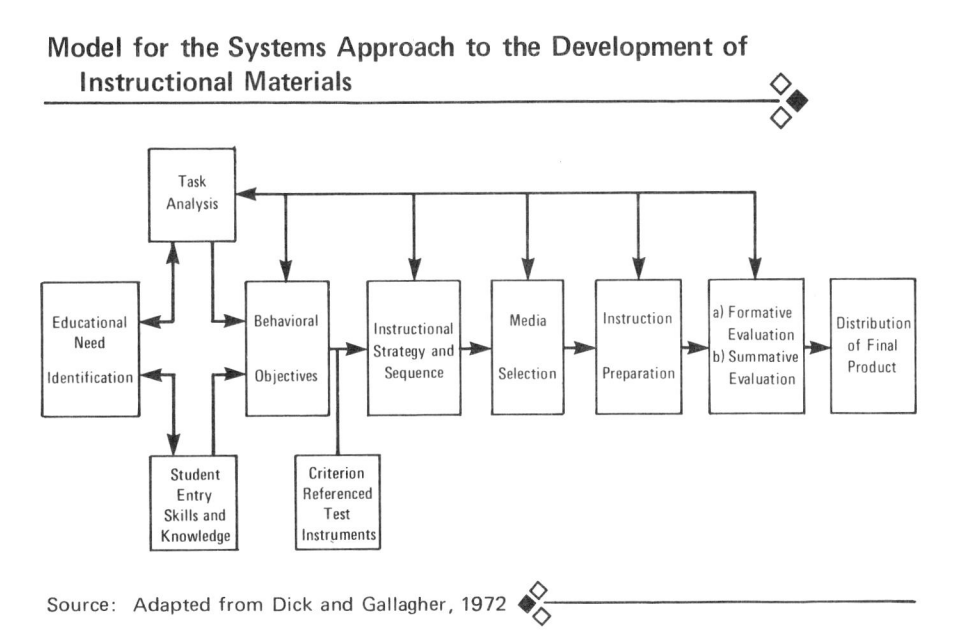

[Flow diagram: Educational Need Identification → Behavioral Objectives → Instructional Strategy and Sequence → Media Selection → Instruction Preparation → a) Formative Evaluation b) Summative Evaluation → Distribution of Final Product. Task Analysis feeds into the process from above; Student Entry Skills and Knowledge, and Criterion Referenced Test Instruments feed in from below.]

Source: Adapted from Dick and Gallagher, 1972

Figure 24

An "ideal" systems approach would begin with a statement of an educational *need* on the part of a particular population or client. A careful analysis would be made of the learner-teacher population, their environment, resources, and problems. *Objectives* of the project would be based on this analysis. A number of possible *alternative approaches* to meeting these objectives would be assessed. (Theoretically, a wide

---

*For discussions of the systems approach see Dick, 1969; Hagerty, 1970; Tennyson and Boutwell, 1971; and Tuckman and Edwards, 1971.

range of alternatives would be considered, not all of which would involve development of new curricular materials, and not all of which would involve computer-based materials.) Assuming that development of new computer-based materials was *selected* as the best *alternative*, a *detailed analysis* of learning needs and learner capabilities would be made. *Detailed objectives* for the curricular materials (and the instructional system of which they are a part) would be prepared. Preliminary materials and related system components would be prepared according to carefully specified procedures. The materials would be tested with students and revised, probably in several iterations. Careful methodology for formative evaluation would be followed.

The project director for the effort would probably be a systems-oriented person with broad background in education, curriculum development, and technology, but not necessarily in the subject-matter of materials. He would draw on the capabilities of a full-time, in-house, multidisciplinary team of discipline experts, educators, psychologists, technologists, and computer scientists. Considerable reliance would be placed on efficient procedures for development and quality control of the materials.

In the "ideal" case, the advantages of a systems approach are that the end product would most closely satisfy the needs of the learner population, and the best available resources and skills would be brought to bear on the solution. Given the many specific procedures and staffing requirements compared to the development of materials by the individual teacher, the costs of the systems approach are relatively high. However, the relatively high cost of development is justified if the end product in fact meets the needs of a large learner population. Carefully specified development procedures would help ensure an efficient development process and quality control over the end product.

When addressing a need or problem of any magnitude, this approach requires a fairly high level of funding over a period of several years. In these conditions, the incentives for the team members include a salary which enables them to devote full attention to the project, the considerable satisfaction of working on an innovative project, the personal and professional stimulation of a multidisciplinary team environment, and the belief that the end product will be useful and beneficial to the user. In the "idealized case," the systems approach could have a high payoff for society in general, the specific learner population, and the developers themselves. In "reality," there cannot be any such idealized project in education. First of all, education is not a "system" in the sense that systems engineering implies, so it is not even theoretically possible to follow a strict systems approach. Arguments abound concerning the inability to identify even equivalent measures of system inputs and outputs (Alkin, 1970). Second, funding sources always predispose the solution to one extent or another. Third, it takes a long time to put together a well-working multidisciplinary team—funding is rarely predictable and reliable enough to maintain the team for the duration of a long-term project. Fourth, there are usually trade-offs between encouraging creativity and inventiveness in the project on the one hand and adherence to well-defined procedures on the other, and the need to produce a usable product within a given time frame. Because of the interdependence of the several team members' work, certain aspects of pedagogy or style may be prematurely standardized, thus precluding the evolution of innovations as the project members gain insight and experience.

Subject-matter, pedagogy, instructional strategies, and computer hardware/software facilities are highly interdependent. Each team member, be he computer programmer, media expert, discipline expert, or instructional writer, can severely constrain as well as enhance the creativity of the others. Extreme flexibility is required in all working relationships.

In "reality," the process and procedures followed in a development project are tailored to the people, the purposes, the scope, the pedagogy, the computer system, the dissemination plan, and many other factors. A good example is the case of the TICCIT courseware development, in which a carefully engineered development process is highly tailored to the pedagogy, the TICCIT computer system, and many practicalities of production scheduling requirements. (The process is heavily influenced, for example, by the fact that the hardware/software system development is proceeding in parallel with course development.)

Formative Evaluation and Revision

> The Purpose of Evaluation
> Is Not to Prove
> But to Improve
>
> Phi Delta Kappan National Study
> Committee on Evaluation
> (Stufflebeam, *et al.*, 1971)

There are several characteristics of computer-based learning materials and related projects that would suggest the need for a systematic approach and careful attention to the processes of formative evaluation and revision. Some of these characteristics are:
- novelty of the instructional techniques being used,
- technical complexity of the materials and systems,
- novel approach to the subject matter,
- new roles for instructors and students,
- opportunity to have the computer collect a considerable amount of data on use and student performance and costs, and
- the demand for evidence of quality and information on costs on the part of potential users.

Although the process of formative evaluation and revision is important for any curriculum development project, it would appear to be even more important in the case of computer-based materials. An "extremely desirable" educational improvement to which the computer can make a "substantial" contribution, is that the computer "would make it possible for educational programs to be more accurately and significantly evaluated, allowing systematic revision of course material to optimize teaching effectiveness." This was one of the consensual opinions of the EDUCOM study of *Factors Inhibiting the Use of Computers in Instruction* (Anastasio and Morgan, 1972).

Although many computer-based instruction projects in the past did not put much formal emphasis on formative evaluation and revision, it is reasonable to assume that projects which aim toward development of materials for widespread use and impact will become more and more concerned with this topic. Furthermore, the federal government in its funding policies and programs is becoming insistent on accountability on the part of developers and educational innovators for assessment of the quality, contribution, and costs of their innovations. Therefore, it seems reasonable to expect that far more serious attention will be paid by developers to the evaluation and revision processes in the future than is reflected in much of the work to date. General comments by developers such as "our students seem to like the materials" are not useful for improvement of materials or for making decisions on adoption.

Past and Present Activities

About half of the projects in our "sample development stories" had some kind of systematic approach to evaluation and revision. The Stanford Reading program had many levels and cycles of evaluation-revision, from laboratory research to pilot school tryout, resulting in a complete redesign of the system, including teacher role, type of computer materials, and terminal design.

The Huntington Two materials underwent extensive tryout and revision throughout the development period. Following this, the materials were tried out in about 100 high schools all over the country. Although there was no systematic means set up for feeding back the results of this use into program revisions, there have been a number of changes in the packages as a result of this widespread tryout. Further, the feasibility of using the packages in a variety of school contexts and computer environments has been demonstrated.

The Pillsbury materials benefitted greatly from the field test in three quite different college environments, in areas of technical refinement, completeness of the total package, and marketing.

Project IMPACT, an advanced development effort in CAI at the Human Resources Research Organization, evolved a detailed systematic formative evaluation and revision procedure using the computer. IMPACT established formative development procedures which included a series of checkpoints to pin down the focus of a problem area—number of students having problems, type of student, what parts of the materials are candidates for review, etc. A three-part criterion was established for determining the worth of a course segment. This was based on percent of students passing the material on the first try, percent passing on second try, and opinions of the students. To facilitate course development, text management, and analysis of student generated data, a number of software support capabilities were developed, such as on-line authoring techniques, student files based on prerequisites passed or failed plus various intersegment controls, and three different off-line file update control programs. The course was tested and revised using feedback from almost 200 students.

The courseware developers of the TICCIT program are attempting to substitute carefully controlled development procedures for tryout-revision in the formative stages of the materials. The approach was apparently necessitated by the fact that the computer hardware and software components of the system are being developed in parallel with the course materials, and by the fact that the materials are being developed in a university setting where the developers do not have access to junior college students representative of the target population. An extensive evaluation of the programs is being planned by an independent agency, to take place in the large-scale demonstrations of the system in two junior colleges. The purpose of this evaluation, however, is primarily to provide summative type information for use by potential users in making adoption decisions, and is not primarily designed to feed back to the developers for program improvement purposes.

In planning a development project, there is a considerable amount of guidance available on the subject of formative evaluation-revision cycles. A general discussion of formative evaluation in a number of past developmental curriculum projects is provided by Grobman (1970). Grobman raises many practical problems in evaluation-feedback-revision, and suggests some useful compromises among various points of view. The Phi Delta Kappa National Study Committee on Evaluation has provided a useful and comprehensive book of guidance on evaluation (Stufflebeam, *et al.*, 1971) with primary emphasis on the feedback-revision process. *Calipers*, a publication of the Southwest Regional Educational Laboratory (1969), offers a set of procedures designed for testing, feedback, and revision of educational products. Gropper (1975) examines the diagnosis and revision of instructional materials in great detail. Borich, *et al.* (1974) provide a comprehensive treatment of product evaluation. We will address only a few issues which have been especially problematic in the field of computer-based learning materials.

The Problem of the Research Model

This problem is well presented by the Phi Delta Kappa committee, which stated: "Perhaps the greatest challenge facing the evaluator is overcoming the idea that evaluation methodology is identical to research methodology. Equating them forces certain constraints inimical to the purposes of evaluation and makes it impossible to meet certain of the needs served by good evaluation" (Stufflebeam, *et al.*, 1971, p. 22).

The primary purpose of curriculum evaluation (at least insofar as we are using the term here) is to provide information on which developers and users can make judgments about a program, in order to make improvements in the product or its use. As such, evaluation must be carried out in conditions which invite interference from all sources which might influence the learning situation. Research, on the other hand, is conducted primarily for the purpose of providing new knowledge. Its methods often require experimentally contrived situations which have little relevance to the actual world in which the program is to be used. Controlled experimental "treatments" produce data at the termination of the experiment. The evaluator cannot wait for the end of the experiment to know what is happening to the students—they are not a crop of grain to be measured at the end of the growing season and compared with grain from the untreated plot.

In following classical experimental design precepts, an evaluator may try to achieve comparability of control and experimental groups by some matching or pairing process—classrooms of equal size, serving culturally similar communities, with similar numbers of boys and girls or similar intelligence and motivation, and so on. "It is no surprise that comparative experiments conducted under such circumstances fail to yield meaningful results. When the researcher has achieved such a 'sea of homogeneity' by virtue of his efforts to produce comparability, it is little wonder that his differentiated treatments, however powerful, cause only tiny and hardly observable ripples" (Stufflebeam, *et al.*, 1971, p. 25).

The most important requirement for evaluation procedures is that they facilitate the continual improvement of the product and its use. A research design which disallows changes during the course of the "experiment" hampers this revision process.

Whether or not there is a carefully controlled situation—whether or not the activity is research or curriculum evaluation—a key activity in formative evaluation is collecting and reporting as much descriptive information about the population as feasible. Telling the educator something worked last week or last year is meaningless unless he has detailed information on the context. Yet this is often seriously neglected in collecting data and, even when such data are collected, in analyzing and presenting it.

Sometimes the developer or evaluator gets so enmeshed in a rigorous, detailed, statistically sophisticated evaluation at the micro-level that the entire educational context is forgotten. Computer-based materials, especially tutorials and drills, make it easy to do this because it is tempting to base evaluation around what is easily measured, and the computer program can be designed to collect all kinds of data on a micro-level. Although evaluation and revision on a micro-level—that is, internal to the program—are important, it will probably be the higher-level aspects which will determine the eventual impact of the program. At the state level, for example, a decision-maker would be interested not in the cost per student hour of an individual instructional program which was used in a developmental setting on a special computer system, but rather he would need information on the costs of the overall delivery system acquisition and implementation for the state, presuming the program had potential applicability statewide. By considering cost information at this macro-level, improvements and modifications in the program might be made in the light of the larger delivery system considerations. Seen in this light, the revisions to the program might not be toward improving student performance on the program objectives, but rather toward making the overall package more feasible for widespread implementation.

Another evaluation issue which often arises is whether to evaluate the innovative course by comparison with a traditionally taught course (e.g., see Schurdak, 1967). Such comparisons more often than not are inappropriate because of two fundamental issues: differences in educational models which the traditional material and the CBLM were designed to serve, and ambiguities of the dimensions even where the models are not in conflict.

The first issue is highlighted where models of "open education" and traditional education may be involved. Traub, *et al.* (1972) ascribe the many failures in educational innovation to lack of detailed considerations of the educational environments into which the innovation is placed. There are many dimensions which differentiate open education from traditional education. Any of these could easily affect the outcome of an attempt at educational innovation. To our knowledge no comparison studies have explicitly dealt with them.

The second problem, ambiguities when a similar model is involved, is illustrated in a study by Schurdak (1967). He was comparing relative achievements in FORTRAN programming across groups of students taught with CAI, programmed text, or conventional text, yet without detailing the dimensions of difference in the instruction. In many instances the comparisons take the form of careful instructional development for the innovative materials (e.g., using the systems approach described earlier) while nothing is done to the old, traditional instruction. This sometimes results in a favorable outcome for the computer-based course but comparisons are from results on tests of mastery for specific objectives at which the computer-based learning material was aimed (see, for example, Mitzel, *et al.*, 1971). In other cases, the computer-based material was added to a standard course and the result was that more instruction increased achievement. But this has also been found by supplementing the instruction with programmed booklets (Vinsonhaler, 1970). In other instances, when the same developmental care in developing the computer-based material has been done for the traditional course as well, results have shown little or no difference (see, for example, Hansen, *et al.*, 1970). But even this neglects the likelihood that there are as many teachers with their own pedagogies and biases as there are points on a normal curve. The results of these studies have usually turned up "no significant differences." As has been said in a previous critique, "Logically this is equivalent to evaluating the potato-holding capacity of a sack, a box, and a barrel" (Kopstein and Seidel, 1967, p. 414). If the dimensions are not known, any comparisons are meaningless.

Planning for Dissemination

Diffusion or dissemination of any innovative educational product is a complex and difficult problem. The fact that a curricular product involves use of a computer enormously complicates an already difficult matter. Therefore, if the aim of the project is to provide materials which can and will be widely used, *it is critical that the planning for dissemination begin at the outset of the project.*

Widespread dissemination is not always thought of as a primary part of the development process. This is particularly the case when the individual instructor is designing new materials for use in one of his specialty courses.

However, early planning for dissemination will affect the contracts for funding, the design of the product itself, the publicity efforts during development, the selection of development sites, the design of tryout and revision processes, the selection of project personnel, the selection of computer hardware and software, and in fact nearly every possible aspect of development itself. Once the project has begun without planning for dissemination, it is very likely that the product will never reach more than a handful of users. There are so many variables involved in successful dissemination of a computer-based product that it is highly unlikely that it will be achieved by accident.

A number of alternative strategies and mechanisms for disseminating computer-based materials are discussed in Chapter 5 of this book. Careful and early consideration of these and other alternatives for dissemination will greatly affect the development process itself. The following points are merely illustrative of the myriad ways in which dissemination plans affect development and vice versa.

Funding arrangements. Contracts or grants with any funding agency, whether federal, private, or state, will be either unwieldy because of their ambiguity or will make unnecessary constraints on dissemination, if the plan for dissemination is not accounted for in the contract. Costs and delays involved in renegotiating contracts later may result in many lost opportunities. Federal agencies have shown increasing flexibility in the last two or three years with regard to copyrights and royalty arrangements, so as to encourage dissemination of research and development products.

Also, the cost of dissemination activities must be accounted for in the development plan. Although in the past (Grobman, 1970) the legislative authority for some grants and contracts did not include support for dissemination, this is increasingly less true. Many federal agency programs now actively encourage dissemination of research and development products.

Design of the Product. Early planning for dissemination will help the project to focus on certain user-oriented issues in the design of the materials, which otherwise might be given little attention. Some of these design considerations are:
- cost and complexity of implementation;
- skills required of instructor—in computing, in instructional management, in subject-matter;
- compatibility with existing curricula and textbooks;
- flexibility and divisibility of package—ease of tailoring by user;
- operational costs;
- facilities and equipment access requirements;
- evaluative information needed to make adoption decisions;
- mechanisms for user evaluation of materials;
- compatibility with school structures, schedules, and classes;
- information needs of support personnel for implementation, operations;
- information, demonstration needs of administrators for decision-making, implementation, operations; and
- requirements of the dissemination strategy, e.g., if commercial publisher is involved, is package designed to be profitable?

Project Personnel. Does anyone on the project staff have a stake in dissemination? The staff may be motivated to improve a course of instruction; to advance the state-of-the-art in instructional computing; to develop innovative instructional strategies; to find out how students learn using computing; to share some exciting new ideas with their own students; or to learn more about computer applications themselves. But if no one on the staff actually is motivated to see people *use* the product, or motivated to achieve personal or professional rewards from disseminating it, then dissemination is not likely to happen.

One hypothesis about dissemination/adoption is that the closer the interpersonal and intergroup relationships between developer and users, the more likely the product will be used effectively (Havelock, 1973). According to this linkage hypothesis, the developer team should include people who either have close ties to, or represent in some manner, the target user groups.

Selection or Design of Hardware and Software. When dissemination is considered at the outset, the selection of the computer hardware and software base for the materials is made largely on the basis of an analysis of the potential user population and the feasibility of their having access to the type of system required. When dissemination is *not* considered early, the primary criteria for selection of hardware and software base are often such factors as convenience to the developer, familiarity of the system to the developer personnel, or advanced technical capabilities which suit the pedagogical needs of the developer. The history of computer-based instruction development is replete with examples of materials developed on special systems—powerful terminals no one can afford, sophisticated systems software that is prohibitive to transport, configurations no one would reproduce, or inefficient author languages.

Materials developed on such systems can, of course, be redesigned later to operate on less expensive systems, but often with serious degradation of the pedagogical design.

The developers of the materials, if they have a dissemination strategy at the outset, will as part of that strategy have a delivery system approach as an integral part of the strategy. There are many alternatives, as discussed in Chapters 5 and 6—program packages to be implemented on the individual user institution's computer; textbooks and problem statements that are essentially system-independent; delivery via commercial time-sharing services; delivery via academic computer networks; or design of a complete package including the computer hardware and software to be installed with the materials. There have been successful cases of dissemination of computer-based materials under each of these approaches, but the role of the computer in the instruction, the design of the materials package, the pedagogy of the program, will be quite different in each case.

Chapter 5

WAYS OF ACHIEVING MORE WIDESPREAD BENEFIT FROM COMPUTER-BASED LEARNING MATERIALS

PERSPECTIVE

Educational research does not stand very well on Capitol Hill for several reasons, one of which is, we do not know what it is. Another is that whatever it is, we do not think it makes much difference. And another... is that we have the apprehension that the fruits of investment in educational research are not really translated into the system (Hon. John Brademas, Chairman, H.R. Subcommittee on Education, in Wentworth, 1972).

Congressman Brademas' apprehensions are confirmed by those who have looked "behind the classroom door" in the United States for evidence that the most well-known and widely discussed reforms in school practice are actually in use (Goodlad, 1966; Goodlad, *et al.*, 1970; Hart, 1969; Jackson, 1970). Based upon observations in 150 classrooms in 67 schools selected from major population centers of the country (a third of which were selected because they were claimed to be "innovative"), Goodlad, *et al.* (1970, p. 97) drew the following conclusion:

One conclusion stands out clearly: many of the changes we have believed to be taking place in schooling have not been getting into classrooms; changes widely recommended for the schools over the past 15 years were blunted on school and classroom door. Second, schools and classrooms were marked by a sameness regardless of location, student enrollment, and "typing" as provided initially to us by an administrator.

The resistance to change that characterizes our schools has been analyzed and discussed in numerous conferences, studies, and books (e.g., Bushnell and Rappaport, 1971; Kozol, 1972; Oettinger, 1969; O'Neill, 1969; Saxe, 1972). Havelock, Huber, and Zimmerman (1969) have annotated and indexed 38 of the major references from the large number of sources on varying aspects of educational innovation. Miles (1964) has cited representative samples of several viewpoints. Almost everything that is said is an elaboration of this statement by Goodlad (1970, p. 100):

> Perhaps the most telling observation about our educational system is that there is not, below the level of intense criticism and endless recommendations for improvement, any effective structure by means of which countervailing ideas and models may be pumped in and developed to the point of becoming real alternatives. Stated conversely, the system is geared to self-preservation, not to self-renewal.

It is against this backdrop that we come now to consider the subject of disseminating computer-oriented learning materials and systems. Most of the innovations that have been introduced in education over the past 15 years require far less capital investment, far less change in school administration and classroom practice than is called for by the adoption of computer-based systems. Hence, a certain modesty of aims in terms of widespread adoption and pace of adoption is appropriate.

A second area where modesty of aims is called for is in the hoped-for educational benefits of computer-based systems and materials. The fact that materials and systems are computer-based or computer-oriented says little about the educational benefits that may be obtained by using them. Computer-based curricula can be as irrelevant to the learning needs of people in this society as any other innovation. Although there have been a number of research studies on the effectiveness of particular computer-assisted instruction (CAI) programs (usually as compared to "traditional" instruction in the same course) in reaching specified subject-matter objectives, there have been no large-scale investigations of the more important general educational effects of adopting computer-based systems and curricula of various kinds (Anastasio and Morgan, 1972). In the present study, we did not go "behind the classroom door" in any systematic way to determine what real effects, if any, the computer-based innovation was having on curriculum content or methods, activities and achievement of students or school organization, management, and goals. We also do not know of anyone who has done this.

WHY IS DISSEMINATION OF COMPUTER-ORIENTED CURRICULA A NATIONAL CONCERN?

In general, none of the traditional organizations and mechanisms by which curricular materials and educational innovations ordinarily get from developer to user have been adequate in the case of computer-oriented curricular materials. Existing mechanisms have not satisfied the needs of either the potential *users* or the *developers* of computer-oriented materials and systems.

Indeed, the dissemination of computer-oriented curricula is a complex issue not just because of the technical complexities, cost, and innovative content. Computer-oriented materials are intimately bound up in a host of educational reforms and issues, including the role of the classroom teacher, the paradigm of the classroom, and the whole lock-step framework of grades, groups, credits, and degrees. Because of the technical complexities of the computer systems and applications themselves, the real educational issues involved are usually obscured. Thus, a computer-based system being hailed as a great innovation in education may actually be used to shore up an obsolete educational practice or institution.

To summarize reasons for national concern with dissemination of computer-based curricula:
1. There is a need for such materials, and this need is only partly being satisfied through a large number of local efforts.
2. The cost of continual re-creation and re-invention, on a local basis, of applications, techniques, and materials, can be seen from a national standpoint to be prohibitive, and unnecessary when compared to the costs and potential payoff of making the best materials and techniques widely available.
3. Traditional mechanisms for dissemination of curricular materials are not adequate in the case of computer-based materials, and piecemeal efforts to augment traditional mechanisms have not been successful.

4. Far more awareness on the part of educators as to the nature and roles of computing in education is essential, in order to ensure that computers are used in ways that are *beneficial* to learners and to society. To create this awareness, a massive national effort in computing literacy of educators is required.

PURPOSE AND ASSUMPTIONS OF THIS CHAPTER

This chapter is addressed to those who are or will be concerned with disseminating or adopting computer-oriented curricula. Our purpose is to assist in planning and implementing the activities needed to accomplish dissemination, on a national scale.

An underlying assumption in this chapter is that a large number and variety of computer-oriented curriculum packages will be developed in the next few years. In the past, neither the developers of computer-based curricular materials nor their sponsors and funding sources placed much emphasis on widespread diffusion of the materials. For the most part, they were experimenting with innovations on a small-scale, local basis in order to advance and evaluate the state-of-the-art.

However, it is believed that the next wave of development will have as a central purpose the development of materials for widespread adoption, and the dissemination of those materials. We assume that the readers of this chapter are already motivated to disseminate. Hence, we are addressing the mechanisms and strategies for accomplishing this purpose, and we are not concerned with the historical lack of motivation and incentives for dissemination. We have been concerned with presenting a current picture of the field. However, change is so much a part of the computer world that some of the examples cited may not be up-do-date.

ORGANIZATION OF THIS CHAPTER

The organization of this chapter (Figure 25) reflects the overall logic of our approach to dissemination.

First, we provide an overview of the state-of-the-art of dissemination. Next, an overview is given of the adoption process as it exists today. These two sections offer an introduction to the key factors in dissemination, which should be taken into account in planning national strategies.

Achieving More Widespread Benefit from Computer-Based Learning Materials 211

Organization of the Chapter

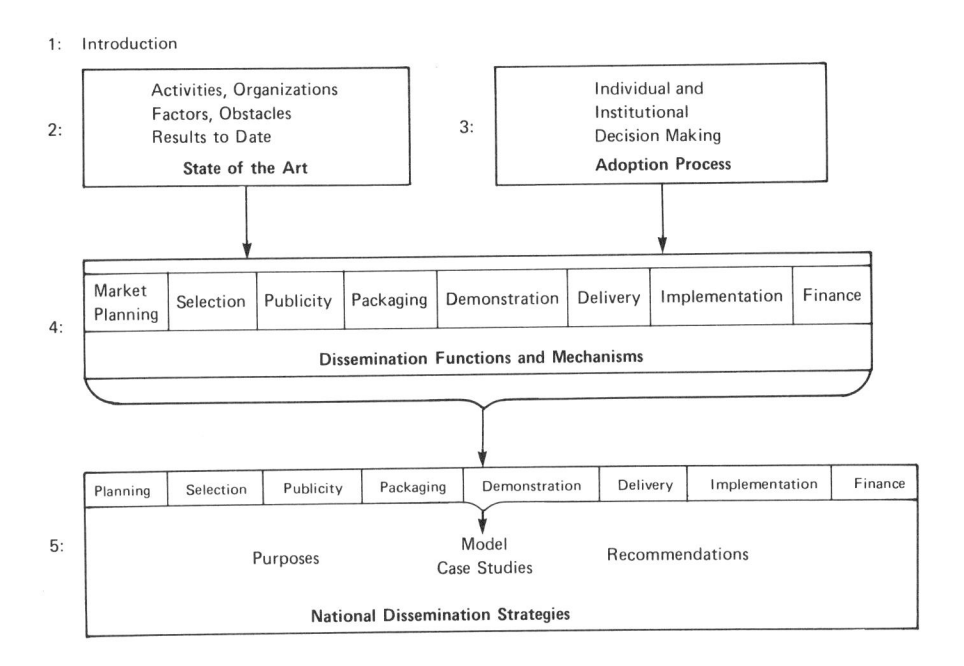

1: Introduction

2: **State of the Art** — Activities, Organizations, Factors, Obstacles, Results to Date

3: **Adoption Process** — Individual and Institutional Decision Making

4: **Dissemination Functions and Mechanisms** — Market Planning | Selection | Publicity | Packaging | Demonstration | Delivery | Implementation | Finance

5: **National Dissemination Strategies** — Planning | Selection | Publicity | Packaging | Demonstration | Delivery | Implementation | Finance; Purposes, Model Case Studies, Recommendations

Figure 25

Then, dissemination is analyzed into nine major functions. Alternative ways of accomplishing each function are suggested through examples of present-day activities.

Finally, the nine major functions provide the framework for the presentation of alternative national strategies. Each "strategy" includes an educational purpose, an organizational plan, and a unique set of mechanisms for carrying out the nine functions. The strategies are based on three case studies that are included in the chapter:

(1) South-Western Publishing Company,
(2) North Carolina Educational Computing Service, and
(3) Houghton Mifflin/Time Share Corporation.

STATE-OF-THE-ART OVERVIEW
Dissemination Activities

Thousands of organizations in the United States are now involved, in one way or another, in disseminating computer-oriented curricular innovations. These organizations have evolved an array of dissemination mechanisms including conferences, educator workshops, newsletters, catalogs, clearinghouses, journals, computer networks, consulting services, standards, demonstration centers, copyright arrangements, mailing lists, and many more to be discussed later in this chapter. These activities have focused on the dissemination of instructional strategy ideas, computing techniques, computer hardware and software, cost-effectiveness information, instructional computer programs, computer-oriented textbooks and problem sets, data bases, and guidance for administrators and teachers. Appendix 2 provides contact information for some of these organizations and activities.

The following illustrative examples further describe the range and nature of present dissemination activity:

- The Center for Exchange of Chemistry Computer Programs (CECCP) at Eastern Michigan University produced a catalog of abstracts and a monthly newsletter. One of the difficulties with this exchange, and others like it, is that there is no incentive for the developer to document his programs so that potential users can evaluate or implement them. Because the file of abstracts has not grown and the newsletter has not appeared for some time, one also wonders about the incentives for the manager of a program exchange. CECCP receives no outside financial support.

- The *Index to Computer Based Learning* (Hoye and Wang, 1973), now in its fourth edition, provides a number of items of information regarding CAI programs at all levels of education and in all disciplines. Many of these programs are not actually available to potential users, however, for a variety of reasons—they were developed as a learning exercise in computing for the developer and do not have educational value, they are dependent on unique or obsolete equipment, they are not documented, or the developer will not release them for use because they are not tested.

- The American Chemical Society Division and the National Research Council Division of Chemistry and Technology sponsored a

Achieving More Widespread Benefit from Computer-Based Learning Materials 213

Conference on Computers in Chemical Education and Research in July 1971 (Conference on Computers in Chemical Education and Research, 1971). This conference might have been an excellent vehicle for exchange of ideas among chemists with both research and education orientation. However, attendance is reported to have been very low, and the *Proceedings* have not been widely distributed.

• Houghton Mifflin publishers have made a joint arrangement with Time Share, Inc. in which Houghton Mifflin provides marketing services for Time Share's computer-based educational products, and in which Time Share provides technical support for Houghton Mifflin's computer-oriented curricular products. (This arrangement is described further below, in the section on "Case Studies in Dissemination.")

• The Kansas State Board of Education is supporting a statewide project to establish a computing network among public schools, for the purpose of sharing curricular materials among the schools (Denny, *et al.*, 1972).

• The Association for Computing Machinery (ACM) has formed several special interest groups for sharing information relevant to computers in education (see Appendix 2).

• The American Journal of Physics has initiated a monthly column on computers in Physics Instruction.

• The National Science Foundation is sponsoring a project for the transport of computer-related curricula between five university networks (CONDUIT).

• The role of commercial publishers and manufacturers has been of special concern for many years (Locke and Engler, 1968). Notable failures to achieve a market success after extensive investment have been experienced by IBM-SRA, Harcourt Brace Jovanovich, and General Learning Corp. It must be pointed out, however, that these notable failures have been in the area of CAI and not with computer-oriented texts and other "supplemental" computer-oriented curricula. The most notable market "success" has been *CompuGuide, Computer Augmented Accounting*, published by South-Western publishers. Some of the publishers currently involved in dissemination of computer-oriented curricular materials are listed in Appendix 2.

It is difficult to assess the results of these activities because the goals of each are different and usually implicit. The actual channels by which computer programs and materials for student use are moved from developer to user are varied and often informal. Few existing organizations carry out all dissemination functions needed to actually move a package from the hands of the developer to the hands of a using student in another institution.

The vast majority (perhaps 95 percent) of existing materials and computer applications to learning were developed by small projects at an individual institution and are used, if at all, only at that institution.

There is a small, but important, class of materials that have achieved fairly widespread recognition, at least within the discipline, and have been moved to a dozen or so universities. "Statistical Programs for the Social Sciences" (SPSS) is an example of such a package. (Such compelling examples, including SPSS, are described in Chapter 3 of this book.) Such cases of dissemination usually involve personal contact among the developer, his computer center, the receiving computer center, and faculty users at the adopting school.

In addition to the large class of home-grown, locally used materials and the smaller group of significant packages which have been transported to a dozen or so schools, there is a third, smaller class of more widely disseminated materials. The most successful of these has been *Computer Augmented Accounting*, which has been adopted by about 10 percent of U.S. colleges and universities. The most widely disseminated CAI package is probably Stanford elementary arithmetic, marketed by Computer Curriculum Corporation, which is being used in about 20 public school systems.

A more intangible result of the various dissemination activities has been the rapidly increasing *awareness* of computer applications to learning on the part of teachers and administrators. There have been no broad-based attempts to measure the nature and growth of this awareness, or what effect it has on actual educational practice.

Nor has there been any attempt to assess the *educational* results of disseminating computer-oriented curricula. Nearly all the studies which evaluate CAI do so on a micro level—that is, they evaluate the effectiveness or efficiency of the instruction within the context of the particular course of instruction involved. The effects on education in terms of such dimensions as programs of study, overall curricula, school organization, scheduling, grading, enrollment, staffing, overall learning environment, educational premises and goals, and so forth, have yet to receive serious investigation. Hence, it is difficult to assess the present or future educational results of disseminating computer-oriented curricular materials.

Obstacles to Dissemination and Adoption

Obstacles and barriers to widespread adoption of computer-based innovation in education have been analyzed and summarized in several studies. The summary of obstacles that follows is a synthesis of findings from studies by Anastasio and Morgan (1972), Carnegie Commission (1972), Denk (1971a), Levien (1972), Luskin (1970), Wilcox (1972), and Zinn (1970). These seven studies used different methods for arriving at their conclusions.

Joseph Denk cited obstacles relevant to his experiences at North Carolina Educational Computing Service (NCECS) using computers in education. Ernest Anastasio compiled barriers using the Delphi technique with experts in the field of CAI. Bernard Luskin's procedure included interviewing 127 individuals, with the final list being compiled by a three-panel jury—educators with CAI expertise, junior college administrators, and people in industry with an interest in CAI. Jarrod Wilcox gathered his data with a simplified Delphi questionnaire that was mailed to technologists and a broad sample of college faculty, librarians, and controllers. The obstacles cited from Levien, Zinn, and the Carnegie Commission were based upon expert opinion of those involved in these federally sponsored studies.

Adoption Obstacles

Materials. A major barrier to dissemination has been the lack of high quality, readily available materials (Anastasio and Morgan, 1972; Carnegie Commission, 1972; Levien, 1972). A related problem has been the absence of a variety of materials to offer a choice to the user in terms of pedagogical techniques, instructional strategies, and subject-matter content (Anastasio and Morgan, 1972; Levien, 1972).

Overlooked Materials. Developers direct their attention to the creation of new instructional uses of the computer that extend the ideas contained in the earlier versions of their works. The earlier versions are improperly considered obsolete (Denk, 1971a) since, in terms of educational value, the materials are significantly advanced over instructional materials in actual use.

Relationship of Materials to Curricula. The lack of standardized curriculum is a major obstacle to widespread adoption of individual packages (Luskin, 1970; Zinn, 1970). The traditional attitude of educators has been to oppose any standardization. This problem is acute for mainline instruction and to a lesser extent for supplemental materials, which in many cases are not easily integrated into curricula.

Documentation. The lack of clear, comprehensive documentation is a major obstacle to adoption (Denk, 1971a; Luskin, 1970). Developers have a notorious reputation for being poor documentors. Developers are creativity-oriented and generally look upon documentation as a distasteful and unnecessary chore.

Attitudes. The fear of role reduction by faculty has been a difficult obstacle to acceptance of mainline instruction systems in which the computer acts as a surrogate teacher (Anastasio, 1972; Carnegie Commission, 1972; Luskin, 1970; Wilcox, 1972). Another attitude often raised as a barrier to adopting computer-based instructional materials is the charge that computers dehumanize education. This attitude is considered a minor obstacle (Levien, 1972; Luskin, 1970; Wilcox, 1972). The attitude of administrators toward computers is an obstacle of some importance. Some administrators hold the view that computers are an add-on cost to be treated separately from the normal cost of school operation (library, student union, labs). The natural feelings of uncertainty that some faculty have toward the effectiveness of newly developed computer-based materials (Anastasio and Morgan, 1972) has also hindered their widespread use.

Skilled Personnel. A persistent problem of adoption has been the lack of skilled, technical support personnel to assist faculty implementation of computer-based instruction (Anastasio and Morgan, 1972; Carnegie Commission, 1972; Denk, 1971a; Levien, 1972, Luskin, 1970).

A companion problem has been the reluctance of computer centers to train faculty in the use of computer-based materials (Anastasio and Morgan, 1972; Denk, 1971a). Related is the obstacle concerning the shortage of skilled new recruits to satisfy the growing need for personnel (Levien, 1972).

Effectiveness Evidence. A current-day problem is the lack of a sufficient number of well-known examples of high-quality computer-based materials (Anastasio and Morgan, 1972; Carnegie Commission, 1972). A corollary obstacle is the insufficiency of evaluation measures to determine educational validity (Anastasio and Morgan, 1972; Carnegie Commission, 1972; Luskin, 1970).

Finally, there is the lack of evidence that computer-based materials are more effective than other materials (Anastasio and Morgan, 1972; Carnegie Commission, 1972; Wilcox, 1972). This argument is mainly applicable to mainline instruction in which effectiveness is an important factor, for example, individualized versus group instruction. The argument for supplementary computer use is usually made on the grounds of enhancement of curriculum rather than cost-effectiveness.

Cost. The high capital investment required to purchase a computer is an obstacle to their adoption, especially in public schools (Anastasio and Morgan, 1972; Luskin, 1970). Generally, CAI systems require a large capital investment (the terminals are a major portion of the cost) and have yet to reach the cost-effectiveness level that could justify the investment.

Dissemination Obstacles

Organization. There is currently no central exchange agency for computer-based materials (Anastasio and Morgan, 1972; Denk, 1971a; Zinn, 1970). While there are many clearinghouses that provide limited information about these materials, there is *no* national organization that today provides a total dissemination service (reproduction, publicity, technical transport, support, training, etc.).

Incentives. Because of the lack of royalties from commercial sales, and lack of professional prestige value, developers are not anxious to "push" dissemination (Anastasio and Morgan, 1972; Zinn, 1970).

Technical Transport. Necessary technical changes when computer programs are run on different manufacturers' machines are another barrier (Anastasio and Morgan, 1972; Carnegie Commission, 1972; Denk, 1971a; Levien, 1972; Luskin, 1970). There are incompatibilities between central computer systems and, in addition, materials designed to operate on one terminal type will not operate on another type without sizable modifications. These problems are usually compounded by lack of technical support information (Denk, 1971a; Zinn, 1970).

Selection. The "sifting" barrier concerns the problem of examining a large array of instructional materials to find materials suitable for educational use (Denk, 1971a). The individual user, after determining that particular computer-based materials will meet his particular course needs, finds, after installation, that they are unsuitable.

Commercial Outlets. The current programs are not sophisticated enough for traditional publishing organizations (Denk, 1971a). Materials do not provide information to reach teachers (Denk, 1971a) and are not integrated into a comprehensive package for a commercial offering. The commercial publishers have shied away from publishing materials without copyright protection (Anastasio and Morgan, 1972; Luskin, 1970; Zinn, 1970). This problem is accentuated by the fact that to date, most computer-based materials have been developed under government auspices, in which case issues of public domain and ownership rights arise.

Emerging Solutions

The barriers to dissemination sound formidable and therefore it would be logical to come to the conclusion that widespread national dissemination of computer-based materials is impossible, undesirable, or both. *The outlook is actually quite different. The emerging solutions indicate major breakthroughs to widespread dissemination, as discussed below.*

Technology

Several important technological developments are beginning to reduce certain obstacles (see Chapter 6 for further discussion of technology):

1. *Lower cost computer systems and components.* The development of reliable, low-cost terminals, mini-computers, and bulk storage (over the operating costs for computer-based curricula).

2. *Communications.* A number of breakthroughs in communications, including two-way cable TV and microwave and satellite transmission, provide the potential for a variety of networking arrangements that would reduce the technical barriers and costs of sharing computer-oriented curricula among institutions nationally.

3. *Networks.* A base of technical and organizational expertise in

networking has been built up, at least in higher education, with the regional and state academic computing networks, the ARPA net (Roberts, 1971), Michigan's MERIT network (Herzog, 1972), and the biomedical national network (The Lister Hill Center, 1972).

The regional networks provide built-in technical compatibility within the network user community.

Another method of obtaining technical compatibility is through the use of high-level programming language that eliminates many of the technical barriers to the exchange of programs.

Computing Literacy. The computing literacy of college-level student and faculty is increasing rapidly. Today's college student accepts the computer as part of academic life. The growing level of computing literacy has ameliorated barriers in attitude and the amount of technical support required. The computing literacy barrier is still severe at the public school level.

Demonstrated Commercial Profitability. Financial awards are possible. This message is just beginning to be felt, with the unqualified market success of the Pillsbury materials (see Chapter 3). Competing products also are emerging.

Novel Copyright Arrangements. The problems of ownership and copyright protection have not proved insurmountable. The government, developing organizations, and individual authors have been able to devise novel royalty-sharing arrangements (e.g., REACT, COMPUTe, Huntington Two).

New royalty arrangements can also aid in finding solutions to the lack of incentives problem, as exemplified by Project COMPUTe:

> It has been COMPUTe's intention from the start to uncover the market for computer-based materials in order to entice the commercial sector to commit front-end money in the form of royalty advances to support writing efforts. In the meantime, what incentive can we provide to potential authors to encourage them to spend the time necessary to document their experiences for the benefit of others? In the firm belief that money in the pocket is a far greater motivator to faculty than release time (which mostly benefits his institution), COMPUTe decided to offer summer salaries to participating faculty and to pay for housing for writers

and their families during their stay at Dartmouth. The icing on the cake, however, was provided by the National Science Foundation within the last few months in the form of an amendment to the terms of the grant. Briefly, COMPUTe now has authority to seek commercial publishers and distributors for these materials on a competitive basis and, concomitantly, to "enter into individual agreements with each author under which the author may receive a portion of the royalties received by the grantee up to a ceiling amount to be agreed to by the author and grantee." This, we feel, is a strong incentive to most authors to complete a writing task they have begun (Morton, from *ACM SIGCUE Bulletin*, October, 1972, p. 29).

New Documentation Techniques. Dissemination organizations have just begun to recognize that new approaches to obtaining well-documented computer programs are needed, and that there are alternatives to waiting for the professor-developer to document his work. Packaging can be expected to become a recognized function of exchange organizations. CONDUIT is developing documentation guidelines.

Marketing Strategies. Developers have become more sophisticated in their approaches to disseminating computer-based instructional materials. They have begun to show a deeper understanding of *who* must be reached with *what* kind of product (Stetten, 1972).

Computer Center Activity. Traditionally, computer centers have been more concerned with software/hardware problems and research applications than with the needs of student users. Many computer centers, however, have begun to take an active role in promoting and supporting educational uses of the computer (e.g., the CONDUIT Project).

New Organizational Forms. People active in educational computing have devised new organizational forms to overcome some of the dissemination barriers. Organizations are now being created that carry out many more of the functions necessary to disseminate materials (e.g., selection, publicity, packaging, training, technical transport, etc.).

Barriers Without Emerging Solutions. Professional recognition for creativity in applying the computer in educational environments has yet to be obtained. The professional recognition problem is critical to the future enrichment of computer-based education, since tenure, recognition, and incentives are interwoven.

Inadequate funding, both locally and from federal agencies, currently prohibits the adoption of computer-related learning resources in the public schools. The few schools that have developed or have access to computer resources do not maintain any budget for dissemination of their materials.

Surprisingly, none of the studies of obstacles singled out the lack of computing literacy on the part of educational decision-makers. Although this barrier is implied in the literature under categories such as "lack of skilled personnel," we feel that the impact of the obstacle is such that careful attention should be given to the issue of computing literacy for educators, especially the administrators who make decisions on adoption.

ADOPTION PROCESSES

The overall purpose of dissemination is to make it possible for someone to adopt the materials or systems in question. A major portion of dissemination activities is designed to provide the information and support an educator needs in order to decide on and plan for adoption of these materials and systems.

Although the subject of educational change and the adoption of innovations is of considerable national interest at present, this study did not uncover any reports or analyses that would be directly useful for understanding the adoption process for computer-based innovations (J.S. Hall, 1970; Schmuck, 1972; Woollatt, 1967). It seemed important, however, to learn more about the processes that school administrators, educational technologists and curriculum developers, computer support staff, and faculty might go through in making adoption decisions. To shed some light on this subject, several versions of a Decision Guide for the adopting of computer-based curricular materials were evolved (see Appendix 4).* The Guide contains fairly broad statements of considerations, such as:

---

*HumRRO. "Decision Guide and Considerations List for Planning and Adopting Computer-Oriented Curricular Innovations," presented at Annual National Educational Technology Conference, New York, N.Y., March, 1972, conducted by *Educational Technology* Magazine.

- What teacher support materials are included in the package?
- What support is available for implementing the materials?
- For what student population are the materials designed?

These general statements of considerations, and the example details, had been collected from hundreds of conversations, articles, papers, and books on computers in education. They reflected the interests and concerns primarily of those who have *developed* computer-based materials. The Guide, then, does not reflect an opinion as to what *should* be considered, but rather a "menu" of things that might be considered when adopting computer-based systems and materials.

The Guide was tried out in workshop settings on four separate occasions, with a total of about 100 educators—school administrators, educational technologists, teachers, state planners, computer center people, all with widely varying degrees of sophistication as regards computer-based materials.

This was not a formal study. The format of the Guide and the procedures of the workshop and the composition of the group changed with each workshop. Only the considerations questions and example details remained the same. *Therefore, the following subjective impressions and conclusions are stated quite tentatively and are intended to stimulate further inquiry*:

1. Each decision-maker is such a unique constellation of role interests, personal interests, background, and knowledge, that it is not possible to predict on the basis of his formal position what considerations are most important to him or how he will look for information.

2. Except for people who have been working directly in the field of computer-oriented materials, most participants had an extremely difficult time understanding the nature, purpose, and operation of a particular computer application to learning. Written descriptions, such as reprints of conference papers on the application, were not sufficient for the participants to gain an understanding of the application. A live, two-hour demonstration and discussion of IMPRESS, however, was comprehensible to most participants.

3. Many participants resisted or resented the idea of making an adoption decision on an individual package or system. They wanted to be able to compare or relate it to some alternative.

4. Most participants did *not* become enamored with the novelty,

gadgetry, or uniqueness of the computer application itself, but rather attempted, under the often adverse conditions of the workshop setting, to relate the innovation to a realistic educational problem or goal. In the shorter (two-hour) workshops, in fact, many participants never proceeded past the stage of defining the problem situation—and did not want to go on to consider the computer application until they felt satisfied that they knew what they wanted to accomplish.

5. Many participants were very unsure of the role they might have in making adoption decisions. One indication of this is that almost no one was willing to write "not applicable" in response to a considerations question, even though there appeared to be obvious and valid reasons why an individual decision-maker would regard some of the considerations as unimportant or as not in his province.

The reader may draw his own conclusions from these observations. One conclusion drawn is that the decision process in education is an obscure and murky process involving many human variables unique to an individual in a particular setting. This is particularly true with regard to adoption of an innovation which is only dimly understood by the decision-makers, and which is not clearly related to their particular problem situation.

One implication of this for dissemination strategies is that the strategy should be flexible, and allow for a range of individually tailored, personal contacts between "disseminator" and adopter.

A related conclusion drawn from this experience is that practice in developing and applying a considerations guide, such as this, would be a useful exercise as part of an educator computing literacy training program. As an aid to meeting such literacy needs of potential adopters of computer-based materials, the Decision Guide is included at the end of this book as Appendix 4.

Adoption Process for Individual Faculty

Although the adoption process for an institution or multi-institution group is complex and unique to the situation and type of materials, the majority of existing computer-oriented curricular materials are presently adopted by an individual teacher or professor for use in a course over which he has a fair degree of autonomous authority. Although he may have to obtain concurrence or support on the part of administrators and staff in his institution, the teacher has primary authority for the decision to adopt these materials. Important steps in faculty adoption might be described as follows:

1. *Awareness.* The teacher hears about a particular package or class of applications, usually from colleagues in his discipline.

2. *Motivation.* The teacher becomes convinced of the potential *educational value* of the application; he believes it is financially and technically *feasible* to use it in his environment; he learns that the materials are actually *available*; he actually or vicariously *samples* the learning experience, through demonstrations, conversations with colleagues, or perusing the materials and documentation.

3. *Education.* The teacher learns how to use the materials/programs—through documentation, workshops, training films, personal consultation with the developer, or trial-and-error tryout on his own. Although some degree of computing literacy on the part of the teacher is prerequisite throughout the adoption process, it is usually critical at this step. Some familiarity with computing, whether it consists of simple terminal operation or computer programming or operating systems, is nearly always required in order to complete this step.

4. *Decision.* Final decision on adoption of a program or package requires that several types of questions be answered, for example:
- How will I integrate this material into my course?
- Is required computer system and technical support available for implementation and operation of the programs?
- Are funds available for implementation and operation of the materials?
- What administrative requirements are there?

5. *Implementation.* This step involves acquisition of computer programs and text materials; getting programs operational; debugging or modifying programs; pilot tryout with students. It may involve acquisition of equipment (e.g., terminal), communications facilities (e.g., leased line to computer center), or software (e.g., language compiler). Existing dissemination mechanisms for computer-based curricula do not satisfy faculty adoption requirements for many reasons. At the awareness level, there are dozens of mechanisms—which is amply demonstrated in Appendix 2. Conferences, professional journals, user groups, and newsletters all provide information on the

existence of materials. A faculty member with a minimum of computing literacy can usually learn of the existence of materials and developers.

Motivation, Education, Decision, and Implementation steps are not well supported by existing mechanisms, except in a few cases. The next section of this chapter describes the dissemination functions and mechanisms that would have to exist on a national scale if the adoption process were to be supported adequately.

DISSEMINATION FUNCTIONS AND MECHANISMS

The term "dissemination" covers a broad spectrum of activities, beginning with selection of materials to be disseminated and either ending with operational use by students or continuing with revisions and improvements. In this section, nine basic dissemination functions are defined, and alternative mechanisms for accomplishing the functions are discussed. The function breakdown is:

1. *Planning a marketing strategy*. This function includes analysis of goals, target audience, dissemination resources, alternative mechanisms for each function, and establishment of mechanisms to carry out each function.
2. *Identification and selection* of materials to be disseminated. This function includes identification of user needs, solicitation of materials to satisfy the needs, and clarification of criteria for selection.
3. *Publicizing* materials through appropriate channels enables potential adopters to become aware of the materials and become motivated to learn about them.
4. *Packaging* materials involves arranging the content and format of all components of the materials into useful form.
5. *Demonstrating* materials, or in other ways enabling potential adopters to sample the learning experience, is more than a publicity function. It enables the decision-maker to learn about the materials or system and therefore be better qualified to evaluate it.
6. *Reproducing* materials involves physical production of the package and is more or less complex depending on package components, which may range from traditional texts to computer hardware and software.

7. *Distribution or delivery* of the package may be as simple as mailing a book or as complex as installing a computer system. "Delivery" of computer-oriented curricular materials may mean providing the users with access to the materials via a time-sharing system.
8. *Implementation support* functions include technical, administrative, and educational support, ranging from modifying a computer program to training faculty or designing a pilot test in the adopting school.
9. Financing the dissemination activities involves a host of considerations from federal funding to school budgets and copyright arrangements.

A discussion of existing and potential mechanisms for each of these functions is presented below.

Planning a Marketing Strategy

Many organizations currently involved in dissemination focus on only one or two specific services and functions. In many cases the strategy fails because all functions have not been planned for or cannot be carried out, since the strategy does not take into account real-world constraints.

The clearest example of this phenomenon in the past has been clearinghouses for dissemination of materials. Most of the materials listed in the clearinghouse catalogs are either not available or not packaged, supported, technically transportable, debugged, or usable as educational materials.

All too often, organizations have relied upon an implicit strategy for dissemination, with the assumption that their approach will be successful. For example, clearinghouses have depended upon author support for materials contained in the clearinghouse catalog. The fact of the matter is that authors have no incentive to spend time and energy to support the user.

An example of activities for which there is a successful implicit strategy is the series of conferences on Computers in Undergraduate Curricula (*Proceedings*, 1970, 1971, 1972). These conferences provide information for user awareness, motivation, and contact for followup on specific packages. This strategy concept—that materials are best described through personal contact with the developer—appears to work.

Levien (1972) presents an example of a planned, explicit strategy concept in the Rand study. A key aspect of this strategy involves libraries of instructional materials to be delivered by commercial time-sharing companies. Detailed plans for materials selection, arrangements with publishers, financing dissemination activities, and other dissemination functions should be made on the basis of the overall strategy concept.

In the next section of this chapter, the concept of strategies is discussed in further detail. Case studies of strategies are presented and proposed national strategies are described.

Selection of Materials to Be Disseminated

Who selects what for whom?

The "Who" may refer to a discipline expert, an educational technologist, an author, or an editor of a publishing firm. This individual sets the path as to "What" will be provided for "Whom."

The "What" may be, for example, information on computer-administered instruction programs, selected computer materials for a discipline, or a large instructional system.

The "Whom" may be any particular group of potential users—college physics students, little children, high school math teachers, or APL users. Table 4 shows some examples of Who-What-Whom.

A first step in selection is the search for candidate materials. A major difficulty encountered in such a search is to identify people with good materials. At present, there are no standardized procedures, or centers within an institution, for locating such materials. Consequently, survey forms are often sent to research centers, computer centers, department heads, faculty members, or routed through administrative personnel aware of the appropriate offices within their institutions.

A publisher selects materials according to the potential profitability in commercial returns. The Mitre Corporation did a market analysis in order to select the courses for development in TICCIT. The criterion was to reach a wide audience with course materials that would be significantly less expensive if offered via computer control. Ludwig Braun's Huntington Two project (Polytechnic Institute of Brooklyn,

Who Selects What for Whom

Name	Who Selects	What	For Whom
National Council of Teachers of Mathematics	Discipline experts	Annotated Bibliography on Computers in the Mathematics Classroom	Secondary School Mathematics Teachers
CONDUIT	Discipline experts	Packages of COCM for classroom use	Faculty and students within CONDUIT network
CACHE	Discipline experts	Selected programs currently used in chemical engineering classrooms	Chemical engineering students and faculty
Index to Computer Based Learning	Educational technologists	Information on existing CAI programs	Users and developers of CAI materials
APL User's Group	User group members	Programs written in the APL computer language	People using APL
Commercial Publishers	Editors	Materials with market potential	Established and potential clientele
Huntington Two	Participating classroom teachers	Adjunct materials for classroom use	High School teachers
DECUS	Users of DEC equipment	Materials developed for a particular computer	User of DEC machine
NCECS	Students and faculty in workshops and curriculum coordinator	Computer-oriented curricular materials	Faculty and students in NC network
SECOS	SECOS personnel	Materials in APL or Coursewriter that have an application for users	Member schools (SECOS network)

Table 4

1971) sponsored the development of a wide range of materials. Then in a pilot test of 100 schools using a standard questionnaire, teacher and student reactions on the value of particular modules determined those preferable for packaging and widespread dissemination. Joseph Denk at NCECS has a twofold approach to selection of materials. He pre-selects materials that are technically feasible on the available delivery system. He then test-markets the materials through workshops, with user (faculty and students) reactions determining those to be supported by NCECS. SECOS, which concentrates on having APL applications in its system, considers the technical feasibility of implementing materials on its computers as well as the potential of the materials for satisfying user needs. CONDUIT established committees of well-known faculty experts in a particular discipline to select from available materials a discipline-oriented package for transport to other schools.

Publicity

Publicity enables potential adopters to become aware of materials and motivated to learn about them. The types of information and the publicity channels needed depend on both the nature of the product and the situation of the adopter.

Of all existing dissemination activities, most have focused on publicity and information exchange. The publicized information often reaches only those that have already been involved in using the computer-oriented materials and are thus aware of channels for gathering information on them. This is the case in organizations such as ACM (see Appendix 2), with its special interest groups, or ADCIS. As current users, they exchange new ideas among themselves.

There are those who believe that publicity and information exchange should be the primary purpose of dissemination. The specific ideas and the spirit behind the innovations (and not curricular materials per se) are what are disseminated. Examples of this include Project SOLO, where the idea of having students develop their own materials and, in the process, computer expertise, is an end in itself.

David Engler* has pointed out the close relationship between the complexity of a product and the ability to sell it via written material.

*Conversation, January, 1972.

The more complex the product, the greater is the "need to provide human interaction and involvement in the information-providing process." He feels, therefore, that dissemination mechanisms for CAI must be human-based. Publicity becomes a matter not only of creating awareness, but educating the customer as well. The burden of providing computer literacy (an understanding of computer applications) for educator-customers falls on the dissemination organization.

Brochures are limited in their ability to provide evaluation and other types of pertinent data for decision-makers, such as where materials are currently being used. If an individual faculty member is the user, then the likely channels would be either discipline-based or a particular organization's user group (see Appendix 2 for a list of user groups). Discipline-based channels include conferences, professional societies and journals (Appendix 2 lists catalogues, summer institutes, workshops, and newsletters).

Conferences provide publicity for ideas and their specific applications, and opportunity for personal contacts, often with the developer of particular materials. Published conference proceedings provide further dissemination of the ideas and applications discussed.

Professional journals are potentially an excellent channel for the future dissemination of discipline-based information. Until recently, the use of a computer within a discipline was not considered a scholarly topic for publication in journals. Now, however, the *American Journal of Physics* has a column on the use of computers in Physics instruction. The column, edited by Donald L. Shirer of Valparaiso University, is called "Computer Notes," and describes computer assistance to learning in physics. Nearly every issue of the *Journal* now also has several articles on instructional users of computers in physics. Appendix 2 lists a sample of professional journals now publishing computer applications to education.

Project C-BE at the University of Texas published an advertisement in the *Journal of Chemical Education*, the purpose of which was to foster its goal of transferring computer techniques to other environments. The ad served to make the public aware of the programs and provided a means of "seeing" them without their physical transfer. By January 1973, 30 requests had been received, and each was answered with an introductory packet. Interested people can obtain free computer time from the University of Texas to sample the materials.

Catalogs are available to publicize descriptions of programs or modules and usually reach already interested people. The early catalogs often provided inadequate information to a potential user. CONDUIT has developed and is pilot testing a survey form that includes data on usage, operational costs, necessary support requirements, educational purpose, and evaluation test results.

Newsletters are another widely used mechanism for information exchange. University computer centers publish newsletters for their particular computing community, with information on new programs and technical matters such as new procedures for running jobs, and equipment changes. This information is rarely applicable outside the range of the center.

Other publicity mechanisms include workshops, seminars, and summer institutes. Dartmouth is holding summer institutes in educational computing. ENTELEK, CONDUIT, and manufacturers such as IBM also use this publicity mechanism.

An underlying requirement of the dissemination process is the need for computer literacy within the educational community. Without this, publicity falls upon uncomprehending ears. User education, therefore, is an overriding requirement that must either precede or parallel the publicity and demonstration activities. With only a meager number of grants awarded by the U.S. Office of Education and the National Science Foundation to educate educators about computers, and with the lack of any initiative on the part of schools of education, the burden has fallen on dissemination organizations.

Sales representatives from commercial organizations (such as publishers, computer manufacturers, and time-sharing companies), provide an important service by making their clients aware of the materials that are available.

Packaging

Packaging is a major contributor to the success or failure of the widespread use of materials. There are several reasons for packaging being a key issue in dissemination; the first is the radical difference between traditional texts and CBLM packages. Many more people are involved in the implementation of such a package—not only student users, but also teachers and computer center personnel. The wide range of support information needed for these groups increases the complexity of the packaging function. Documentation of computer programs in itself has long been a problem, but is only one component of an integrated package. Educationally, the more innovative the package, the more difficult it is to adapt the materials to existing curricula.

There are no standards for a comprehensive package of CBLM. A package may vary in form and content according to the kind of materials, the type of user, and whether it is being packaged for local or widespread dissemination.

A package may contain different items for the varied personnel involved in the implementation and management of the computer materials. Such a combination might include teacher guides or teacher training manuals, proctor guides, student problem sets, tests that address the subject matter, program documentation for technical transport, sample program runs and listings, hardware and software specification, descriptions of the program concepts, or actual hardware.

The potential contents listed above can be packaged in a wide array of forms, including hardbound books, films, program listings, card deck, magnetic tape, etc. The formats of these items influence development cost, cost to user, and nature of the environment in which the materials are to be used (Grobman, 1970). Books may be hardbound or softcover, expendable or permanent, films on 16mm, with or without sound, color, etc. These descriptions do not answer the question of what is an integrated package. For any specific materials, an integrated package would provide the necessary implementation and support information for students, teacher/managers, administrators, and technical personnel.

It is difficult for an individual faculty member to develop an integrated package. His computer program, even if well-documented, does not provide technical, student, and teacher support. In the present state of affairs the individual faculty member has no incentives to document and package his materials for others. A viable dissemination strategy should not depend on individual professor-developers for documentation packaging.

Project COMPUTe at Dartmouth, funded by NSF (see Chapter 4) is aiding individual faculty authors to develop and package the materials for publishing. COMPUTe assistance includes standards and guidelines, salary and travel reimbursements, housing, computer time, a portable terminal, editorial and secretarial assistance, and programming support.

Technical considerations enter into packaging. Materials may be packaged to be more technically adaptable; for example, programming in BASIC rather than ALGOL language. System-dependent subroutines can be identified. A package can make the "bits and bytes" of the program either opaque or transparent to the user, and thus easier or harder to install and run.

Demonstration

"The potential user has to be able to sample the product. In the case of a book, he looks at it and leafs through it. You have to give him a chance to apply his own criteria to evaluate the product. The more complex the product, the harder it is to provide a sample for him to evaluate. Demonstrations and validation data are required in order to provide a sample of information on an educational system as opposed to a textbook or a film. In the case of an educational system, the people have to be able to sample it in some way in their own shop." These comments on production demonstration, by David Engler,* point out the uniqueness of this dissemination function when it is related to computer-oriented materials. Using computer materials can so drastically change a learning environment that a potential user needs to sample, if only vicariously, the new learning experiences in an appropriate setting.

Possible means for sampling materials would include remote access via telephone, portable terminals, or a visit to a center where the materials are running.

At conferences and workshops the materials and the associated learning experiences can also be sampled and manipulated by faculty, peers, and other decision-makers. Videotapes, films, and closed circuit television offer means of experiencing a learning environment—a demonstration of the materials or students using the materials.

*Conversation, January, 1972.

Demonstration schools and projects allow a prospective user to sample not only the materials, but the learning experiences and environment as well.

Reproduction

The reproduction or copying of instructional materials may be as simple as arranging for printing production or as complex as replicating hardware and software. In the case of the former, the printing of instructional materials poses no problem unless this function is left to the author, who is not geared to handle this type of operation. In the latter situation, considerable thought must be given as to how the hardware and software will be assembled, tested, and maintained at remote sites. The Computer Curriculum Corporation has this task so refined that an entire instructional system (both hardware and courseware) can be made operational in only two or three days. The hardware system is specifically designed for simple maintenance procedures* and the reliability is such that maintenance is seldom needed.

Distribution of Educational Programs

The means of distributing educational programs from developing institutions to other sites have included physical transport of programs; communications networks; moving the entire delivery system; and replication of a total system. The distribution problem has received a great deal of publicity because of the concern about the incompatibility of computer systems. The Anastasio and Morgan (1972) findings rank incompatibility as a "moderately" important obstacle. Coupled with lack of skilled support personnel and program documentation, this obstacle becomes more critical.

Programs can be physically transported (in forms such as card decks, magnetic tapes, disks, program listings, and specifications) and implemented on the user's system.

The physical transportability of educational computer programs is determined by a number of factors:

---

*Although maintenance per se is not a reproduction function, it is mentioned here in the interest of completeness of thought.

Achieving More Widespread Benefit from Computer-Based Learning Materials   235

- the programming language in which the programs are written;
- the complexity of the instructional program logic;
- the type of terminal required by the program;
- the quality of program documentation;
- the use of predefined (canned) subroutines;
- the core requirements;
- the type of program—that is, interactive or batch; and
- number of system-dependent subroutines used.

The physical transportation of complete instructional programs may be, in some instances, the most convenient and inexpensive means of moving programs between computer environments, depending upon the characteristics of the instructional materials and their implementation.

Ludwig Braun, the developer of the Huntington Two computer program simulations, wished to reach the widest possible educational audience. He designed the simulation programs to operate with the BASIC language, a teletype terminal, and a paper tape reader. The Huntington Two Project chose a least-common-denominator configuration, normally found on almost every educational mini-computer installation, including an effort to use BASIC language features universally available. In other cases, the instructional materials must be *converted* to the receiving institution's computer environment. This may require reprogramming and, in some cases, partial redesign.

The key to unlocking the physical barriers (incompatible computer environments) is good documentation. The successful technical implementation of Wilbur Pillsbury's accounting materials in a wide range of computer environments can be credited largely to good, complete documentation.

Not all instructional materials move easily by means of physical transport. Joseph Denk, when importing IMPRESS from Dartmouth, found it necessary to rewrite all the programs. In this case, the only thing that was transported was the developer's pedagogy (Denk, 1972).

There are differences in computing environments; this is a major barrier to transport for some materials. Some schools use an *interactive* process while others use *batch*. In many cases, the instructional pedagogy is based upon the student-computer dialogue. While it may be technically feasible to convert an *interactive* to a *batch* program, key pedagogical elements may be lost.

Access to programs can be made available via communication networks.

Networking avoids many *technical* constraints of physically transporting computer programs. An educational user can access the materials through a *physical* connection between the host computer and the remote user.

The primary limiting factor to distributing instructional programs through a network is economic. This method must be compared with other methods of distributing instructional programs as well as other methods of instruction. The distribution/delivery costs include data communication costs, network management costs, terminal rental, and computer costs.

When these costs are combined, they amount to more than most institutions are willing to pay per instructional hour. Federal subsidies will be necessary until these costs are reduced through large-scale implementation.

Another factor in the use of networks is terminal compatibility. For example, the University of Illinois has a wide range of instructional materials that have been designed to use the unique features of the PLATO IV terminals. While terminal incompatibilities can be overcome, this adds another dimension of difficulty.

The delivery system itself (including the programs) can be transported to the user site.

This approach to distribution is attractive for special situations. The Pennsylvania State University CAI Laboratory developed a mobile delivery system to provide training for teachers in remote rural areas, as noted earlier in this book. The main drawback is that the mobile vans require individual design, since there is no mass production. Costs will remain high unless a large-scale program is instituted.

The total computer system (including hardware, software, and instructional programs) is replicated at each user site.

This is a turnkey approach, in which a total instructional system is furnished to the user, to be utilized without alternation. Patrick Suppes has pioneered this method of distributing CAI material. The method eliminates the data communications cost element of a network distribution approach. It also simplifies technical complexities that are inherent to a large network. The TICCIT experiment is using a similar approach to distribute CAI instruction at the junior college level. The primary advantage to the total system approach, aside from overcoming technical program transport problems, is that the total system is optimized for efficient performance with the particular type of programs and terminals involved. General purpose software is avoided.

This approach may prove highly advantageous where the following conditions hold:
- The instructional materials satisfy a recognized learning need by many students throughout the country, and therefore system development costs can be amortized over many installations.
- The instructional materials themselves are flexible enough to be used by many different students without program alteration. TICCIT programs, for example, incorporate "student control options" intended to provide this flexibility.
- The total system demonstrates a clear-cut cost or performance advantage over alternative instruction—enough to outweigh the disadvantages of a computer system tailored to a specific application.

Technical and Educational Implementation Support

The technical implementation support required depends on the type of materials, type of distribution, and the user's need for support. Included are activities such as assistance in acquiring access to a machine, program debug, conversion, or implementation, communications support, terminal operations and maintenance, and program language training for faculty.

Technical implementation support is usually provided through institutional computer centers which are primarily operations-oriented. Neither their personnel nor those of the computer manufacturer are trained to support discipline-oriented materials, or to provide education in computing literacy for users. Exceptions to this include Digital Equipment Corporation and Hewlett-Packard, who have designed hardware systems specifically for the educational market. (IBM used to have one also, the 1500 System.)

In some computer centers, a "curriculum coordinator" provides technical support for instructional applications. In many cases, students provide these services. Curriculum coordinators are people within a regional computer center who have the explicit mission of interfacing with operations personnel, programmers, faculty users, and subject-matter experts. Their role is to facilitate the technical transport of discipline-oriented packages. They also may host a national workshop with faculty from other networks, to introduce and practice with the materials for future use in the classroom.

In both Project DELTA and SECOS, Inc., student volunteers implement materials. DELTA has a student-staffed systems group for system maintenance, and contact students (one in each school) to interface between the school and DELTA. The high school students traveled to Dartmouth to acquire a subset of IMPRESS, which they implemented on the DELTA computer.* At SECOS, the student volunteers program two-thirds of the time for SECOS and are given a third of their working hours to use the system for their own pleasure.

Joseph Denk at NCECS uses "circuit riders" as technical support personnel who travel between the schools in the network. Commercial organizations can provide field representatives to their clientele. Other technical assistance can be in the form of packaged instructions, phone consultations with developers and other users, or workshop practice.

With all the attention on technical matters, the educational side of implementation has often been overlooked or underemphasized. Many of the materials themselves were designed in a research effort, and must be revised for educational use and curricular applicability. The nature of the teacher role and the classroom environment often change with their adoption and implementation. Educational users must be supported as they adapt to the new nature of role and environment.

After selling a package, McGraw-Hill selects enthusiastic teachers and trains them as regional consultants to support other educators. Expensive support personnel are avoided in South-Western Publishing Company's marketing strategy of *CompuGuide*. Only one interested faculty member is allowed to implement the materials the first year.

*Telephone conversation with Teresa Green, Project DELTA, University of Delaware, Newark, Delaware, July 24, 1974.

This individual is provided with personal attention as well as a comprehensive package. This innovator then supports his colleagues when they are ready to use *CompuGuide*.

Time Share, Inc. is training the current Houghton Mifflin marketing representatives to provide some support to current clientele if they indicate interest in the Guidance Information System, which is being marketed by Houghton Mifflin. In the area of computer materials, where such a large proportion of a commercial organization's overhead is being spent for customer education, reluctance to enter the field is understandable.

Computer centers in general have been slow to perceive that need and to allocate funds to hire educational support personnel. However, a number of centers have for some time maintained joint appointments with various departments or schools to serve the interface role. The Carnegie Commission recommends that colleges and universities add qualified technologists and specialists to instructional faculty staffs (Carnegie Commission on Higher Education, 1972). One of the products expected from the CONDUIT experiment is a documented description of roles, tasks, and skills required of curriculum coordinators. It is very unusual to find individuals who have both the necessary computer technical capability and enough depth in the disciplines to provide educational as well as technical support.

Grobman discusses several approaches to teacher training. For relatively short projects the only practical kind of orientation might be a teacher manual or training film. Other materials may require an organized kind of course work activity. These may include inservice institutes, workshops, open-circuit television, and briefing sessions (Grobman, 1970).

CONDUIT is exploring the value of workshops for training with computer materials. Follow-up evaluations will determine if participants feel that face-to-face contact is a much-preferred alternative strategy.

The Center for Research in College Instruction of Science and Mathematics (CRICISAM) had a newsletter describing experiences, problems, and quotations from users, in order to establish communication links between the teachers using the materials.

The Carnegie Commission (1972), recognizing the current need for educational support when using innovative technologies, recommends the incorporation of this training into the curricula of schools of education.

Financing Dissemination Activities

Commercial publishers, traditionally, have been the primary disseminators of instructional materials. Profit has provided the motivation for the large investment required for widespread dissemination of these materials.

The commercial publishers derive their incomes from selling text materials, and have serious reservations about the feasibility of selling instructional materials that are in the form of computer programs or data bases.

With a few exceptions, commercial publishers are not equipped to provide technical or educational implementation support for instructional computer programs. Further, the cost of educating potential users in the nature of computers and related materials entails an abnormally high investment in marketing activities relative to more traditional materials.

Harcourt Brace Jovanovich recently abandoned the marketing of CAI materials. A recent private survey of commercial publishers reveals that the commercial publishers do not perceive that a commercially viable market for CAI materials will exist before the mid 1980's. (The survey explicitly did not include computer-*oriented* texts and the like.) Only one "traditional" publisher attended the bidder's conference for the Huntington Two materials—the others were a new educational firm and a hardware manufacturer.

It is clear, then, that a commercially viable market for most computer-based instructional materials cannot exist under these current conditions:
- lack of computing literacy of potential users;
- lack of technical support capabilities within present commercial publisher organizations;
- lack of commercial organizations for distributing instructional programs with the knowledge of educational applications and understanding of the market; and
- lack of sophistication on the part of materials developers as

to arrangements for rights and royalties; lack of experience on part of publishers in working out complex contractual agreements which do not fit the single-author model.

A further complexity surrounding the commercial role in CBLM is the fact that the federal government is involved in development of the materials. Commercial publishers must have exclusive rights to distribution in order to protect their investment in packaging, reproduction, and distribution. In the past, explicit contractual arrangements were rarely made in advance as to ownership, rights, and royalties on materials and programs. These are difficult to arrange after the fact.

In the past, one way of coping with this problem was to prepare an essentially unusable draft version of materials for public domain, with a reworked version being published commercially. This arrangement has not required any special negotiations with sponsors.

The U.S. Office of Education and the National Science Foundation have recently taken more positive action to encourage dissemination of curriculum products.

The Biological Sciences Curriculum Study (BSCS) has an arrangement with NSF whereby some of the royalties are returned to a special project fund for further development and modifications (Grobman, 1970).

The U.S. Office of Education and the Northwest Regional Education Laboratory made an arrangement for the REACT materials in which Technica Education Corporation would have exclusive rights for distribution for a period of five years. A portion of the royalties is placed in escrow, to be used in future revision and update.

In the case of the Huntington Two Project, agreements were made with NSF to have DEC publish and market the materials packages exclusively and return royalties to the State University of New York (holder of the contract with NSF) to use for continuing work on the grant.

NSF has recently amended the PROJECT COMPUTe grant to provide further incentives with new royalty arrangements.

Commercial publishers are gaining new awareness of the potential of computer-based instructional materials for capturing a significant share of the market. The commercial publishers are beginning to recognize the emergence of an important new market for text materials (textbooks, workbooks, manuals, code books, etc.) to accompany instructional computer programs.

For the present it is clear that federal support is required to finance many dissemination activities until the commercial marketplace is firmly established. As the financial incentives become apparent, the commercial organizations will rapidly take over individual functions performed by government-sponsored organizations. Commercial publishers will take over the packaging, publicity, and distribution of instructional text materials. Hardware manufacturers and time-sharing companies will take over the delivery and implementation support of the accompanying computer programs.

GOALS AND STRATEGIES

It should be clear from the preceding sections that there are a variety of existing and possible mechanisms for dissemination. It should also be clear, however, that no one mechanism in itself is sufficient to get curricular materials from developer to students. In order to achieve widespread availability and adoption of materials, *coherent strategies* that take into account all dissemination functions are needed.

What Is a Coherent Strategy for Dissemination?

In order to successfully move computer-oriented curricular materials from developer to student users, all the dissemination functions discussed in the previous section must be accounted for. The way in which these functions are performed depends upon the type of materials, the potential user population, and the purposes and resources of those who take responsibility for dissemination. The phrase "coherent strategy" is used to denote a plan for dissemination that is coherent in the following ways:
- all the basic functions are planned for;
- the mechanisms and activities planned for accomplishing the functions, are appropriate for the particular individuals and institutions that may be adopting the materials;
- the mechanisms and activities planned are appropriate for the particular type of materials being disseminated; and
- the plan is consonant with the particular educational

purposes of the developer, the disseminator, and the users.

Table 5 sketches the main features of some existing dissemination strategies. Consider, for example, Computer Aids for Chemical Engineering (CACHE) with a goal of enhancing chemical engineering curricula through computer materials and programs.

Consistent with this goal is the *selection* process for materials, which is performed by a committee of recognized experts in the discipline. The *packaging* approach, again consistent with the goals, is to organize the computer problems and programs into several volumes corresponding to topic sequences typical of chemical engineering curricula. *Publicity* channels used are those appropriate to the adopting audience, namely chemical engineering faculty, through professional society meetings and direct mail to the faculty. *Distribution* is accomplished through direct mail of the printed volumes (which include program listings) to chemical engineering faculty. *Delivery* assumes availability of suitable computer facilities at adopting institutions. *Implementation* support is provided indirectly through the standards of programming and documentation required of each application. Educational implementation support is minimal and provided mainly through packaging. Financing of the dissemination activities is provided by the National Science Foundation and the National Academy of Engineering Commission on Education.

In the case of Mitre-TICCIT, on the other hand, the general goal is to provide more cost-effective education through computer-based systems. A more specific goal for the community college TICCIT system is to catalyze the commercial market for such systems. The manner in which dissemination functions are carried out reflects these goals. *Selection* of curricular materials is performed by the developer on the basis of a market analysis, and materials are developed in accordance with this analysis of national needs for curricula and the potential market for the materials. *Packaging* is comprehensive, because the total system must be cost-effective in order for the strategy to work. In this case, the package includes not only computer-based courses of instruction (mainline CAI), but also the computer hardware and software required to implement the instruction. *Publicity* involves large-scale, high-visibility pilot demonstrations of the system, and extensive documentation of evaluative information regarding costs and

Examples of Existing Dissemination Strategies

Package	Identification/ Selection	Potential Market	Packaging	Publicizing	Demonstrating	Reproducing	Delivery Distribution	Implementation/ Support	Financing
Guidance Information System Time Share Corporation Hanover, N.H.		All high schools and junior colleges.	Entire system includes: teletypewriter terminal; installation and service for terminal; four data banks software specific no. hours of computer time preliminary study books instruction manual	TSC Application Bulletin Academic computing Bulletin Houghton Mifflin brochures, reps. Seminars and classes for educators provided by company	Reps give live demos		Via time-sharing terminal	Included in the package—little support required	User schools' budgets
TICCIT Mitre Corporation McLean, Va.	Market study (for wide audience cost-effectiveness by computer)	Potential market is all junior colleges. Marketing aimed at administrators	Total package includes: Hardware (2 minis, 128 terminals) Software 4 complete courses Equipment maintenance	Mitre Corp. documents for public distribution Conference proceedings NSF news bulletins Educational media, e.g., journals	Mini-demo at Mitre full-scale demo at 2 community colleges	Total system reproduction	2 mini-computers time-shared, 128 terminals Dedicated system serving one institution	Tailored to individual institutions requirements	NSF (seed money from Mitre)

Table 5

Table 5 (continued)

Package	Identification/ Selection	Potential Market	Packaging	Publicizing	Demonstrating	Reproducing	Delivery Distribution	Implementation/ Support	Financing
Elementary Reading (decoding) and Mathematics Computer Curriculum Corporation Palo Alto, California	Developer (Institute for Mathematical Studies in the Social Sciences)	All elementary schools Administrators	Alternate levels (according to what is purchased by the user): a. program documentation b. programs c. computer and programs	Published books Teacher journals *Index to Computer Based Learning*	Potential users visit user schools	CCC—fabricates hardware	Via CCC computer or user can implement programs on his own computer	Provided by CCC consultants in technical, administrative, and instructional areas Manufacturer will support program implementation 2-day teacher training free	CCC overhead User pays per terminal or per course per terminal
CompuGuide Accounting Workbook Published by South-Western Publishing Co., Cincinnati, Ohio	Selected by Publisher on basis of profit potential and pilot tests at several schools	Introductory Accounting professors; All introductory Accounting	Computer program documentation *CompuGuide* workbooks Instructor manuals Computer Center personnel manual Computer Programs	Publisher brochures, reps	Documentation Satisfies need to sample product	South-Western Publishing facilities	Tapes provided by publisher user, installs on his own computer	Included in package complete program documentation	Royalties on workbooks, pay for workbooks, get computer tapes free

(Continued)

Table 5 (continued)

Package	Identification/ Selection	Potential Market	Packaging	Publicizing	Demonstrating	Reproducing	Delivery Distribution	Implementation/ Support	Financing
NCECS Programs Reseach Triangle, North Carolina	Users at workshops, Test marketing with faculty and students	Service for NCECS customers only (50 N.C. institutions)	Computer-program and minimum documentation by a user	ECS Newsletter PALS Catalog, Direct mail to users	Faculty and students at workshops		Programs delivered via NCECS regional computing network	Provided by circuit riders in technical areas	N.C. State Board of Education
Huntington Two Programs Ludwig Braun Polytechnic Institute of Brooklyn Published by Digital Equipment Corporation (DEC)	Users in large-scale pilot test	Teachers and school administrators of any secondary school by DEC marketing reps	Teacher Guide Student Guide Resource manual on subject Paper tape in BASIC	DECUS users' group DECUS newsletter Large pilot test (100 schools national)		DEC publishing division	Program on paper tape in BASIC sold with package, user implements on his own machine	Provided by DEC reps in area	DEC overhead
CACHE Computer Aids for Chemical Engineering Education Commission on Education National Academy of Engineering Washington, D.C.	Professional Society Committee Selected from programs submitted by C.E. Professors	All chemical engineering faculty in U.S.	Program listings (7 volumes in FORTRAN) and standardized documentation organized in curricular sequence	Professional society meetings Newsletter, Direct mail to users			Printed volumes by mail	CACHE designed documentation standards	NSF

(Continued)

Table 5 (continued)

Package	Identification/ Selection	Potential Market	Packaging	Publicizing	Demonstrating	Reproducing	Delivery Distribution	Implementation/ Support	Financing
Sample CONDUIT package: COEXIST University of Iowa, Iowa City, Iowa	Committee of discipline experts	Faculty at network schools	Workbooks by discipline committee Documentation by CONDUIT Center	CONDUIT newsletter sent to potential faculty through curriculum coordinator at their own network Phone calls to potential faculty	User faculty at workshop	At receiving network	Each network uses its own delivery system, packages distributed through CONDUIT programmers at each network convert programs	Implementation at each network Curriculum coordinator interfaces between computer center faculty user Programmer developer Workshops for faculty for technical and educational support	NSF all computing time to faculty is free. CC salary paid by CONDUIT

effectiveness of the system in the pilot implementation. *User sampling* of the system will be provided through site visits to the demonstration schools. *Distribution* of the materials involves installation of the total system on a campus. *Implementation support* will be extensive and tailored to the needs of the individual adopting institution. *Financing* of dissemination activities is provided initially by NSF but eventually should be supported through sales of the system.

Strategy Case Studies

Three case studies of dissemination strategies are presented below. The purposes are, first, to further illustrate the concept of "coherent strategies," and second, to suggest these (or aspects of them) as potential models of national dissemination computer-oriented educational materials and systems. The cases are:
 (1) South-Western Publishing and Computer Augmented Accounting
 (2) North Carolina Educational Computing Service
 (3) Houghton Mifflin and Time Share Corporation

South-Western Publishing Company and Computer Augmented Accounting

The purpose of the developer of *CAA*, Wilbur Pillsbury, was to improve accounting curricula in a variety of ways with the computer support package. The goal of South-Western was to make a profit on the package through market success. The package was selected by South-Western primarily on the basis of its success during pilot tests of the material at several colleges (see development stories, Chapter 4). The materials came to the attention of South-Western through a field representative of the company who was servicing one of the pilot schools. The marketing strategy for *CAA* was based on the traditional textbook model used by South-Western. The potential market included all introductory accounting classes in institutions of higher education. Information on the *CAA* package is disseminated to accounting faculty through South-Western's regular channels: brochures, catalogs, and field representatives. The package includes a series of softbound *Compu-Guides*, instructor manuals, computer center personnel manual, and a package of 80 FORTRAN IV programs for use on a range of computers. The potential user appears not to need a live demonstration of the computer programs in order to sample the materials. Examination of the teachers' manual, student booklets, and publicity information is sufficient in most cases to sample the materials. The package is distributed in the traditional textbook manner, with the following exception: South-Western provides, at cost of reproduction, program card deck or tape in FORTRAN for the IBM 1130. Institutions with a different type of computer either convert the program to their own machine or obtain converted programs from another institution with a similar machine. Technical implementation of the programs is easily handled by any computer center. The programs are extremely well documented. South-Western's only involvement in technical implementation is to provide contacts with other institutions who have converted the programs to a computer configuration comparable to the adopting institution's machine. *CAA* has now been implemented on nearly every major manufacturer's equipment.

The mechanism for educational implementation support is highly effective, yet does not require a costly or time-consuming investment on the part of South-Western. The mechanism, designed by Pillsbury, involves controlled marketing and implementation. Each new adopting institution conducts a one-year pilot classroom implementation of *CAA*, with one or two highly interested and innovative faculty in the department. The technical, logistical, and classroom implementation of the *CAA* approach is thus worked out on a small scale by the faculty who are best able to experiment. Their implementation thus becomes a model for the rest of the department, and the innovators provide consulting and guidance to the remaining faculty, in a manner appropriate to the particular institution's needs.

The cost to South-Western of marketing *CAA* is comparable to the cost of marketing any of their traditional products (textbooks) and is paid for through sales of the package.

The success of *CAA* is reflected in the fact that South-Western is preparing to market other packages similar to the *CAA* model. Other publishers are preparing competitive packages.

North Carolina Educational Computing Service (NCECS)

NCECS is a nonprofit agency sponsored by the General Administration of the University of North Carolina and supported by the State of North Carolina. This agency provides computing service to 42 institutions of higher education, 23 of them technical institutes and community colleges as well as to 10 high schools, through the Triangle Universities Computation Center (TUCC) network. The unique dissemination strategy for computer-oriented curriculum materials was set up by Joseph R. Denk, the Curriculum Development Manager. Almost totally user-oriented, the strategy involved over 1,500 faculty from over 75 institutions of higher education in North Carolina.

Before this strategy is analyzed, certain significant characteristics of NCECS, which make such a strategy possible, should be made clear.

NCECS is organizationally independent of the institutions it serves. This has been the case for the entire seven years of the network's history and has enabled experimentation and innovation in ways that would be impossible within traditional controls. Freedom in the selection of subject matter and introduction of interdisciplinary materials is therefore possible. Vital to the dissemination strategy were the unique skills and discipline background of Denk himself, all of which made it easier to relate to the human needs of the target population in the regional network.

The following outlines salient aspects of the way in which each dissemination function is carried out in NCECS.

The educational goals of NCECS are to provide computing opportunity and an undergraduate applications library to the faculty and students of the institutions served. The materials are preselected from what is available nationally, mostly by Dr. Denk, but with the significant aid of faculty members funded to aid NCECS in its library construction. Since no national clearinghouse activity for such materials existed during the execution of the NCECS model, this process was random. A sifting activity was then employed to market what materials seemed to be the most educationally promising. This sifting was for the most part done by Denk with some consultation from funded faculty. Sifting also was dependent on what could be made operational under reasonable cost and time considerations. Both marketing and a further selection of materials was accomplished through workshops in which user acceptance was tested. In 3½ years, 45 workshops were run to elicit indicators of acceptance of materials from attending faculty and students. These workshops (usually two days) involved 1,500 faculty and students. Preparation for workshops involved NCECS staff efforts and over 40 funded projects involving faculty in selecting materials (or designing new materials), getting the materials operational, and training faculty in the workshops. While the NCECS staff was responsible for the majority of the materials involved, the review process by the funded faculty was significant.

Packaging by NCECS was done only for a selected few materials with higher promise. For the most part, the original documentation was preserved as far as possible. Publicizing curricular materials was accomplished through workshops, newsletters, and through a current awareness journal, Program and Literature Service (PALS) (Denk 1971b). The large number of materials collected were selectively put under limited support and finally full support through the final sifting process involving the workshops. Programs in PALS are categorized into three levels: IC—no support, IB—low support, and IA—full support. Final sifting to IA represents a library entry as supported by some degree of faculty interest. Section II of PALS, Literature, attempts to correlate descriptions of relevant implementation techniques with the programs in Section 1.

Because of its regional orientation, NCECS can also take advantage of existing local channels of information such as regional meetings of professional societies and student clubs.

Distribution/Delivery of curricular materials and computer programs is provided through the Triangle Universities Computer Center (TUCC), a regional computing network. Clearly, this relationship with the computer delivery system has been a critical element in the success of ECS dissemination of curricular materials.

Demonstration and Implementation support performed in a complex manner. Workshops are not only statewide but are also run regionally and at single institutions through a "circuit-rider" function. These functions cover technical aspects of computing and curriculum materials. Further, WATS-line telephone service makes three experts in the supported curriculum materials available free by phone at all times. Users are notified that they can request a regional workshop of their own design.

Such support takes a staff of 12. Financing such curriculum-oriented service is unusual. After three years of NSF funding, the Legislature of North Carolina voted in support of such a centralized support function. The activity could not have been self-supporting at the current state-of-the-art. Computer centers could not justify this support without a return on cost.

By this strategy, NCECS collected over 2,000 program packages, 1,000 of which are listed in PALS. Of the 381 entities in full support, IA, 320 have found some kind of classroom usage. Almost all of these 320 entities have no proof of supplying educational validity but have indicators of faculty interest and support.

The Houghton Mifflin Company-
Time Share Arrangement

Time Share Corporation is a commercial time-sharing company established in 1966 for the primary purpose of serving educational computing needs. Time Share currently provides low cost time-sharing services to about 120 high schools in the Northeastern United States. A major product is an interactive guidance information system for two- and four-year college and occupational information.

Because the lack of available computer-oriented curricular materials is a major obstacle to instructional computing, Charles Morrissey, Vice President of Time Share, felt it was essential to get commercial publishers involved in computer-oriented materials. His efforts were successful, in mid-1971, in establishing a joint working agreement between Time Share and Houghton Mifflin Company and the sale of nine percent of Time Share stock to Houghton Mifflin. The Senior Vice President of Houghton Mifflin is on the Board of Directors of Time Share.

The dissemination strategy which is emerging from this relationship promises to be beneficial both to the field of educational computing and to the corporations involved.

The purposes of both companies are to establish a viable market for computing services and educational materials, and to realize a profit on these services and materials. Both Time Share and Houghton Mifflin seek out text materials and programs through the personal contacts of their field representatives at educational institutions. In addition, authors of computer-oriented text materials seek out Houghton

Mifflin's interest. Time Share provides the expertise to evaluate materials from a technical standpoint—both in terms of the accuracy and appropriateness of the technical content and in terms of feasibility of implementing and operating the materials in a variety of schools and on a variety of computer systems. Houghton Mifflin evaluates materials on the basis of editorial, packaging and support requirements and potential market and profitability. Both companies provide publicity mechanisms. Houghton Mifflin, of course, has the traditional publisher mechanisms of brochures, catalogs, and personal contact of field representatives. Because Houghton Mifflin has a substantial interest in guidance and testing, their field representatives provide an excellent mechanism for publicizing the Time Share Guidance Information System.

Time Share publishes an "Academic Computing Bulletin" for its client schools, which publicizes new products and curricular materials, including those published by Houghton Mifflin. Time Share provides a lecture service for state and regional educational societies and meetings. In addition, the informal channels of communication among administrators of school districts help to publicize Time Share's services among user and potential user schools. Packaging can take a variety of forms, depending on the product. Houghton Mifflin publishes self-contained textbooks. An example is a Guidance Information System which consists of the computerized data bank of occupational and college information, an interactive search and retrieval program operating on Time Share's system, and user instruction booklets. Time Share issues updates and modifications to the guidance file about four times a year.

Access to the Guidance Information System and other products like it is provided to the user in several ways. In one instance, the user may lease a line to the Time Share computer center, in which case he has unlimited use of the system and all programs in the Time Share library.

Time Share computer facilities include nine Hewlett Packard 2000's, which provide the low-cost, time-sharing capability required for school applications. The primary language used is BASIC, and most instructional programs are written in BASIC.

For users who have their own computer system or wish to use another time-sharing service, Time Share will rent the package for implementation on that computer system.

Little implementation support is required in the case of a package being used directly from Time Share's system. Time Share provides field representatives and telephone consultations for matters concerning terminal operations, communications, etc. Houghton Mifflin sales representatives receive training from Time Share in terminal and system operations.

In the case of computer programs and programming systems to be implemented on the user's computer, Time Share provides technical support for program conversions or modifications.

A major proportion of Time Share's operating expenses is required for training and orientation of educational administrators and teachers. In 1972, Time Share staff provided seminars, workshops, and training programs for about 2,000 school personnel in the application of the computing facilities and materials to the instructional and guidance programs of the schools.

As part of its service, Time Share provides a "core curricular kit" of self-study texts on BASIC programming and instructional applications for use by classroom teachers and their students.

The need for educational implementation support has been one of the major factors in the Time Share dissemination strategy. Attempts to get college and university schools of education to assist in educator training in computing literacy have been unsuccessful. The lack of educator computing literacy has been a major obstacle to the successful marketing and beneficial use of computing in the schools.

User schools pay a fixed rate of $600 per month for unlimited use of the system on one dedicated port (terminal line). All programs on the Time Share system library are available to the user, except materials in other users' private libraries. The system is operational three hours per day, seven days per week. Hence actual cost per student hour depends on the number of hours the school chooses to make the terminals available for student and teacher use. In a recent, promising innovation, some schools are providing portable terminals which students can take home and dial into the system for evening work. The charge for renting the Guidance Information System, for implementation on the user's computer, is approximately $9,000 a year for a system with up to 32 terminal ports.

Compared to other commercial ventures into the educational computing market, the Houghton Mifflin/Time Share Corporation approach has been promising to date. The Guidance Information System has been implemented on a PDP/10 time-sharing system for a community college and has been rented to the TIES network in Minnesota.

Chapter 6

WAYS OF PROVIDING COMPUTER SERVICES

PERSPECTIVE

Our focus throughout this study has been on learning experiences made feasible through computer systems, and the curricular materials needed to make those learning experiences possible. Although the computer system itself is a major and essential element in these learning experiences, technical issues regarding computer systems have not been a central concern in this study. In general, the state-of-the-art of computer technology is quite adequate to support the curricular advances discussed here. For those who are planning educational computer use, a major problem at present is in deciding among a range of alternative approaches to providing computing power for instructional use.*

The system which provides the computing power to the user has several types of components: hardware, software, communications, financial, and administrative arrangements. A computer system may be designed to serve a classroom, a school, or several hundred schools. The computer system may be physically in the same room as the students, or it may be thousands of miles away. The terminals can range in price from $500 for the simplest typewriter to $100,000 for experimental three-dimensional graphics. A great variety of sizes, speeds, and costs of central computer are available. There are dozens of computer languages.

---

*For a comprehensive review of the technological aspects of instructional computing, the reader should consult the study of the Rand Corporation, *The Emerging Technology: Instructional Uses of the Computer in Higher Education* (Levien, 1972).

In the ideal case, from a technical point of view, the educational planner would have a well-defined set of requirements against which to evaluate alternative systems and approaches. The requirements would state such factors as number of students to be served by the system in a given period of time; average amount of use per student in that time period; the geographical location of the students; terminal features required for the planned curricular materials; and so forth, for data storage, computer language requirements, cost requirements, and compatibility with other systems.

Many of these requirements can be stated with some precision. However, for most educational environments instructional computing is in its infancy. The actual extent and nature of computer use in a particular curriculum cannot be predicted in advance, unless it is established arbitrarily by policy. Therefore, it is rarely the case that a detailed set of requirements covering all system parameters can be set out in advance of selecting or designing a computer system for a particular educational environment—whether that environment be a department in a college, a statewide university system, a national consortium of professional schools, or any other organizational entity.

Therefore, the educational planner who is making decisions on the selection or design of computer system facilities for instruction will not be able to make the rigorous analysis of trade-offs that is expected in, for example, the design of computer systems for military or industrial applications. In fact, the selection of a system often begins not with a set of requirements specifications, but rather with a survey of available alternatives. For example, a public school district may consider buying services from a commercial time-sharing company, leasing a medium size computer to serve all schools in the district via telecommunications lines, or placing a mini-computer in each school. There are some general trade-off considerations to be made regarding each approach. In addition, the choices are further limited by specific requirements which can be identified. For example, not all computer systems support the APL language. If curricular materials using APL are specifically desired, this will limit the available choices.

This chapter identifies some of the alternative approaches to providing computing facilities for instruction, and some general advantages and disadvantages. Special attention is given in the first half of the chapter to the subject of sharing resources among institutions via a variety of computer network arrangements.

RESOURCE SHARING VIA NETWORKS*

Computer system hardware, software, and computer-based learning materials, although they are physically located at individual educational institutions or other organizations, can be developed and used by individuals in other organizations and other physical locations. This is what is meant by the phrase "resource sharing."

The term "network" has several definitions:
- *A physical computer network* ("hardwired network") is an inter-connection of computers, transmission facilities, terminals, and data communications equipment, which communicate with each other to allow remote users to access computer system facilities.
- A *user network* ("user group") is a coalition of computer users who share common interests or goals. It is composed of individuals or organizations who have established some formal or informal lines of communication and resource sharing among its members (example: economists who exchange econometric models).

There are many different types of physical network arrangements. The most common is a *star network*, such as the one shown in Figure 26. The network user nodes are connected to a large central computer through the telephone dial-up network or through leased lines that are rented from the common carrier. The digital computer signals are converted to a voice signal for transmission over the phone network. They are then converted back to a digital signal, using a device known as a modem, before they are entered into the computer.

Most of the NSF-sponsored Regional Computing Networks are star-type networks. Batch and/or interactive terminals and applications are supported. The capability of a star network to support educational users is expanded by the use of *satellite computers*. The satellite computer may serve as an input/output terminal, or as an independent

*A list of organizations and networks providing computing services to education is shown in Appendix 3.

Star Network

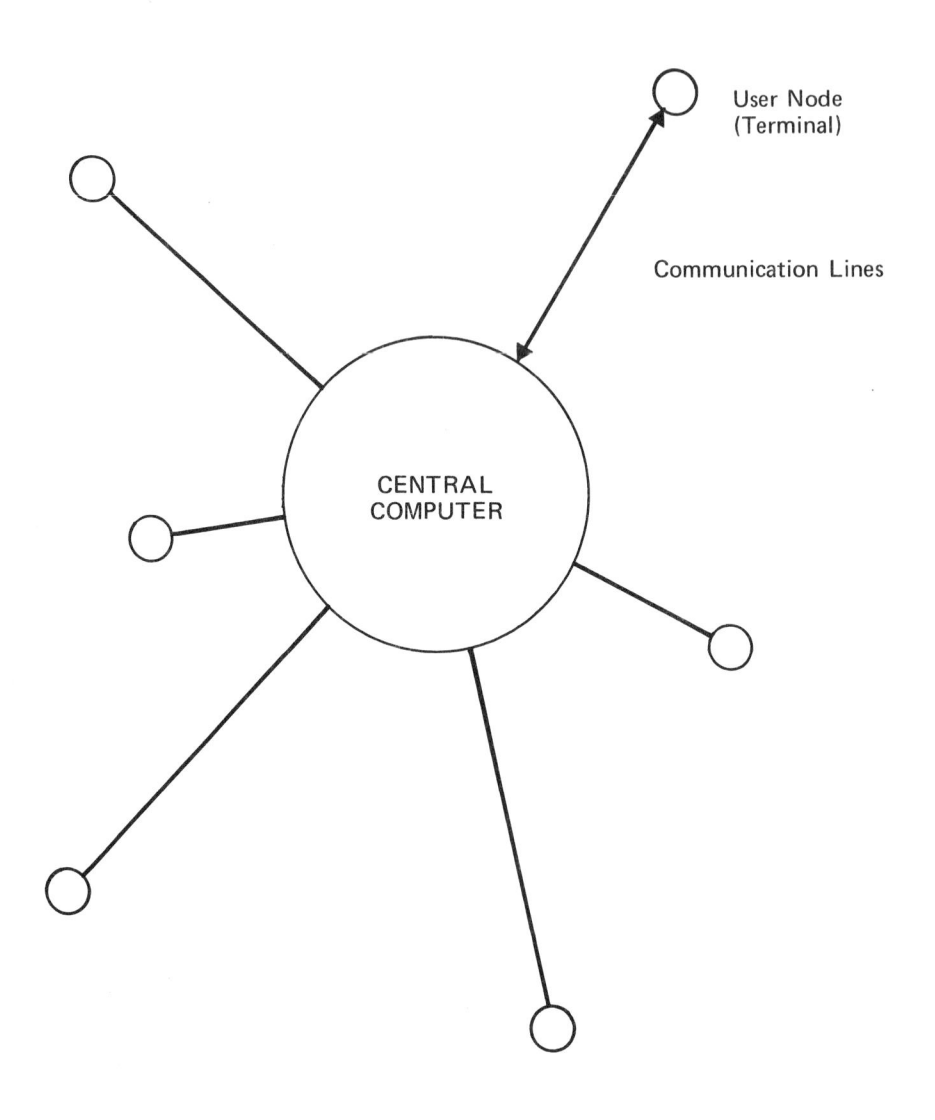

Figure 26

processor, or function in a dual capacity as a terminal and separate processor.

The satellite computer configuration is advantageous because it allows certain programs to be economically processed on a small computer without incurring communications charges, but, at the same time, provides access to the facilities of a large computer complex. Also, the satellite computer can be dedicated to performing specialized functions; e.g., graphics software support, not performed satisfactorily by the central computer. Figure 27 illustrates this type of network arrangement. The satellite computers are located at remote sites or on the campus where the central computer is located.

A more sophisticated network arrangement is one which uses a number of large central computers. Users who are connected to the individual computers may share the resources of all the other computers. Such networks are known as *distributed networks*, because the computing facilities are distributed among network nodes. Figure 28 illustrates one type of distributed network arrangement.

The MERIT Computer Network Project is a cooperative venture among Michigan State University, the University of Michigan, and Wayne State University. MERIT is a pioneering effort in the direction of large-scale resource sharing. The project's purpose is to develop an educational computer network connecting the existing central computing facilities of these universities. Funded by the State of Michigan and NSF, MERIT's broad objective is to gain through research, development, and implementation of a physical network, knowledge about, and possible solutions to, the problems of network operation in an established educational computing environment. The following benefits are expected to result from this network:

1. The network will augment the computing resources of each participating institution with those available elsewhere in the net. Thus, a user at any point of entry to the network could conveniently access the composite resources of the entire system.
2. The achievements of students, faculty, and/or researchers at any institution can be shared, instead of duplicated, by others in the net—examples are the mutual use of special programming languages, data bases, unique software, and

Satellite Network

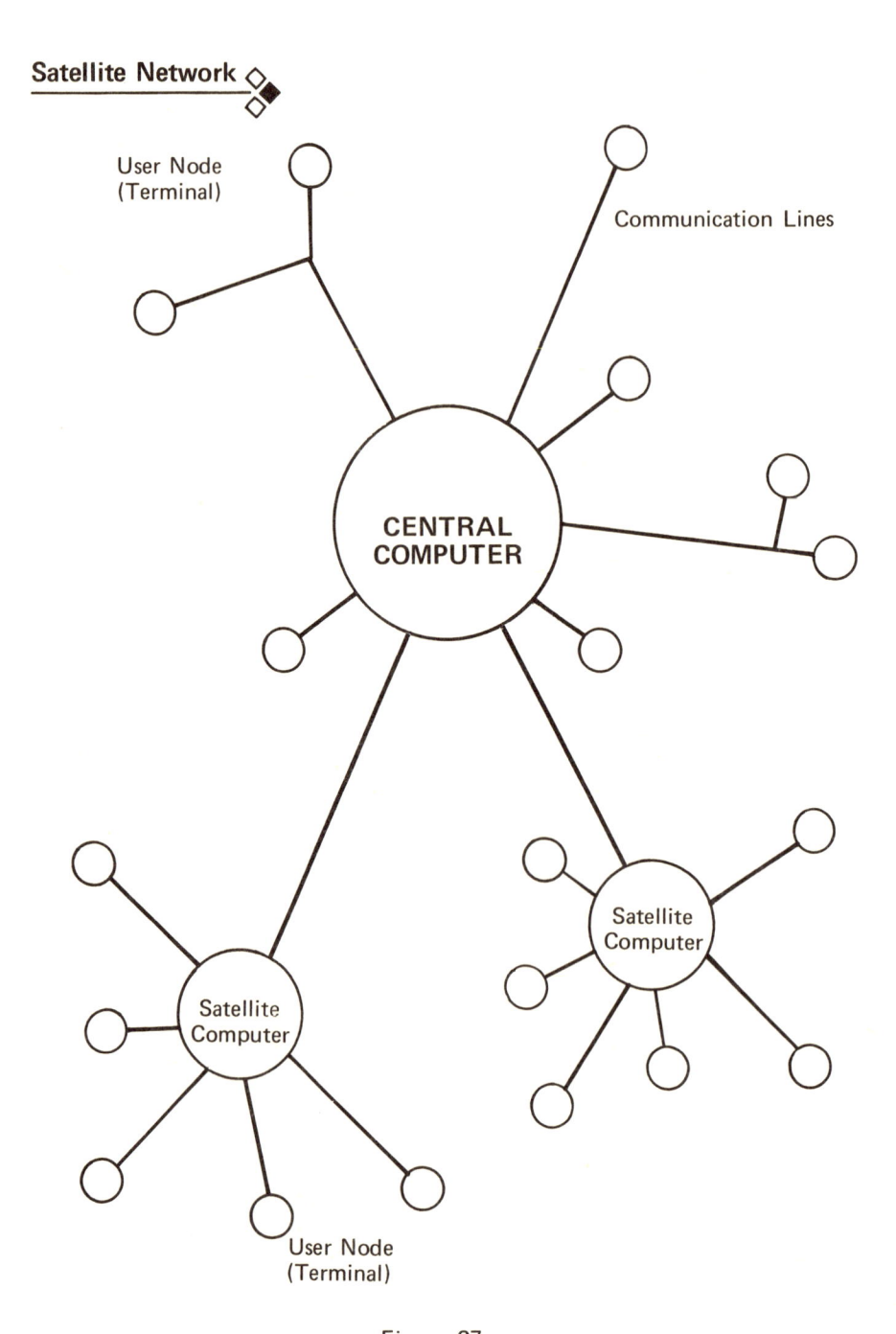

Figure 27

Distributed Computer Network

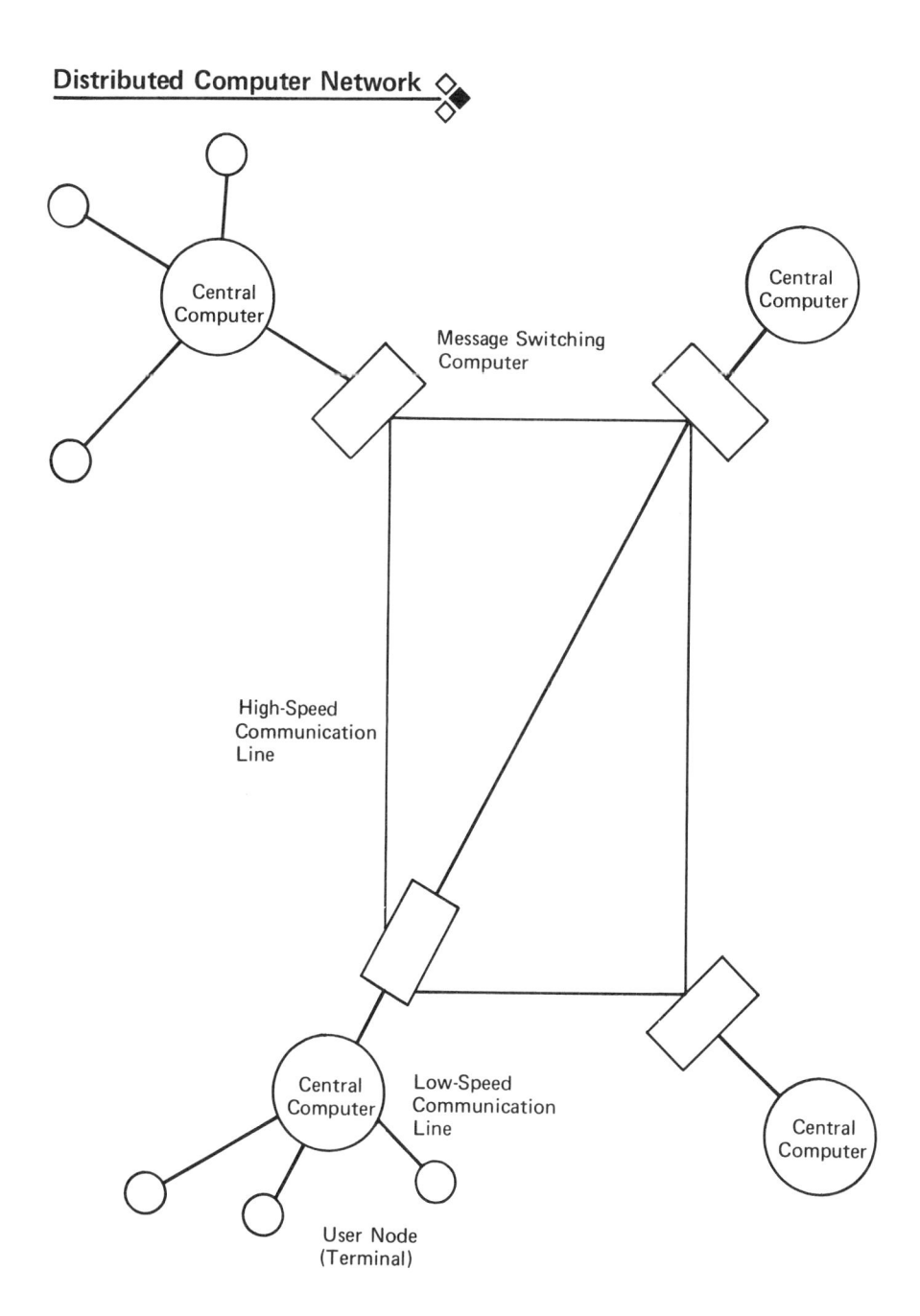

Figure 28

even standard mathematical and statistical procedures.
3. The network eases the joint preparation, testing, and maintenance of computer-aided instruction programs. It is hoped that the network would overcome the geographical barriers between institutions and lead to more rapid, economical, and scholarly developments in these areas.

From the viewpoint of the network user, the primary advantage of a distributed network is the tremendous expansion in capabilities that the user may access.

While the distributed network concept has substantial appeal, there are some potentially difficult barriers to sharing. The MERIT network user has the burden of learning the protocol of the remote network center in addition to knowing that of his home computer center. For example, a student at Michigan State University accustomed to CDC-system procedures requests a connection with the University of Michigan. Once the connection is made, the student must communicate with the University of Michigan computer in the command language of the IBM system in use there. In the MERIT network the problem of learning multiple protocols is reduced by the fact that Wayne State University and the University of Michigan both use the same time-sharing software.

It would appear that a longer learning curve will be required for substantial sharing to occur in a distributed network than with a star network.

The Advanced Research Projects Agency (ARPA) experience of a relatively low level of usage for the first two or three years of operation, followed by a rapid expansion in growth, supports this thesis. While ARPA is a research network, the users share the same problems as educational users in that they must become familiar with the protocols of the network computers and must have access to documentation that explains the operation of the programs.

Project EXTEND, under the direction of Karl Zinn, has been developing information about network node computer operating system and application software. The information requirements of a distributed network have not been ignored. Project EXTEND is fulfilling this role through the development of a set of training and reference materials on the computer-based learning aids from the three MERIT network nodes.

Regional Networks

Leadership in networking has been taken by many organizations, including federal agencies, state governments, commercial organizations, educational institutions, and discipline groups.

For colleges and universities, the establishment of the Regional Computing Program by the NSF in 1968 was a major step in the direction of resource sharing. Hundreds of colleges and universities now have access to instructional computing facilities through NSF-sponsored regional networks.

Most of the regional networks have been built around an already existing computing facility, where an experienced staff is available to handle technical problems in establishing the network. These regional networks typically serve small colleges with an enrollment of 1,000 to 3,000 students, with the majority of the faculty having no prior experience using computers before joining the network. A user college typically will concentrate its educational computing activity in three or four disciplines (e.g., mathematics, physics, biology, and political science).

A typical regional network makes the central facilities of a large college or university available to a dozen or more colleges within a 200-300 mile area, via teleprocessing lines. Remote user institutions typically have two or more batch or teletype terminals.

The University of Texas network "average" institution user logged 634 hours of connect time during the 1970-71 fiscal year and spent $66.41 per student on a total of 3,407 jobs. The "average" college spent $11,954 per user on computing, with average session costing $3.58 (Weingarten, *et al.*, 1973).

The remote user has the advantage of access to a full range of capabilities and support services of a large computer center, and the university supplier has a larger user base for spreading the cost of computer operations. Typical services that the network supplier may provide are debugging assistance, information newsletters, short courses, seminars on using instructional materials, and consulting on technical problems.

The decision to join a network involves a trade-off analysis on the relative advantages and disadvantages of each choice.

When a user institution joins a network, it gives up control over the computer's resource to another institution. This means that the institution cannot direct the operation and the money is not spent internally. On the other hand, there are many advantages which a user gains from belonging to a network (Weingarten, *et al.*, 1973, p. 14):

1. Access is gained to facilities of a large central computer with greater hardware speed or size, which permits a wider range of applications than are possible with a smaller central computer.

2. Network membership eliminates the overhead cost of a computer center staff. The weekly computer center payroll at a university with a large computer facility (IBM 370/155) will typically run between $4,000 and $8,000. The network center benefits from the economies of scale, as the staff members can specialize in a particular area. For instance, the center may have an on-line system specialist, or a specialist in CAI language.

3. The network user pays only for services used. This advantage is important to a new user who does not have a history of use on which to estimate his needs.

4. The network center can provide technical and educational support to network users. This support may include computer programming courses, workshops on educational applications, consultation services on the use of the operating system, and the center's application program.

5. The network center will undertake the conversion and installation of application software packages. This service is of particular value for the user in a small college setting, where it is not possible for him to independently convert and install the packages on his own system and where local computation centers do not have the incentive to undertake this unpleasant chore (Weingarten, *et al.*, 1973). In contrast, a network center as a distributor desires to make such packages available to a wide community of users.

6. Large computers (annual rental above $200,000; e.g., IBM 370/165) provide greater cost performance than small computers (with annual rental below $25,000; e.g., PDP-11). Larger computers operate at a far lower cost per computation than small computers. The cost per student on a small computer, for the compilation of a FORTRAN program, would run from $0.25 to $0.50. Contrastingly, the cost on a large computer would only be $0.05 to $0.10 using a fast in-core

compiler. A counter-factor is the cost of communications, which may offset the savings in computation cost, depending on the distance from the network center. At distances greater than 200 miles, the cost may exceed the savings, depending on the type of telephone service used and the line usage.

The network provides both *service* and *economic* advantages over a stand-alone computer center. However, there are a number of potential disadvantages to network participation:

1. In most network arrangements the network user pays for the services he uses but has no ownership in the network facilities. In the University of Texas network, the network college on the average spent $11,954.00 for FY 1970-71 (Weingarten, *et al.*, 1973, p. 55). This money could have been applied on a lease-purchase agreement in which the college would *own* the computer for a nominal payment at the end of the lease period.

2. The network college does not have an opportunity to develop its own expert staff of computer scientists to consult on research projects. The network user, instead, depends on the hardware, software, and language experts at the network center. For many colleges this is an advantage, since someone else worries about the technical problems, but others may find the lack of a campus computer science expertise to be a disadvantage.

3. The *prestige* value of a college having its own computer may be viewed as a negative factor to joining a network.

Networks Which Do Not Own Computing Facilities

Most networks have their own computing facilities and, therefore, control the network resources. However, there are network organizational arrangements in which the network provides services without owning the computing facilities. These networks provide a variety of services, including training, orientation on network use, and documentation of instructional computer programs.

The New England Regional Computing Program (NERComp) is a nonprofit organization that serves as a broker. NERComp provides access to five major computer centers, including the Dartmouth College net through its leased lines. The advantages to the user are:

(1) access to six different computer centers;
(2) special contract features;
(3) free evaluation and orientation period; and
(4) the use of a leased line.

NERComp permits a user college to have access to a host computer at another college through a leased communication line without having to make a long-term commitment. Depending on the user college location, NERComp's leased lines may be cheaper than a direct leased line to their college. The NERComp's leased lines are shared by 46 colleges.

The NERComp user currently places a dial-up call to the NERComp central office and then is manually switched to a leased line connecting the central office to the appropriate network node. Plans have been formulated to automate this switch using a mini-computer.

North Carolina Educational Computing Service (NCECS) sponsors a network that, like NERComp, does not have its own computing facility. However, the functions of NCECS and NERComp are quite dissimilar. NCECS is committed to the educational side of computing where emphasis is placed on the instructional requirements of the individual disciplines. NCECS has collected a large array of instructional computer programs, and has produced the educational documentation for selected computer programs to guide the teachers on the classroom utilization of these materials. NCECS is a notable exception to the general lack of effort on documentation of programs.

NCECS obtains computer time for its users from the Triangle Universities Computation Center (TUCC). TUCC is a sophisticated computer complex which provides computing power primarily to these three large universities and a network of smaller colleges throughout North Carolina. The central computer is an IBM 370/165 installed at Research Triangle Park. The University of North Carolina, Duke University, and North Carolina State all have IBM computers which are compatible with the main computer and are linked to the main computer by a high-speed (40,800 bits per second) line. The advantage of this network configuration is the elimination of compatibility problems that arise in non-homogeneous computer networks.

CONDUIT (Computers at Oregon State, North Carolina Educational Computing Service, Dartmouth, and the Universities of Iowa and Texas) is a consortium of five regional computer networks sponsored by the National Science Foundation. The five regional networks in the CONDUIT consortium serve a total of approximately 100 institutions of higher learning comprising nearly 300,000 students. CONDUIT may be considered a softwired network, since the five regional computer networks are *not* connected by *hardwired* communications facilities.

CONDUIT was funded as an experiment to identify the factors, educational and technical, related to the transfer of computer-related curriculum materials. CONDUIT sponsored national workshops in seven fields attended by 52 professors within the five regional networks, of which 50 professors subsequently adopted the materials for classroom use. Altogether, approximately 5,000 students have participated in the CONDUIT experiment.

Preliminary data indicate that the technical problems of transporting the instructional computer programs were minor. The most frequently encountered technical problem was documentation inaccuracies, which resulted in some wastage of staff time. It has been found that the computer programs were transported between computer environments for about two percent to four percent of their original development cost.

Discipline Networks

Networks may be organized according to disciplines. For example, an experimental Chemistry Network was organized to develop instructional programs and share them among member nodes.* Eight centers of excellence were provided with Culler-Fried terminals on which to do their development work. Each center independently developed its own instructional computer programs. A good portion of the total project time of two years was used in learning how to use the ARPA Communications Network, in learning how to use the Culler-Fried terminal system, in developing the materials, and in trying them out at the home institution in experimental sections.

Another example of a discipline-oriented network is the educational network sponsored by the Lister Hill Center. The Lister Hill network provides educational services to a variety of institutions in the

---

*Final Report: "On-Line Computer Network for Chemistry Education," National Science Foundation, Grant GJ-693, David O. Harris, undated.

health profession, including medical schools, nursing schools, and hospitals.

The educational network uses the Biomedical Communications facilities of the National Library of Medicine. These facilities are furnished by a commercial time-sharing corporation, Tymshare, which has a nationwide hook-up of leased line facilities (Department of Health, Education, and Welfare, 1972).

The Lister Hill network has unusual arrangements under which participants use materials provided by the network servers (contract school). The network user must apply to the Lister Hill Center to be either a trial or operational user. The trial users must obtain a terminal on which they can try out the network-provided curricula but they are not obligated in any other way.

In order to become an operational user, an institution must agree both to evaluate existing network materials and to contribute to the expansion of these materials. Before being accepted as an operational user, the institution must submit a formal evaluation plan describing plans for evaluating the educational effectiveness of the instructional materials. Some of the evaluation plans have included in-depth, two-way interviews of students, performance evaluation of control and experimental groups on standardized tests, and so forth.

The operational user institutions are required to add to the repertoire of materials currently available from the service providers. For example, the University of Illinois Medical Center provides the CASE program, which simulates a clinical encounter. The operational user is required to submit additional medical case histories to expand the range of experience the student can obtain. The Director of the Lister Hill network, Dr. Harold Wooster, feels that user-developed materials are a key to the long-term success of the network.

The service suppliers were carefully selected on the basis of the quality of materials which they could offer the network users. The contractors agree to share their materials, and their computer facilities, and to provide consulting services to the network users. One important circumstantial finding interesting to note is that usage of materials on the Lister Hill Network (and the CONDUIT project described elsewhere) is directly related to adequacy of user documentation.

The network user accesses the network by dialing the mini-computer (a special communications processor) nearest to his institution. This mini-computer is attached to a Tymshare leased line which connects the user to the contractor school. The user has to pay for the dial-up call only, and the Lister Hill center pays for the leased line communications that is a major component of the Center's cost.

The popularity of the service has introduced some problems with the network. The network providers have a limited number of ports (access lines to the computer), and during the busy periods the users are frequently unable to gain access. The biggest problem is the cost of communications, which is now approximately 40 percent of total costs.

National Educational Networks

Currently, there is no national educational network that is equivalent in scope to the ARPA research network. The major problem blocking the introduction of an educational network is the cost. At the present time, transmission costs are on the order of four to 10 times the magnitude of the computer processing costs. While the costs can be expected to drop with the introduction of alternative communications facilities, there must be a special rationale for supporting a national network.

One of the greatest potential areas for a national educational network is knowledge sharing. We can speculate on the possibilities of a student being able to access data banks pertinent to his individual study interests.

In the social sciences, for example, the student may be conducting a study in such subject areas as:
- factors affecting voting behavior,
- consumer protection,
- the rights of the American Indian, or
- land utilization policies in the United States.

The student will need real-life data to support his research:
- party affiliations of voting groups (e.g., labor, farmers),
- consumer buying habits,
- history of treaties with American Indians, or
- land utilization (zoning) records in the Western United States.

This data requirement can be fulfilled through a national educational network tied to specialized data centers.

In the field of social science, there are many archives with holdings which are potentially valuable to a national educational network. Some examples are:*

>Latin American Data Bank
>University of Florida, Gainesville
>
>National Opinion Research Center
>University of Chicago
>
>Polimetrics Laboratory
>Ohio State University
>
>Political Data Archive
>Michigan State University
>
>Regional Social Science Data Archive
>University of Iowa
>
>Roper Public Opinion Research Center
>Williams College

Data bases like the ones described above generally cannot be used "as is" for educational purposes. These data bases may require a massive clean-up task to fill in missing data cells or eliminate incomplete records. It may be necessary to develop a smaller data set than the original research data base to reduce the search time.

At the University of Iowa, considerable work has been expended on cleaning up data files and developing code books and other materials to assist the students in their research work. If the University of Iowa were tied into a national network, the benefits of this work could be shared by sociology students throughout the nation (ignoring the question of costs).

*Information can be obtained from John Kolp, Laboratory for Political Research, University of Iowa, Iowa City, Iowa 52240.

DATA COMMUNICATIONS COSTS

The common carrier data communications costs are based on distance, time of day, and length of call. Tariff schedules depend on the type of service used.

The dial-up network is prohibitively expensive, except for extremely limited use. The utilization of Wide Area Telephone Service (WATS) would reduce the cost by as much as 40 percent, but this is still high for educational usage.

A third alternative is leased line service, in which the user pays a fixed charge per mile per month. If a leased line is 75 percent loaded on a single shift, eight-hour basis, the cost of the three-minute "conversation" is about $0.12.

The telephone line charges increase rapidly with distance. The table below shows the cost per hour, for a voice grade leased line assuming single shift usage with a 75 percent line loading (Datapro, 1973):

Distance in Miles from Network Center	$/hour
50	1.17
100	1.97
250	3.69
500	6.37
1000	8.59
2000	14.33

The common carrier's leased line cost per mile per month decreases with increasing distances. A low-speed, 55-bit-per-second line costs $1.40 per mile per month for distances up to 100 miles, while the cost per mile of line between 100 and 250 miles drops to $0.98 per mile per month. A 100-mile line would cost $140.00 per month and a

250-mile line would cost $250.00. Several schools may be connected to the same line, thus creating a multidrop line which allows costs to be shared although the common carriers make a surcharge for each drop.

It was mentioned earlier that line cost varies with the type of service used. The three basic types of service are low-speed, voice grade, and wideband facilities.

Low-speed services are used with slow mechanical devices like typewriters or teletypes. The voice grade facilities are compatible with medium-speed devices like CRT's. The wideband channels are normally reserved for high-speed computer-to-computer communications, but these channels can be multiplexed to carry a large number of lower-speed conversations, as is done in the PLATO system, over limited distances with a concentrated group of users.

Illustrations of actual computer costs will help to clarify the relative importance of communications cost to total costs. In the Iowa network the dominant cost is the terminal equipment rental. The network schools are using expensive remote batch terminals or small computers with a rental range of $4,000 to $12,000 per year.

Dartmouth presents a different picture from Iowa. The computer connect charges (the central facility costs) are the dominant costs while communications are only 10 percent to 17 percent of total hardware costs. This compares with 11 percent to 32 percent for the selected colleges at Iowa.

The basic factor explaining this difference is that Dartmouth operates in a *conversational* processing mode, while Iowa primarily operates in a *batch* processing mode. Dartmouth College users employ inexpensive teletype terminals with an annual cost of only $780 to $3,120 for a college with four terminals. Also, Dartmouth may incur higher computer costs to support interactive processing, including a large mass storage.

Telephone and telegraph communications facilities completely dominate data transmission today. However, alternative communications channels may some day play an important role in data transmission. Satellite transmission, microwave, cable TV, and special digital communications networks are some of the possibilities for solving the communications cost bottleneck.

The previous discussion has pointed out that conventional

transmission media are prohibitively expensive for long distance transmission. Satellite transmission offers the promise of providing a low-cost communications alternative to conventional telephone channels for transcontinental and international data transmission. The federal government in the United States has been slow to act on the potential of satellites for low-cost transmission but NASA and HEW have organized a joint domestic satellite project as an experimental undertaking, and the first U.S. educational satellite was launched successfully into orbit in May, 1973.

Canada has plans for offering a long-distance satellite transmission at substantial savings over conventional ground transmission cables. A trans-Canada digital communications service has plans to offer low-speed channels compatible to teletype terminals at up to 80 percent cost reduction over conventional telephone channels. The higher-speed channels may be offered at 45 percent of the cost of conventional ground communications facilities.

At Washington University, a number of organizational strategies are being studied for using communications satellites for education (Morgan and Singh, 1972). A pilot project using satellite transmission was operational for a short time, in which instructional materials from the Institute for Mathematical Studies in the Social Sciences were transmitted to schools in New Mexico (Ball and Jamison, 1973).

Cable TV is a wideband coaxial cable that provides a high bandwidth so that a single channel can provide the equivalent bandwidth of 1,008 voice grade channels. The PLATO IV communications network uses the coaxial channel in this manner. Under optimum conditions the cost of communications for PLATO IV services using cable television is estimated to add only $0.06 per terminal hour (Alpert, 1971). Considering current-day communications cost, this appears to be an optimistic estimate, unless the terminals are situated in clusters within a reasonably short distance of the central computer site.

PROGRAMMING LANGUAGES

Languages are a key link in curriculum development. The choice of programming language may have a substantial effect on curriculum development time. The characteristics of a particular language may be such that a 20 to 30 percent saving in coding time can be achieved over some other language less suitable to the task.

Another major factor in curriculum development is the skill level of the personnel who are assigned as instructional programmers. Some programming languages are designed for use by inexperienced programmers, while others can be effected only when used by highly experienced information scientists. The type of development staff to be used is dictated by the programming language. Conversely, the type of staff at hand can determine the language to be used.

The selection of a language has impact beyond development aspects. It is a primary consideration in the transportability of curricula materials to institutions which do not have the same computer configuration as that of the developing institution. The most popular and generally used languages, such as BASIC and FORTRAN, are implemented on virtually all machine configurations. Among the languages that have been developed in the past few years, BASIC has had by far the greatest impact on educational computing in terms of student use, since it is an easily learned, interactive language. The Conference Board of the Mathematical Sciences, Committee on Computer Education, recommended in 1972 a universal computer literacy course for junior high school students and a follow-up course with problem-solving experiences using BASIC. Nearly every commercially available interactive computing system has a BASIC language capability.

There are drawbacks to relying on one language, since other languages may have capabilities that students can use to solve different classes of problems. For example, a language with list processing capabilities would be advantageous in solving operations research type problems.

A large number of languages have been developed to accommodate a variety of purposes such as conversational processing, graphics, and CAI. Karl Zinn at the University of Michigan has developed a structure that shows the main avenues of language development, as depicted in the tree structure in Figure 29 (Zinn, 1972).

One of the main lines of language development affecting curricula has been "author" languages. For over a decade, pioneers in computer-assisted instruction applications have invested substantial efforts to

Program Language Tree Structure

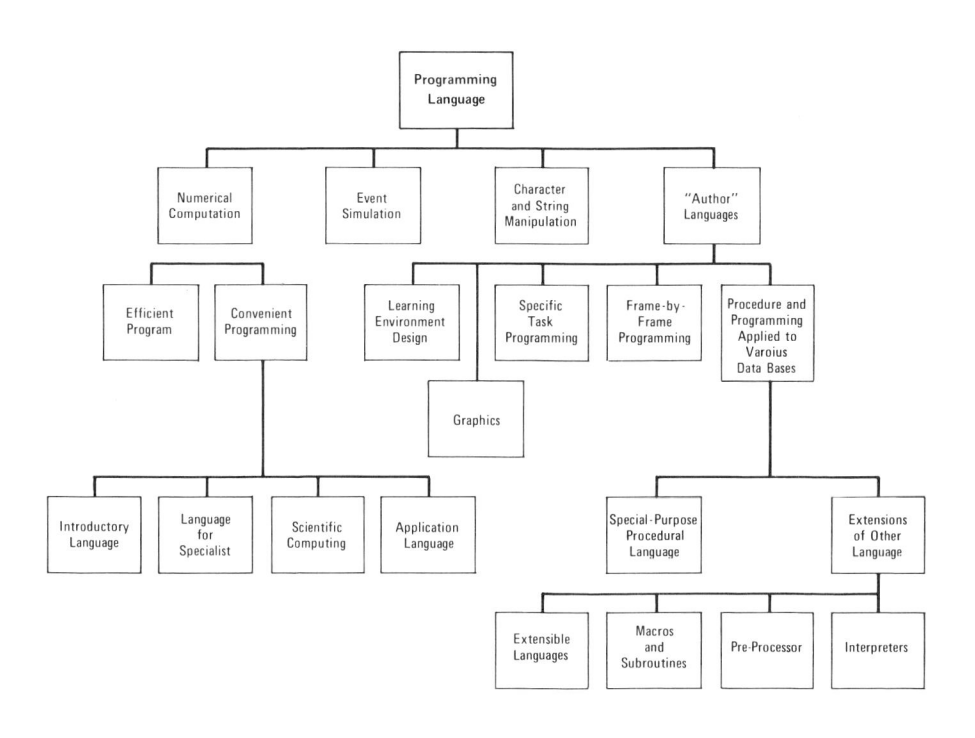

Source Data: Zinn, 1972 (unpublished)

Figure 29

develop author languages to simplify the process of preparing tutorial instructional materials. Dozens of such languages have been developed. Zinn provides an analysis of the requirements for and suitability of types of languages suitable for CAI (Zinn, 1971).

These languages allow teachers who are novices to the computer to translate their pedagogy to instructional logic to be presented by the computer. PLATO system users can create and store graphic images on-line, using simple procedures, store the images, and later call them out in a TUTOR instructional program (CERL, 1972). The MENTOR language is designed so that the author can provide a student with the capability for a fairly natural dialogue with the computer, in which the student can pose questions as well as participate in the conventional dialogue, in which the computer does all the questioning (Frye, 1969).

Coursewriter III, developed by IBM, is one of the best known frame-oriented languages, in which information is presented to the student a frame at a time. More recent language developments, such as TUTOR, have attempted to expand the language facilities to allow flexibility beyond a frame-by-frame presentation and response analysis. Pittsburgh Interpretive Language (PIL) is a procedural language that is particularly suitable for interactive time-sharing use. The language commands include those required for simple, calculator-like computations. Programming systems and languages designed especially for a particular problem area or subject matter have many obvious advantages over frame-oriented CAI languages for special learning environments. Many subject areas require computation, manipulation of data structures, and access to mass storage files, which cannot be facilitated by frame-by-frame languages.

Political and social science students may use the computer to analyze data, and to test the impact of, for example, various measures for the conservation of natural resources. A student might wish to further his studies by building a model to simulate energy use under varying policies. Specialized languages such as those suitable for student model building would be an essential component of the learning environment. Special purpose languages make it possible for the student to communicate in terms and concepts natural to the subject matter he is studying. An example is COGO, a problem-oriented language, subset of Integrated Civil Engineering System (ICES). A student can specify design and computation in such areas as highway design or engineering surveys, using a language natural to geometrics (*General ICES Information*, 1971).

ARTSPEAK was designed for the humanities student. He can describe artistic designs for execution by a computer-controlled plotter with only a few hours' training in the language (Mullish and Lewis, 1972).

LOGO, a language developed by Seymour Papert of the Massachusetts Institute of Technology, is a component of a total learning environment in which young children program a variety of procedures that control the manipulation of such devices as a "turtle," a music box, and a set of lights (Papert and Solomon, 1972).

How Does One Choose a Language?

There are approximately 50 languages from which a user can make a selection. Often it is the case that half a dozen languages or more may be able to handle the problems which arise in a particular learning environment. A management simulation may be programmed in BASIC, FORTRAN, ALGOL, or a special simulation language such as SIM-SCRIPT. The selection of a language is basically a trade-off situation in which different choices must be analyzed against the user's objectives. These objectives might be machine independence, ease of learning the language, built-in documentation, general acceptance of the language by the educational community, hardware requirements of the language, and running time efficiency.

An examination of some of the trade-offs between BASIC and APL will serve as an illustration. BASIC is one of the most popular instructional languages, but APL has a large following of dedicated instructional users. BASIC and APL are both conversational languages but APL is more interactive and BASIC is an easier language for inexperienced instructional developers to learn. APL is by far the most concise language. With a single statement, a routine can be written to read a set of numbers, calculate their mean, and print the results. BASIC, on the other hand, would require 10 statements to perform the same function. APL sacrifices readability with the use of special symbols such as Φ and Δ. These symbols lead to the requirement for a special APL keyboard, and make concise programs difficult to read, even by their programmers.

The above discussion points out that there are many complex trade-offs between languages, and no one language satisfies all requirements (Zinn, 1971).

TERMINALS

The mainstay of interactive computing has been the teletypewriter terminal. An ASR 33 Teletype terminal can be purchased for under

$1,000.00. This is the most common interactive terminal found in the regional networks. The instructional user trades off *cost* against terminal *features* and the *reliability*. A teletype can be rented for as little as $75.00 per month. Besides being inexpensive, the device provides hard copy of interactions, and is easy to use in either a batch or a conversational mode.

The disadvantage of the teletype is primarily its slow speed (e.g., 10 characters per second on the ASR 33, 15 characters per second on the ASR 37, or possibly the 30 characters per second on the TI 733 for $1,500). Also, the teletype machine is a poor graphics device, even though users have attempted to work in this mode using characters instead of line segments.

How does the alphanumeric CRT compare with the teletype or other typewriter-like device? The CRT could present material a page at a time, which would provide definite pedagogical advantages in a tutorial mode of instruction. The teletype operates at slower speeds than a person normally reads. This forces the terminal user to sit and wait until the terminal catches up with the human operator. On the other hand, with a CRT and the proper communications channel, a full screen of data (perhaps 20 lines) may appear in a second or two.

The alphanumeric CRT has not been a popular educational terminal. What are the drawbacks? Generally speaking, a CRT costs much more than a typewriter-like device, although this price differential is continually decreasing. Clustering of display units has the effect of making the price differential of less significance. Another drawback is the lack of hard copy output for the student to carry away for future reference. The CRT's can be equipped with an auxiliary printing device that would make the CRT even less cost competitive.

CRT Features

There are many features about a CRT-type terminal which offer potential for improving the man-machine interface:
(1) light pens or other pointing devices for either selecting out information or drawing on the screen;
(2) special function keys which can be given special application meaning, e.g., a DICTIONARY or HELP key;
(3) color displays for highlighting information;

(4) individually addressable screen positions or areas that allow new information to be added while previous information remains displayed;
(5) interchangeable character sets;
(6) special keyboard designs tailored to an application;
(7) joy stick, "mouse," or track-ball control that allows the user to skip around the terminal screen at will; and
(8) special editing features like erase and close text.

The problem for the educator is to determine the features which are important to his application. Some features may be nice to have but may have little instructional value. If a terminal is difficult to use, the terminal user may become distracted from the learning task at hand. Is the cost for a specially designed keyboard justified from the human engineering standpoint or is it justifiable only for a special application as are the math functions and structure for the Culler-Fried terminal? These are questions for further research.

There are special instructional applications areas in which special features are either desirable or mandatory.

A person learning Russian needs a keyboard that contains the Russian alphabet. The physics student should be able to work with symbols that are natural to his discipline. There is no need to limit the student to the standard set of symbols found on a typewriter. This unnecessarily constrains the student-computer communication by making it difficult to enter student replies to responses (Bork, 1972). Special keyboard designs are available for different types of applications, such as mathematics, but educator desire is not always matched with economic feasibility.

In scientific and mathematical notation, superscripts and subscripts have an important meaning. This capability is not generally available but it is found on the PLATO IV terminal and the new ASR 37 teletype.

Graphic Terminals

Graphic terminals vary in capability from being able to create simple line drawings to terminals which can display some image, rotate the image to show a different perspective, blow up a portion of the image being displayed, display a surface view of an object (instead of a line drawing), and allow the operator to manipulate the object at will. Graphic terminals have been developed which can provide a 3-D view of an object in color.

At the low end of the spectrum, simple line graphic terminals can be purchased for as little as $4,000, while sophisticated graphic terminals may cost a minimum of $20,000 and can run as high as $100,000. One of the problems with graphic terminals is the time that it takes an object to appear. Thousands of bits of data may be required to describe the picture. Therefore, data communication and terminal speed are important features for some applications. HumRRO is currently developing a high-speed 3-D, low cost (under $10,000) graphic terminal which can display objects with as many as 4,000 surfaces.

This terminal acts as a window into a 3-D world; a world which is stored in the computer. The objects of the world can have dynamic parameters, such as velocity and acceleration. Objects can be programmed to obey physical laws which include collision dynamics, where an object bounces according to the conservation of momentum and energy.

The objects of a world as observed at a terminal actually can be simulating or representing other users of the system. Thus, many terminals together can be observing the same sub-world, each seeing the other. This permits, for instance, driver training where each driver finds himself in a real-world situation where others are involved, producing the dangers and the problems associated with learning to drive. It can act as a pilot trainer where other planes controlled by other terminals are within the same world and act as real-life obstacles within the learning environment.

Via a joy stick or keyboard, the user can alter the position of objects via commands; he can alter his position and orientation within the world, including velocity and acceleration, etc. He can dissect an object, peer from any point within the object and, in general, have all the degrees of freedom conceivable.

The full extent of educational value of terminals that are able to operate in the 3-D domain is not yet known. Experimental applications will be required to exploit their potential. But obvious immediate applications which come to mind are medical simulations and engineering design.

There has been considerable work with more conventional graphic terminals and pen-and-paper plotters that provides some clue as to the educational potential of graphics. This work includes the development of software to take advantage of the terminal hardware. This is a *major* factor in capitalizing on hardware features. Much work remains to be done in developing easy to use graphic languages. The terminal user must have a language which allows him to draw objects, store objects, scale objects, or alter the shape of an object.

ARCH:GRAPHIC is a system which illustrates the type of software support that must be behind the terminal. ARCH:GRAPHIC allows the user to manipulate a set of elementary objects such as cubes, quarter circles, octahedrons, stick figures, and any other unit he creates. The user can pile up these shapes to form larger objects, draw buildings, or design whole cities on the face of the cathode ray tube (CRT) or with a computer-driven digital plotter. The program permits display of an object with sun and shade in relation to latitude, season, day, and hour. The architecture student can see his designs in time as well as space. The computer is capable of generating alternative views and perspectives. The student can investigate in the abstract many more designs and more complex problems in one course than he would otherwise experience in an entire program of architectural studies, or perhaps in an entire career without computer simulation. More importantly, the student is learning computer-aided techniques of design in which the computer becomes an integral part of his own creative capabilities. The traditional reliance on static sketches and manually built models is replaced by dynamic, computer-generated spatial views. At the University of Michigan, the ARCH:GRAPHIC is used in two "architectural computing" courses.

Although the dynamic qualities of sophisticated display systems are essential to some learning experiences involving graphics, simple pen-and-paper plotters can also greatly enhance a learning experience. For example, the authors of COEXIST materials and their students have found that it is much easier to learn basic concepts such as in physics when a simple analog x-y plotter is used to draw the results of simulated laboratory experiments in such subjects as classical mechanics, fluid flow, and geometrical optics.

The value of graphics in a learning experience is not restricted to the one-to-one interaction of the student and the computer. Computer-animated films enable many persons to experience the phenomena simultaneously, but *interactive* systems with many individuals are possible as well. The interactive classroom graphics system at Oregon State University provides three-way interactions—among students, teacher, and computer. Through careful design of the instruction and innovative classroom management, the traditional passive learning environment of a lecture classroom can, even with a large group, be transformed into an active, creative experience. The hardware for the classroom graphics system includes a Textronix computer graphics display terminal, and the equipment necessary to project the CRT image onto a large wall screen to function as an electronic blackboard. The image on the graphics display is converted from digital to analog by a scan converter and is projected into a large movie-size screen (Kelley, 1971).

The total cost of the equipment is roughly $15,000.00. When this course is spread over a large number of users, the graphics terminal is reasonably priced (Kelley, 1971).

A special graphics language was developed to allow the instructor to dynamically control the display of a program solution. The LIMITS command, for example, allows the instructor to specify the range of the independent variable.

The instructor is able to interact with the computer and maintain the attention of the students at the same time.

MINI-COMPUTER DEVELOPMENTS

Computer complexity and cost have been obstacles to widespread use of computers in learning, particularly for smaller institutions. Expertise in operating systems, computer languages, computer operations, and computer applications has been difficult to assemble for the typical smaller educational institution, particularly public schools.

Mini-computers are appearing in a rapidly increasing number of the nation's schools and colleges as an inexpensive method of obtaining educational computing power. They combine low-cost computer power with simplicity of operation. Mini-computers today come equipped with an easy-to-use operating system, the BASIC computer language, and a growing complement of instructional materials.

Simulation materials developed by Huntington Two (see Chapter 3) take advantage of these mini-computer features. The computer programs, written in BASIC, are distributed on punched tape with the text packaged separately. In the future, the added convenience of magnetic tape cassettes may be available.

In 1967 there were fewer than 100 mini-computers in colleges and universities, but five years later the figure had grown to over 400. A major attraction of mini-computers is that they are a manageable budget item. Mini-computers can now be purchased for as low as $5,000, with a typical configuration costing around $75,000 to $100,000. Large, fully equipped mini-computers which are able to support up to a 32-terminal interactive computing environment can be obtained for under $200,000 including the cost of the terminals.

If mini-computer costs continue to decline as they have in the past (20 percent a year since 1965), it is reasonable to expect that mini-computers will eventually become a consumer item where each user will have his own personal educational computer system consisting of a small TV set, a typewriter-like keyboard, and cassette tape player.

Large Central Facility
Versus Mini-computer

The computer user often has a choice of whether to use a large central facility or to obtain a mini-computer for his exclusive use.

The mini-computer approach has a number of advantages:

1. The systems do not use highly complex system software that requires the knowledge and skills of operating system experts.

2. The computers can be used in special applications, e.g., a laboratory data acquisition system.

3. The system is cost-effective at the lower end of the range of the number of simultaneous users supported. An inexpensive mini-computer system (under $50,000) can be configured to support one to four terminals.

4. The student users can get "hands on" experience in using a computer.

The mini-computer user makes an implied trade-off between the simplicity of use and the capabilities of the system.

5. Because of the small size of the mini-computer and con-

sequently small cost, it can be *controlled* by a small number of users, and dedicated to a particular purpose.

The large central system has a number of advantages:

1. The system can be designed to provide continuous operation, e.g., the Dartmouth College system has back-to-back central processors. Normally, the second processor performs background work but is automatically switched over in the case of a failure of the first processor.

2. The large central facility can provide special capabilities not found on mini-computers. The large computation center can provide a larger variety of languages, canned packages, and special application programs than can a small independent center. Large regional computer centers usually offer most of the common programming languages such as FORTRAN, BASIC, PL/1, COBOL, ALGOL, and APL to their users as fully supported languages. In addition a larger center will have a limited selection of specialized languages like LISP, CLICK, SNOBOL, and simulation languages such as GPSS.

3. Large central computers can handle a greater variety of instructional applications than can a small mini-computer. These greater performance capabilities permit sophisticated systems to develop which use large matrices, lists, large-scale simultaneous equations systems, and sophisticated file-searching techniques.

Specialized Mini-computer Applications

Mini-computers are often used as a major component of a total instructional system consisting of computer hardware, software, and courseware. One such example is the targeted instructional system specifically designed to meet the requirements of a particular segment of the educational community. Key elements of this approach as employed with the TICCIT system being developed jointly by Mitre Corporation and Brigham Young University are:

(1) identification of a widespread educational need, and targeting the system design and marketing to fill that need;

(2) development of an efficient system for a specific instructional purpose, through a total systems design approach (computer hardware, software, instructional programs);

(3) demonstrated cost/effectiveness over traditional instruction in

the target institutions by providing "mainline" computer-assisted instruction which supplants many faculty functions and thereby the educational system becomes more capital intensive and less labor intensive; and

(4) mass dissemination of the curricula through installation of the total system at many institutions.

This approach to delivery systems eliminates many technical problems of transporting the instructional materials from one institution to another, since it is the total system that is transported. Because the system is tailored to a specific application, the per-student cost for instruction should be competitive with, if not cheaper than, conventional classroom instruction. One problem, however, is that in order for such a system to prove cost-effective, the user institution must allow for self-paced scheduling and grading of students. If the TICCIT type of system is used in a lock-step environment, the cost savings cannot be fully realized.

A potential disadvantage to the total instructional system approach is in the trade-off between efficiency and flexibility. In order for such a system to be highly efficient for student operations, the design does not allow for experimentation and course development at the user installation.

The TICCIT system separates the authoring subsystem from the operational delivery system. The authoring of course materials using this strategy is performed by a team of professionals on a different computer system. Thus, the successful mass dissemination of the material depends heavily on the design of courses that will be adaptable for students in a variety of educational settings. The TICCIT system deals with this problem by incorporating an extensive set of "learner control" mechanisms into the instructional strategy and into the system software.

TRADE-OFFS REVISITED

The basic theme discussed in the foregoing sections is expressed by a single sentence: *There is no absolute answer to the choice of hardware, software, or the use of computers in education.* Persons or institutions entering the field of computers in education must ask a number of questions related to how they wish to take advantage of the computers to amplify the quality of the instructional environment. Generally, the questions can be grouped into two categories: user requirements and facilities considerations. Figure 30 illustrates the number of contingent issues to be considered but suggests no necessary order in which they must be taken. Thus, one can start with any specific category and move around the circle, just making certain that no category is neglected. In addition, the user must establish the relative importance of the questions. For example, the instructional implications of choosing a small, inexpensive minicomputer as the central processor is to limit almost totally the development of materials to *adjunctive* or supplementary instruction (as opposed to full tutorial). With respect to terminals, lack of graphics implies development of only limited simulations which do not portray dynamic physical phenomena. However, teletypewriters with no graphic capability are more common from system to system and, thus, facilitate communication and sharing of materials.

Taken together, the issues discussed above are also relevant to the degree of control the user has over the technological base as well as the nature of instructional use. The decision is relevant to the dollars it will cost to use that technology and it is relevant to the availability and priority of the system, as well as pedagogical interests.

In short, the user must decide: How does the simulation, the drill and practice, the tutorial, or the inquiry mode fit into his pedagogical scheme? One can then determine the capabilities and constraints of particular hardware and software which will support it satisfactorily. The computer technology is available. It is a question of purposes, which only the instructional designer, the administrator, faculty, and student users can answer.

As noted earlier, networking adds some dimensions to the trade-off decision-making. Networking can provide the user with the capability for sharing resources not possessed locally. Applied to national instructional needs, it could enable the teacher or the student to access a widespread library of courses and support programs that may be available elsewhere. To bring this concept to operational reality will require considerable planning, dollar investment for feasibility analyses, breakthroughs in long-distance communication costs, and heavy investment in cooperative programs by potential suppliers and users.

A Potpourri of Decisions for the Potential Educational User of Computers

USER REQUIREMENTS

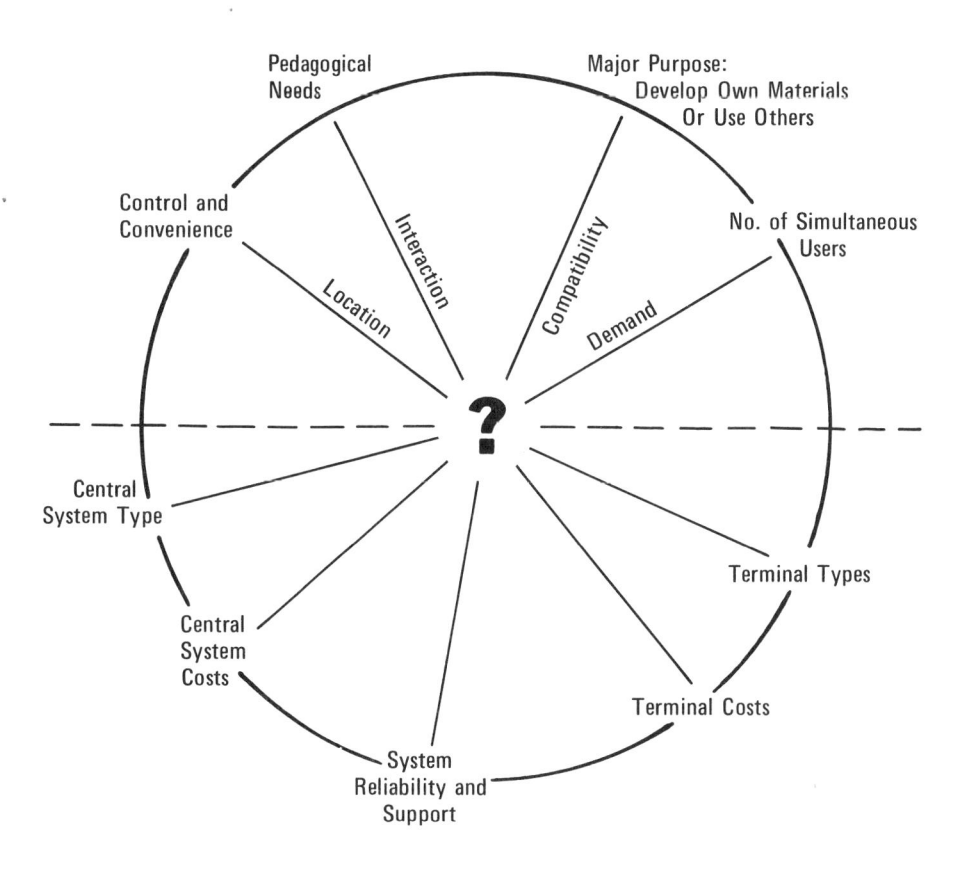

- Pedagogical Needs
- Major Purpose: Develop Own Materials Or Use Others
- Control and Convenience
- No. of Simultaneous Users
- Interaction
- Location
- Compatibility
- Demand
- Central System Type
- Terminal Types
- Central System Costs
- Terminal Costs
- System Reliability and Support

SYSTEM CONSIDERATIONS

Source: Seidel, 1974

Figure 30

The rationale for establishing national academic networks for instruction is clear: Where the capabilities do not exist on campus they can be obtained by going to other institutions. This can be accomplished at a lower cost, but they are then duplicated locally. Additionally, forming cooperative groups to combine the kinds of user capabilities on a super-institutional basis can greatly enhance discipline identification and, in turn, discipline-oriented curricular developments. Thus, for example, embryologists at one school of medicine can talk on-line to embryologists at another school on a joint curriculum development project. On a national scale, resources can be pooled to create critical masses of personnel expertise and facilities to further curriculum reform. An excellent example of a beginning in the medical school area is the Lister Hill network sponsored by the National Library of Medicine. It would be instructive for federal and state administrators to monitor this effort closely to determine the prospects for a network to become self-sustaining once the National Library of Medicine withdraws financial support. The CONDUIT project warrants similar attention as an alternative "soft-wired" national network.

Speculating further, the most far-reaching implications of national networking are in very broad areas of educational system reform. If successful, they could provide an alternative learning system, and society could take a major step toward implementation of personally relevant instruction. In medicine, as in other fields, they could lead to a nationwide learning resource pool. A student could have access to a library of courses which are not available at a particular institution but are available on a national academic network. This capability could be augmented by local subject-matter consultants available only on a part-time basis. The student could obtain education on demand. This concept has the possibility for becoming a reality, but it will take the intense kinds of exploration noted above to make it an operational delivery system.

The essence, then, is that recent advances in computer hardware (and software) are adequate to support a wide range of learning experiences. At the present stage of educational technology, the real concerns are for educators, institutions, and state and federal decision-makers to consider the user arrangements which are required and desirable. Thus, the technical capabilities that are available can be made pedagogically useful for the desired learning and development activities of the student and faculty members. As will be discussed in the next chapter, this approach will require careful consideration of alternative comprehensive national strategies to take into account the various facets of development and delivery of quality CBLM.

SUMMARY

Recent advances in computer hardware and software are adequate to support a wide range of learning experiences. At the present stage of technology, the major concerns for education relate to the organizational arrangements whereby these technical capabilities may be made available to students for the desired learning activities. In order to advance the state-of-the-art in instructional computing through continued research and development, and at the same time provide for more widespread access to computer-based learning materials, resource sharing on an unprecedented level is required nationally.

Computer networks provide the technical foundation for resource sharing. Considerable work needs to be done by users' groups, institutions, states, and federal agencies in order to work out the organizational and economic arrangements needed to make resource sharing a reality.

Chapter 7

ALTERNATIVE NATIONAL MODELS: STRATEGIES FOR CHANGE

...There is a much better chance that the benefits of instructional technology will be effectively and fully utilized if its introduction and development are coordinated and planned than if it is allowed to follow its present, largely uncontrolled course...

(Carnegie Commission on Higher Education, *The Fourth Revolution*, June 1972, p. 46)

The decade of the 1960's showed an acceleration in instructional uses of computers in education. With this acceleration came literally thousands of individual local development efforts accompanied by a corresponding proliferation of reports, general articles, and other sporadic attempts at communicating results. We have now reached the stage where those concerned with computer applications are shifting their attention to designing better ways of sharing information and resources among educational institutions.

A large number of small experimental efforts are currently underway in the nation's schools and colleges. Few have led to the adoption of the computer as an instructional aid on a national scale. Barriers and obstacles to the more rapid implementation of computer applications in instruction were discussed in Chapters 4 and 5. Briefly reviewing these obstacles, they are: current development efforts are small-scale and widely dispersed; many of the instructional materials or software are of marginal or untested quality; potential users need to be trained to exploit the computer's potential as an instructional aid; and a coordinated dissemination capability is lacking. Ways in which these barriers can be overcome, in order to facilitate the adoption of computer-based instructional materials and procedures, need to be explored.

Systematic, coordinated development, dissemination, and utilization programs are outlined in this chapter. Alternative strategies are examined in terms of their advantages and disadvantages for accomplishing different goals.

Current Attempts at Development and Dissemination

In order to evaluate the need for comprehensive national programs, first it is necessary to have a perspective on current attempts and the problems which have been encountered. The most pervasive model for developing and disseminating educational materials is the "textbook model" in which the principal agents are the professor and the commercial publisher. Oversimplified, the development process goes something like this: First the author draws up an outline, perhaps even finishes the draft of a first chapter and shows it to a publisher's representative. The publisher ascertains the potential market and sends out the chapter for review. If accepted by the publisher, the author takes pen (and sometimes graduate students) in hand and grinds out chapter after chapter.

Technically, it is fairly simple to photocopy drafts of chapters or problems for student tryout. The author can test the organization of his ideas through lectures to his own class. Student feedback can be incorporated fairly easily into manuscript revisions.

Once the final manuscript has been sent to the publisher, professional editors have the competence to package the material in the traditional form—the textbook.

Potential users (teachers), when presented with the option of using the text in their courses, can compare the text to others with which they are familiar. They can make the judgment as to whether and how to use the book in their course or school. Success is evaluated by the publisher in terms of a simple optimization function relating dollar volume, number of sales units, share of total possible market, cost to produce, and cost to market. He has a small, known dollar investment with a reasonable projection of return.

In the area of computer-based learning materials, however, there are many reasons why the "textbook model" has not worked. A higher dollar investment is required by the publisher to produce a less predictable sales volume. His editors are not trained to test and debug computer programs. The publisher is forced to fill in a void in computing literacy of potential users. Also, potential users need to try out the materials before adopting them. User sampling costs for computer materials are far higher than the costs of distributing sample copies of a new textbook. These factors, coupled with the innovative nature of computer materials and the ambiguous nature of the market, are the reasons that commercial publishers have not fulfilled their traditional role in providing the incentives for development of curricular materials.

It is interesting to recall some projections made by one expert back in 1968. Rodgers (1968) predicted that the new combinations of hardware manufacturers and publishers were the groups to watch in solving all the complex problems noted in this discussion.

In particular, he noted at that time the merging of Xerox and RCA with publishing houses and the IBM and SRA combine as interesting new development capabilities within the area of CBLM. He also saw Harcourt Brace Jovanovich as an innovative publishing company taking the lead in developing and disseminating CBLM. Today RCA is no longer in the CAI market and Harcourt Brace withdrew from its commitment to developing CAI materials. None of the other traditional publishing houses has either been willing or able to take the required risks.

Educational Institution Role

Individual educational institutions have had a major role in the development of computer-based learning materials. The major question is whether individual educational institutions can accomplish all the functions necessary to develop and disseminate computer-based learning materials. One of the strongest assets of an educational institution is the availability of individual authors, creative instructional designers, and scholars to contribute to the development. Also, there is a ready supply of students on which the materials may be tried out and revised, based on student and teacher evaluation. This is a *must* with computer materials which are highly innovative and complex.

While many individual developments have taken place at educational institutions, and the educational institutions have been the main sponsor of development projects, the financing has come primarily from outside sources. This limitation of institutions is apparent on a large project, where the project is discontinued as soon as the outside financing ends.

Another problem, in many educational institutions, is a structure which rewards research and not curricular development. In fact, the institutional structure may create negative incentives where the innovative teacher may be penalized for trying out new methods of instruction using computers.

Despite the drawbacks, there are still many advantages of institutional sponsorship. The fact that the institutions have the expert personnel and student population makes the institution a natural setting for development. Also, if the college or university has a special influence based on its prominence in a field, there is additional value to institutional sponsorship of projects in that field. In addition, educational institutions with a computer science major have a steady supply of student programmers to participate in development projects.

Many institutions of higher learning are well equipped to provide training in the use of computers in education. The institutions are able to offer educational programs in the development of curricular materials using computer technology. Also, the institutions can provide training support for the adoption of computer-based learning materials since they have the facilities, computer technologists, and educators experienced with the problems of using the innovations.

Cooperative Arrangements
Among Institutions

There are many examples of universities attempting to provide a more comprehensive program through cooperative arrangements. In the CONDUIT Project, sponsored by the National Science Foundation (Weeg, *et al.*, 1973). the participants are sharing instructional programs, with a total of approximately 100 institutions reached altogether. While this arrangement has demonstrated the feasibility of sharing, there have been problems of coordination and financing the activities. The question remains at this writing whether a network of networks is a viable model for national sharing of computer-based learning materials.

It is important to keep in mind that the CONDUIT project does not include support for the development of materials, but only their dissemination. Many problems remain with the identification of existing materials, as well as their packaging and delivery to network participants. These problems are described in detail in Chapter 5. Also, there is the possibility that the well of materials may run dry, or that institutions may not be willing to pay the cost for receiving materials, making it difficult for this type of organization to be self-perpetuating.

Other Resources

Discipline-based organizations are another resource with an active role in the development and dissemination of computer-based learning materials. Associations, committees, commissions, and professional societies have carried out limited functions in this area. Discipline associations have sponsored the preparation of specialized bibliographies of computer programs. Discipline committees have performed an evaluative task as the reviewer of computer-based learning materials.

The principal drawback to broader discipline participation is the frequency with which discipline groups normally meet. It is difficult for a discipline group to take on the responsibility for the actual development work or to carry out a sustained program of dissemination. Despite this constraint, discipline groups should assume a larger role within a more comprehensive program strategy.

Nonprofit educational research and development organizations are another agent to be considered. The nonprofit firm may be the facilitator for a comprehensive program of innovation. For example, Research for Better Schools has organized a large network of experimental schools that facilitates tryout and dissemination of curriculum developments.

Another strength of a nonprofit firm is the availability of a stable research and development staff needed for long-term development. Also, they have an advantage over the commercial publisher in that they are not required to answer to the stockholders at the end of each fiscal year.

The main disadvantage of many nonprofit firms is that they are physically and organizationally removed from the environment where the materials will be used.

One interesting development has been the emergence of special purpose organizations specifically for computer curricula. Computer Curriculum Corporation and Courseware, Inc., are two such examples. The advantage of these organizations is their specialized knowledge in the development and marketing of CAI materials.

From the review above it is evident that a more comprehensive program will have to be undertaken if computer-based curricular materials are to make a significant national impact on learning. Commercial publishers, individual authors, educational institutions, discipline organizations, and nonprofit educational R & D firms do not independently have the resources, organizational structure, and know-how to meet this objective. Further, individual government agencies, whether state or federal, have traditionally not had the legislative authority or financial resources to support comprehensive programs for development and widespread dissemination of innovative curricula. An agency that can support curriculum development, for example, may be limited in its authority to support the teacher training needed for adoption of the materials.

NEED FOR COHERENT STRATEGIES

The current efforts in research, development, and dissemination of computer learning materials have been disappointing from the viewpoint of national impact. While there have been a large number of instructional computer programs developed, only a handful have resulted in widespread advances in the application of computers in education.

From our investigation, we believe the major reason has been the lack of a coherent plan for the development of quality materials justifying widespread adoption. Individual projects have been funded for some special purpose, e.g., research on the pedagogical implications of a particular instructional strategy. Few projects have included all the activities necessary to develop and implement integrated computer-based curriculum packages. In addition, the development projects have occurred under organizational structures not set up for functions required for widespread dissemination.

Alternative National Models: Strategies for Change

A "coherent strategy" for a national program would take into account many dimensions of computer-based curriculum development. These dimensions are summarized in Figure 31.

Dimensions of a Coherent Strategy

Targets	Products	Component Functions	Mechanisms	Organization
Public Education	Adjunct	Sponsor & Approve Projects: Specific CBCM a. Goals b. Scope	Individual	Local
Higher Education	Mainline		Discipline	State
	Program Packages & Support Materials	Finance: Front-end continuing	Professional Society	Regional
Continuing Education	Delivery Systems			National
		Develop Materials	Commercial Publisher	Center
Professional Education	Texts	Package CBCM	Educational Institution	Consortium
	Programs	Disseminate CBCM		Computer Network
Special Education	Problem sets	a. Information Exchange b. Market Packages	Local Government	
	Simulations	Provide Delivery Systems	State Government	Corporation
	Games	Training for		
	Curricula	a. Developer Personnel b. User Personnel	Federal Government	
	Systems	c. Marketing Personnel d. Support Personnel (e.g., computer center people)	Lending Agencies	

Figure 31

To be "coherent," a strategy must tie together all the dimensions into a unified effort. The strategy would begin with the target population and the nature of the products to be developed. A strategy that is used successfully at the higher education level, for example, may not work for secondary education. Similarly, a strategy that works for one type of materials, e.g., adjunct materials used to augment the traditional curriculum, may not work in the case of instructional systems that replace the traditional curriculum.

The *component functions* to be performed must fit into some comprehensive plan if the fragmentation of earlier projects is to be avoided. A comprehensive plan would include goal setting, sponsorship, type of products, the packaging of instructional materials for dissemination, the provision of training for faculty users, and the type of delivery system that will be used.

Our examination of a significant number of computer-based curriculum projects has pointed to the consistent lack of a total program. Each individual project has limited resources and does not include key functions needed to make a significant impact. Since no single organization now in existence is suitable for conducting a total program, a comprehensive program would have to coordinate the efforts of individual agents or form new organizational structures designed to meet the needs.

The organizations selected for carrying out specific functions are a key factor in making an impact. A professional society may be the ideal sponsor for highly innovative instructional programs, while a minicomputer manufacturer may be the best choice for marketing programs written in BASIC.

The last dimension, *organization*, is important because of the problems introduced by the computer. The organizational arrangement is one of the major factors in widespread dissemination. The organization should be able to provide the proper level of support to solve the technical and management problems that arise during the tryout and classroom use of the materials.

ALTERNATIVE NATIONAL MODELS

This chapter presents five alternative models for accomplishing broad-based computer curriculum adoption. These models are a synthesis of the ideas of dozens of educators, developers, and researchers who have addressed the problems of educational innovation, computer-based curricula, and curriculum development.

Taken collectively, these models contain a wide range of alternative approaches, strategies of development, and diffusion of computer innovations. The models suggest many different approaches to organizing concerted programs for using our investment in computer technology. The models are not mutually exclusive, but rather are sets of functions that may be recombined into any number of programs on a federal, regional, state, or discipline basis. The particular program structure and combination of functions would be geared to the goals of

the programs in terms of:
- educational levels reached,
- disciplines involved,
- type of materials developed,
- specific target population,
- comprehensiveness of the curriculum,
- purposes for using computers in the curriculum, and
- sophistication of the technology.

National Program Exchange

The idea of a national exchange, or clearinghouse, for computer-based curricular materials has received considerable attention in the past two or three years. The National Science Foundation's Office of Computing Activities has received dozens of proposals for the establishment of an exchange or clearinghouse. The basic idea behind most such proposals is to make the existing computer-based curricular materials available to more users. The idea of a centralized service, or clearinghouse for materials, sounds rather simple and obvious. However, there are many issues and problems surrounding it. Many earlier attempts at providing similar services have not been entirely successful, for a variety of reasons.

Essentially, an exchange would have to perform the functions that are traditionally performed by commercial publishers—editing, packaging, reproduction, marketing, distribution—plus other functions commercial publishers have been reluctant to perform due to the technical complexity and financial investment required. These include, among others, technical test and debug of computer programs, technical program documentation, and user training in the technical and educational implementation of the materials. One argument against establishment of such an organization with public funds is that it would compete with or discourage the development of commercial market mechanisms.

We believe that an exchange mechanism could be designed to help establish a commercially viable market for computer-based curricular materials. A primary objective of such an organization would be to phase itself out of existence within a specified time period, with commercial organizations taking over the functions of the exchange organization.

A central question about the establishment of an exchange is whether there is a large enough supply of existing materials to justify the expense of setting up the organization. Our study indicates that the number of quality materials is limited, but is sufficient to initiate an exchange provided the exchange organization is set up to package existing materials in a form suitable for distribution.

In Chapter 5 we reviewed the great variety of organizations which are presently involved in some aspects of disseminating computer-based learning materials. These organizations have unique ways of reaching and supporting their users—based on discipline groups, geographic proximity, similar computer systems, networking, and so forth. To be effective, a National Exchange organization should be designed to have close working arrangements with such existing organizations. Table 6 illustrates the possible division of functions between, for example, a National Exchange and a regional or state network such as the North Carolina Educational Computer Service (NCECS) (see Chapter 5 for a description of NCECS).

Where would the financing come from? In all probability, a national exchange would be federally supported. Participating institutions could be expected to furnish some of the funds through a membership fee. It is also possible that the Exchange could be made partially self-supporting by charges for services.

In the past, one of the barriers to national exchange has been the incompatibilities of institutional computer hardware. However, the experiences of CONDUIT indicate that hardware incompatibility is not a significant barrier if the technical support personnel are available to convert programs to run on different machines.

Figure 32 illustrates how the National Program Exchange might provide support for the packaging, dissemination, and training of potential users. It also illustrates the extent to which an exchange is dependent upon existing delivery networks. Institutions, not a member of a network, would have to pay the costs or use their own computer center staff to implement the instructional programs on their machine. This cost could be passed on to the students through a charge for using the computer learning materials in a manner analogous to paying a special lab fee.

Roles of National and Regional Organizations in Proposed National Strategy for Dissemination

Function	National Clearing-House Role	Regional Service Role
Selection of materials to be disseminated	Discipline committees or conferences	Test marketing via faculty and student workshops for the region, or materials provided by national clearinghouses or others.
Publicity	National professional societies and journals; National clearinghouse catalog	Regional subset of catalog; Local communications channels; regional newsletters
Demonstration		Films, videotapes provided by national clearinghouse or development project; regional workshops.
Packaging	In-house staff for documentation; development projects; commercial publishers	Modifications and augmentations to package by Regional Users (operations guides, program conversion, education guides).
Reproduction of materials	In-house staff and facilities; commercial publisher	Regional modifications and augmentations by in-house staff and facilities
Distribution/ Delivery	Distribution of programs and packages to Regional Group	Local channels of distribution and delivery—regional network, commercial time-sharing, institutional computer centers; commercial publishers.
Technical Implementation Support	Standardized program and systems documentation; information on other implementations	Program conversion when required; circuit riders for operations assistance augmentation to operations guides where required.
Educational Implementation Support	Standards for packaging to include teacher guides; teacher and administrator training materials, videotape, etc., as appropriate; training for regional workshop leaders and curriculum coordinators as appropriate.	Local and regional training workshops as appropriate; newsletter containing educational experiences and evaluative information from users in this and other regions.
Financing the Dissemination Activities	Initially, federal support. Continuing, charges for services and products	State and institution support

Table 6

National Program Exchange Model

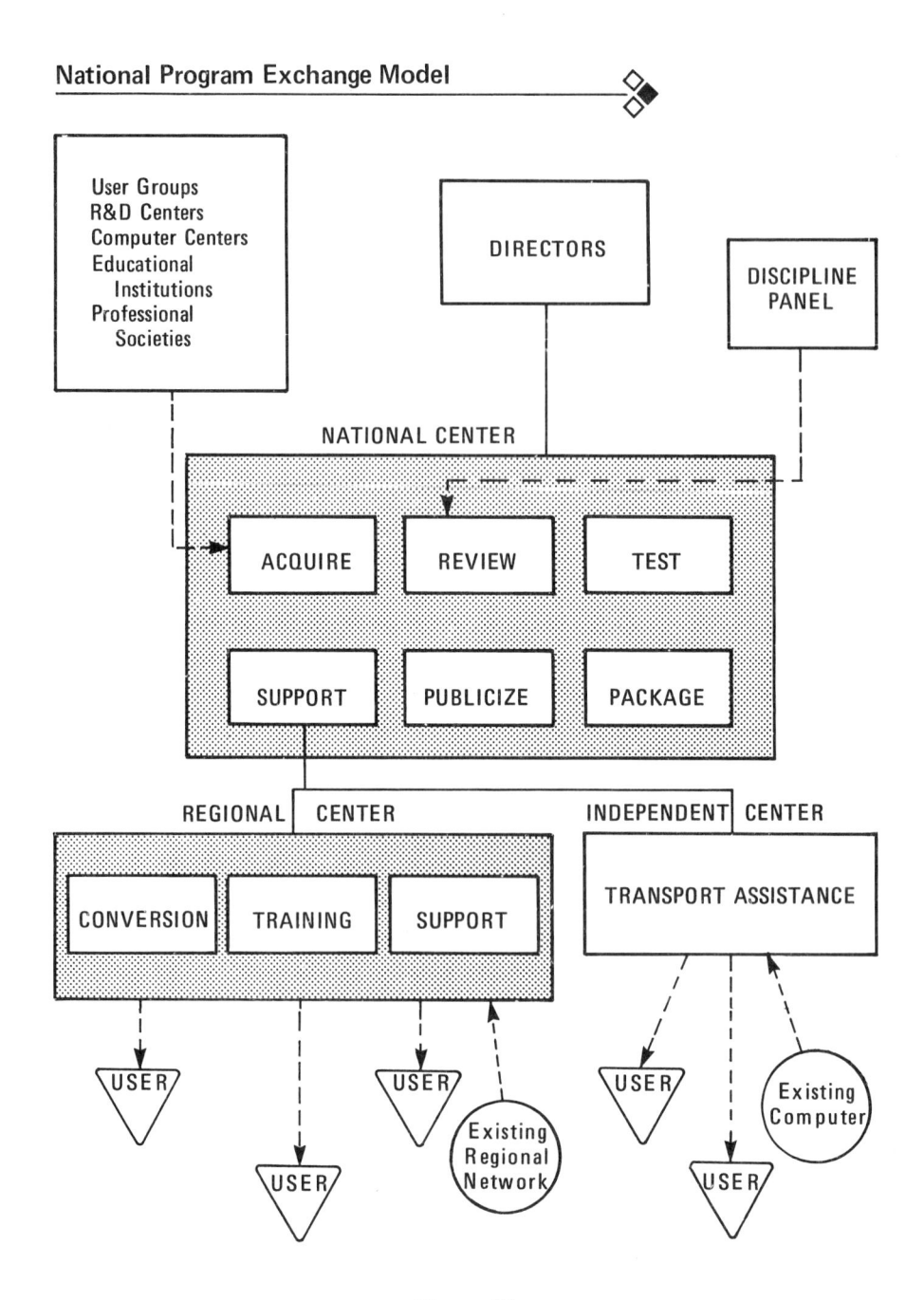

Figure 32

Discipline Center Model

The discipline center model has been proposed as the best way to achieve the development of high quality curricular materials which will be adopted by teaching professors in a particular discipline. This is in contrast to a national exchange which cuts across a large number of subject areas and focuses on the dissemination function. Of course, a discipline center could develop a bibliography of materials available and provide an information service to members of that discipline. However, the organization would not be structured to provide the total support functions that are necessary for exchanging complex computer-based materials.

A professional society would sponsor a center, financed to a limited extent through society dues and, at a later stage, through royalties made available from the sale of curriculum products. It would be necessary for the federal government to assume a major role in the initial financing of such centers.

The principal contributors to each of the discipline-oriented centers would be teaching professors recruited for specific periods of time to develop curriculum materials in their areas of specialization (see Figure 33). A permanent staff of experienced curriculum design specialists would be available to support the teacher-authors. Quality control would be exercised through the use of a professional, discipline-oriented, review panel. Materials developed at the center would be tried out and evaluated at nearby institutions and/or at the author's institution.

One advantage of the discipline center is its emphasis upon the development of quality curriculum materials through the recruitment of outstanding individuals and the imposition of stringent quality controls on the materials developed.

Another strength of a discipline center, compared to a National Exchange, is the professional visibility that participants would obtain by being contributors to a national discipline-based group.

Implicit in the discipline center approach is the assumption that future curriculum development will follow traditional discipline lines, and this does not agree with the recent movement toward an interdisciplinary curriculum. The Center for Unified Science Education, sponsored by the National Science Foundation, illustrates the point.

Discipline Center Model

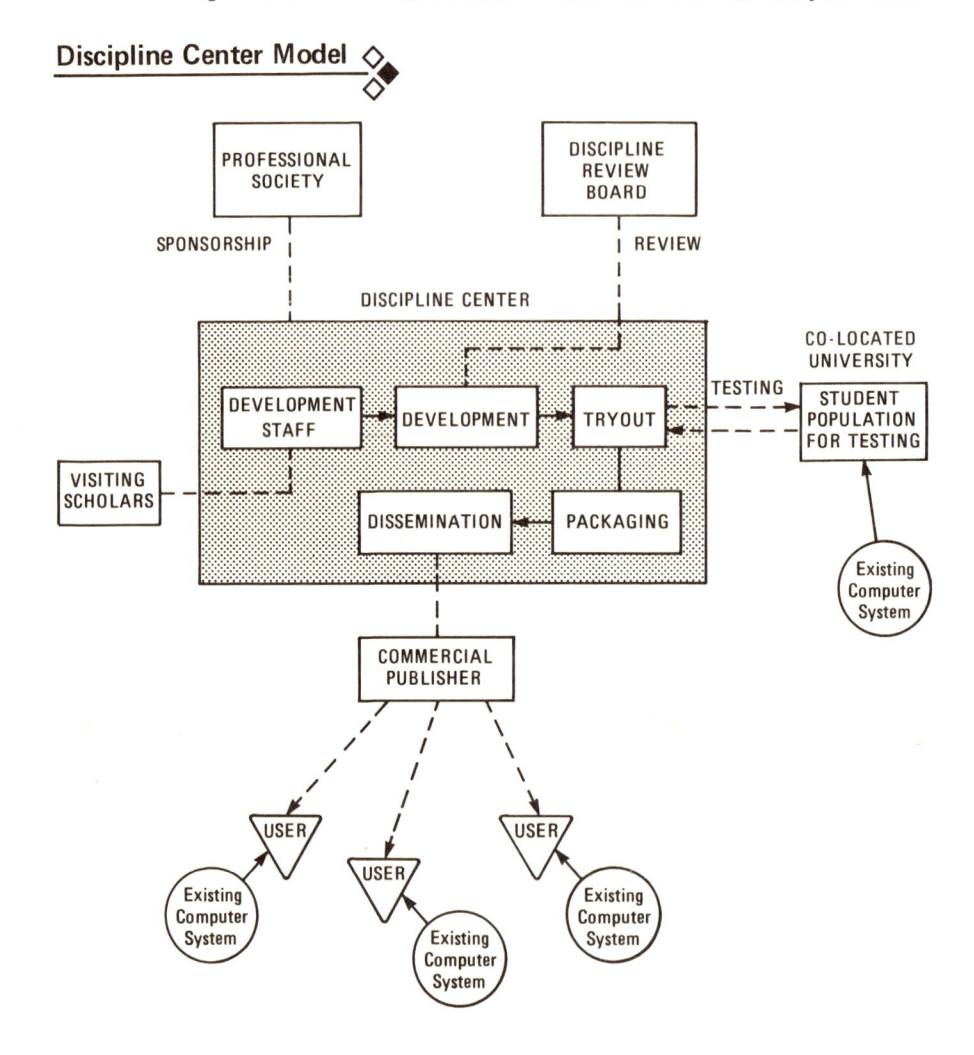

Figure 33

The principal objective of this newly established center is the building of an interdisciplinary curriculum which cuts across the boundaries of physics, chemistry, biology, and the social sciences.

Another potential disadvantage of a discipline center, unless a separate mechanism was available for dissemination, is the possibility

Alternative National Models: Strategies for Change 307

that the staff would focus almost entirely on the problems of development, to the exclusion of any plans for active distribution of the center's products.

The discipline center model as described here is oriented toward higher education.

National Development Center Model

The major distinguishing characteristic of this model compared to other models is the centralization of development at a large national center. The center would have the resources, facilities, and staff required for systematic large-scale curriculum development.

The National Development Center would follow procedures designed to produce quality materials. These procedures might encompass the development of instructional objectives, the design and field testing of total curriculum packages, and a systematic evaluation of the learning outcomes with trial users.

An illustrative organizational arrangement for a National Development Center is shown in Figure 34. The Center would have a staff of highly skilled specialists such as educational psychologists, computer technologists, experts in instructional design, and CAI experts. These staff specialists would share their time among the different projects being undertaken at the Center. Therefore, the project development staffs would be interdisciplinary containing a mix of talents including the content experts and other experts already mentioned.

A National Development Center, like the one envisioned in this particular model, would require access to a large body of students in order to carry out full-scale tryouts of the Center's products. This implies the desirability of a connection to a large academic network. If the network was national in scope, this would be ideal since the Center's products would have national exposure during a large-scale tryout.

A large initial federal investment would be required. Therefore, the center might be established as a permanent or at least semi-permanent institution.

A major program like this might be set up under the aegis of the National Institute of Education. The location under NIE is compatible with the suggestion of the Commission on Instructional Technology

National Development Center Model

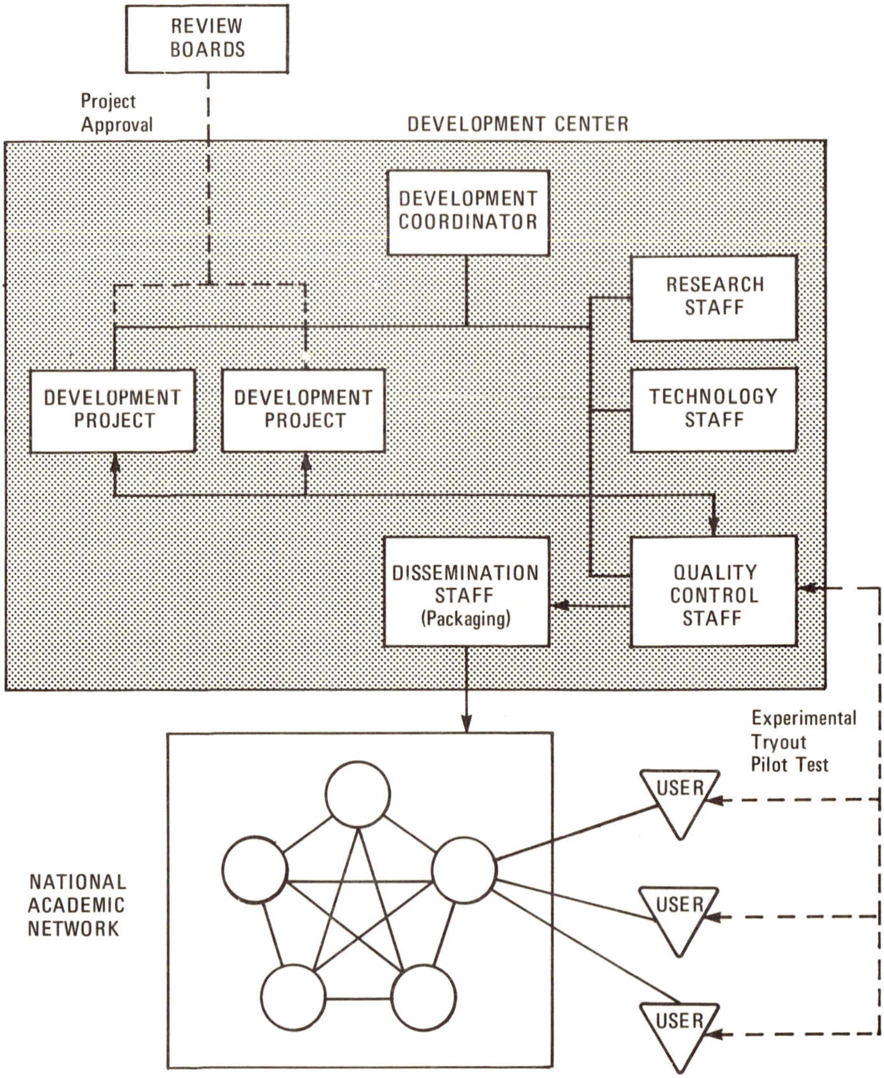

Figure 34

that a National Institute of Instructional Technology be established.

The product of a large, expert team effort could be reasonably expected to be a high impact curriculum that gains wide acceptance because of its superiority over existing curricula. The acceptance of curricula developed by the Center would be helped by the early involvement of potential users in the creation, test, and revision.

A fallout advantage would be greater sophistication of computer-based material developers through their training and experience at the Center. Members of the design teams would assimilate the skills of other team members with skills different from their own.

The National Center would undertake the job of maintaining an inventory of existing curricular materials in order to eliminate the wasteful duplication of efforts which occurs with uncoordinated project development. The Center would be able to evaluate proposals in terms of their overall contribution to the advance of education through computers.

The major disadvantage of such a large program would be the management problems that could arise.

In a large organization, the effort is slowed by bureaucratic procedures. This is especially disrupting in a creative curriculum development project. Another drawback of a National Center approach is the danger that developer personnel, physically removed from an educational environment may get out of touch with the real interests and needs of users. This disadvantage could be overcome by locating the Development Center at an institution that is active in the field.

Lastly, discipline groups may resent the fact that the Development Center is making decisions on the areas in which computers should be used and how they should be used. Therefore, a National Center organizational structure might provide for discipline societies to have a major say in the goals of various curriculum development projects.

The National Development Center, as envisioned here, would be oriented primarily toward developing and disseminating *computer-*oriented materials. It would not be a national curriculum development center in the sense of standardizing curricula in general across the nation. On the contrary, it would be designed to contribute to the overall repertoire of curricular materials available to an educational institution.

Regionally Based Learning Technology Centers

This model has been suggested by the Carnegie Commission report, *The Fourth Revolution* (Carnegie Commission, 1972). The report proposes that several regional centers be established for the purpose of providing instructional technology services to participating states and local institutions. This approach would offer the advantage of amortizing the cost of developing and disseminating technologically oriented materials across a large number of users assuming that the services are widely accepted. The report proposes that the Centers' products would be instructional units varying in degree of comprehensiveness. There would be a library and informational retrieval system provided to the region in which each center is located. The teaching and learning segments would be tried out in schools by the staff of the distribution unit (see Figure 35). The Center would have facilities for the storage of computer programs and would provide on-line computer services for instructional administration. (The Computing Unit would provide the latter services.)

The Carnegie Report estimates that each regional center would require roughly $35 million as an initial capital investment and would also need an annual operating budget in the neighborhood of $150 million. Three sources of financial support would be potentially available. First, the federal government would provide the initial capital investment plus one-third of the total operating budget for a 10-year span. Secondly, the participating institutions would provide support on an as-needed basis. Thirdly, short-term special projects support might be obtained from state governments, foundations, or private industry.

The evaluation of instructional materials developed at the various regional centers would be carried out by independent commissions supported by either the government or a private foundation. Evaluative reports would be widely disseminated to the cooperating institutions and to participating state agencies.

The Regional Centers would differ from the USOE-sponsored Regional Laboratories and the university-based R & D centers in that they would be principally *service*- not *research*-oriented. The principal activities of the regional centers would be to identify, produce, and distribute already developed teaching and learning materials as well as

Regionally Based Learning Technology Center

Source Data: Carnegie Commission on Higher Education, 1972

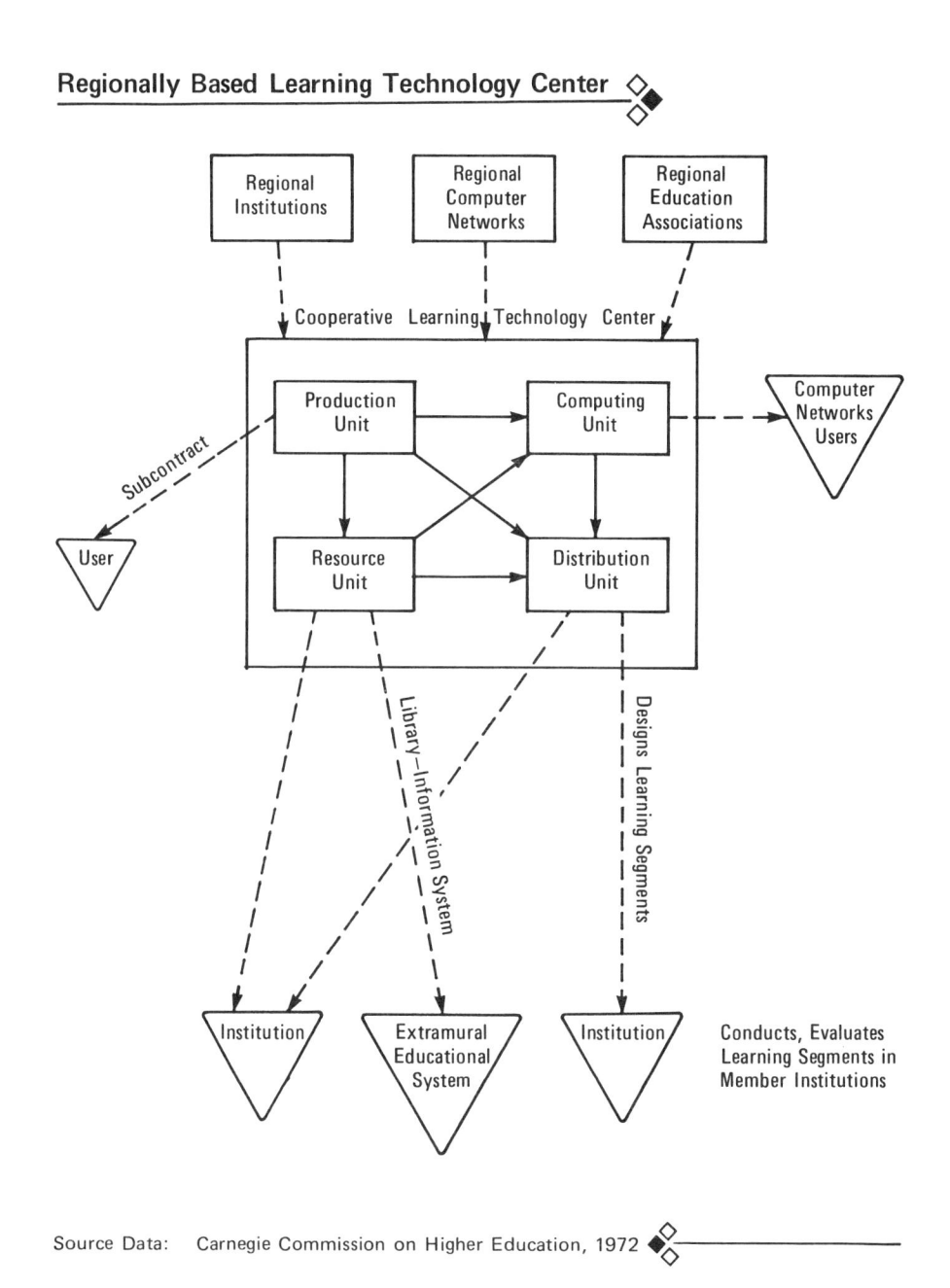

Figure 35

to make available their computing facilities, information retrieval capability, and cataloguing and production capabilities to participating institutions. Teachers wishing to incorporate a variety of materials and resources into their learning program would be provided with professional expertise and advice by the Regional Center. One of the novel features of such a cooperative relationship would be the availability of these resources to private profit-making educational institutions as well as public institutions.

The Regionally Based Learning Technology Centers have an advantage over the National Development Center of being located in closer physical proximity to the institutions which will use the products to be offered. However, the Regional Centers have a major disadvantage of not being part of either the state or the local educational structure. Political maneuvering could arise that would negate the advantages of being a Regional Center.

Another potential trouble with this model is the problem of having a sufficient discipline-based leadership to insure that the products will be favorably received. Unless teachers and curriculum specialists in local schools participate, considerable problems might be encountered.

Ideologically Based Center Model

This model is the most novel of the five presented here because the Center is neither discipline- or geographically based. Instead, the Centers are each organized around a particular educational ideology, e.g., "College Without Walls," and the computer's role would be directed toward supporting specific goals within that ideology.

Multiple centers would be sponsored to encourage a number of different educational philosophies. The federal government would provide the initiative to innovative uses of the computer within new educational systems. In each case the computer would have a central role in carrying out a center's unique educational philosophy. For example, in one center the computer would primarily be a surrogate teacher, in another a place to retrieve knowledge, and in a third situation an educational facilitator. The basic structure of an Ideological Center is shown in Figure 36.

Quality control standards would be employed to review and

Ideologically Based Center Model

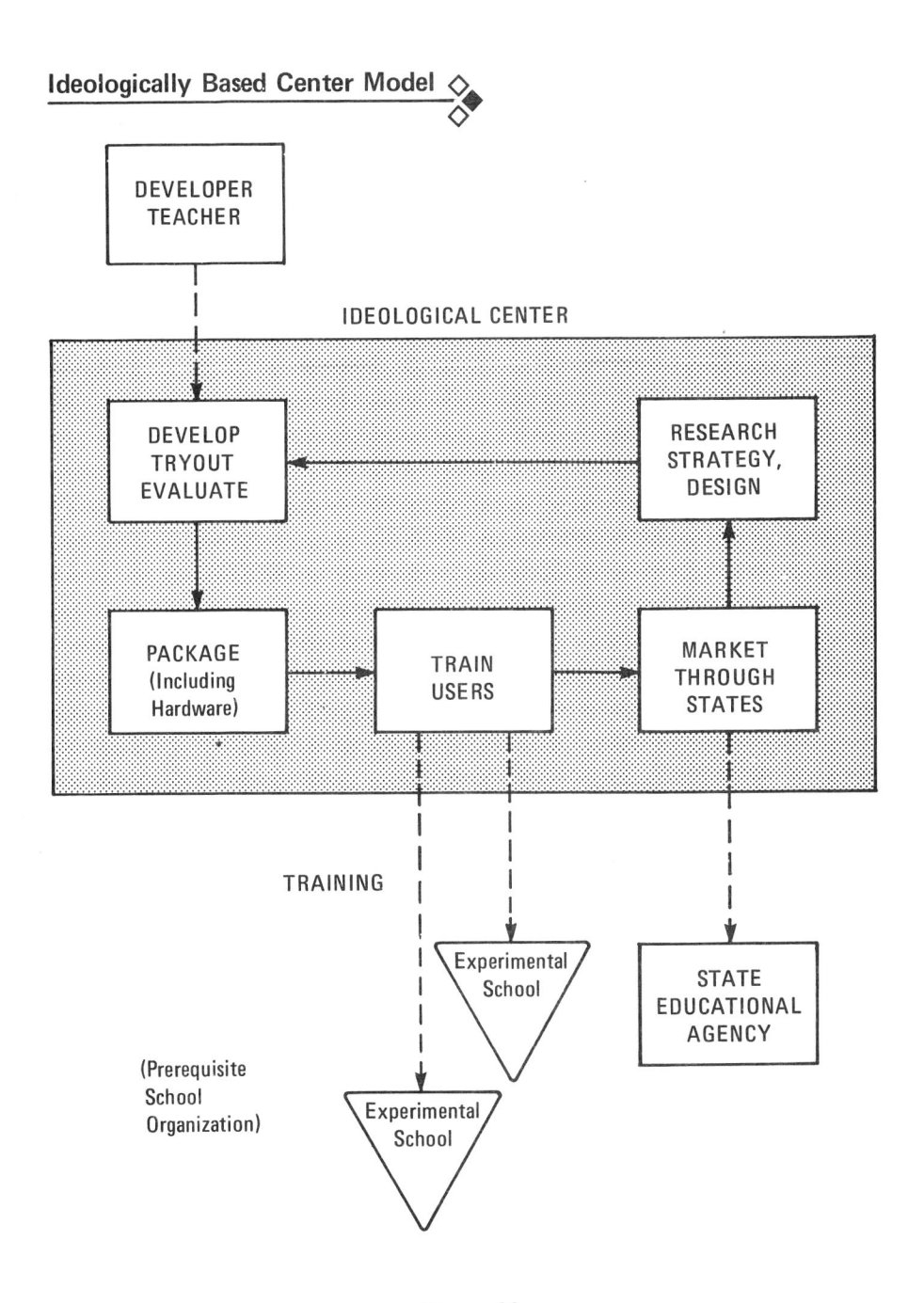

Figure 36

evaluate the entire systems developed to support the educational goals of the Center. Experimental schools would be used to try out the educational system developed by the Center. A linkage with state departments of education would be vital to gain cooperation and financial support for widespread dissemination.

A possible disadvantage of this model is the assumption that experimental schools can be found to try out totally new approaches to education. These schools may be difficult to find, although there is the precedent at the public school level with the network of experimental schools that Research for Better Schools organized.

Another problem would be the potential resistance encountered if a state educational department attempts to coerce local school districts into adopting a new learning system. Without the careful nurturing of teacher interest and acceptance, teachers' unions and professional associations could be expected to react negatively.

FINANCING COMPREHENSIVE PROGRAMS

Without detailed planning it is difficult to give any reliable estimate on project costs to implement programs of the scope of these models. The goals established for a particular program in terms of the type of development and dissemination projects, the number of these projects, and factors related to the national economy must be considered.

An individual curriculum development project may cost anywhere from $20,000 to $10,000,000, depending on the scope of the educational reform, the sophistication of the technology, the methodology of development, and the complexity of the materials.

If the products produced by a concerted federal program are going to have any national impact, financing must be available to package, publicize, and assist teachers to adopt the materials. This assistance might include financial support to try out and evaluate the innovative curricular materials. These costs are dependent upon the number of institutions reached.

If the project requires special computer hardware, e.g., a unique CAI terminal, the total project costs may be doubled because of the actual equipment costs and added technical complexity.

Tangible experience with comprehensive computer-based curricula effort is extremely limited, as there have been almost no large-scale projects. One current fairly comprehensive curricula development effort is for TICCIT, described earlier in this volume. Brigham Young University is contracted by the Mitre Corporation to develop a tutorial freshman year course for both math and English at a current estimated cost in excess of $1.5 million.

Project IMPRESS (Interdisciplinary Machine Processing for Research and Education in the Social Sciences) is an on-line analysis and data base retrieval system that cost $500,000 to develop. The funding did not include funds for dissemination of the system. Because of inflation, this project would run closer to $750,000 today; and if a national dissemination were part of the project, then the costs would be double or triple the development costs.

Experiences with non-computer curricula projects, even though there is no close parallel in terms of complexity level, may provide some guides on the overall scale at which funding is required. The ES-70 project was undertaken by federal and local agencies at a planned cost of $300 million over five years, including the financing for widespread dissemination. The $300 million was to be for the development and dissemination of five curricula covering four years of conventional education. This means that the estimated cost was a little over $10 million per year per curriculum project. The federal funding for this grand-scale project was cut off when development was just getting underway after a year of establishing the organizational structure.

Another example of a non-computer curriculum development is the Biological Sciences Curriculum Study (BSCS), funded at $5 million over five years between 1959 and 1964. BSCS produced three curricular packages that included teacher guides and supplementary materials. Savings were achieved through dual use of materials and development personnel.

TOTAL PROGRAM FUNDING LEVELS

The next question is the federal resources that would be allocated to computer-based education. There is no one answer, as it depends on the value attached to the computer's role in society, the program goals, and the competing demands for educational dollars. There are, however, several commissions which made some recommendations in the broader area of educational technology.

The most encompassing cost projections were suggested by the Commission on Instructional Technology (1970). For the recommended National Institute of Education to conduct the functions of research, curriculum development, and application to school systems, the Commission advocated an initial $565 million. The amount recommended for a National Institute of Instructional Technology (NIIT) within the NIE was $150 million annual funding with a $250 million recommendation for research, development, and implementation during the first year. The functions of the NIIT appear to encompass the proposed National Development Center Model within a broader context of educational R & D involving all forms of technology (e.g., TV, cassettes, etc.).

The Carnegie Commission recommendation for educational technology in only higher education (using the Regional Center approach) was $100 million for 1973 and increasing to one percent of the higher education operational budget. This initial figure appears extremely modest considering the size of the higher education enterprise. Robert Filep, former Director of the National Center for Educational Technology, Office of Education, estimates that the total annual expenditures for higher education in 1971 were $29.9 billion and it is projected that these expenditures will rise to $46 billion by 1981.*

Another approach is to look at the educational enterprise as comparable to the corporate model in which the research and development budget is 3 percent of the total budget (Seidel and Kopstein, 1970). Using this percentage, $870 million should currently be going into higher education R & D.

PROBLEMS OF FINANCE

The problems of finance are particularly severe because of the difficulty of obtaining official support for curriculum development

---

*Presentation at a three-day symposium on technology-based systems for improving instructional productivity in higher education, September 24-26, 1973, State University of New York, Stony Brook. Proceedings available from Educational Technology Publications, Englewood Cliffs, New Jersey 07632, titled *Improving Instructional Productivity in Higher Education.*

projects. Curriculum development projects do not have the high level of visibility of a media-based project. Therefore, it is much easier to obtain large-scale financing for a new hardware application, e.g., an educational satellite program, than it is to obtain money for an innovative curriculum that will use the media, e.g., instructional materials that will be transmitted by satellite.

Perhaps it is necessary to highlight one of the most significant funding issues mentioned in Chapter 1 and implied throughout this report. Total dollar expenditures on technology in education have, indeed, been impressive. Molnar (1971) has indicated that the U.S. Office of Education alone spent in fiscal year 1967 about four-fifths of a billion dollars for educational media funding. However, the accumulative effect of this investment has suffered from fractionalization. For any of the models proposed in this chapter to be brought into being, some *categorical* support would be necessary. Thus, a redirection of programs could accomplish some of the job without additional funding.

Realistically, however, it is still necessary to look to federal and state tax monies to provide the critical funding mass. It will be necessary for educators who understand the fundamental impact computers have on what we do and how we do it to convince government officials of the need to revamp traditional non-computer-based curricula in those areas where the computer is making an impact.

Other than direct federal and state support through tax monies, what other sources of funding can be found to support innovative educational programs? A bank vice-president suggested that a special state bond issue with a guaranteed purchase by banks was a method with real promise.* Recently the state of Virginia sold $20.9 million in higher education bonds to a bank syndicate, which in turn offered them to the public.

Another possibility is that banks and savings and loan institutions could make loans to finance large-scale projects and in this manner have an active role in financing socially useful programs. Because of the risks involved in funding innovations, there would have to be some federally backed guarantee of loans. This technique will not be practical until the

---

*Personal interview with Gorman Donnegan, vice-president, Riggs National Bank, Washington, D.C., May, 1973.

education marketplace develops to the point that a return on investment can be expected.

An even more speculative and yet increasingly employed source today is the lottery. Many states have begun to adopt this approach to raise general revenues, and Mexico has successfully used it for many years to support social programs at the national and local levels. A national lottery to support educational reforms sounds far-fetched, but as the lottery approach to raising money becomes more widely accepted generally, it may make good sense to accomplish educational reform through this mechanism.

Chapter 8

A SUMMARY OF FINDINGS, CONCLUSIONS, AND RECOMMENDATIONS

Major results of our study have implications for nationwide development, dissemination, and implementation of computer-based learning materials and systems. This chapter organizes the findings, interpretations, and recommendations into four broad categories relevant to U.S. education:
- significance of computer-based curricula;
- strategies for information exchange about computer-based education;
- mechanisms for disseminating computer-based curricula; and
- organizational structures to accomplish comprehensive programs of development, dissemination, and implementation.

These areas are addressed in terms of the *varied purposes* for introducing computer-based learning into U.S. education (e.g., *efficiency of instruction* or *educational reform*). They are analyzed with respect to what can be done by existing groups or agencies and what can be accomplished with new organizational structures.

A. What is the importance of, or requirement for, computer-based curricula in U.S. education?

Findings

The importance of computer-based curricula is tied to educational goals, alternative means of accomplishing these goals, and the value placed on the computer's role in society. The importance attached to computer-based curricula depends on the value attached to the computer in information processing, data retrieval, problem-solving and as a tool for augmentation of human intellect. If the assumption is made that the computer is an invaluable tool in solving complex problems, and in handling the accelerated growth of information, then computers are a key factor in education.

The importance of computer-based curricula as a means of making educational processes more cost-effective (cost per student per instructional hour) is based on two assumptions that have not been proven: (a) that computer-based systems are more cost-effective than alternative means, and (b) that cost-effective trade-offs are of major importance in educational decision-making.

The importance of computer-based curricula as a means of providing individualized instruction is based on the assumption that individualized instruction is superior to group instruction in terms of measures of learning outcomes.

Conclusions

The importance of, or need for, computer-based curricula can be stated relative to certain assumptions and purposes.

1. *Computing literacy*. Assuming continued growth of computing in society in general, and continually increasing influence of computer-based systems and methods in most scientific, business, and technological jobs, then a need seems obvious to enable citizens to gain knowledge of computer systems. Insofar as educational curricula are intended to provide students with job-relevant skills, then curricular materials and learning objectives relevant to these skills would be in demand as part of the curriculum at all levels of education. If the trend toward increased dependence on computing systems in society is assumed to continue, one can foresee the time in a decade or two when computing literacy would be as universally required as the ability to read and write. Young school children would learn such basic skills as procedure-writing, retrieving information on-line, requesting computer assistance with computations, and observing the dynamics of computer-based simulations. High school students would use computers routinely as part of their studies in most subject areas, and particularly in mathematics, engineering, sciences, and business subjects.

At the entering college level, a minimal set of computer-related skills on the part of the student would be assumed. Curricula in sciences, mathematics, engineering, and business routinely would

A Summary of Findings, Conclusions, and Recommendations

include computer methods and facilities as part of the subject-matter treatment.

If these assumptions and purposes are accepted, then the need for computer-based educational materials on a very large scale is apparent. For elementary levels, curricular materials to provide basic computing skills would be required. In high school and college curricula, the use of the computer would become part of the discipline or problem area in a way that is unprecedented today. An analogy might be made with reading and writing—most curricular materials assume the ability to read and write. Similarly, the high school and college curricula of the 1990's may be written to assume computing skills. Without such skills, the students would be as unprepared for jobs in business, industry, and government as they would be today without the ability to read and write.

2. *Educational Reform.* If one assumes a massive shift in formal education to individualized learning—including individual objectives, programs of study, and methods of learning, then computer-based systems and curricular materials may be seen as indispensable to the implementation of educational programs. The variety of learning materials and the repertoire of intelligent algorithms which would be needed to meet the diverse needs of all the people could not be stored, retrieved, evaluated, or updated without the aid of computer-based systems.

If this shift toward individualized learning is assumed, the need can be seen for large-scale computer-based systems in education for storage, retrieval, and update of learning materials, management of instruction, and educational guidance. If a need for life-long education on the part of the majority of citizens is assumed, computer-based systems would be in great demand to enable citizens to access learning materials on-line from places and at times convenient to them.

3. *Educational Efficiency.* If it is assumed that computer-based systems will become a cost-effective substitute for many functions a human teacher now performs, and if it is assumed that such cost-effectiveness is of paramount concern among educators, then it can be projected that in the 1990's there will be an enormous demand for computer programs of this type. Basic skills, especially in the elementary grades, would be acquired primarily through the use of

computer-managed or computer-assisted tutorial lessons and drill exercises.

4. *Curriculum Enhancement.* If one assumes the continuation of the information explosion and the pressures on individuals to acquire more and more knowledge in shorter and shorter time, it seems apparent that computer-based methods of learning would be among several innovations much in demand. If students are to acquire two or four times the knowledge in the same amount of time, it seems obvious that they must be armed with more efficient methods of learning than presently seen in traditional curricula. Computers will be used as an everyday tool by the student, not just to perform time-consuming computations and information retrieval, but also to help him focus on major concepts, complex problems, and powerful methods of studying complex phenomena.

Recommendations

1. Professional societies and curriculum development groups might establish committees to examine the above assumptions and purposes. If agreement is found, the implications for curriculum development over the next decade should be published, including comprehensive program recommendations.

2. Commercial publishing firms should reevaluate publishing plans and policies in light of a careful review of the above assumptions to determine whether there are areas of potential commercial development.

3. State departments of elementary and secondary education might take the following steps to ensure adequate provision of computer-based curricula in the schools:
- ensure that adequate computing facilities are available to the schools;
- provide for school administrators and faculty education on the impact of computers on society, education, and curricula;
- encourage or require the use of textbooks with computer-oriented subject-matter treatment, especially in mathematics, sciences, and business subjects;
- consider the adoption of learning objectives in the curriculum relating to skills in computing;

- actively develop logistical, administrative, and pedagogical procedures for accommodating total individualized curricula; and
- require state-supported curriculum development projects to seek inclusion of computing methods and materials.

4. The National Institute of Education should sponsor an investigation of the computer-related skills and knowledge needed by average citizens. These would become objectives for universal computing literacy.

5. The U.S. Department of Labor should sponsor studies of the computer-related skills required in major job and occupation categories. The results of such a study should be disseminated to state boards of education, community colleges, and colleges and universities for use in deriving curriculum objectives.

6. The National Science Foundation might sponsor major curriculum development programs in the basic sciences, which would be specifically designed to integrate the computer into the curriculum.

7. NIE, OE, and NSF might form joint working groups to pool their respective and collective bodies of information relevant to existing and potential computer-based curriculum development and evaluation. Consolidation of programs might be followed by joint sponsorship of major computer-based curricula development.

B. What is the need for and availability of information about computer-based education?

Findings

The demand for information about computer-based education is growing with the general growth in interest in educational uses of the computer. Indicators of this interest include the steadily growing participation in conferences about computers in education and the rise in the number of organizations active in sharing information about computers.

Currently there is no single source of information about computer-based learning materials. A teacher interested in finding out information about developments and materials in a discipline has to research many sources to find information, and often is unaware of some of these diverse sources. Information about computer innovations is rarely found in traditional information sources, such as discipline journals. There is only one professional society which currently publishes a journal for computer-based education; this was initiated in the fall of 1974. Much of the information on computer-based education is not generally available since it is contained in unpublished reports. Publicly available information on the quality of computer-based education materials or their educational benefits is practically non-existent.

Conclusions

Present information sources are not adequately serving information needs. This problem is acute for people who are not currently active in computer-based education, but are interested in information necessary to acquire an understanding of the developments which are occurring.

Research for information is more difficult than normal, because computer-based education cuts across computer science, educational technology, education, and the disciplines to which the materials are related.

Research for information is difficult because the individual information sources are limited in the information they have available, and difficulty is encountered getting information directly from the source.

Needs for information fall at all levels in the educational hierarchy including administrators, state planners, faculty deans, department heads, and individual teachers.

Recommendations

A special form of an information clearinghouse is needed because of the dynamic nature of developments within computer-based education. Possibly a computer-based system with on-line access as well as the usual means of communication would be desirable. An information clearinghouse would have to process information from a large number of published and unpublished sources and condense it into a form usable by people with a limited time to spend on learning about computer developments.

The information clearinghouse(s) would have to be initially

A Summary of Findings, Conclusions, and Recommendations 325

supported by the federal government. Because of the differences in higher education and secondary education, a separate clearinghouse is needed for each level. Because of the differences in relative program emphases by USOE and NSF, each might contribute a portion to the clearinghouse funding and jointly sponsor its establishment.

Analysis of costs and demands should be a requirement of the initial effort. The information clearinghouse could later evolve into a self-sustaining clearinghouse for computer-based materials after demand was established through the distribution of information about educational uses of materials.

C. What strategies and mechanisms might be effective for disseminating computer-based curricular materials themselves (rather than or in addition to information about them)?

Findings

No single organization or strategy is adequate to reach all types of users at all levels of education and all disciplines. It is possible to have two separate organizations to accomplish the unique function of disseminating (1) information about CBLM and (2) the materials themselves. Another approach would be to establish one center and phase the functions so that function No. 1 (publicity) is set in place first and then a second function is added (e.g., packaging). The determination could be made on a basis of feasibility (available dollars, resources, etc.).

There have been a number of limited attempts at dissemination of specific types of materials to specific audiences.

Dissemination of computer-based curricular materials is complex and expensive due to the technical complexity, innovative character of the curriculum, the intended purposes of the materials, and the difficulty in assessing costs and benefits of adoption.

Dissemination and adoption of CBLM requires unprecedented cooperation among educators, publishers, computer manufacturers, funding agencies, and developers of materials.

Successful dissemination strategies provide for several major functions: planning; evaluation and selection of materials; packaging; publicity; demonstration; physical production; delivery, including computer facilities; technical support to users; and educational implementation support to users.

Conclusions

Different strategies for dissemination may be considered depending on purposes.

1. *Computing Literacy and Opportunity.* On a state or regional basis, organizations like the North Carolina Educational Computing Service can provide the technical and educational support functions needed to disseminate CBLM.

In order for such regional organizations to be fully effective, a national capability is required for communication among the regional groups. A national clearinghouse that provides not only information but the programs and materials themselves would greatly enhance the operation of regional groups. On the other hand, regional or state organizations, representing the particular needs and dissemination channels of the regional institutions, would greatly enhance the effectiveness of a national clearinghouse.

2. *Educational Reform.* In order for any single package of curricular materials or computer-based system for learning to be effective in reforming the overall educational system, it must be implemented in a school environment conducive to those aims.

The network-of-schools strategy could be a model for dissemination of computer-based learning materials and systems within a particular reform philosophy and methodology.

3. *Educational Efficiency (instructional cost-effectiveness) Purposes.* The type of national strategy for dissemination of computer-based learning materials and systems which would most likely support the cost-effectiveness goal today is a competitive, open market strategy. Several commercial firms, competing to provide packages which meet the costs and effectiveness criteria of their potential customers, will provide some alternatives from which decision-makers can select the best for their own situations.

One of the most promising strategies for achieving a commercially profitable market for existing organizations is outlined by Levien, *et al.* (1972) and is exemplified in the relationship between Houghton Mifflin and the Time Share Corporation described in Chapter 5 of this volume.

4. *Curriculum Enhancement.* The strategy suggested under computing literacy goals, which involves regional organizations supported by a national clearinghouse, would support curriculum enhancement,

A Summary of Findings, Conclusions, and Recommendations 327

adding the following refinements: the clearinghouse should include selection and review mechanisms which rely on committees or conferences of discipline experts to review the materials submitted. Further, the clearinghouse must have well-established links with developers in the various disciplines in order to search out quality materials that are being developed as part of the research and teaching of individual professors. A national clearinghouse cannot rely on the regional groups entirely for publicity channels. The prestige of national publications and societies in the disciplines must be included in the publicity function.

Recommendations

Federal and state funding agencies could encourage initiatives made by commercial firms to increase cooperation among themselves and with educational institutions. Some examples might be:

1. NSF-funded summer institutes might arrange with a commercial time-sharing company to provide computing facilities for the institute.
2. Educator training programs (such as summer institutes and workshops) that are funded by federal and state agencies might be opened up to representatives of commercial firms.
3. Seed money might be provided to commercial time-sharing companies desiring to enter the education market. Contractual arrangements could be made for reimbursement to the government from profits after the market has been established.
4. A conference on dissemination of computer-oriented materials would enhance communication among commercial publishers, computer manufacturers, communications suppliers, time-sharing companies, professional societies, developers of computer-oriented curricula, and educational users. Presentations and work sessions would be made by representatives of each industry.

A federal agency, such as NIE, USOE, or NSF, might fund a study to analyze existing and potential mechanisms for providing educator training, and recommend national strategies for accomplishing a reasonable set of objectives. *The problem is not primarily one of developing training materials and curricula for educators, but rather the organizational arrangements and communications channels by which educators can be reached, and the incentives they have or do not have for acquiring this literacy.*

D. What are the limitations of current organizational structures? Are new organizational structures needed?

Findings

Curriculum development projects and/or dissemination agencies under current organizational structures are limited in scope.

If widespread national usage of computers in education is a desirable goal, then current organizational structures are not suitable for carrying out a comprehensive strategy that can produce a noticeable national impact. A comprehensive strategy to develop, disseminate, and implement computer-based materials and systems would include such functions as adequate initial financing, curriculum tryout and revision, educational evaluation, packaging of instructional materials, publicity, technical support, and training.

Current organizational structures do not provide financial rewards to developers for producing quality materials. Commercial publishers have not found the distribution of computer-based learning materials to be profitable (with a few notable exceptions) and, therefore, are not fulfilling their traditional role.

Current organizations do not have a structure required to properly serve a national need for computer-based learning materials. Organizations which have attempted to facilitate national exchange of instructional computer programs have not provided all functions required to aid the adoption of complex innovations.

The majority of computer-based learning materials have been developed and used by one institution and by individual authors.

Conclusions

Current organizational structures (e.g., educational institutions, publishers, etc.) are inadequate to the task of dealing with the complexities of computer-based learning materials on a large-scale basis.

The single agent model is not a workable approach to developing and disseminating computer-based materials. Various organizations (discipline groups, educational institutions, R & D centers, exchanges) should pursue cooperative arrangements for providing needed computer-based educational materials.

New organizational structures are needed to implement a comprehensive strategy yielding quality computer-based curricula that will have widespread effects toward individualizing education.

Recommendations

As has been noted, no current agencies have been capable of dealing adequately with all functions related to dissemination or development. But it would be fruitful to examine current organizational structures for possible partial solutions *now*. Thus, it would be reasonable to consider the possibility and feasibility of building the good features of each of the existing organizational structures into new, more comprehensive ones in the near-term future. If computer-based educational advances are to be made, comprehensive federal programs should be established by NSF, NIE, and USOE specifically for the purpose of exploring the computer's potential as a basic force in education. A federal agency could support the establishment of a national organization to implement the clearinghouse strategy suggested earlier. The organization would work closely with regional and state groups to achieve a workable allocation of functions.

The Office of Education and the NIE might support a phased program to:
1. Study existing "experimental" or "reform" schools to determine whether some are candidates to become the basis of a nationwide network of schools and to become the framework for dissemination of computer-based innovations.
2. Study the feasibility of establishing such a network. State departments of education would play a key role.
3. Design an overall strategy which includes organization, funding, and implementation of the network as well as development of the appropriate computer-based learning facilities and other educational technology systems and materials.

These federal programs should establish new permanent organizational structures that use the combined capabilities of organizations, groups, societies, individual developers, institutions, and R & D centers dedicated to advancing education through computer technology. The passage of categorical legislation by the Congress could be an added vehicle for establishing these new organizational structures.

A study group should be formed to consider the goals and the possibilities of a joint federal program, the organizational arrangements, the funding requirements, and the participation of various groups. The exact character of the new structures, regional discipline centers, technology centers or national development center, or some combination, would be an important outcome of this study group.

The new organizational structures for computer-based curriculum development should have access to a large diverse student population for the development phase.

If distributed computer networks are shown to be a feasible means of sharing instructional computer programs, then special consideration should be given to locating development centers at nodes on a distributed educational network.

REFERENCES

Abrahamson, Stephen, Denson, Judson S., and Wolf, Richard M. "Effectiveness of a Simulator in Training Anesthesiology Residents," *Journal of Medical Education*, Vol. 44, 1969, pp. 515-519.

AEDS. *Layman's Guide to the Use of Computers*, The Association for Educational Data Systems, Washington, D.C., 1971.

Alkin, Marvin C. "Evaluating the Cost-Effectiveness of Instructional Programs," in *The Evaluation of Instruction: Issues and Problems*, M.C. Wittrock and David E. Wiley (eds.), Holt, Rinehart, and Winston, Inc., New York, 1970.

Allen, John R. "ELSE at Dartmouth: An Experiment in Computer Aided Instruction in French," *The French Review*, Vol. XLIV, No. 5, April, 1971.

Alpert, Daniel. "Computers and the Future of Education," in *Computers in Instruction: Their Future for Higher Education*, Roger E. Levien (ed.), Proceedings of a Conference, Rand Corp., Santa Monica, California, October, 1971.

Anastasio, Ernest J., and Morgan, Judith S. *Factors Inhibiting the Use of Computers in Instruction*, EDUCOM, Interuniversity Communications Council, Princeton, New Jersey, 1972.

Anderson, Ronald E. *Bibliography on Social Science Computing*, Social Sciences Research Facilities Center, Minneapolis, Minnesota, 1972.

Atkinson, R.C., Fletcher, J.D. Chetin, H.C., and Stauffer, C.M. *Introduction in Initial Reading Under Computer Control: The Stanford Project*, Technical Report No. 158, Institute for Mathematical Studies in the Social Sciences, Stanford University, Stanford, California, 1970.

Automated Education Letter. Vol. 7, No. 10, Automated Education Center, Detroit, Michigan, October, 1972.

Baker, Eva L. "The Technology of Instructional Development," in *Second Handbook of Research on Teaching*, Robert M.W. Travers (ed.), Rand McNally & Co., Chicago, Illinois, 1973.

Ball, John, and Jamison, D. "Computer-Assisted Instruction for Dispersed Populations: System Cost Models," *Instructional Science*, Vol. 1, No. 4, February, 1973.

Berry, William, and Whybard, D. Clay. *Operation and Logistics Management*, South-Western Publishing Co., Cincinnati, Ohio, 1972.

Bishop, Robert L. "Computer Analysis of Natural Language Text for Style and Content in the Context of Instruction in Writing," in *Conference on Computers in the Undergraduate Curricula*, University of Iowa, Center for Conferences and Institutes, Iowa City, Iowa, 1970.

Bloom, Benjamin S. (ed.). *Taxonomy of Educational Objectives, the Classification of Educational Goals, Handbook I: The Cognitive Domain*, David McKay Co., Inc., New York, 1956.

Blum, Ronald (ed.). *Computer-Based Physics: An Anthology*, Commission on College Physics, College Park, Maryland, 1969.

Blum, Ronald, *et al. Introductory Computer-Based Mechanics: A One Week Sample Course*, Commission on College Physics, College Park, Maryland, 1970.

Blum, Ronald (ed.). *Computers in Undergraduate Science Education, Conference Proceedings*, Commission on College Physics, College Park, Maryland, 1971.

Borich, Gary D., *et al. Evaluating Educational Programs and Products*, Educational Technology Publications, Englewood Cliffs, New Jersey, 1974.

Bork, Alfred. "Inexpensive Time-Shared Graphics on the Sigma 7," paper given at XDS Users Group 17th International Meeting, Las Vegas, Nevada, 1971.

Bork, Alfred. "Terminals for Education, Networks, and Disciplines: Terminals—Social Challenge," *EDUCOM*, Vol. 7, No. 4, Winter, 1972.

Bork, Alfred, and Ballard, Richard. "The Physics Computer Develop-

ment Project," brochure, University of California, Irvine, January, 1972.
Boulding, K.E. "The Specialist with a Universal Mind," presentation at The American Association for the Advancement of Science, New York, December 26, 1967.
Bowker Annual of Library and Book Trade Information, Janice Johnson and Frank L. Schick (eds.), R.R. Bowker, New York, 1971.
Bowker Annual of Library and Book Trade Information, Jeanne J. Henderson and Frank L. Schick (eds.), R.R. Bowker, New York, 1973.
Bowles, Edmund A. (ed.). *Computers in Humanistic Research: Readings and Perspectives*, Prentice-Hall, Inc., Englewood Cliffs, New Jersey, 1967.
Brennan, Robert L. "A Model for the Use of Achievement Data and Time Data in an Instructional System," paper presented at the Annual Meeting of the American Educational Research Association, New Orleans, February, 1973. This paper was originally entitled: "The Use of Test Data in Non-Traditional Instruction."
Bunderson, C. Victor. "Justifying CAI in Mainline Instruction," *Proceedings of the Conference on Computers in the Undergraduate Curricula*, June 16-18, 1970, University of Iowa, Iowa City, Iowa, September, 1970.
Bunderson, C. Victor. *Team Production of Learner-Controlled Courseware: A Progress Report*, Brigham Young University, Provo, Utah, 1972.
Burns, Richard W., and Brooks, Gary D. (eds.). *Curriculum Design in a Changing Society*, Educational Technology Publications, Englewood Cliffs, New Jersey, 1970.
Bushnell, David, and Rappaport, Donald (eds.). *Planned Change in Education: A Systems Approach*, Harcourt Brace Jovanovich, Inc., New York, 1971.
CACHE News, News About Computers in Chemical Engineering Education. No. 3, Cambridge, Massachusetts, March, 1973.
Calipers: Planning the Systems Approach to Field Testing Educational Products. Southwest Regional Educational Laboratory, Austin, Texas, 1969.

Carnegie Commission on Higher Education. *Less Time, More Options: Education Beyond the High School*, McGraw-Hill Book Company, New York, 1971.

Carnegie Commission on Higher Education. *The Fourth Revolution: Instructional Technology in Higher Education—A Report and Recommendations*, McGraw-Hill Book Company, New York, June, 1972.

Cartwright, G. Phillip, and Cartwright, Carol G. "A Computer-Assisted Instruction Course in the Early Identification of Handicapped Children," College of Education, Pennsylvania State University, University Park, Pennsylvania, June, 1971.

Cartwright, G. Phillip, and Cartwright, Carol G. "An Undergraduate Computer Assisted Instruction Course in the Early Identification of Handicapped Children," *Proceedings of the 1972 Conference on Computers in Undergraduate Curricula*, Southern Regional Education Board, Atlanta, Georgia, June, 1972.

Center for Research on Learning and Teaching. *Project EXTEND: An Introduction*, University of Michigan, Ann Arbor, Michigan, May, 1972.

Chapanis, A. "Prelude to 200 Explorations in Human Communication," *American Psychologist*, Vol. 26, No. 11, November, 1971.

Commission on Instructional Technology (Sterling M. McMurrin, Chairman). *To Improve Learning, A Report to the President and the Congress of the United States*, Printed for Use of the Committee on Education and Labor, House of Representatives, U.S. Government Printing Office, Washington, D.C., March, 1970.

Committee on the Undergraduate Program in Mathematics. *Recommendations for an Undergraduate Program in Computational Mathematics*, A Report of the Panel on Computing, Mathematical Association of America, Berkeley, California, May, 1971.

Committee on the Undergraduate Program in Mathematics (Alex Rosenberg, Chairman). *Recommendations on Undergraduate Mathematics Courses Involving Computing*, A Report of the Panel on the Impact of Computing on Mathematics Courses, Mathematical Association of America, Berkeley, California, October, 1972.

Computer Applications in Dental Education: A Conference Report (Dale W. Podshadley, Conference Chairman). U.S. Department of

References

Health, Education, and Welfare, Public Health Service, National Institutes of Health, Bureau of Health Manpower Education, Division of Dental Health, Dental Health Center, Professional Education Branch, San Francisco, California, 1971.

Computer-Based Education Research Laboratory (CERL). *TUTOR User's Memo: Introduction to TUTOR*, University of Illinois at Urbana-Champaign, Urbana, Illinois, March, 1973.

Computing Newsletter for Instructors of Data Processing. Center for Cybernetics Systems Synergism (CYSYS), Box 9630, Colorado Springs, Colorado 80909, Vol. VI, No. 1, September, 1972. (J. Daniel Couger, ed.)

Conference Board of the Mathematical Sciences (CBMS), Committee on Computer Education. *Recommendations Regarding Computers in High School Education*, Committee on Computer Education (Edward G. Begle, Chairman), Washington, D.C., April, 1972.

Conference on Computers in Chemical Education and Research: Preliminary Proceedings, DeKalb, Illinois, July, 1971.

Cooley, W.W., and Lohnes, P. *Multivariate Procedures in the Behavioral Sciences*, John Wiley & Sons, Inc., New York, 1962.

Courtney, Harley M. "Remote Time-Sharing for Education in Business Planning and Control," *Proceedings of the 1972 Conference on Computers in Undergraduate Curricula*, June 12-14, 1972, Southern Regional Education Board, Atlanta, Georgia, 1972.

Crawford, Jack J., et al. *Evaluation of the Impact of Educational Research and Development Products: Final Report*, American Institutes for Research, Palo Alto, California, March, 1972.

Csuri, Charles. "Computer Animated Film for Art and Education," *Proceedings of the Conference on Computers in the Undergraduate Curricula*, University of Iowa, Center for Conferences and Institutes, Iowa City, Iowa, 1970.

Darby, Charles A., Jr., Korotkin, Arthur L., and Romashko, Tania. *A Survey of Computing Activities in Secondary Schools: Final Report*, American Institutes for Research, Silver Spring, Maryland, October, 1970.

Datapro Research Corporation. *DATAPRO 70: All About Data Communications Facilities*, One Corporate Center, Route 38, Moorestown, New Jersey 08057, April, 1973.

Davis, James A. "Using the IMPRESS System to Teach Sociology," *Conference on Computers in the Undergraduate Curriculum*, Dartmouth College, Hanover, New Hampshire, June, 1971.

Denk, J.R. "Exchange of Applications Programs for Education—A National Stalemate," *ACM Interface*, Vol. 5, No. 1, February, 1971a.

Denk, J.R. (ed.). *PALS (Program and Literature Service)* 1971, North Carolina Educational Computing Service, Research Triangle Park, North Carolina, 1971b.

Denk, Joseph R. "POISSON—A Daughter of Dartmouth's IMPRESS Has Been Born in the Environment of IBM Time-Sharing," *Proceedings of the 1972 Conference on Computers in Undergraduate Curricula*, Southern Regional Education Board, Atlanta, Georgia, June, 1972.

Denny, Cecil, Converse, Ron, Krieghbaum, Gary, and McMahan, Denis. *Original Presentation to the Kansas State Board of Education*, July 6, 1972.

Department of Health, Education, and Welfare. *Report to the Congress*. Lister Hill National Center for Biomedical Communications. Publication No. (NIH) 72-268, April, 1972, p. 6.

Dick, Walter. "Some Directions for the College of Education in the 1970's," Annual Progress Report, January 1, 1968 through December 21, 1968, Florida State University, Computer Assisted Instruction Center, Tallahassee, Florida, 1969.

Dick, Walter, and Gallagher, Paul. "Systems Concepts and Computer-Managed Instruction: An Implementation and Validation Study," *Educational Technology*, February, 1972, pp. 33-39.

Dorn, William S., Bitter, Gary G., and Hector, David L. *Computer Applications for Calculus*, Prindle, Weber and Schmidt, Inc., Boston, Massachusetts, 1972.

Doyle, Frank J., and Goodwill, Daniel Z. *An Exploration of the Future in Educational Technology*, Bell Canada, January, 1971.

Dwyer, Thomas A. "The Case for Extending BASIC as an Educational Programming Language," Project SOLO Newsletter, No. 18, University of Pittsburgh, September 7, 1971a.

Dwyer, Thomas A. "Some Principles for the Human Use of Computers in Education," *International Journal of Man-Machine Studies*, Vol. 3, No. 3, 1971b, pp. 219-239.

Dwyer, Thomas A., and Critchfield, Margot. *Computer Resource Book–Algebra*, Houghton Mifflin, Boston, Massachusetts, 1973.

Dyer, Charles A. *Preparing for Computer Assisted Instruction*, Educational Technology Publications, Englewood Cliffs, New Jersey, 1972.

EDP Industry Report. Vol. 8, No. 11, March 30, 1973.

Eichhorn, Mary M., and Reinecke, Robert D. "Vision Information Center: A User Oriented Data Base," *Science*, July 3, 1970, Vol. 169, pp. 29-31.

Engleman, Carl. "The Mechanization of Mathematics," in *Computers in Undergraduate Science Education*, Conference Proceedings, Ronald Blum (ed.), Commission on College Physics, College Park, Maryland, 1971.

Engler, David. "Monoliths Mishmashes and Motivations," in *Computers in Instruction: Their Future for Higher Education*, R.E. Levien (ed.), The Rand Corporation, Santa Monica, California, July, 1971.

English, Fenwick W., and Sharpes, Donald K. *Strategies for Differentiated Staffing*, McCutchan Publishing Corp., Berkeley, California, 1972.

ENTELEK. *Computer-Assisted Instruction, Computer-Managed Instruction, CAI/CMI Information Exchange*, ENTELEK, Inc., Newburyport, Massachusetts, 1965-1973.

Feurzeig, Wallace. "Decision-Making," in *Computer-Assisted Instruction in the Health Professions*, Lawrence M. Stolurow, Theodore I. Peterson, and Anne C. Cunningham (eds.), ENTELEK, Inc., Newburyport, Massachusetts, 1970, pp. 114-124.

Feurzeig, Wallace, and Lukas, George. *A Programmable Robot for Teaching*, paper prepared for the Proceedings of the World Congress on Cybernetics and Systems, Oxford, England, September, 1972.

Fielding, Gordon J., and Rumage, Kenneth W. (eds.). *Computer Assisted Instruction in Geography*, Technical Paper No. 2, Commission on College Geography, American Association of Geographics, Washington, D.C., 1969.

Fielding, Gordon J., and Rumage, Kenneth W. (eds.). *Computerized Instruction in Undergraduate Geography*, Technical Paper No. 6,

Commission on College Geography, American Association of Geographics, Washington, D.C., 1972.

Frye, Charles H. "CAI Languages: Their Capabilities and Applications," in *Computer-Assisted Instruction, A Book of Readings*, Richard C. Atkinson and H.A. Wilson (eds.), Academic Press, New York, 1969.

Fuller, R. Buckminster. *Education Automation: Freeing the Scholar to Return to His Studies*, Doubleday/Anchor, New York, 1971.

Fuller, R. Buckminster. "The Meaning of Wealth," *World*, Vol. 2, No. 3, January, 1973.

Futurist. August, 1970, Vol. IV, No. 4, World Future Society: An Association for the Study of Alternative Futures, Washington, D.C.

Gagné, R.M. "The Acquisition of Knowledge," *Psychological Review*, Vol. 69, 1962, pp. 335-365.

Gagné, R.M. *The Conditions of Learning* (1st ed.), Holt, Rinehart, and Winston, New York, 1965.

Gagné, R.M. *The Conditions of Learning* (2nd ed.), Holt, Rinehart, and Winston, New York, 1970.

Geis, George L. "Premature Instruction," in *Curriculum Design in a Changing Society*, Richard W. Burns and Gary D. Brooks (eds.), Educational Technology Publications, Englewood Cliffs, New Jersey, 1970.

General ICES Information. Civil Engineering Systems Laboratory, Department of Civil Engineering, Massachusetts Institute of Technology, Cambridge, Massachusetts, September, 1971 (unpublished report).

Gill, Robert W., Bryant, Stephen H., and Mellon, Terry F. "Uses of Computers in the Teaching of Ecology," *Proceedings of the Conference on Computers in the Undergraduate Curricula*, Hanover, New Hampshire, Dartmouth College, Computer Oriented Materials Production for Undergraduate Teaching, 1971, pp. 171-175.

Goodlad, John. *School, Curriculum, and the Individual*, Blaisdell Publishing Co., Waltham, Massachusetts, 1966.

Goodlad, John. "Perspective on Curriculum Design," in *Curriculum Design in a Changing Society*, Richard W. Burns and Gary D.

Brooks (eds.), Educational Technology Publications, Englewood Cliffs, New Jersey, 1970.
Goodlad, John, and Klein, M. Frances and Associates. *Behind the Classroom Door*, Charles A. Jones Publishing Co., Worthington, Ohio, 1970.
Gray, Clifford, and Graham, Robert. *Business Games Handbook*, American Management Association, Inc., New York, 1969.
Grayson, Lawrence P., and Robbins, Janet B. *U.S. Office of Education Support of Computer Projects, 1965-1971*, U.S. Government Printing Office, Washington, D.C., 1972.
Green, B.F., Jr. *Digital Computers in Research*, McGraw-Hill Book Co., Inc., New York, 1963.
Greenlaw, P., and Frey, M. *FINANSIM: A Financial Management Simulation*, International Book Company, Chicago, Illinois, 1967.
Greenlaw, P., and Kniffin, F. *MARKSIM: A Marketing Decision Simulation*, International Book Company, Chicago, Illinois, 1964.
Greeslin, Robert H. "Preparing Mathematics Teachers to Use the Computers in Secondary Schools," *Proceedings of the 1972 Conference on Computers in Undergraduate Curricula*, Southern Regional Education Board, Atlanta, Georgia, June, 1972.
Grobman, Hulda. *Developmental Curriculum Projects: Decision Points and Processes*, F.E. Peacock Publishers, Inc., Itasca, Illinois, 1970.
Gropper, George L. *Diagnosis and Revision in the Development of Instructional Materials*, Educational Technology Publications, Englewood Cliffs, New Jersey, 1975.
Hack, Walter G., et al. *Educational Futurism 1985: Challenges for Schools and Their Administrators*, McCutchan Publishing Corporation, Berkeley, California, 1971.
Hagerty, Nancy K. "Development and Implementation of a Computer-Managed Instruction System in Graduate Training," Tech Report No. 11, Florida State University, Tallahassee, Florida, June 30, 1970.
Halas, John, and Manwell, Roger. *Techniques of Film Animation* (2nd ed.), Hastings House Publishers, New York, 1968.
Hall, John S. *Models for Rational Decision Making Analysis of Literature and Selected Bibliography*, ERIC Clearinghouse on Educational Administration, University of Oregon, Eugene,

Oregon 97403, September, 1970.

Hall, Michael. *Social Sciences Instructional Programming Project: Final Report*, August 1968 through August 1970, Michael A. Hall (Project Director), Beloit College, August, 1970.

Hall, Michael. "Meeting the Need for a Better Front End," in *Computing in Higher Education 1971: Successes and Prospects*, Proceedings of the EDUCOM 1971 Fall Council Meeting and Conference, the Interuniversity Communications Council, Inc., 1971.

Hamblen, John W. *Inventory of Computers in U.S. Higher Education, 1969-70: Utilization and Related Degree Programs*, Survey Report for the National Science Foundation, U.S. Government Printing Office, Washington, D.C., March 1, 1972.

Hammadi, Ibrahim B., and Fonkalsrud, Eric W. "Case Studies in Surgery," in *Computer-Assisted Instruction in the Health Professions*, Lawrence M. Stolurow, Theodore I. Peterson, and Anne C. Cunningham (eds.), ENTELEK, Inc., Newburyport, Massachusetts, 1970, pp. 125-141.

Hammond, Allen L. "Computer-Assisted Instruction: Two Major Demonstrations," *Science*, Vol. 176, No. 4039, June 9, 1972.

Hanna, Thomas. *Bodies in Revolt*. Holt, Rinehart, and Winston, Inc., New York, 1970.

Hansen, Duncan, *et al. Conference on Computers and Undergraduate Science Education: A Computer-Assisted and Managed Course in Physical Sciences*, Tech. Memo No. 23, Florida State University CAI Center, Tallahassee, Florida, October 30, 1970.

Harless, William G., *et al.* "CASE: A Computer Aided Simulation of the Clinical Encounter," *Journal of Medical Education*, Vol. 46, May, 1971, pp. 443-448.

Harris, Ray D., and Maggard, Michael. *Computer Models in Operations Management*, Harper and Row, New York, 1972.

Hart, Leslie A. *The Classroom Disaster*, Teachers College Press, New York, 1969.

Havelock, Ronald G. *The Change Agent's Guide to Innovation in Education*, Educational Technology Publications, Englewood Cliffs, New Jersey, 1973.

Havelock, Ronald G., Huber, Janet, and Zimmerman, Shaindel. *Major

Works on Change in Education, An Annotated Bibliography and Subject Index, Center for Research on Utilization of Scientific Knowledge, University of Michigan, Ann Arbor, Michigan, 1969.

Hege, Molly, and Denk, Joseph R. *PALS 1972: Program and Literature Service*, North Carolina Educational Computing Service, Research Triangle Park, North Carolina, October, 1972.

Hellerstein, Earl E. "CAI at Harvard University," in *Computer-Assisted Instruction in the Health Professions*, Lawrence M. Stolurow, Theodore I. Peterson, and Anne C. Cunningham (eds.), ENTELEK, Inc., Newburyport, Massachusetts, 1970, pp. 31-44.

Henshaw, Richard C., Jr., and Jackson, James R. *The Executive Game*, Richard D. Irwin, Inc., Homewood, Illinois, 1966 (revised, 1972).

Hertlein, Grace C. "Computer Aided Graphics as an Art Form for the Artist," *Proceedings of the 1972 Conference on Computers in the Undergraduate Curricula*, Atlanta, Georgia, Southern Regional Education Board, 1972.

Herzog, B. *Computer Networks*, May, 1972. Proceedings of the 1972 International Computer Symposium, ACM and AICA, Venice, Italy, 1972.

Hewlett-Packard. *Newsletters, HP Educational Users' Group*, Hewlett-Packard Company, 11000 Wolfe Road, Cupertino, California, Vol. II, No. 7, March 15, 1972.

Hicks, B.L., and Hunka, S. *The Teacher and the Computer*, W.B. Saunders Company, Philadelphia, Pennsylvania, 1972.

Hill, Joseph E. *The Educational Sciences*, Descriptive Brochure, Institute for Educational Sciences, Oakland Community College, Oakland, Michigan, February, 1971.

Hokkanen, Dorothy B. "American Book Title Output—A Ninety-Year Overview," reprinted from July 1970 issue of *Printing and Publishing* in *The Bowker Annual of Library and Book Trade Information*, R.R. Bowker, New York, 1971.

Howland, Howard C. "Digital and Analog Computing in General Animal Physiology," *Proceedings of the 1972 Conference on Computers in Undergraduate Curricula*, June 12-14, 1972, Southern Regional Education Board, Atlanta, Georgia.

Hoye, Robert E., and Wang, Anastasia C. *Index to Computer Based Learning*, Educational Technology Publications, Englewood Cliffs, New Jersey, 1973.

Huke, Robert E. "Climate Types: Recognition and Classification," *Computer-Assisted Instruction in Geography*, Technical Paper No. 2, Association of American Geographers, Commission on College Geography, Washington, D.C., 1969.

Huntington Two Computer Project. *GENE1: A Simple Genetics Program*, developed and programmed by Ludwig Braun, Polytechnic Institute of Brooklyn, June 1, 1971.

Huntington Two Computer Project. *STERL: A Pest Control Simulation*, developed by Austin M. Frishman, Ludwig Braun, and Charles Losik, Polytechnic Institute of Brooklyn, September 1, 1971.

Huntington Two Computer Project. *POLUT: Resource Handbook*, Polytechnic Institute of Brooklyn, September 15, 1971.

Illich, Ivan. *Deschooling Society*, Harper and Row, New York, 1970.

Illinois Institute of Technology, Information Science Center. *Cooperative Venture in College Curriculum Development, Final Project Report*, Illinois Institute of Technology, Chicago, Illinois, July, 1971.

Ingellsore, Ralph. "CAI at Ohio State University," in *Computer-Assisted Instruction in the Health Professions*, Lawrence M. Stolurow, Theodore I. Peterson, and Anne C. Cunningham (eds.), ENTELEK, Inc., Newburyport, Massachusetts, 1970, p. 49.

Jackson, Philip W. *Life in Classrooms*, Holt, Rinehart, and Winston, Inc., New York, 1970.

Janda, K. *Data Processing Applications to Political Research*, Northwestern University Press, Evanston, Illinois, 1969.

Jason, Hillard. "Introductory Remarks," in *Computer-Assisted Instruction in the Health Professions*, Lawrence M. Stolurow, Theodore I. Peterson, and Anne C. Cunningham (eds.), ENTELEK, Inc., Newburyport, Massachusetts, 1970, pp. 22-29.

Johnson, David C., and Koetke, Walter J. *Computers in the Mathematics Classroom, Selected Bibliography (8/15/68, revised 5/1/71)–Annotated*, National Council of Teachers of Mathematics, Washington, D.C., 1971.

Johnson, M. Clemens. *Educational Uses of the Computer: An Introduction*, Rand McNally & Co., Chicago, Illinois, 1971.

Johnson, Richard. "DATACALL: A Computer-Based Simulation Game for Teaching Strategy in Scientific Research," *Proceedings of the Conference on Computers in Undergraduate Curricula*, Dartmouth College, Hanover, New Hampshire, 1971.

Jung, Steven M. *Individually Prescribed Instruction—Mathematics (IPI-Math)*, Product Development Report No. 17, American Institutes for Research, Palo Alto, California, January, 1972.

Kapfer, Philip G. "Behavioral Objectives and the Curriculum Processor," in *Curriculum Design in a Changing Society*, Richard W. Burns and Gary D. Brooks (eds.), Educational Technology Publications, Englewood Cliffs, New Jersey, 1970.

Kelley, Tim G. "On-Line Classroom Graphic Display," in *Computers in Undergraduate Science Education Conference Proceedings*, Ronald Blum (ed.), Commission on College Physics, College Park, Maryland, 1971.

Kelley, Tim G., Grillot, David, Ballance, Jeffrey, and Hubble, Larry. "Interactive Classroom Graphics," *Proceedings of the 1972 Conference on Computers in the Undergraduate Curricula*, Southern Regional Educational Board, Atlanta, Georgia, 1972, pp. 383-396.

Kemeny, John G. *Man and the Computer*, Charles Scribner's Sons, New York, 1972.

Kiewit Computation Center. *Kiewit Comments*, Vol. 5, No. 8, Dartmouth College, Hanover, New Hampshire, March, 1972.

Kopstein, Felix F., and Seidel, Robert J. "Comments on Schurdak's 'An Approach to the Use of Computers in the Instructional Process and an Evaluation,'" *American Educational Research Journal*, Vol. 4, No. 4, November, 1967, pp. 413-416.

Kozol, Jonathan. *Free Schools*, Houghton Mifflin, Boston, Massachusetts, 1972.

Kratochvil, Daniel W. *Sesame Street*, Product Development Report, American Institutes for Research, Palo Alto, California, December, 1971a.

Kratochvil, Daniel W. *The Frostig Program for Perceptual-Motor Development Developed by the Marianne Frostig Center of Educational Therapy*, Product Development Report, American Institutes for Research, Palo Alto, California, December, 1971b.

Kratochvil, Daniel W. *Arithmetic Proficiency Training Program (APTP)*, developed by Science Research Associates, Inc., Product Development Report, American Institutes for Research in the Behavioral Sciences, Palo Alto, California, January, 1972.

Kratochvil, Daniel W., and Crawford, Jack J. *Intermediate Science Curriculum Study*, Product Development Report, American Institutes for Research, Palo Alto, California, November, 1971.

Leinbach, L. Carol. "Calculus as a Laboratory Course," *Proceedings of the Second Annual Conference on Computers in the Undergraduate Curricula*, June 23-25, 1971, Arthur W. Luehrmann (ed.), Dartmouth College, Hanover, New Hampshire, 1971.

Leonard, George B. *Education and Ecstasy*, Delacorte Press, New York, 1968.

Levien, Roger E. (ed.). *Computers in Instruction: Their Future for Higher Education*, Proceedings of a Conference held in October, 1970, sponsored by the National Science Foundation, the Carnegie Commission on Higher Education, and the Rand Corporation. The Rand Corporation, Santa Monica, California, July, 1971.

Levien, Roger E. *The Emerging Technology: Instructional Uses of the Computer in Higher Education*, A Carnegie Commission on Higher Education and Rand Corporation Study, McGraw-Hill Book Company, New York, 1972.

Licklider, J.C.R. "Preliminary Experiments in Computer-Aided Teaching," in *Programmed Learning and Computer-Based Instruction*, John E. Coulson (ed.), John Wiley and Sons, Inc., New York, 1962.

Licklider, J.C.R. "A Crux in Scientific and Technical Communication," *American Psychologist*, 1966, Vol. 21, pp. 1044-1051.

Lincoln, Harry B. (ed.). *The Computer and Music*, Cornell University Press, Ithaca, New York, 1970.

Lister Hill National Center for Biomedical Communications, *Report to the Congress*, U.S. Department of Health, Education, and Welfare, Public Health Service, National Institute of Health, National Library of Medicine, Bethesda, Maryland, 1972.

Lockard, J. David (ed.). *Seventh Report of the International Clearinghouse on Science and Mathematics Curricular Developments, 1970*, a joint project of the American Association for the Advancement of Science and the Science Teaching

Center, University of Maryland, 1970.

Lockard, J. David (ed.). *Eighth Report of the International Clearinghouse on Science and Mathematics Curricular Developments, 1972*, a joint project of the American Association for the Advancement of Science and the Science Teaching Center, University of Maryland, 1972.

Locke, R.W. "Has the Education Industry Lost Its Nerve?," *Saturday Review*, January 16, 1971.

Locke, Robert W., and Engler, David. *Run, Strawman, Run*, McGraw-Hill Book Company, Inc., New York, 1968.

Luehrmann, Arthur W. (ed.). *Proceedings of the Second Annual Conference on Computers in the Undergraduate Curricula*, COMPUTe, Dartmouth College, Hanover, New Hampshire, 1971.

Luehrmann, Arthur W. "Should the Computer Teach the Student or Vice Versa?," Proceedings of the Spring Joint Computer Conference, AFIPS Press, Montvale, New Jersey, 1972.

Luskin, Bernard J. *An Identification and Examination of Obstacles to the Development of Computer Assisted Instruction*, unpublished Ed.D. Thesis, University of California, Los Angeles, California, 1970.

Lykos, Peter. "Networking and Chemistry," Networks and Disciplines, *Proceedings of the EDUCOM Fall Conference*, October 11-13, 1973.

MARKET Resource Manual. Huntington Two Computer Project, Polytechnic Institute of Brooklyn, May 1, 1972a.

MARKET Teacher Handbook. Huntington Two Computer Project, Polytechnic Institute of Brooklyn, May 1, 1972b.

McLuhan, Marshall, and Fiore, Quentin. *The Medium Is the Massage*, Bantam Books, New York, 1967.

Meany, John O. "Man-Machine Alternatives in Computer Based Counselor Training Systems," *Counselor Education and Supervision*, December, 1972, Vol. 12, No. 2.

Meredith, J.C. *The CAI Author/Instructor*, Educational Technology Publications, Englewood Cliffs, New Jersey, 1971.

Merrill, John R. "Inexpensive, Interactive Graphics on Telephone-Connected, Time-Shared Computers," in *Computers in Undergraduate Science Education Conference Proceedings*, Ronald Blum (ed.), Commission on College Physics, College Park, Maryland, 1971.

Merrill, M. David. "Necessary Psychological Conditions for Defining Instructional Outcomes," *Educational Technology*, August, 1971.

Merrill, M. David. "Content and Instructional Analysis for Cognitive Transfer Tasks," *AV Communication Review*, Vol. 21, No. 1, Spring, 1973, pp. 109-125.

Merrill, Paul F. *Task Analysis—An Information Processing Approach*, Tech. Memo No. 27, Florida State University, Tallahassee, Florida, April 15, 1971.

Mesthene, Emmanuel. "Instructional Technology and the Purposes of Education," in *To Improve Learning, An Evaluation of Instructional Technology, Vol. II,* Sidney G. Tickton (ed.), R.R. Bowker, New York, 1971.

Meyers, E.D., Jr. "IMPRESS and Undergraduate Education in the Social Sciences," *Proceedings of the Conference on Computers in the Undergraduate Curricula*, University of Iowa, Iowa City, Iowa, 1970.

Mikkelson, R.C. "A Simulated Accelerator Laboratory," in *Computer-Based Physics: An Anthology*, Ronald Blum (ed.), Commission on College Physics, College Park, Maryland, September, 1969, pp. 85-105.

Miles, Matthew B. (ed.). *Innovation in Education*, Bureau of Publications, Teachers College, Columbia University, New York, 1964.

Mitzel, Harold E., *et al.* "A Commonwealth Consortium to Develop, Implement, and Evaluate a Pilot Program of Computer-Assisted Instruction for Urban Schools," Final Report, Report No. R-47, College of Education CAI Laboratory, University Park, Pennsylvania, July, 1971.

Mitzel, Harold E. "The Potential Contribution of Computers to Instruction Reform," *Alternative Futures in American Education*, Appendix 3 to Hearings on H.R. 3606 and Related Bills to Create a National Institute of Education Before the Select Subcommittee on Education, January, 1972.

Molnar, Andrew R. "Computer Based Instruction and the Knowledge Society," in *Computers in Education: Conference Proceedings*, Aldo Romano and Sergio Rossi (eds.), Bari, Italy, 1970.

Molnar, Andrew R. "Critical Issues in Computer-Based Learning," *Educational Technology*, August, 1971.
Molnar, Andrew R. *Computer Innovations in Education*, National Science Foundation, Washington, D.C., January, 1972.
Morgan, Robert P., and Singh, Jai P. *A Guide to the Literature on Application of Communications Satellites to Educational Development*, Washington University, St. Louis, Missouri, February, 1972.
Morton, A. Kent (ed.). "SIGCUE 1: Large Scale CAI–The NSF Program." *ACM SIGCUE Bulletin*, Vol. 6, No. 3, June, 1972a, pp. 5-13.
Morton, A. Kent (ed.). "Students and Computers–Toward a Deeper Involvement," *ACM SIGCUE Bulletin*, Vol. 6, No. 3, June, 1972b, pp. 14-20.
Morton, A. Kent. "Project COMPUTe: Objectives, Rationale, and Procedures," *ACM SIGCUE Bulletin*, Vol. 6, No. 4, October, 1972c.
Moxley, Nancy, and Denk, Joseph R. "Fox and Rabbit Ecology Model," *Computer Based Educational Guide*, CEG-BIOLO-01, North Carolina Educational Computing Service, Research Triangle Park, North Carolina, undated. (Originally authored by Biology Curriculum Group, Harold Kerster, Group Leader, University of Illinois.)
Mullish, Henry, with Lewis, Jimmy. *A Short Course in ARTSPEAK*, University Computing Center, New York University, New York, 1st Edition, February, 1972.
Northwest Regional Educational Laboratory. *Book I: REACT and the Computer in Education–Course I, Administrators and Teachers, Computers in Education: A Survey*, Technica Education Corporation, Portland, Oregon, 1971.
Nyren, Karl. "Library and Book Trade Information," News Report: 1972, *Library Journal*, January 1, 1973.
Oettinger, Anthony G., with Marks, Sema. *Run, Computer, Run: The Mythology of Educational Innovation*, Harvard University Press, Cambridge, Massachusetts, 1969.
Ogborn, Jon M., Hopgood, F. Robert, and Black, Paul J. "Chance and Thermal Equilibrium," in *Conference in Undergraduate Science Education Conference Proceedings*, Ronald Blum (ed.), Commis-

sion on College Physics, College Park, Maryland, 1971, pp. 181-192.

Okey, James R. "Developing and Validating Learning Hierarchies," *Audio-Visual Communication Review*, Vol. 21, No. 1, Spring, 1973, pp. 87-108.

Olivier, W.P. "Learner and Program-Controlled Sequences of Computer-Assisted Instruction," paper presented at American Educational Research Association Annual Meeting, New York, February, 1971.

O'Neill, William F. *Selected Educational Heresies*, Scott, Foresman and Co., Glenview, Illinois, 1969.

Owen, H. Malcolm. "The Computer in Undergraduate Genetics," *Conference on Computers in the Undergraduate Curricula*, Dartmouth College, Computer Oriented Materials Production for Undergraduate Teaching, Hanover, New Hampshire, 1971, pp. 176-180.

Papert, Seymour, and Solomon, Cynthia. "Twenty Things to Do with a Computer," *Educational Technology*, April, 1972.

Pillsbury, Wilbur F. "Computer Augmented Accounting Education at Knox College," in *Conference on Computers in the Undergraduate Curricula*, Dartmouth College, Hanover, New Hampshire, June, 1971, pp. 516-521.

Polytechnic Institute of Brooklyn. *Huntington Two: Teacher Reaction Inventory*, Brooklyn, New York, 1971.

President's Science Advisory Committee. *Computers in Higher Education: Report of the Committee to the White House*, February 1967, U.S. Government Printing Office, Washington, D.C., 1970.

Proceedings of the Conference on Computers in the Undergraduate Curricula, June 16-18, 1970, University of Iowa, Iowa City, Iowa, September, 1970.

Proceedings of the Second Annual Conference on Computers in the Undergraduate Curricula, June 23-25, 1971, published by COMPUTe, Dartmouth College, Hanover, New Hampshire, 1971.

Proceedings of the 1972 Conference on Computers in the Undergraduate Curricula, June 12-14, 1972, Southern Regional Education Board, Atlanta, Georgia, 1972.

Proceedings of the Fourth Conference on Computers in the Under-

References 349

graduate Curricula, June 18-20, 1973, The Claremont Colleges, Claremont, California, 1973.

Prueitt, Melvin. "Fantastic Computer Pictures Give Us a New Look at Numbers," *Popular Science*, February, 1973.

Rappaport, Paul N. "The Dynsim System: A System for Student Investigation of Economic Models," in *Conference on Computers in the Undergraduate Curricula*, Dartmouth College, Hanover, New Hampshire, June, 1971.

Roberts, Lawrence. "ARPA Network Implications," *EDUCOM, Bulletin of the Interuniversity Communications Council*, Vol. 6, No. 3, Fall, 1971.

Roberts, Lawrence. "ARPANET: Current Status, Future Plans," *Networks for Higher Education*, Proceedings of the EDUCOM Spring Conference, EDUCOM, Interuniversity Communications Council, Inc., Princeton, New Jersey, 1972.

Robinson, Isaiah E. "Redesigning Public Education Via Technology," *Journal of Educational Technology Systems*, June, 1972.

Rodgers, James L. "Current Problems in Computer-Assisted Instruction," *Datamation*, September, 1968.

Rossman, Michael. "How We Learn Today in America," *Saturday Review*, August 19, 1972.

Salter, Ernest M., Pitts, Gerald N., and Bateman, Barry L. "Computerized Ecology Simulation," in *Proceedings of the 1972 Conference on Computers in Undergraduate Curricula*, Atlanta, Georgia, Southern Regional Educational Board, 1972, pp. 33-35.

Saxe, Richard W. (ed.). *Opening the Schools: Alternative Ways of Learning*, McCutchan Publishing Corp., Berkeley, California, 1972.

Scanlon, Robert. "The Expansion of an Innovation," Research for Better Schools, Inc., Philadelphia, Pennsylvania, 1968.

Schey, Harry M. "The Use of Computers in Teaching Calculus," in *Computers in Undergraduate Science Education Conference Proceedings*, Ronald Blum (ed.), Commission on College Physics, College Park, Maryland, 1971.

Schmuck, Richard. "Developing Collaborative Decision-Making: The Importance of Trusting, Strong, and Skillful Leaders," *Educational Technology*, October, 1972.

Schurdak, John J. "An Approach to the Use of Computers in the

Instructional Process and an Evaluation," *American Educational Research Journal*, Vol. 4, 1967, pp. 59-73.

Schwartz, J.T. "Prospects of Computer Science," in *The Mathematical Sciences, A Collection of Essays*, M.I.T. Press, Cambridge, Massachusetts, 1969.

Schwartz, W.B. "Medicine and the Computer," *New England Journal of Medicine*, Vol. 283, December, 1970.

Seidel, Robert J. "Theories and Strategies Related to Measurement in Individual Instruction," *Educational Technology*, September, 1971a.

Seidel, Robert J. "Who Should Develop Instructional Materials for CAI?," *Computers in Instruction: Their Future for Higher Education*. Proceedings of a Conference Held in October, 1970, R.E. Levien (ed.), Rand Corporation, Santa Monica, California, July, 1971b.

Seidel, Robert J. "Hardware Technology for Computers in Education: One of the Soluble Problems," Professional paper 7-74, Human Resources Research Organization, Alexandria, Virginia, May, 1974.

Seidel, Robert J., et al. *Project IMPACT: Computer-Administered Instruction Concepts and Initial Development*. Technical Report 69-3, HumRRO Division No. 1 (System Operations), The George Washington University, Human Resources Research Office, Alexandria, Virginia, March, 1969.

Seidel, Robert J., and Kopstein, Felix F. *Resource Allocations to Effect Operationally Useful CAI*, Professional Paper 12-70, Human Resources Research Organization, Alexandria, Virginia, April, 1970.

Seider, Warren D., Evans, Lawrence B., and Westerberg, Arthur W. *Origins and Organizations of the CACHE Committee—A Report*, Cambridge, Massachusetts, January, 1972.

Select Subcommittee on Education of the Committee on Education and Labor, House of Representatives, 91st Congress (2nd Session on H.R. 8838, March 12, 1970). *Educational Technology Act of 1969*, U.S. Government Printing Office, Washington, D.C., 1971.

Sheepmaker, B., and K.L. Zinn (eds.). *World Conference on Computer Education 1970*, Papers of the First International Federation for

Information Processing (IFIP), August 24-28, 1970, Amsterdam, The Netherlands, Distributed by Science Associates/International, New York, 1970.
Silber, Kenneth. "The Learning System: A New Approach to Facilitating Learning Based on Freedom, the Future, and Educational Technology," *Audiovisual Instruction*, September, 1972.
Silberman, Charles E. *Crisis in the Classroom*, Random House, New York, 1970.
Slack, Warner. "Computer-Based Interviewing System Dealing with Nonverbal Behavior as Well as Keyboard Responses," *Science*, Vol. 171, No. 3966, 1971.
Spain, J.D. "The Use of the Olivetti-Underwood Programma 101 for Mathematical Modeling of Biological Processes," *Proceedings of a Conference on Computers in the Undergraduate Curricula*, University of Iowa, Iowa City, Center for Conferences and Institutes, September, 1970, pp, 6.1-6.7.
Standards of Quality and Objectives for Public Schools in Virginia, 1972-74. Enacted by the General Assembly of Virginia, 1972.
Stenberg, Warren, Walker, Robert, *et al. Calculus: A Computer-Oriented Presentation*, Part 1 and Part 2, The Center for Research in College Instruction of Science and Mathematics (CRICISAM), Florida State University, Tallahassee, Florida, 1968.
Stetten, Kenneth J. *Toward a Market Success for CAI: An Overview of the TICCIT Program*, the MITRE Corporation, June, 1972.
Stolurow, Lawrence M. "Application of Psychology to Educational Technology," *Educational Technology*, December, 1972.
Stolurow, Lawrence M., Peterson, Theodore I., and Cunningham, Anne C. (eds.). *Computer-Assisted Instruction in the Health Professions*, ENTELEK, Inc., Newburyport, Massachusetts, 1970.
Stoner, Ronald E. "Simulated Visual Appearance of Rapidly Moving Objects," *Computers in Undergraduate Science Education Conference Proceedings*, Ronald Blum (ed.), Commission on College Physics, College Park, Maryland, 1971, pp. 247-256.
Stufflebeam, Daniel L., *et al. Educational Evaluation and Decision-Making*, F.E. Peacock Publishers, Inc., Itasca, Illinois, 1971.
Syracuse University LOGO Project Report No. 2, Progress Report, Syracuse University, Syracuse, New York, August, 1972.

Syracuse University LOGO Project Report No. 3, Final Report (Report No. NSF-TIE-GJ 32222-3), Syracuse University, Syracuse, New York, June, 1973.

Tan, J.C. "Applications of a Wang Calculating/Computing System in the Undergraduate Genetics and Biometry Laboratory Instructions," in *Proceedings of the Conference on Computers in the Undergraduate Curricula*, Dartmouth College, Hanover, New Hampshire, 1971, pp. 181-186.

Taylor, Edwin F. "History of a Failure in Computer Interactive Instruction," *Computers in Undergraduate Science Education*, Conference Proceedings, Commission on College Physics, American Institute of Physics, 1970.

Tennyson, Robert D., and Boutwell, Richard C. "A Quality Control Design for Validating Hierarchical Sequencing of Programmed Instruction," *NSPI Journal*, Vol. 10, No. 4, 1971, pp. 5-10.

The MERIT Computer Network. *Progress Report for the Period July 1969-March 1971*, Publication 0571-PR-4, Ann Arbor, Michigan, May, 1971.

The University of Michigan. *ON-LINE*, News on Educational Use of Computers Among Michigan Colleges and Universities, Vol. 2, No. 2, Ann Arbor, Michigan, March, 1973.

Thomas, David B. "Computer-Based Instructional Design," presentation at American Educational Research Association Annual Meeting, 1973.

Thompson, Lorna J. *The Sullivan Reading Program*, Product Development Report No. 5, American Institutes for Research, Palo Alto, California, November, 1971.

Thorelli, Hans B., and Graves, Robert L. *International Operations Simulation*, The Free Press of Glencoe, Macmillan Company, New York, 1964.

Tickton, Sidney G. (ed.). *To Improve Learning, An Evaluation of Instructional Technology*, R.R. Bowker, New York, 1970.

Toffler, Alvin. *Future Shock*, Random House, New York, 1970.

Traub, Ross E., *et al*. "Closure on Openness: Describing and Quantifying Open Education," *Interchange*, Vol. 3, Nos. 2, 3, 1972.

Tuckman, Bruce W., and Edwards, Keith J. "A Systems Model for Instructional Design and Management," *Educational Technology*, September, 1971, pp. 21-30.

U.S. Department of Health, Education, and Welfare. *Support for Research and Related Activities*, Office of Education, April, 1969.

U.S. Department of Health, Education, and Welfare. *Experimental Schools Program 1971, Experimental School Projects, Three Educational Plans*, DHEW Publication No. (OE) 72-42, Washington, D.C., 1972.

Vargus, Brian S., and White, Douglas. "Report on an Attempt to Utilize Computers in Urban Affairs Education," in *Conference on Computers in the Undergraduate Curricula*, Dartmouth College, Hanover, New Hampshire, June, 1971.

Vinsonhaler, John F. "Nothing Succeeds Like Success: On the Evaluation of CAI Drill and Practice," paper presented at Association for the Development of Instructional Systems Meetings, Chicago, Illinois, 1970.

Watson, Paul G. *Using the Computer in Education: A Briefing for School Decision Makers*, Educational Technology Publications, Englewood Cliffs, New Jersey, 1972.

Wedemeyer, Charles A. "Teaching-Learning Environments (The Enigma Behind the Enigma)," *Proceedings of the Third Annual Frontiers in Education Conference*, 1972, Institute of Electrical and Electronic Engineers, 345 East 47 Street, New York 10017, pp. 8-10.

Weeg, Gerard P., *et al*. "Panel: Disseminating Computer Based Curriculum Materials for the Social Sciences," *Proceedings of a Fourth Conference on Computers in the Undergraduate Curricula*, The Claremont Colleges, Claremont, California, June, 1973, pp. 443-447.

Weingarten, Fred W., *et al. A Study of Selected Regional Computer Networks*, with Partial Support of the National Science Foundation, University of Iowa, Iowa City, Iowa, 1973.

Wentworth, Eric. "National Institute Stresses R & D to Improve Education," article in *Washington Post*, September 3, 1972.

White, Roscoe B., and Fried, Burton D. "Mathematical On-Line Systems as a Tool for Teaching Physics," in *Computers in Undergraduate Science Education, Conference Proceedings*, Ronald Blum (ed.), Commission on College Physics, College Park, Maryland, 1971.

Whithed, Marshall H. "Political Simulation and the Mini-Computer: A Challenge to the Industry," in *Proceedings of the 1972 Conference on Computers in the Undergraduate Curricula*, Southern Regional Education Board, Atlanta, Georgia, 1972.

Wilcox, Jarrod W. *A Survey Forecast of New Technology in Universities and Colleges*, Working Paper, Alfred P. Sloan School of Management, Massachusetts Institute of Technology, Cambridge, Massachusetts, January, 1972.

Williamson, J. Peter. *Investments–New Analytic Techniques*, Praeger, New York, 1971.

Williamson, J. Peter, and Downes, David H. *Manual for Computer Programs in Finance and Investments (User Guide)*, The Amos Tuck School, Dartmouth College, Hanover, New Hampshire, 1971 (2nd ed.).

Woollatt, Lorne H. "Expediting Decision-Making at the State Department Level," in *The Computer in American Education*, Don Bushnell and Dwight Allen (eds.), John Wiley and Sons, Inc., New York, 1967.

Zinn, Karl L. *An Evaluative Review of Uses of Computers in Instruction*, Project CLUE (Computer Learning Under Evaluation), Final Report, USOE Project No. 8-0509, University of Michigan, Ann Arbor, Michigan, December, 1970.

Zinn, Karl L. "Requirements for Programming Languages in Computer-Based Instructional Systems," Center for Educational Research and Innovation, Organization for Economic Cooperation and Development, Technical Report, March, 1971.

Zinn, Karl L. *A Personal View of Computing Software for Use in the Instructional Process*, Paper for the International Computing Symposium, Venice, Italy, April 12-15, 1972.

APPENDIX 1

SOURCES OF INFORMATION USED TO IDENTIFY COMPUTER-ORIENTED CURRICULAR MATERIALS

Center Catalogs and Newsletters

Bowdein Public Program Library. NERComP, Inc., Cambridge, Massachusetts.

Catalog of Program Library in the Dartmouth Time-Sharing System. Kiewit Computation Center, Hanover, New Hampshire.

Computing Newsletter. School of Business Administration, University of Colorado, Colorado Springs.

Demonstration and Experimentation in Computer Training and Use in Secondary Schools. Dartmouth College, Hanover, New Hampshire.

Descriptive List of PLATO Programs. Computer Based Research Laboratory, University of Illinois, Urbana.

Newsletter. Regional Social Science Data Archive, University of Iowa, Iowa City, Iowa.

North Carolina Educational Computing Service (NCECS) Memoranda Index. NCECS, Box 12175, Research Triangle Park, North Carolina.

Northern California Regional Computer Network Newsletter. Stanford University Computation Center, Campus Facility, Stanford, California.

PALS (Program and Literature Service) 1971. North Carolina Educational Computing Service, Research Triangle Park, North Carolina.

Project SOLO *Newsletter*. Department of Computer Science, University of Pittsburgh.

A Representation Sample of Facilities and Activities at the University of Michigan Bearing on Instructional Uses of Computing. MERIT Applications Office, Ann Arbor, Michigan.

Temple University Computer Activity Newsletter. Temple University, Philadelphia.

University Computer Center Newsletter. University of Iowa Computer Center, Iowa City.

Discipline-Based Catalogs, Journals, Newsletters, and Conferences

American Journal of Physics

American Psychologist

Arithmetic Teacher

Computer Applications in Dental Education—A Conference Report. Department of Health, Education, and Welfare, 1971.

Computer Applications for Mathematics Education—Selected Bibliography. National Council of Teachers of Mathematics (NCTM), Reston, Virginia.

Computer Assisted Instruction in Geography, Technical Paper 167. Commission on College Geography, Association of American Geographers, Washington, D.C., 1969.

Computers in Undergraduate Science Education—Conference Proceedings. College Park, Maryland: Commission on College Physics, 1971.

Computerized Instruction in Undergraduate Geography: Technical Paper No. 6. Commission on College Geography, Association of American Geographers, Washington, D.C., 1972.

Guide to Computer Assisted Instruction in the Health Sciences. Department of Community Medicine, College of Medicine and Dentistry of New Jersey, Rutgers Medical School, Piscataway, New Jersey, and Office of Information Systems, University of California at San Francisco, December, 1972. (This document is available from the National Technical Information Service, Springfield, Virginia.

IBM—Digital Computer in Introductory General Physics, IBM Corporation, White Plains, New York.

Journal of Business Education

Journal of Chemical Education

Journal of Economic Education

Journal of Medical Education

Library of Computer Programs. Center for the Exchange of Chemistry Computer Programs (EMU-CEECP), Eastern Michigan University, Ypsilanti, Michigan, 1970.

Manuals for Computer Programs in Finance and Investments. Dartmouth College, Hanover, New Hampshire, 1971.

The Mathematics Teacher

NPL/CPIS: A National Program Library and Central Program Inventory Service for the Social Sciences. University of Wisconsin, Madison, 1971.

Preliminary Proceedings—Conference on Computers in Chemical Education and Research. Northern Illinois University, DeKalb, Illinois, 1971.

Seventh Report of the International Clearinghouse of Science and Math Curriculum, University of Maryland, 1970.

Social Sciences Instructional Programming Project (SSIPP). Beloit College, Beloit, Wisconsin, 1970.

General Catalogs, Newsletters, Journals, Books, and Conferences

Audiovisual Instruction

Automated Education Letter

The Case for a Computer Animation Resource Center: A Report to the National Science Foundation. The CARC Committee, Ludwig Braun, Chairman, Polytechnic Institute of Brooklyn, 1971.

Datamation.

Educational Technology Magazine.

EIN Software Catalog, EDUCOM.

ENTELEK CAI Research Abstracts.

Index to Computer Based Learning. Educational Technology Publications, Englewood Cliffs, New Jersey, 1973.

Nation's Schools.

Proceedings of a Conference on Computers in the Undergraduate Curricula. University of Iowa, Center for Conferences and Institutes, Iowa City, 1970.

Proceedings of the Second Annual Conference on Computers in the Undergraduate Curricula. Dartmouth College, Hanover, New Hampshire, 1971.

School and Society.
World Conference on Computer Education—1970. International Federation for Information Processing, Amsterdam, 1970.

APPENDIX 2

A. PROFESSIONAL AND COMMERCIAL ORGANIZATIONS WHICH PROVIDE MECHANISMS FOR INFORMATION EXCHANGE

Name/Location	Mechanisms
Academic Press Inc. Berkeley Square House Berkeley Square London, W 1, England and 111 Fifth Avenue New York, New York 10003	*International Journal of Man-Machine Studies*
American Educational Research Association 1126 16th Street, N.W. Washington, D.C. 20036	*The Educational Researcher* *The American Educational Research Journal*
American Federation of Information Processing Societies Montvale, New Jersey 07645	The *Conference Proceedings* are published by the AFIPS Press.
American Psychological Association	Newsletter–*Educational Psychologist* *The Journal of Educational Psychology*
The Association of American Geographers 1710 Sixteenth Street, N.W. Washington, D.C. 20009	*Computer Assisted Instruction in Geography: Computer Instruction in Undergraduate Geography*

Association for Computing
Machinery
    1133 Avenue of the Americas
    New York, New York 10036

Association for the Development
of Computer-Based Instructional
Systems
    Dr. Ronald Christopher
    Ohio State University
    1080 Carmack Road
    Columbus, Ohio 43210

Association for Educational
Data Systems
    1201 Sixteenth Street, N.W.
    Washington, D.C. 20036

Capitol Publications, Inc.
    Suite G-12
    2430 Pennsylvania Avenue, N.W.
    Washington, D.C. 20037

Center for Exchange of Chemistry
Computer Programs
    Eastern Michigan University
    Ypsilanti, Michigan 48197

Computing Newsletter for Schools
of Business
    School of Business Administration
    University of Colorado
    Cragmor Road
    Colorado Springs, Colorado 80907

Conference Board of the
Mathematical Sciences
    2100 Pennsylvania Avenue, N.W.
    Suite 834
    Washington, D.C. 20037

Cooperative Program Exchange
Service

The *Journal of the ACM*
Computing Review
Computing Survey
(SIGCUE) Bulletin

ADCIS News Letter
(as of September, 1974,
Journal of Computer-Based Instruction)

AEDS Monitor

AEDS Journal

CAI Reporter

Catalog of Program Abstracts

Publication containing evaluative reports, descriptions.

Recommendations Regarding Computers in High School Education

Printed listings

Appendix 2

Regional Computer Network
Illinois Institute of Technology
Chicago, Illinois 60616

Digital Equipment Computer *DECUSCOPE*, a monthly journal and
   Users Society   the annual *DECUS Proceedings*
Maynard, Massachusetts 01754

Educational Systems Corp. The *Journal of Education Data*
   P.O. Box 2995   *Processing*
   Stanford, California 94305

Educational Technology Publications *Educational Technology* Magazine
   140 Sylvan Avenue
   Englewood Cliffs, New Jersey 07632

The Educational Users Group Monthly newsletter
   Hewlett-Packard
   ATTN.: Mrs. Jean Danver
   11000 Wolfe Road
   Cupertino, California 95014

EDUCOM–Interuniversity Communi- *EDUCOM*–Bulletin
cations Council, Inc.
   100 Charles River Plaza
   Boston, Massachusetts 02114

ENTELEK Incorporated ENTELEK CAI/CMI Information
   42 Pleasant Street   Exchange Catalog
   Newburyport, Massachusetts 01950

Inter-university Consortium Archives free to students and
for Political Research   faculty at member institutions
   P.O. Box 1248
   Ann Arbor, Michigan 48106

Joint Users Group of the Association *Computer Programs Directory/71*,
for Computing Machinery   published by CCM Information
   c/o ACM Headquarters   Corporation
   1133 Avenue of the Americas
   New York, New York 10036

Mathematical Association of Report with recommendations on
America   the use of computers in under-
   CUPM   graduate mathematics curricula

P.O. Box 1024
Berkeley, California 94701

National Council of Teachers of
Mathematics
   Reston, Virginia 22091

Computers in the Mathematics Classroom Selected Bibliography— Annotated

National Council for Educational
Technology
   160 Great Portland Street
   London, W 1, England

The British Journal of Educational Technology

National Opinion Research Center
   Roper Center
   P.O. Box 624
   Williams College
   Williamstown, Massachusetts 01267

Survey free upon request

National Program Library and
Central Program Inventory Service
   University of Wisconsin
   Madison, Wisconsin 53706

Catalog of Program Abstracts

North Carolina Educational
Computing Service
   P.O. Box 12175
   Research Triangle Park
   North Carolina 27709

PALS Journal—Program and Literature Service

Regional Social Science Data
Archive
   321A Schaeffer Hall
   University of Iowa
   Iowa City, Iowa 52240

Newsletter—*SS Data*

Relevant Educational Applications
of Computer Technology
   Technica Education Corporation
   655 Sky Way
   San Carlos, California 94070

Courses

Society for Automation in
Business Education
   c/o Dr. E. Dana Gibson

SABE Data Processor

Appendix 2 363

San Diego State College
San Diego, California 92115

Society of Data Educators
2-76 Union
Northfield, Vermont 05663

Journal of DATA Education,
monthly magazine

Time Share, Inc.
Lime Road
Hanover, New Hampshire 03755

Academic Computing Bulletin,
monthly newsletter

B. USERS GROUPS

Name/Contact	Description
APL Users Group Tom McConnel Atlanta Public Schools 218 Pryor St., S.W. Atlanta, Georgia 30303	APL users, programmers
College and University Eleven Thirty Users Group Richard Wood Gettysburg College Gettysburg, Pennsylvania 17325	For sharing experiences and program library among IBM 1130 users.
COMMON Mr. M.K. O'Heeron Computer Center University of South Dakota Vermillion, South Dakota 57069	Users of IBM 360, 1130, 1800 and up to 360/30. Publishers newsletter, CAST. Program library. Four divisions: (1) administrative; (2) systems; (3) applications; (4) installation management.
Cooperative Users of Burroughs Equipment W.H. Eichelberger Computer Center University of Denver Denver, Colorado 80210	Burroughs users, maintains program library.
Digital Equipment Computer Users Society	Maintains a user library, mechanism for feedback to manufacturer on user

146 Main Street, Bldg. 3-5
Maynard, Massachusetts 01754

Educational Users Group
  Mrs. Jean Danver
  Hewlett-Packard
  11000 Wolfe Road
  Cupertino, California 95014

Forum of Control Data Users
  Mr. Abe Hiebert
  Control Data Corporation
  13145 Porter Drive
  Palo Alto, California 94304

Guidance Information System
Users Group
  375 Concord Avenue
  Belmont, Massachusetts 02178

GUIDE
  Mr. T.E. Wiese
  University of Wisconsin
  1558 Van Hise Hall
  1220 Lindeu Drive
  Madison, Wisconsin 53706

ICES Users Group
  CLM/Systems, Inc.
  292 Main Street
  Cambridge, Massachusetts 02142

Joint Users Group

National Association of Users
of Computer Applications to Learning
  Mr. Harry Strasbourg
  Chicago Board of Education
  228 N. LaSalle Street
  Chicago, Illinois 60601

needs, publishes DECUSCOPE (monthly) and DECUS proceedings (annually).

Software library, monthly newsletter for the use of H-P equipment in instruction.

Medium for exchange of ideas, experiences, and computer programs. Mainframe and special interest groups.

Users of Time Share Corporation's Guidance Information System, a proprietary data base for guidance counselors.

Users of IBM 360/40 and larger. Information exchange, evaluation, feedback to IBM.

Exchange of information pertaining to the use of all components of ICES, formulating and enunciating the views of the ICES community.

JUG's members are 16 user organizations of ACM. Publishes computer program directory, establishes communications among user groups.

Members are large school systems having CAI projects.

Appendix 2 365

SHARE
  George Gorsline, Jr.
  Ohio University Computer Center
  Clipping Research Labs
  Athens, Ohio 45701

Users of IBM 350/44, IBM/370 and higher. Maintains program library.

V.M. Users of CDC 6000 Series
  Dr. Loren Meissner
  Building 50B, Rm. 3245
  Lawrence Radiation Laboratory
  University of California
  Berkeley, California 94720

Maintains library.

XDS Users
  Mr. Scott Wheeler
  Computer Center
  University of Texas at Arlington
  Arlington, Texas 76010

Users of XDS computers for interchange of information, establishing standards and maintaining a program library.

C. MAJOR PROFESSIONAL JOURNALS WITH ARTICLES ON COMPUTERS IN EDUCATION

BEHAVIORAL AND SOCIAL SCIENCES

American Psychologist
American Psychological Association
1200 17th Street, N.W.
Washington, D.C. 20036

The Journal of Educational Psychology
American Psychological Association
1200 17th Street, N.W.
Washington, D.C. 20036

BUSINESS EDUCATION

Journal of Business Education
15 S. Franklin Street
Wilkes Barre, Pennsylvania 18701

EDUCATION

The American Educational Research Journal (AERA)
1126 16th Street, N.W.
Washington, D.C. 20036

Audiovisual Instruction (NEA)
Association for Educational Communications and Technology
1201 16th Street, N.W.
Washington, D.C. 20036

Educational Technology
　140 Sylvan Avenue
　Englewood Cliffs, New Jersey 07632

The Instructor
　P.O. Box 6099
　Duluth, Minnesota 55806

Nation's Schools
　P.O. Box 666
　Hightstown, New Jersey 08520

NSPI Journal (NSPI)
　Cardinal Station
　Catholic University
　Washington, D.C. 20017

School Management
　22 W. Putnam Avenue
　Greenwich, Connecticut 06830

School and Society
　Society for the Advancement of
　Education, Inc.
　1860 Broadway
　New York, New York 10023

ENGINEERING

Journal of Engineering Education
American Society for Engineering Education
　1 Dupont Circle
　Suite 400
　Washington, D.C. 20036

HUMANITIES

Computers and the Humanities
　Queens College
　Flushing, New York 11367

INTERDISCIPLINARY

The American Journal of Computer Applications Computerworld
　797 Washington Street
　Newton, Massachusetts 62158

Computers and Automation
Berkeley Enterprises
　815 Washington Street
　Newtonville, Massachusetts 02160

Computer Decisions
Hayden Publishing
850 Third Avenue
New York, New York 10022

Datamation
　P.O. Box 2000
　Greenwich, Connecticut 06830

Data Processing Magazine
　N. American Publishing Co.
　134 N. 13th Street
　Philadelphia, Pennsylvania 19107

Appendix 2 367

Instructional Science
Elsevier/North Holland
  335 Jan Van Galenstraat
  Amsterdam, The Netherlands

LIBRARY SCIENCE

Journal of Library Automation
American Library Association
  So. E. Huron Street
  Chicago, Illinois 60611

MATHEMATICS AND PHYSICAL SCIENCES

AEDS Journal
Association of Educational Data Systems
  1201 16th Street, N.W.
  Washington, D.C. 20036

AEDS Monitor
  1201 16th Street, N.W.
  Washington, D.C. 20036

American Journal of Physics
American Institute of Physics, Inc.
  335 E. 45th Street
  New York, New York 10017

Journal of Chemical Education
Business and Publications Office
  20th and Northampton Streets
  Easton, Pennsylvania 18042

School Science and Mathematics
  P.O. Box 246
  Bloomington, Indiana 47401

Science
American Association for the Advancement of Science
  1515 Massachusetts Avenue, N.W.
  Washington, D.C. 20005

Science Education
John Wiley & Sons, Inc.
  605 3rd Avenue
  New York, New York 10016

Science Teacher
National Science Teachers Association
  1201 16th Street, N.W.
  Washington, D.C. 20036

MEDICINE

Journal of Medical Education
Association of American Medical Colleges
  1 Dupont Circle, N.W.
  Washington, D.C. 20036

APPENDIX 3

ORGANIZATIONS AND NETWORKS PROVIDING COMPUTING SERVICES TO EDUCATION

Cooperative Arrangements Providing Service to School Districts, Towns

Name/Location	Description/Services
Computer Instruction Network Marion County Intermediate Education District Salem, Oregon	This network serves 40 high schools in the district, using a mobile van housing four small computers.
DICE Newark, Delaware	DICE is a nonprofit consortium that provides educational data processing services to five Delaware school districts.
Division of Instructional Systems School District of Philadelphia Philadelphia, Pennsylvania	All grade levels of public schools in Philadelphia are serviced by this system.
Metropolitan Dayton Educational Cooperative Association Dayton Board of Education Dayton, Ohio	Instructional use of the computer in and around the Dayton area. Terminals serve elementary and high school students.
Middle-Atlantic Educational and Research Center P.O. Box 1372 Lancaster, Pennsylvania	MERC has nine participating colleges as members. Each pays a small amount of money for services from the cooperation.

National Educational Computing Service
   Western Institute for Science and Technology
   P.O. Box 1591
   Waco, Texas

National Educational Computing Service is funded by the U.S. Office of Education to provide services to colleges, junior colleges, senior high schools, and vocational institutions nationwide.

New England Regional Computing Project, Inc.
   Massachusetts Institute of Technology
   Cambridge, Massachusetts

NERComP is a network with 25-30 members sharing six large university computer centers. It is funded by NSF.

Northeast Rhode Island Computer Project
   Lincoln, Rhode Island

Offers computer training to every high school student in four Rhode Island towns.

Northwest Educational Cooperative
   Chicago, Illinois

Consortium of eight grade schools and two high school districts, which serve 93 elementary and nine high schools with a total enrollment of 90,000 students.

Project LOCAL
   44 School Street
   Westwood, Massachusetts

Project LOCAL provides educational computer services to member towns in Massachusetts.

Shared Educational Computer System, Inc.
   P.O. Box 204
   Poughkeepsie, New York

SECOS has 32 typewriter terminals installed in 19 schools (public and private elementary and secondary schools, private colleges, a community college, and within the state university of New York's system).

Total Information for Educational Systems
   Thomas Campbell, Director
   1925 W. County Road, B2
   St. Paul, Minnesota

TIES is administered by the Minnesota School Districts Data Processing Joint Board to provide complete computer services to 27 independent Minnesota school districts.

Uni-Coll Corporation
   University of City Science Center
   University of Pennsylvania
   Philadelphia, Pennsylvania

Uni-Coll is a non-profit subsidiary computing service, serving institutions in the metropolitan Philadelphia area.

Appendix 3

University/College-Based Delivery Systems

Name/Location	Description/Services
Academic Computer Group Babson College Babson Park, Massachusetts	Serves some 10 colleges in the Boston area from Babson College's computer center. Financed solely by member schools.
Willis H. Booth Computing Center California Institute of Technology Pasadena, California	CIT serves 10 schools and 19 teletypes. One group of six colleges is part of Claremont College, with one teletype each. The University of Redland has five; LaVerne College two; Occidental College four; and California Lutheran, two.
Colorado State University Fort Collins, Colorado	Regional consortium in which Colorado State University serves nine junior colleges and two four-year colleges.
Dartmouth Time-Sharing System Kiewit Computation Center Dartmouth College Hanover, New Hampshire	DTSS provides computing resources for Bates, Berkshire Community, Bowdoin, Colby Junior, Middlebury, Mount Holyoke, New England and Vermont Technical Colleges, Norwich University of Vermont, plus some 35 secondary schools.
Florida State University CAI Center Tallahassee, Florida	Florida State CAI Center has done a wide variety of experimentation with CAI and CMI materials for all levels of education.
Information Science Center Illinois Institute of Technology Chicago, Illinois	Nine Chicago City Colleges, Dominican, Elmhurst, Monmouth, Mundelein, Quincy, Ripon, and St. Xavier Colleges, and Loyola University.
Lehigh Valley Regional Computer Network Lehigh University Bethlehem, Pennsylvania	Consortium of seven colleges in the Lehigh Valley area.

MERIT Computer Network
   Michigan Education Research and
   Information Triad
   611 Church Street
   Ann Arbor, Michigan

MERIT is a university-based network research project to link University of Michigan, Michigan State, and Wayne State for the purpose of resource sharing. It is funded by NSF, the state, and three schools. MERIT, Inc. was formed as an administrative body to submit proposals.

Computer Center
   Oregon State University
   Corvallis, Oregon

Oregon College of Education, Land Community College, Portland State University, Eastern Oregon College, Southern Oregon College, Oregon Technical Institution are sharing the resources of the Oregon State regional network.

PLATO Project
   University of Illinois
   Urbana, Illinois

PLATO is an NSF-sponsored development project of a large computer-based teaching system. PLATO has developed its own language and graphics to support up to 4000 terminals.

Pennsylvania State University,
   University Park, Pennsylvania

Pennsylvania State University serves local institutions in the Williamsport area and five four-year institutions of higher learning.

Rippon College
   Rippon, Wisconsin

Rippon has used a mini-computer to set up a network for local high schools.

Stanford Bay Area Educational
Computer Network
   Stanford Computation Center
   Stanford University
   Stanford, California

A consortium of 17 four-year colleges and one junior college within the Stanford Bay area. The network was started in 1971.

Computation Center
   Stanford University
   Stanford, California

San Francisco State, University of San Francisco, Mills College, California State College at Hayward, and Henry M. Gunn Senior High School.

Appendix 3

Triangle Universities Computation Center P.O. Box 12175 Research Triangle Park, North Carolina	University of North Carolina, Duke and North Carolina State University. The North Carolina Computer Center Orientation Project (NCCOP) is associated with TUCC and purchases computer service through dial-up teletype.
UCLA Campus Computing Network University of California at Los Angeles Los Angeles, California	Links UCLA's main computer to the data processing system of the 19 California state colleges through the two CSC regional data centers at San Jose State and California State Colleges.
TEXAS/RCP Computation Center University of Texas Austin, Texas	There are 11 State Colleges and one high school presently using the system, 11 in Texas.
University of Wisconsin LaCrosse Computer Center John Storlie, Director LaCrosse, Wisconsin	A recent time-sharing service available to school districts of any size for any length of time.
Washington State University Computing Center Pullman, Washington	A consortium of eight four-year institutions of higher learning, a community college and a teacher college.

APPENDIX 4

DECISION GUIDE AND CONSIDERATIONS

Introduction

More and more educators are becoming convinced of the potential usefulness of computer applications in curricula. The job of deciding *which* materials would be desirable and feasible to adopt or develop is a difficult one, due to the complexity and novelty of the materials themselves, the variety of factors which enter into decision-making, and the various people entering into the decision process.

This Appendix contains a set of questions about students, education, and computer-oriented curricular materials. The organization of the questions is intended to be useful to people who are making decisions about adopting or developing computer-oriented innovations. The people who should use this list are education planners, administrators of educational institutions, teachers, curriculum planners, education computer center directors, industry representatives, and others concerned with the adoption of curricular innovations.

The considerations are organized into four main categories as illustrated in Figure 37:

1. Questions about the TARGET SITUATION into which the innovation may be introduced. Answers to these questions, such as who are the students you want to serve, establish the ground rules for evaluating an innovation.
2. Questions about the PURPOSE of the INNOVATION.
3. Questions about the CHARACTERISTICS of the INNOVATION.
4. Questions about the cost and support REQUIREMENTS of the INNOVATION.

Decision Strategy for Evaluating Computer-Oriented Curricular Innovation ◇◆◇

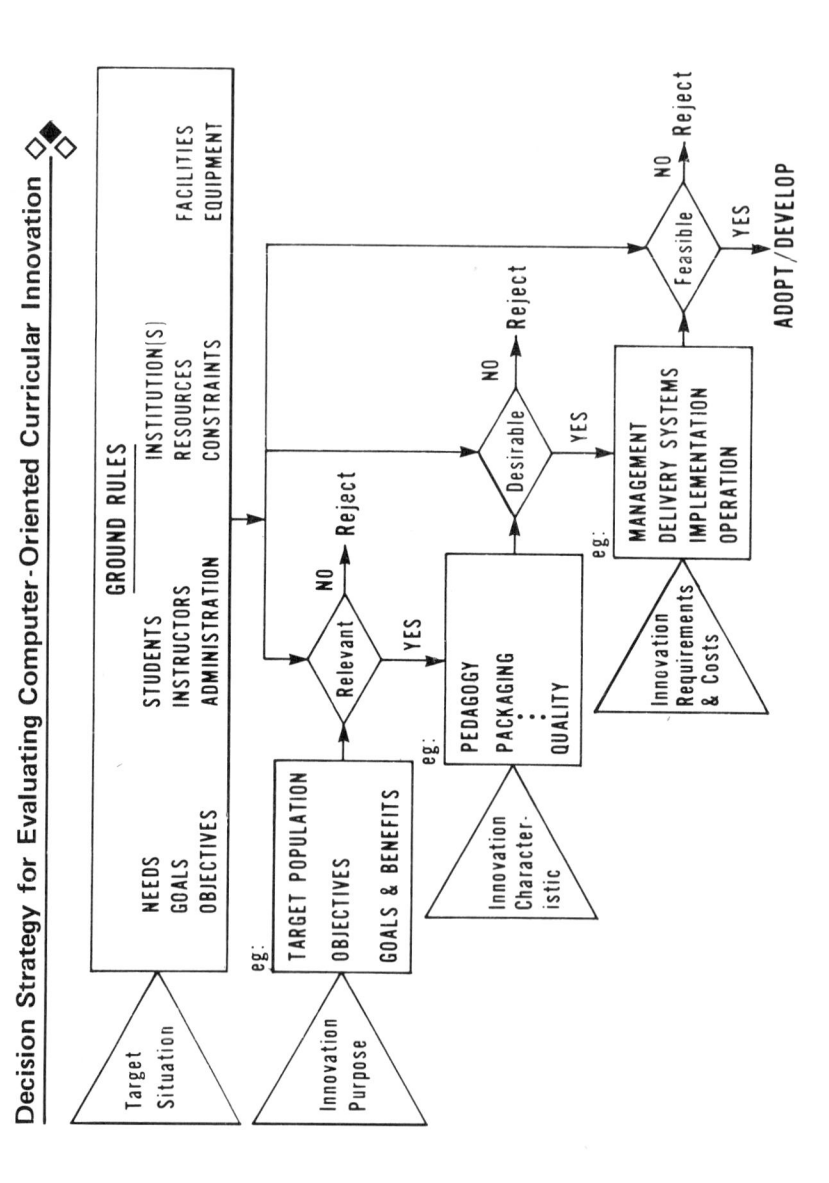

Figure 37

Appendix 4 377

Category I: The Target Situation

Answers to questions about the target situation help to bring into focus the educational needs and problems being addressed by the evaluator. They also establish some of the ground rules under which an innovation will be evaluated—such as resources available for, and constraints on, curricular innovation.

1. For purposes of this evaluation, what are the educational needs and goals being addressed?

    Example Details
    - Improve a specific course?
    - Major curriculum reform?
    - Subject areas involved?
    - Develop variety of intellectual skills?
    - Encourage learner independence?
    - Increased relevance of curriculum?
    - Improve efficiency of a course or program?
    - Make learning available to more people?

2. What are the characteristics of the student population whose needs and goals are being addressed in this evaluation?

    Example Details
    - Age or grade level?
    - Academic background?
    - Career interests?
    - Major field of study?
    - Demographic characteristics?
    - Regional background?
    - Computing skills?

3. What are the characteristics of the instructors involved in this subject area?

    Example Details
    - Subject matter background?
    - Instructional management skills?
    - Computing skills?
    - Pedagogical biases?

4. What incentives are there for the instructors and support staff to adopt innovations into the curriculum?

Example Details
- Professional advancement?
- Intrinsic interest?
- Release time?
- Sabbatical?
- Funding support?
- Promotion possibilities?

5. What computing facilities are presently accessible to the instructors/staff/students in the target situation?

   Example Details
   - Any computer available?
   - Terminal time available?
   - What model computer?
   - Interactive capability?
   - Keypunch machines?
   - What is the typical batch turnaround time?
   - Programming languages available?
   - Location of equipment?

6. What types of personnel are available with technical computer skills?

   Example Details
   - Systems/program analysts?
   - Systems programmers?
   - Hardware maintenance personnel?
   - Faculty with programming skills?
   - Student programmers?

7. What is the acceptable cost per student in this program or institution?

   Example Details
   - Annual?
   - Term?
   - Course?
   - Hour?

8. What sources of financial support are potentially available for instituting curriculum innovation in the target situation? Extent? When?

   Example Details

Appendix 4

- Departmental budget?
- Institutional funds?
- Local, state funds or programs?
- Federal agency grants?
- Foundation support?
- Commercial organization?

Category II: The Purpose of the Innovation

Answers to these questions should be compared to the target situation, in order to determine whether there is a match between the needs and goals of the situation, and the designed purpose of the innovation/materials. For example, if the students we are concerned with in the target situation are physics majors, but the materials were designed for non-science majors taking a science course, then some question is raised as to the relevance of the materials to the target situation.

1. What student population are the materials designed for?
    Example Details
    - Age or grade level?
    - Academic background?
    - Career interests?
    - Major field of study?
    - Demographic characteristics?
    - Regional background?
    - Computing skills?
2. What instructor population are the materials designed for?
    Example Details
    - Subject matter knowledge?
    - Instructional management skills?
    - Computing skills?
    - Pedagogical biases?
3. Is the innovation part of a major curricular or educational reform?
    Example Details
    - Are the goals of the curriculum changing?
    - Are subjects to be introduced at an earlier age?
    - Is an interdisciplinary curriculum being established?

- Is the focus changing from group study to independent study?
- Is a new program of studies being introduced?

4. What intellectual skills will students develop by using these materials?

   Example Details

   Will students:
   - Develop a variety of cognitive tools for describing phenomena (e.g., graphic, mathematical, modeling, statistical, logical)?
   - Learn to handle large volumes of data with computers as data reduction tool?
   - Learn new methods, e.g., mathematical methods in solving large systems of equations?
   - Learn how to deal with factors which limit and define experimental accuracy; e.g., learn to distinguish systematic from random errors in data and processing?
   - Become masters of the computer as an intellectual tool?
   - Develop richer intuitive grasp of physical phenomena (e.g., behavior of magnetic force fields)?

5. Will the materials result in greater learner independence?

   Example Details
   - Will they enable students to perform more independent research projects?
   - Will they enable institutions to establish "independent study" curricula?

6. Do the materials increase the "relevance" of the curriculum?

   Example Details

   Will students:
   - Solve more realistic problems instead of pedagogically oversimplified problems (e.g., physics)?
   - Apply skills and knowledges learned in class (e.g., business games)?
   - Address complex social problems (e.g., through modeling; access to demographic data bases)?
   - Practice applying skills in a setting similar to that he will encounter upon graduation?

Appendix 4 381

- Experience greater variety of problems (e.g., simulation of a variety of diseases in a clinical encounter)?

7. Do the materials help students learn to deal with real-world complexity?

   Example Details
   - Does the (game) provide a realistic understanding of real-world complexity or is it oversimplified?
   - Does the model provide ways of introducing sufficient uncertainty into a subject to enable the student to get a feel for the complexity of the real-world phenomena?
   - Does the model provide a framework for making real-world observations?
   - Can parameters be easily added to increase the complexity of the model?
   - Does the simulation enable students to see the implications of theory?
   - Does the application provide the opportunity for students to learn to deal with various types of error (measurement error, data base error, computer rounding error)?

8. Will the materials improve the efficiency of education?

   Example Details

   Will they:
   - Accomplish learning objectives in less student time?
   - Accomplish greater learning objectives in same amount of student time?
   - Accomplish same learning objectives with lower cost per student (teacher time, facilities costs, program costs, amortized development costs, etc.)?
   - Accomplish greater learning objectives with same total cost per student?

9. Will the materials make education available to more people?

   Example Details

   Will they:
   - Bring educational programs to learners outside the traditional institutions (e.g., Penn State's mobile van)?
   - Make it possible for more students to master the

objectives of a course (e.g., Suppes' math drills; Pillsbury accounting package)?
- Enable non-science majors to master principles of science (e.g., COEXIST; animated films)?
- Make information accessible in an educational setting that would not be provided otherwise (e.g., on-line data base)?
- Make new subject matter accessible to students (e.g., quantitative methods in a business curriculum; concepts in fluid mechanics for undergraduates; ecology models in elementary schools)?

10. What are the learning objectives of the materials?
    Example Details
    - What is the student supposed to be able to do as a result of having used the materials?
    - What tasks or problems is it appropriate to assign a student with respect to the program?
    - What evidence is there that the materials assist students in achieving the objectives?

11. What is the role of the computer in the learning objectives?
    Example Details
    - Is the student supposed to achieve objectives through writing computer programs?
    - Does the student use the computer to do computations?
    - Is the computer an object of study?
    - Is the computer a teacher-surrogate?
    - Does the student use the computer to structure and retrieve information?
    - Are the computer algorithms and models intended to be visible to the student?
    - Does the computer control the students' path of study?

12. What is the relation of the materials' learning objectives to the objectives of a course of instruction?
    Example Details
    Are they:
    - The same as a portion of an existing course?
    - A potential replacement for existing course objectives?

Appendix 4

- A potential addition to the curriculum?
13. What is the relation of the materials to existing course materials?
    Example Details
    Will they:
    - Replace some existing course materials?
    - Be used as a supplement to existing materials?
    - Replace the existing course with a revised course?
    - Add a new course to the curriculum?

Category III: Characteristics of the Innovation

These considerations relate to various characteristics of the materials and the way in which they would be used in the target situation. Various aspects of packaging, pedagogy, use, and quality are considered, so that desirability of the materials can be evaluated from several points of view.

1. What teacher support materials are included in the package?
    Example Details
    Does package include:
    - The author's concept of the *course* to which the materials are suited?
    - Caveats and warnings to the teacher regarding potential trouble spots (e.g., types of mathematical problems not handled by canned routines; common student programming errors; types of experiments the simulation handles poorly)?
    - Guidance to the teacher on instructional management (e.g., time to allot to a game; criteria for student evaluation; possible groupings of students)?
    - Instructional objectives?
    - Mechanisms for teacher to evaluate student progress (tests; computer-generated reports; guides for evaluating problem solutions)?
    - Mechanisms for the teacher to tailor materials to his course (add parameters to a model; select modules; add problem sets; keys to standard textbooks)?

2. What is the role of the instructor in using these materials?
   Example Details
   - Does use of the materials entail new roles which the instructor is reluctant to assume (helping students debug programs; managing a game)?
   - Does the content of the materials do violence to the instructor's concept of the subject matter?
   - Can the materials be easily tailored by the instructor to suit his course and students (e.g., sequence of topics; add parameters to a model; modify problem sets)?
   - Is there a mechanism for the instructor to monitor student progress?
   - Do the materials increase instructor workload?
3. Can the materials be tailored to suit your student/instructor population?
   Example Details
   - Can instructor easily select/rearrange modules?
   - Can complexity of the models be varied?
   - Can problems be keyed to standard textbook?
   - Can instructor modify drill-and-practice sets?
4. What student materials are included in the package?
   Example Details
   - Does package include student user guides?
   - Can student determine instructional objectives?
   - Are there mechanisms for student to tailor materials to suit his needs?
   - Are homework problems provided?
   - Are solutions to homework problems provided?
   - Are workbooks provided?
5. What computer-related skills are required on the part of the student in order to use the materials?
   Example Details
   Does he have to:
   - Have programming skills?
   - Know a particular programming language?
   - Know how to use computer systems?
   - Operate hardware devices?

Appendix 4

- Keypunch cards?
- Know a job control language?

6. Do the materials enable students to get a wider variety of experience?

    Example Details
    - Does the game encourage the learner to try out alternative solutions rather than depend on a single one?
    - Can the student use the computer to relieve him of time-consuming computations, thereby freeing him to study more problems?
    - Can the student address more complex and realistic problems than he otherwise could?
    - Can the student perform a larger variety of laboratory experiments than otherwise?

7. Do the materials capitalize on individuality of the learner?

    Example Details
    - Does system allow students to master prescribed learning objectives at their own individual pace (e.g., Suppes math drills)?
    - Does system allow for independent study by students who work best under this approach (e.g., Ohio Medical Independent Study Program)?
    - Do materials provide individual diagnosis and prescriptions?
    - Does computer-supplied information make it possible for teacher to provide individual attention to students (e.g., CMI systems)?
    - Do materials provide remedial work for students who need it, not for entire class?

8. Are the materials designed to increase student motivation to learn?

    Example Details
    - Is the turnaround time (computer response time) appropriate to the task student is performing? Is motivation lowered by too long turnaround (feedback) from computer?
    - Does system provide immediate feedback to student on his performance (e.g., drills)?

- Do technical tasks, e.g., programming, interfere with student's motivation to learn the main subject matter?
9. Are the materials designed to provide students with an understanding of the learning objectives and a knowledge of how well they are achieving the objectives?

    Example Details
    - Are objectives stated in student materials?
    - Does computer give student feedback?
    - Does computer enable instructor to give student feedback?

10. What is the potential extent of use of these materials in your situation?

    Example Details
    - How many students per term would be using them?
    - Would students' use be optional or required?
    - How many faculty will adapt the materials?
    - What is the expected life of the materials?

11. What evaluative information is available regarding the materials?

    Example Details
    - Does package include information on the student population and institutional environment the materials were tested on?
    - Does package include information on the results of trial use of materials with students? with teachers?
    - Have the capabilities, limitations, and support requirements been described specifically enough so that a school or department may judge the suitability of the materials for their needs?
    - Have all computer programs been well debugged and tested?

12. Who developed the materials?

    Example Details
    - Are teachers who will use the materials being consulted in design?
    - Do students have a role in planning and developing the materials?
    - How many students were involved in tryouts?

Appendix 4 387

- Have materials been reviewed by content experts to assess the accuracy of the content?
- Have the computer programs been reviewed by content experts to assess the accuracy of results produced by the algorithms, acceptability of rounding errors, etc.?

13. What information is available regarding acceptance of the materials by others?

    Example Details
    - Number of institutions using the materials?
    - Number of delivery systems or different manufacturers' equipment the materials are implemented on?
    - Number of courses the materials have been incorporated into?
    - Number of faculty using the materials after they were made available within the institution?
    - Number of students using the materials within the adopting institution?
    - Statistics on student use of the programs?
    - Student reactions/evaluations of the materials?
    - Financial support provided by institution or local or state government after initial federal funding?

14. What is the acceptability of computer uses in this subject area?

    Example Details
    - Have computers had substantial impact on this discipline/subject area in either research or applied settings?
    - What is the acceptability of computer techniques to researchers and teaching professors in this subject area?
    - Have professional societies and journals in this discipline encouraged the use of computing techniques in this subject area? (e.g., conferences, journal articles, sponsored studies, curricula recommendations)

15. How efficient is the material approach?

    Example Details
    - How much of the total course time will student spend on the materials?
    - Is amount of student/instructor time spent on materials

proportionate to amount of learning objectives achieved?
- Can the objectives be achieved through less expensive means?

Category IV: Cost and Support
Requirements of the Innovation

Requirements for implementing and operating the materials are considered, in relation to the resources provided by both the target situation and the innovation package.

1. Are the materials compatible with existing institutional/curricular constraints?

    Example Details
    - Is effectiveness of the materials contingent upon existence of preconditions in the instructional setting: scheduling, space, groupings, credit requirements, budgeting?
    - Can the game be played in a 2-3 times a week class meeting schedule? Are decision periods conveniently scheduled in the traditional one-hour class meeting period?
    - Does use of the materials require reorientation of course management from a group-oriented instruction to an individual-oriented program?
    - Are materials compatible with existing departmental/institutional credit requirements?
    - Are materials compatible with existing textbooks?
    - Does use of the materials entail unusual organizational arrangements within the institution such as interdepartmental cooperation?

2. What are the requirements for student access to equipment in order to use the materials?

    Example Details
    - Do students need to interact with computer via a terminal?
    - How much time will a student spend on a terminal? (per day, week, year?)

Appendix 4

- How many terminals would be needed to provide ready access for all students who require use?
- How many students need to be using the computer simultaneously? Why?
- Can computer facilities be made available to enough students to justify cost of implementation?
- If batch mode operation of computer is to be used, will students have turnaround time appropriate to the task they are performing?
- Are administrative procedures for getting access to computing facilities so complex as to discourage users?
- Can students work in teams without degrading the use of the materials?
- Are terminals conveniently located for instructor and students?

3. What are the computer system requirements of the materials?
   Example Details
   - What central computer hardware/software capabilities are required by the application (storage; operating systems; compilers; cpu; I/O channels; library routines)?
   - What terminal capabilities are required (interactive; hard copy; graphic; visual; audio)?

4. What support is available for implementing the materials?
   Example Details
   - Can all parties interested in the progress and possible adoption of the materials be provided with a precise and complete listing of all support requirements?
   - Does package support include user-staff training or workshops?
   - What is the training time required for teachers? staff?
   - Are program listings provided in the language of the delivery system to be used?
   - Are programs described in hardware/software independent form for easy implementation on user delivery system?
   - Is documentation of computer programs sufficient for user staff to make necessary modifications or improvements?

5. What are the initial implementation costs?
    Example Details
    - Does the implementation/operation of the program require professional personnel having unusual experiential and academic qualifications and capabilities?
    - What special costs are associated with the delivery system (special space arrangements; communications costs; system software modifications)?
    - What are the time and manpower requirements to implement the application on the delivery system?
    - Will computer programs have to be rewritten to run on the delivery system available?
6. What are the operating costs for using the materials?
    Example Details
    - What is the cost per student hour, including overhead?
    - What is the marginal cost if one student uses the facility for one additional hour?
    - What is the additional capital cost, above present investments, to provide the service to 10 students? 100 students? 1000 students?
    - Can the application be redesigned for cheaper delivery system (e.g., TTY; small computer; subset data base for smaller files)?
    - Are operating costs at a level acceptable to the school/department administration?
    - Do specific plans exist for obtaining financial resources to support long-term continuance of the program?
    - What unusual organizational or financial arrangements will be required in order to pay for the materials?
7. If the materials entail introduction of new hardware devices, what are the maintenance considerations for the devices?
    Example Details
    - If maintenance and repair are to be provided by the school, what is the average annual salary of the staff person needed for this purpose?

Appendix 4

- Are materials using established technology: for which commercial troubleshooting and repair is quickly available?
- Can the materials be adapted to a more established technology with only slight sacrifice of its central educational features?

INDEX

Accounting curricula, 78, 79, 149-153
ACM (*see* Association for Computing Machinery)
ADCIS (*see* Association for Development of Computer-Based Instructional Systems)
Adoption of CBLM (*see* Dissemination of CBLM)
AERA (*see* American Educational Research Association)
Affective learning, 132-135
American Accounting Association, 88
American Association of Geographers, 116
American Chemical Society, 63
American Educational Research Association, 17
American Institute of Certified Public Accountants, 88
American Institute for Decision Sciences, 88
American Institutes for Research, 16, 182, 189, 190
APL language, 228, 258, 279
APTP (*see* Arithmetic Proficiency Training Program)
ARCH:GRAPHIC language, 283
Archives (*see* Data bases)
Arithmetic Proficiency Training Program (APTP), 75-76, 148, 172-174

ARPA Network, 18, 219, 264
Art curricula, 103-104
ARTSPEAK language, 278
Association for Computing Machinery (ACM), 17, 213
Association for Development of Computer-Based Instructional Systems (ADCIS), 17, 229
Association for Educational Data Systems, 120
Author languages (*see* Programming languages)

Babson Institute of Business Administration, 88
Barriers to computer use (*see* Obstacles to computer use)
BASIC language, 60, 61, 168, 233, 235, 253, 276, 279, 284
Behavioral objectives (*see* Objectives, learning)
Beloit College, 153
Books, computer-oriented, 49, 50
Bowling Green State University, 65
BRAIN system, 64
Brigham Young University, 170
Brooklyn Polytechnic Institute, 69, 161
Business curricula, 49, 53, 78-88, 149-153

Cable television, 169, 218, 275
CACHE (*see* Computer Aids for Chemical Engineering)
CAI (*see* Computer-Assisted Instruction)
California, University of, 63
Canned programs, 51
CARE, 149, 176-177
Carnegie Commission on Higher Education, 6, 13, 16, 126, 239, 293, 310
Catalogs, CBLM, 231, 355-358
CATALYST language, 51, 62
CECCP (*see* Center for Exchange of Chemistry Computer Programs)
Center for Exchange of Chemistry Computer Programs (CECCP), 63, 212
Center for Research on Learning and Teaching (*see* Michigan, University of)
Chemistry curricula, 54, 55-63
Chicago Public Schools, 173
Chicago, University of, 84, 116
Chico State College, 103, 142
Civil engineering, 278
Clearinghouses, 226, 324, 326-327, 359-368
Coast Community College, 116, 141
COEXIST, project, 69, 145, 192
Cognitive learning, 132-135
COGO language, 278
Coherent strategy, 242, 298-300
College-level materials, 54, 74, 78, 93-95, 103-105, 111-121, 149-153, 153-155
Commercial organizations (*see* Private industry)
Commission on College Geography, 116, 148, 155-156
Commission on College Physics, 17, 68
Commission on Instructional Technology, 16, 126
Communications facilities, 218, 273-275

Community college curricula, 141, 169-170
Compulsory education, 35
COMPUTe, project, 138, 141, 156-157, 219, 233, 241
Computer Aids for Chemical Engineering (CACHE), 63, 228, 243, 246
Computer-Assisted Instruction, 50, 56-57, 62, 63, 64, 75, 96, 108-109, 118-119, 144, 169-172, 213
Computer Augmented Accounting, 213, 214
case study, 79, 148-153, 213
case study, 248-249
Computer-based learning materials, 6, *definition* 47, Chapter 3
Computer Curriculum Corporation, 19, 167, 244
Computer-managed instruction, 52, 96
Computer science, 77
Computers (*see* Technology)
Computing literacy, 10, 14, 117, 145, 167, 219, 231, 320, 326
Computing opportunity purposes, 9
CONDUIT, 18, 213, 220, 228, 229, 239, 247, 268-269, 290, 296-297
Conferences, 17, 213, 226, 230, 327, 355-358, 359-368
Copyrights for CBLM, 204, 219
Cost-effectiveness, 10, 40, 62, 143, 172, 177, 320, 321, 326
(*see also* Evaluation of materials)
Courses using computers, 4, 52, 60, 66, 72, 74, 79, 80, 89, 93, 115, 117
Coursewriter language, 278
CRICISAM
case study, 74-75, 145-148, 159-160, 239
CRT (*see* Terminals)
Culler-Fried system, 61, 64, 70, 269
Curricular materials (*see* Computer-

Index 395

based learning materials)
Curriculum enhancement (*see* Discipline advancement purposes)

Dartmouth College, 18, 60, 88, 104, 108, 116, 145, 156, 231, 267, 274
Data bases, 51, 80, 111, 271, 272
Data communications (*see* Communications facilities)
Data reduction programs, 58-60, 61
DELTA, project, 238
Demonstration of CBLM, 233-234
Developers of CBLM, 178-188
Development process, 188-206
Development strategies, 293-330
Dialogues (*see* Computer-Assisted Instruction)
Digital Equipment Corporation (DEC), 19, 161, 162, 228, 237
Discipline advancement purposes, 9, 144, 269, 322, 326
Discipline center model, 305-307
Dissemination functions, 225-242
Dissemination of CBLM, 204-255
Dissemination strategies, 242-255, 301-304
Distribution of CBLM, 234-237
Drills (*see* Computer-Assisted Instruction)

Eastern Michigan University, 212
Ecology, 88
Economics curricula, 114
Education curricula (*see* Teacher training)
Educational reform, 11, 124, 125-126, 132, 146, 209, 321, 326
Educational Testing Service, 172
EDUCOM, 17, 18, 187, 189, 198
Effectiveness of CBLM (*see* Cost-effectiveness)
Elementary school materials, 20, 23, 52, 71, 75-76, 106-109, 165-167, 172-174, 322
Engineering curricula, 53
English curricula, 54, 169
ENTELEK, 102, 231
Evaluation of materials, 62, 85-87, 101-102, 115-116, 143-147, 172, 198-203, 214
    (*see also* Cost-effectiveness)
Examinations, computer-generated, 57
Exchange of CBLM (*see* Dissemination of CBLM)
Expenditures for computers in education, 3, 4, 5, 19
EXTEND, project, 264

Films, computer-animated, 52, 65, 103
Finance curricula, 79
Finance for CBLM (*see* Funding for CBLM)
Florida State University, 69
Formative evaluation (*see* Evaluation of materials)
FORTRAN language, 58, 154, 248, 276
Funding for CBLM, 178-188, 204-205, 240-242, 314-318

Games (*see* Simulations)
General Learning Corporation, 213
Genetics curricula, 93
Geography curricula, 116, 155-156
Graphics, 61, 64, 67, 68, 93, 94, 103, 281-284
GROPE system, 64

Harcourt Brace Jovanovich, 213, 240, 295
Harvard University, 64, 99
Health professions curricula, 96-102, 174-175
Hewlett-Packard Corporation, 19, 161, 237, 253
Houghton Mifflin Company

case study, 213, 239, 252-255, 326
Humanism, 29-32, 39
Humanities curricula, 53, 54, 103-111, 169
Huntington projects
    case study, 90, 131, 148, 160-162, 199, 227, 235, 240, 246

IBM Corporation, 76, 151, 155, 166, 172-174, 213, 231, 266, 268, 295
Ideologically based center model, 312-314
Illinois Institute of Technology
    case study, 69, 89, 141, 157-159
Illinois, University of, 97, 102, 236, 270
IMPRESS, project, 111, 192, 235, 315
Individualization of education, 34
Information explosion, 26-27
Information retrieval, 12, 29, 38, 99
Instructional methods, 130
Iowa, University of, 18, 96, 112, 116, 272

Journalism curricula, 110

Kansas State Board of Education, 213
Kansas, University of, 111
Knowledge explosion (*see* Information explosion)
Knox College, 150

Laboratory (*see* Simulations)
Language curricula, 108
Learning System, the, 37
Life science curricula, 53, 54, 88-96
Linguistics, 111
Lister Hill Biomedical Network, 102, 149, 174-175, 269-271
LOGO system, 71-73, 106, 278

Marketing (*see* Dissemination of CBLM)
Massachusetts General Hospital, 98, 102
Massachusetts Institute of Technology, 70
Mathematical Association of America, 78
Mathematics curricula, 49, 53, 69-78, 159-160, 169, 172-174
MATHLAB, 69-70
McGraw-Hill Publishing Company, 187, 238
Medical professions curricula (*see* Health professions curricula)
MERIT network, 219, 261, 264
Michigan State University, 117
Michigan, University of, 82, 110, 113, 114, 116, 276, 283
Mini-computers, 61, 95, 169, 235, 284-287
Minnesota Council of Teachers of Mathematics, 78
Minnesota, University of, 88, 116
Mitre Corporation, 69, 227
Models (*see* Simulations)
Music curricula, 104-108

National Council of Teachers of Mathematics, 78, 228
National development center model, 307-310
National Institute of Education (NIE), 307, 323, 329
National Library of Medicine, 102
National program exchange model, 301-304
National Science Foundation, 4, 16, 18, 19, 78, 150, 153, 155, 160, 161, 166, 169-170, 178-184, 213, 241, 243, 323, 327
National Science Information Network, 19
NCECS (*see* North Carolina Edu-

Index

cational Computing Service)
NERComp (*see* New England Regional Computing Program)
Networks, 218, 236, 259-275, 290, 330, App. 3
  (*see also* names of specific networks)
New England Regional Computing Program, 267-268
Newsletters, 212, 355-358, 359-368
New York University, 104
Non-profit organizations, 297
North Carolina Educational Computing Service
  case study, 215, 228, 245, 249-252, 268
North Carolina, state of, 250
Northern Virginia Community College, 170
Northwest Regional Educational Laboratory, 117, 167, 241
Notre Dame University, 116
Numerical analysis, 60

Oberlin College, 114
Objectives, learning, 135-139, 163, 196
Obstacles to computer use, 6-8, 215-221
Oceanography, 93
Ohio State University, 88, 96, 102
Operations management, 84
Oregon State University, 18, 64

Packaging of CBLM, 231-233
PCDP (*see* Physics Computer Development Project)
Pennsylvania State University, 118, 124, 176, 236
Philadelphia School District, 124, 125
Phoenix Junior College, 170
Physics Computer Development Project, 63-64, 69
Physics curricula, 63-69

PIL language, 57, 62, 278
Pittsburgh School District, 124, 162
Pittsburgh, University of, 57, 58, 69, 116, 141
PLATO, 18, 63, 236, 274, 277
President's Science Advisory Committee, 16
Private industry, 4, 19, 241, 322, 327
Problem-solving applications, 14, 56, 60, 63, 69-70, 77, 149-153
Professional journals, 230, 355-358, 359-368
Professional societies, 155, 355-358, 359-368
Programming languages, 275-279
Projections of computer use in education, 19-45
Psychomotor learning, 132-135
Publicity, 229
Publishers, 359-368
  (*see also* Dissemination of CBLM)
Purposes for using computers, 8-12, 25-45, 123-139

Quantum Chemistry Program Exchange (QCPE), 63

RAND Corporation (study), 13
RCA Corporation, 295
REACT, project, 148, 167-168, 241
Reading curricula, 109
Regional computing networks, 18, 157-158, 259, 265-267
Regionally based learning technology centers, 310-312

Satellite communications, 275
Science Research Associates (*see* IBM Corporation)
Secondary school materials, 20-22, 52, 63, 75, 82, 90-93, 124-125, 160-162, 162-165, 168
SECOS, 238
Simulations, 50, 51, 56, 58-60, 62,

65-66, 80-87, 88-93, 95, 97-98, 113, 114, 138, 141
Social science curricula, 111-117, 153-155, 271-272
Social Sciences Instructional Programming Project (SSIPP), 148, 153-155, 192
SOLO, project
    case study, 75, 78, 137, 140, 148, 162-165, 192, 229
Southern California, University of, 98
Southern Regional Education Board, 4, 15, 49
South-Western Publishing Company, 79, 152, 213, 238, 245, 248-249
SPSS (*see* Statistical Programs for the Social Sciences)
Stanford Initial Reading Project, 148, 165-166, 199
Stanford University, 109, 125, 165-167, 214
Statistical Programs for the Social Sciences, 112, 116, 214
Strategies for developing and implementing CBLM, 15
Studies of computer use in education, 15-17
Stylistic analyses, 109
Syracuse University, 72
Systems approach to development, 195-197

Taxonomies of learning outcomes, 132
Teacher training, 117-121, 167-169, 176-177, 239, 296, 327
Technical support, 217, 237, 240
Technology, 218, 257-291
Teletypewriter (*see* Terminals)
Terminals, 257, 279-284
Texas, University of, 230, 265
Textbook model, 294-295
TICCIT
    case study, 18, 144, 148, 169-172, 193, 197, 200, 227, 237, 286-287
Time Share Corporation
    case study, 19, 213, 239, 244, 252-255, 316
Transport of CBLM (*see* Distribution of CBLM)
Trends, 25-45
    (*see also* Projections of computer use in education)
Tuck, Amos School of Business Administration, 79, 88
Turtle (*see* LOGO system)
TUTOR language, 278
Tutorials (*see* Computer-Assisted Instruction)

Users Groups, 17, 359-368
U.S. Office of Education, 3, 19, 127, 166, 167, 176, 178-184, 241, 323, 328, 329

Values (*see* Purposes for using computers)

Washington, University of, 93, 275
Western Washington University, 120
Wisconsin, University of, 99, 111, 116

DATE DUE

0 2001

JUN 2 0 2001
JUL 1 0 2001

81138

370.2
L47